CLYMER®

SUZUKI

OUTBOARD SHOP MANUAL
2-140 HP • 1977-1984

The world's finest publisher of mechanical how-to manuals

CLYMER®

P.O. Box 12901, Overland Park, KS 66282-2901

FIRST EDITION
First Printing April, 1985
Second Printing January, 1989
Third Printing July, 1991
Fourth Printing July, 1995
Fifth Printing May, 1999
Sixth Printing June, 2006

Printed in U.S.A.

CLYMER and colophon are registered trademarks of Prism Business Media Inc.

ISBN: 0-89287-406-6

TOOLS AND TEST EQUIPMENT: Thorsen Tool, Dallas, Texas, and Dixson, Inc., Grand Junction, Colorado.

TECHNICAL ILLUSTRATIONS: Courtesy of U.S. Suzuki Motor Corporation with additional illustrations by Mitzi McCarthy. Thanks to Marina Specialties, Sun Valley, California, and Ken's Boat Center, Burbank, California.

COVER: Photographed by Michael Brown Photographic Productions, Los Angeles, California. Boat driven by Ray Wittbrod. Nova inflatable boat courtesy of Regency Boats & Motors, Marina del Rey, California.

CLYMER®

Publisher Shawn Etheridge

EDITORIAL

Managing Editor
James Grooms

Associate Editors
Richard Arens
Steven Thomas

Technical Writers
Jay Bogart
Jon Engleman
Michael Morlan
George Parise
Mark Rolling
Ed Scott
Ron Wright

Group Production Manager
Dylan Goodwin

Senior Production Editors
Greg Araujo
Darin Watson

Production Editors
Julie Jantzer-Ward
Justin Marciniak
Holly Messinger

Associate Production Editor
Susan Hartington

Technical Illustrators
Steve Amos
Errol McCarthy
Mitzi McCarthy
Bob Meyer

MARKETING/SALES AND ADMINISTRATION

Sales Channel & Brand Marketing Coordinator
Melissa Abbott Mudd

Art Director
Chris Paxton

Sales Managers
Justin Henton
Dutch Sadler
Matt Tusken

Business Manager
Ron Rogers

Customer Service Manager
Terri Cannon

Customer Service Representatives
Felicia Dickerson
Courtney Hollars
April LeBlond

Warehouse & Inventory Manager
Leah Hicks

PRISM
BUSINESS MEDIA™
P.O. Box 12901, Overland Park, KS 66282-2901 • 800-262-1954 • 913-967-1719

The following books and guides are published by Prism Business Media

More information available at *clymer.com*

Contents

Quick Reference Data

MODEL HISTORY

	1977	1978	1979	1980	1981	1982	1983	1984
DT 2	X	X	X	X	X	X	X	X
DT 3.5			X	X	X	X	X	X
DT 4.5	X							
DT 5		X	X	X	X	X	X	
DT 6								X
DT 7.5	X	X	X					
DT 8				X	X	X	X	X
DT 9	X	X	X					
DT 9.9	X	X	X	X	X	X	X	X
DT 15							X	X
DT 16	X	X	X	X	X	X		
DT 20	X	X	X	X				
DT 25	X	X	X	X	X	X	X	X
DT 30							X	X
DT 40				X	X	X	X	X
DT 50/50M	X	X	X	X	X	X	X	X
DT 60							X	X
DT 65		X	X	X	X	X		
DT 75							X	X
DT 85			X	X	X	X	X	X
DT 115					X	X	X	X
DT 140					X	X	X	X

BATTERY CAPACITY (HOURS)

Accessory draw	80 Amp-hour battery provides continuous power for	Approximate recharge time
5 amps	13.5 hours	16 hours
15 amps	3.5 hours	13 hours
25 amps	1.8 hours	12 hours

Accessory draw	105 Amp-hour battery provides continuous power for	Approximate recharge time
5 amps	15.8 hours	16 hours
15 amps	4.2 hours	13 hours
25 amps	2.4 hours	12 hours

MAINTENANCE SCHEDULE*

At first 10 hours	• Change gearcase lubricant
Every 10 hours	• Retighten bolts and nuts • Check wire harness connections • Check idle speed (DT 2-DT 16) • Check and adjust carburetors (DT 20-DT 140) • Check propeller for damage • Lubricate propeller shaft splines • Check fuel lines for leakage • Check intake manifold hose for deterioration • Lubricate steering handle • Check neutral start interlock switch operation • Check emergency switch operation (if so equipped) • Check and adjust remote control linkage (if so equipped) • Check engine key and choke operation (if so equipped) • Check starter button and choke operation (if so equipped)
Every 50 hours	• Clean and regap spark plugs • Decarbonize the piston(s), cylinder and cylinder head • Change gearcase lubricant • Check fuel strainer or filter • Check steering handle preload • Check starter rope condition • Check tilt mechanism preload
Every 100 hours	• Check and adjust ignition timing • Check water pump impeller
Every week	• Check oil injection lines (if so equipped)
Every month	• Lubricate carburetor and choke linkage • Lubricate clamp screws
Every 3 months	• Lubricate swivel bracket • Lubricate support tube • Lubricate shift lever
Once each season	• Change starter rope • Check fuel tank condition • Replace water pump impeller

* Not all items apply to all engines. Perform only those pertaining to your engine.

RECOMMENDED LUBRICANTS

Type	Part No.
Water-resistant grease	99000-25170
Outboard Motor Gear Oil	99000-22540
Suzuki CCI 50:1 Outboard Oil	99105-00153
Super Grease "A"	99000-25010
Silicone Seal	99000-31120
Bond No. 4	99000-31030
Cemedine 366E	99000-31090
Thread Lock 1342	99000-32050
Thread Lock Super 1333B	99000-32020
DEXRON automatic transmission fluid	—

RECOMMENDED SPARK PLUGS

	NGK part No.	Gap (in.)
DT 2	B5HS, BR5HS	0.028
DT 3.5		
1979-1981	BPR6HS	0.028-0.031
1982-on	BP6HS	0.024-0.028
DT 4.5	B6HS	0.028
DT 5		
1978-1980	BPR6HS	0.028
1981-on	BP6HS	0.036
DT 6	BP6HS	0.036
DT 7.5	B6HS	0.028
DT 8		
1980	BPR6HS	0.028
1981-on	BP6HS	0.036
DT 9	B6HS	0.028
DT 9.9		
1977-1982	B6HS	0.028
1983-on	BR7HS-10	0.040
DT 15	BR7HS-10	0.040
DT 16		
1977-1981	BR7HS	0.028
1982	B7HS	0.028
DT 20	B7HS	0.028
DT 25		
1977-1982	B7HS	0.028
1983-on	BR7HS-10	0.040
DT 30	BR7HS-10	0.040
DT 40		
1980-1983	BR8HS	0.036
1984	B8HS	0.036
DT 50		
1977-1983	B8HS	0.036
1984	B8HS-10	0.040
DT 60, DT 65	B8HS-10	0.040
DT 75-DT 140	B8HS	0.036

SPARK PLUG CROSS-REFERENCE CHART*

NGK	Champion	AC
B4HS, BR5HS	L81, L88A	44F, 44FF
B6HS, BR6HS	L9J, QL7J, RL7J	42F, 42FF
BP6HS, BPR6HS	RL12Y, RL87Y, L66Y	42FS, 43FS, R43FS
B7HS, BR7HS	L5, L7J	M42FF, S42FR
BR7HS-10	—	—
B8HS, BR8HS	L4J, RL4J, L78, RL78	S41FR, S40FR, M41FF

* The cross-referenced spark plugs are not exact replacements for original plug heat range and should be used only as a temporary replacement.

IGNITION TIMING

Model	Maximum retard @ 1,000 rpm	Maximum advance @ 5,000 rpm
DT 25		
1983-on	2° ATDC	25° BTDC
1977-1982	TDC	25° BTDC
DT 30	2° ATDC	25° BTDC
DT 40	6° ATDC	25° BTDC
DT 50	4° ATDC	25° BTDC
DT 50M	8° BTDC	25° BTDC
DT 60	4° ATDC	21.5° BTDC
DT 65	3° ATDC	25° BTDC
DT 75	7° ATDC	21.5° BTDC
DT 85		
1979-1982	7° ATDC	21.5° BTDC
1983-on	3° ATDC	23° BTDC
DT 115, DT 140	3° ATDC	23° BTDC

IDLE AIR SCREW ADJUSTMENT

Model	Turns out from lightly seated position
DT 20	1-1 1/2
DT 25	
1977-1982	1 1/4-3/4
1983-on	3/4-1 1/4
DT 30	1 1/4-1 3/4
DT 40	
Independent ignition	1 3/4-2 1/4
Simultaneous ignition	1 7/8-2 3/8
DT 50, DT 65	1 3/4-2 1/4
DT 60	1 5/8-2 1/8
DT 75	1-1 1/2
DT 85	1 1/4-1 3/4
DT 115	1 1/2
DT 140	1 3/8

SELF-DISCHARGE RATE

Temperature	Approximate allowable self-discharge per day for first 10 days (specific gravity)
100° F (37.8° C)	0.0025 points
80° F (26.7° C)	0.0010 points
50° F (10.0° C)	0.0003 points

CLYMER®

SUZUKI

OUTBOARD SHOP MANUAL
2-140 HP • 1977-1984

Introduction

This Clymer shop manual covers Suzuki 2 to 140 hp outboard engines from 1977-1984. Step-by-step instructions and hundreds of illustrations guide you through jobs ranging from simple maintenance to complete overhaul.

This manual can be used by anyone from a first time do-it-yourselfer to a professional mechanic. Easy to read type, detailed drawings and clear photographs give you all the information you need to do the work right.

Having a well-maintained engine will increase your enjoyment of your boat as well as assure your safety when offshore. Keep this shop manual handy and use it often. It can save you hundreds of dollars in maintenance and repair bills and make yours a reliable, top-performance boat.

Chapter One

General Information

This detailed, comprehensive manual contains complete information covering maintenance, repair and overhaul. Hundreds of photos and drawings guide you throughout every procedure.

Troubleshooting, tune-up, maintenance and repair are not difficult if you know what tools and equipment to use and what to do. Anyone not afraid to get their hands dirty, of average intelligence and with some mechanical ability can perform most of the procedures in this manual. See Chapter Two for more information on tools and techniques.

A shop manual is a reference. You want to be able to find information quickly. Clymer books are designed with you in mind. All chapters are thumb tabbed and important items are indexed at the end of the manual. All procedures, tables, photos and instructions in this manual assume the reader may be working on the machine or using the manual for the first time.

Keep the manual in a handy place in your toolbox or boat. It will help you to better understand how your boat runs, lower repair and maintenance costs and generally increase your enjoyment of your boat.

MANUAL ORGANIZATION

This chapter provides general information useful to boat owners and marine mechanics.

Chapter Two discusses the tools and techniques for preventative maintenance, troubleshooting and repair.

Chapter Three provides troubleshooting and testing procedures for all systems and individual components.

Following chapters describe specific systems, providing disassembly, inspection, assembly and adjustment procedures in simple step-by-step form. Specifications concerning a specific system are included at the end of the appropriate chapter.

NOTES, CAUTIONS AND WARNINGS

The terms NOTE, CAUTION and WARNING have specific meanings in this manual. A NOTE provides additional information to make a step or procedure easier or more clear. Disregarding a NOTE could cause inconvenience, but would not cause damage or personal injury.

A CAUTION emphasizes areas where equipment damage could cause permanent mechanical damage; however, personal injury is unlikely.

A WARNING emphasizes areas where personal injury or even death could result from negligence. Mechanical damage may also occur. WARNINGS *must* be taken seriously. In some cases, serious injury or death has resulted from disregarding similar warnings.

TORQUE SPECIFICATIONS

Torque specifications throughout this manual are given in foot-pounds (ft.-lb.), inch-pounds (in.-lb.) and newton meters (N•m.). Newton meters are being adopted in place of meter-kilograms (mkg) in accordance with the International Modernized Metric System. Existing torque wrenches calibrated in meter-kilograms can be used by performing a simple conversion: move the decimal point one place to the right. For example, 4.7 mkg = 47 N•m. This conversion is accurate enough for most mechanical operations even though the exact mathematical conversion is 3.5 mkg = 34.3 N•m.

ENGINE OPERATION

All marine engines, whether two or four-stroke, gasoline or diesel, operate on the Otto cycle of intake, compression, power and exhaust phases.

Two-Stroke Cycle

A two-stroke engine requires one crankshaft revolution (two strokes of the piston) to complete the Otto cycle. All engines covered in this manual are a two-stroke design. **Figure 1** shows gasoline two-stroke engine operation.

Four-Stroke Cycle

A four-stroke engine requires two crankshaft revolutions (four strokes of the piston) to complete the Otto cycle. **Figure 2** shows gasoline four-stroke engine operation.

FASTENERS

The material and design of the various fasteners used on marine equipment are carefully thought out and designed. Fastener design determines the type of tool required to work with the fastener. Fastener material is carefully selected to decrease the possibility of physical failure or corrosion. See *Galvanic Corrosion* in this chapter for information on marine materials.

Nuts, bolts and screws are manufactured in a wide range of thread patterns. To join a nut and bolt, the diameter of the bolt and the diameter of the hole in the nut must be the same. It is just as important that the threads are compatible.

The easiest way to determine if fastener threads are compatible is to turn the nut on the bolt, or bolt into its threaded opening, using fingers only. Be sure both pieces are clean. If much force is required, check the thread condition on each fastener. If the thread condition is good but the fasteners jam, the threads are not compatible.

Four important specifications describe the thread:

1. Diameter.
2. Threads per inch.
3. Thread pattern.
4. Thread direction

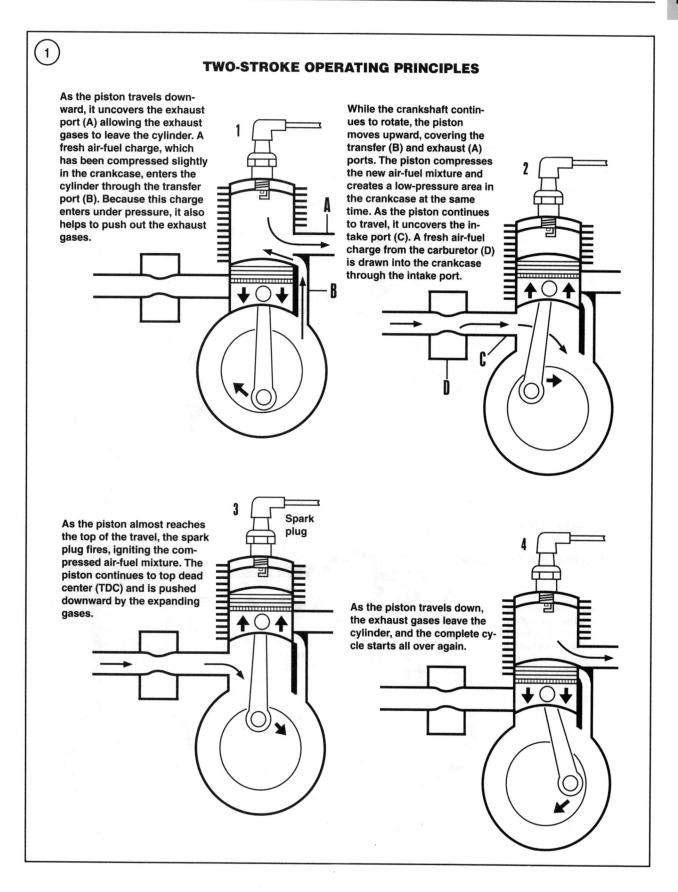

TWO-STROKE OPERATING PRINCIPLES

As the piston travels downward, it uncovers the exhaust port (A) allowing the exhaust gases to leave the cylinder. A fresh air-fuel charge, which has been compressed slightly in the crankcase, enters the cylinder through the transfer port (B). Because this charge enters under pressure, it also helps to push out the exhaust gases.

While the crankshaft continues to rotate, the piston moves upward, covering the transfer (B) and exhaust (A) ports. The piston compresses the new air-fuel mixture and creates a low-pressure area in the crankcase at the same time. As the piston continues to travel, it uncovers the intake port (C). A fresh air-fuel charge from the carburetor (D) is drawn into the crankcase through the intake port.

As the piston almost reaches the top of the travel, the spark plug fires, igniting the compressed air-fuel mixture. The piston continues to top dead center (TDC) and is pushed downward by the expanding gases.

As the piston travels down, the exhaust gases leave the cylinder, and the complete cycle starts all over again.

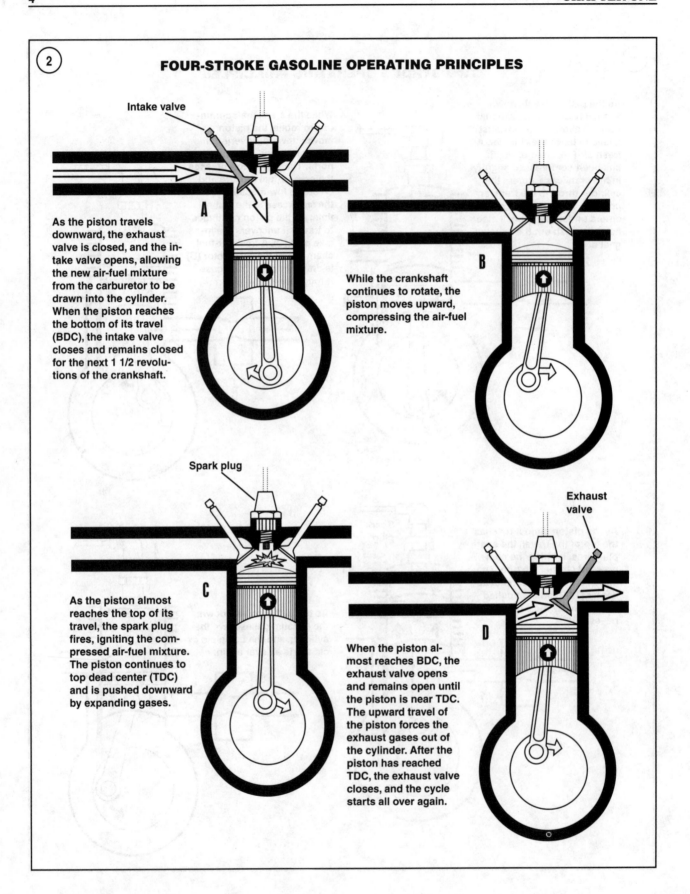

FOUR-STROKE GASOLINE OPERATING PRINCIPLES

Intake valve

A

As the piston travels downward, the exhaust valve is closed, and the intake valve opens, allowing the new air-fuel mixture from the carburetor to be drawn into the cylinder. When the piston reaches the bottom of its travel (BDC), the intake valve closes and remains closed for the next 1 1/2 revolutions of the crankshaft.

B

While the crankshaft continues to rotate, the piston moves upward, compressing the air-fuel mixture.

Spark plug

C

As the piston almost reaches the top of its travel, the spark plug fires, igniting the compressed air-fuel mixture. The piston continues to top dead center (TDC) and is pushed downward by expanding gases.

Exhaust valve

D

When the piston almost reaches BDC, the exhaust valve opens and remains open until the piston is near TDC. The upward travel of the piston forces the exhaust gases out of the cylinder. After the piston has reached TDC, the exhaust valve closes, and the cycle starts all over again.

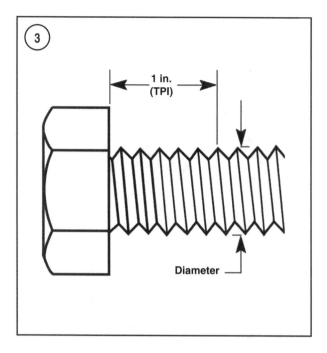

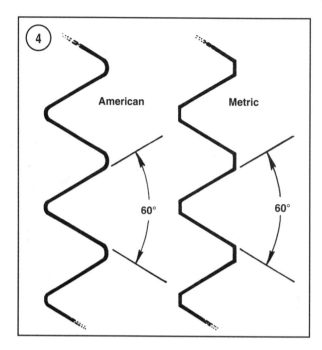

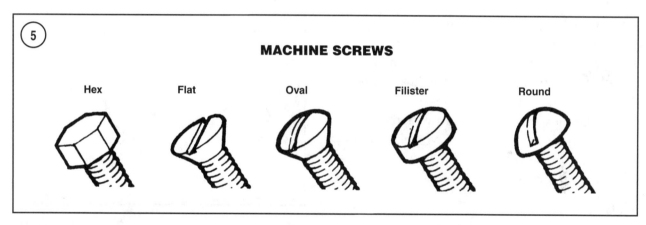

Figure 3 shows the first two specifications. Thread pattern is more subtle. Italian and British standards exist, but the most commonly used by marine equipment manufactures are American standard and metric standard. The root and top of the thread are cut differently as shown in **Figure 4**.

Most threads are cut so the fastener must be turned clockwise to tighten it. These are called right-hand threads. Some fasteners have left-hand threads; they must be turned counterclockwise to tighten. Left-hand threads are used in locations where normal rotation of the equipment would tend to loosen a right-hand threaded fastener. Assume all fasteners use right-hand threads unless the instructions specify otherwise.

Machine Screws

There are many different types of machine screws (**Figure 5**). Most are designed to protrude above the secured surface (rounded head) or be slightly recessed below the surface (flat head). In some applications the screw head is recessed well below the fastened sur-

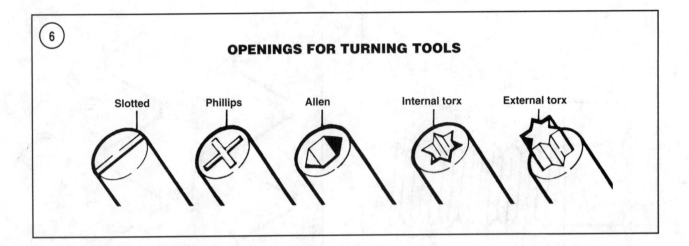

OPENINGS FOR TURNING TOOLS

Slotted Phillips Allen Internal torx External torx

face. **Figure 6** shows a number of screw heads requiring different types of turning tools.

Bolts

Commonly called bolts, the technical name for this fastener is cap screw. They are normally described by diameter, threads per inch and length. For example, 1/4-20 × 1 indicates a bolt 1/4 in. in diameter with 20 threads per inch, 1 in. long. The measurement across two flats of the bolt head indicates the proper wrench size required to turn the bolt.

Nuts

Nuts are manufactured in a variety of types and sizes. Most are hexagonal (six-sides) and fit on bolts, screws and studs with the same diameter and threads per inch.

Figure 7 shows several types of nuts. The common nut is usually used with some type of lockwasher. Self-locking nuts have a nylon insert that helps prevent the nut from loosening; no lockwasher is required. Wing nuts are designed for fast removal by hand. Wing nuts are used for convenience in non-critical locations.

To indicate the size of a nut, manufactures specify the diameter of the opening and the threads per inch. This is similar to a bolt specifi-

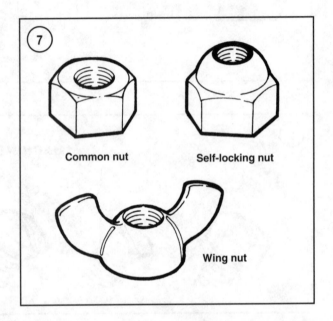

Common nut Self-locking nut Wing nut

cation, but without the length dimension. The measurement across two flats of the nut indicates the wrench size required to turn the nut.

Washers

There are two basic types of washers: flat washers and lockwashers. A flat washer is a simple disc with a hole that fits the screw or bolt. Lockwashers are designed to prevent a fastener from working loose due to vibration, expansion and contraction. **Figure 8** shows several types of lockwashers. Note that flat washers are often

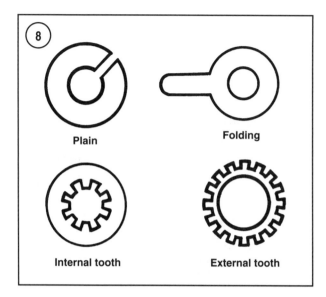

Plain

Folding

Internal tooth

External tooth

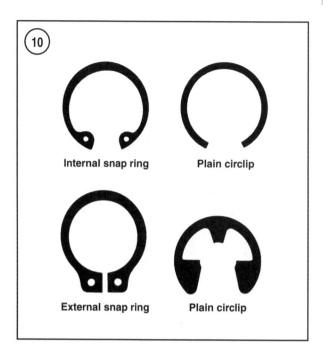

Internal snap ring

Plain circlip

External snap ring

Plain circlip

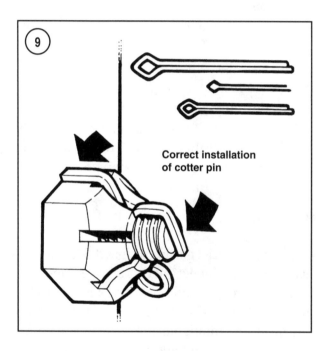

Correct installation of cotter pin

used between a lockwasher and a fastener to provide a smooth bearing surface. This allows the fastener to be turned easily with a tool.

Cotter Pins

In certain applications, a fastener must be secured so it cannot possibly loosen. The propeller nut on some marine drive systems is one such ap-

plication. For this purpose, a cotter pin (**Figure 9**) and slotted or castellated nut is often used. To use a cotter pin, first make sure the pin fits snugly, but not too tight. Then, align a slot in the fastener with the hole in the bolt or axle. Insert the cotter pin through the nut and bolt or propeller shaft and bend the ends over to secure the cotter pin tightly. If the holes do not align, tighten the nut just enough to obtain the proper alignment. Unless specifically instructed to do so, never loosen the fastener to align the slot and hole. Because the cotter pin is weakened after installation and removal, never reuse a cotter pin. Cotter pins are available in several styles, lengths and diameters. Measure cotter pin length from the bottom of its head to the tip of its shortest prong.

Snap Rings

Snap rings (**Figure 10**) can be an internal or external design. They are used to retain components on shafts (external type) or inside openings (internal type). Snap rings can be reused if they are not distorted during removal. In some applications, snap rings of varying thickness (selective fit) can be selected to position or control end play of parts assemblies.

LUBRICANTS

Periodic lubrication helps ensure long service life for any type of equipment. It is especially important with marine equipment because it is exposed to salt, brackish or polluted water and other harsh environments. The type of lubricant used is just as important as the lubrication service itself, although in an emergency, the wrong type of lubricant is better than none at all. The following paragraphs describe the types of lubricants most often used on marine equipment. Be sure to follow the equipment manufacture's recommendations for the lubricant types.

Generally, all liquid lubricants are called *oil*. They may be mineral-based (including petroleum bases), natural-based (vegetable and animal bases), synthetic-based or emulsions (mixtures). *Grease* is lubricating oil that has a thickening compound added. The resulting material then usually enhanced with anticorrosion, antioxidant and extreme pressure (EP) additives. Grease is often classified by the type of thickener added; lithium and calcium soap are the most commonly used.

Two-stroke Engine Oil

Lubrication for a two-stroke engine is provided by oil mixed with the incoming air/fuel mixture. Some of the oil mist settles out in the crankcase, lubricating the crankshaft, bearings and lower end of the connecting rod. The rest of the oil enters the combustion chamber to lubricate the piston, rings and the cylinder wall. This oil is then burned along with the air/fuel mixture during the combustion process.

Engine oil must have several special qualities to work well in a two-stroke engine. It must mix easily and stay in suspension in gasoline.

When burned, it cannot leave behind excessive deposits. It must also withstand the high operating temperature associated with two-stroke engines.

The National Marine Manufacturer's Association (NMMA) has set standards for oil used in two-stroke, water-cooled engines. This is the NMMA TC-W (two-cycle, water-cooled) grade. It indicates the oil's performance in the following areas:

1. Lubrication (preventing wear and scuffing).
2. Spark plug fouling.
3. Piston ring sticking.
4. Preignition.
5. Piston varnish.
6. General engine condition (including deposits).
7. Exhaust port blockage.
8. Rust prevention.
9. Mixing ability with gasoline.

In addition to oil grade, manufactures specify the ratio of gasoline and oil required during break-in and normal engine operation.

Gearcase Oil

Gearcase lubricants are assigned SAE viscosity numbers under the same system as four-stroke engine oil. Gearcase lubricant falls into the SAE 72-250 range. Some gearcase lubricants are multigrade. For example, SAE 80-90 is a common multigrade gear lubricant.

Three types of marine gearcase lubricants are generally available; SAE 90 hypoid gearcase lubricant is designed for older manual-shift units; type C gearcase lubricant contains additives designed for the electric shift mechanisms; high-viscosity gearcase lubricant is a heavier oil designed to withstand the shock loads of high performance engines or units subjected to severe duty use. Always use the gearcase lubricant specified by the manufacturer.

Grease

Greases are graded by the National Lubricating Grease Institute (NLGI). Greases are graded by number according to the consistency of the grease. These ratings range from No. 000 to No. 6, with No. 6 being the most solid. A typical multipurpose grease is NLGI No. 2. For specific applications, equipment manufactures may require grease with an additive such as molybdenum disulfide (MoS_2).

GASKET SEALANT

Gasket sealant is used instead of preformed gaskets on some applications, or as a gasket dressing on others. Three types of gasket sealant are commonly used: gasket sealing compound, room temperature vulcanizing (RTV) and anaerobic. Because these materials have different sealing properties, they cannot be used interchangeably.

Gasket Sealing Compound

This nonhardening liquid is used primarily as a gasket dressing. Gasket sealing compound is available in tubes or brush top containers. When exposed to air or heat it forms a rubber-like coating. The coating fills in small imperfections in gasket and sealing surfaces. Do not use gasket sealing compound that is old, has begun to solidify or has darkened in color.

Applying Gasket Sealing Compound

Carefully scrape residual gasket material, corrosion deposits or paint from the mating surfaces. Use a blunt scraper and work carefully to avoid damaging the mating surfaces. Use quick drying solvent and a clean shop towel and wipe oil or other contaminants from the surfaces. Wipe or blow loose material or contaminants from the gasket. Brush a light coating on the mating surfaces and both sides of the gasket. Do not apply more compound than needed. Excess compound will be squeezed out as the surfaces mate and may contaminate other components. Do not allow compound into bolt or alignment pinholes.

A hydraulic lock can occur as the bolt or pin compresses the compound, resulting in incorrect bolt torque.

RTV Sealant

This is a silicone gel supplied in tubes. Moisture in the air causes RTV to cure. Always place the cap on the tube as soon as possible if using RTV. RTV has a shelf life of approximately one year and will not cure properly after the shelf life expires. Check the expiration date on the tube and keep partially used tubes tightly sealed. RTV can generally fill gaps up to 1/4 in. (6.3 mm) and works well on slightly flexible surfaces.

Applying RTV Sealant

Carefully scrape all residual sealant and paint from the mating surfaces. Use a blunt scraper and work carefully to avoid damaging the mating surfaces. The mating surfaces must be absolutely free of gasket material, sealant, dirt, oil grease or other contamination. Lacquer thinner, acetone, isopropyl alcohol or similar solvents work well to clean the surfaces. Avoid using solvents with an oil, wax or petroleum base as they are not compatible with RTV compounds. Remove all sealant from bolt or alignment pinholes.

Apply RTV sealant in a continuous bead 0.08-0.12 in. (2-3 mm) thick. Circle all mounting bolt or alignment pinholes unless otherwise specified. Do not allow RTV sealant into bolt holes or other openings. A hydraulic lock can

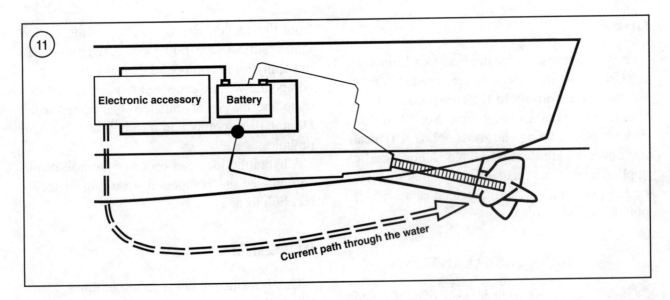

Current path through the water

occur as the bolt or pin compresses the sealant, resulting in incorrect bolt torque. Tighten the mounting fasteners within 10 minutes after application.

Anaerobic Sealant

This is a gel supplied in tubes. It cures only in the absence of air, as when squeezed tightly between two machined mating surfaces. For this reason, it will not spoil if the cap is left off the tube. Do not use anaerobic sealant if one of the surfaces is flexible. Anaerobic sealant is able to fill gaps up to 0.030 in. (0.8 mm) and generally works best on rigid, machined flanges or surfaces.

Applying Anaerobic Sealant

Carefully scrape all residual sealant from the mating surfaces. Use a blunt scraper and work carefully to avoid damaging the mating surfaces. The mating surfaces must be absolutely free of gasket material, sealant, dirt, oil grease or other contamination. Lacquer thinner, acetone, isopropyl alcohol or similar solvents work well to clean the surfaces. Avoid using solvents with an oil, wax or petroleum base as they are not compatible with anaerobic compounds. Clean a sealant from the bolt or alignment pinholes. Apply anaerobic sealant in a 0.04 in. (1 mm) thick continuous bead onto one of the surfaces. Circle all bolt and alignment pin openings. Do not apply sealant into bolt holes or other openings. A hydraulic lock can occur as the bolt or pin compresses the sealant, resulting in incorrect bolt torque. Tighten the mounting fasteners within 10 minutes after application.

GALVANIC CORROSION

A chemical reaction occurs whenever two different types of metal are joined by an electrical conductor and immersed in an electrolytic solution such as water. Electrons transfer from one metal to the other through the electrolyte and return through the conductor.

The hardware on a boat is made of many different types of metal. The boat hull acts as a conductor between the metals. Even if the hull is wooden or fiberglass, the slightest film of water (electrolyte) on the hull provides conductivity. This combination creates a good environment for electron flow (**Figure 11**). Unfortunately, this electron flow results in galvanic corrosion of the metal involved, causing one of the metals to be corroded or eroded away. The amount of electron flow, and therefore the amount of corrosion, depends on several factors:

1. The types of metal involved.
2. The efficiency of the conductor.
3. The strength of the electrolyte.

Metals

The chemical composition of the metal used in marine equipment has a significant effect on the amount and speed of galvanic corrosion. Certain metals are more resistant to corrosion than others. These electrically negative metals are commonly called *noble*; they act as the cathode in any reaction. Metals that are more subject to corrosion are electrically positive; they act as the anode in a reaction. The more *noble* metals include titanium, 18-8 stainless steel and nickel. Less *noble* metals include zinc, aluminum and magnesium. Galvanic corrosion becomes more severe as the difference in electrical potential between the two metals increases.

In some cases, galvanic corrosion can occur within a single piece of metal. For example, brass is a mixture of zinc and copper, and, when immersed in an electrolyte, the zinc portion of the mixture will corrode away as a galvanic reaction occurs between the zinc and copper particles.

Conductors

The hull of the boat often acts as the conductor between different types of metal. Marine equipment, such as the drive unit can act as the conductor. Large masses of metal, firmly connected together, are more efficient conductors than water. Rubber mountings and vinyl-based paint can act as insulators between pieces of metal.

Electrolyte

The water in which a boat operates acts as the electrolyte for the corrosion process. The more efficient a conductor is, the more severe and rapid the corrosion will be.

Cold, clean freshwater is the poorest electrolyte. Pollutants increase conductivity; therefore, brackish or saltwater is an efficient electrolyte. This is one of the reasons that most manufacturers recommend a freshwater flush after operating in polluted, brackish or saltwater.

Protection From Galvanic Corrosion

Because of the environment in which marine equipment must operate, it is practically impossible to totally prevent galvanic corrosion. However, there are several ways in which the process can be slowed. After taking these precautions, the next step is to *fool* the process into occurring only where you want it to occur. This is the role of sacrificial anodes and impressed current systems.

Slowing Corrosion

Some simple precautions can help reduce the amount of corrosion taking place outside the hull. These precautions are not substitutes for the corrosion protection methods discussed under *Sacrificial Anodes* and *Impressed Current Systems* in this chapter, but they can help these methods reduce corrosion.

Use fasteners made of metal more noble than the parts they secure. If corrosion occurs, the parts they secure may suffer but the fasteners are protected. The larger secured parts are more able to withstand the loss of material. Also major problems could arise if the fasteners corrode to the point of failure.

Keep all painted surfaces in good condition. If paint is scraped off and bare metal exposed, corrosion rapidly increases. Use a vinyl- or plastic-based paint, which acts as an electrical insulator.

Be careful when applying metal-based antifouling paint to the boat. Do not apply antifouling paint to metal parts of the boat or the drive unit. If applied to metal surfaces, this type of paint reacts with the metal and results in corrosion between the metal and the layer of paint. Maintain a minimum 1 in. (25 mm) border between the painted surface and any metal parts. Organic-based paints are available for use on metal surfaces.

Where a corrosion protection device is used, remember that it must be immersed in the electrolyte along with the boat to provide any protection. If you raise the gearcase out of the water with the boat docked, any anodes on the gearcase may be removed from the corrosion process rendering them ineffective. Never paint or apply any coating to anodes or other protection devices. Paint or other coatings insulate them from the corrosion process.

Any change in the boat's equipment, such as the installation of a new stainless steel propeller, changes the electrical potential and may cause increased corrosion. Always consider this when adding equipment or changing exposed materials. Install additional anodes or other protection equipment as required ensuring the corrosion protection system is up to the task. The expense to repair corrosion damage usually far exceeds that of additional corrosion protection.

Sacrificial Anodes

Sacrificial anodes are specially designed to do nothing but corrode. Properly fastening such pieces to the boat causes them to act as the anode in any galvanic reaction that occurs; any other metal in the reaction acts as the cathode and is not damaged.

Anodes are usually made or zinc, a far from a noble material. Some anodes are manufactured of an aluminum and indium alloy. This alloy is less noble than the aluminum alloy in drive system components, providing the desired sacrificial properties. The aluminum and indium alloy is more resistant to oxide coating than zinc anodes. Oxide coating occurs as the anode material reacts with oxygen in the water. An oxide coating will insulate the anode, dramatically reducing corrosion protection.

Anodes must be used properly to be effective. Simply fastening anodes to the boat in random locations will not do the job.

First determine how much anode surface is required to adequately protect the equipment's surface area. A good starting point is provided by the Military Specification MIL-A-818001, which states that one square inch of new anode protects either:
1. 800 square inches of freshly painted steel.
2. 250 square inches of bare steel or bare aluminum alloy.
3. 100 square inches of copper or copper alloy.

This rule is valid for a boat at rest. If underway, additional anode area is required to protect the same surface area.

The anode must be in good electrical contact with the metal that it protects. If possible, attach an anode to all metal surfaces requiring protection.

Good quality anodes have inserts around the fastener holes that are made of a more noble material. Otherwise, the anode could erode away around the fastener hole, allowing the anode to loosen or possibly fall off, thereby loosing needed protection.

Impressed Current System

An impressed current system can be added to any boat. The system generally consists of the anode, controller and reference electrode. The anode in this system is coated with a very noble

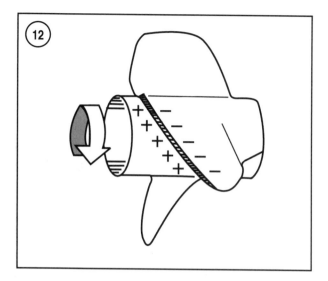

metal, such as platinum, so that it is almost corrosion-free and can last almost indefinitely. The reference electrode, under the boat's waterline, allows the control module to monitor the potential for corrosion. If the module senses that corrosion is occurring, it applies positive battery voltage to the anode. Current then flows from the anode to all other metal component, regardless of how noble or non-noble these components may be. Essentially, the electrical current from the battery counteracts the galvanic reaction to dramatically reduce corrosion damage.

Only a small amount of current is needed to counteract corrosion. Using input from the sensor, the control module provides only the amount of current needed to suppress galvanic corrosion. Most systems consume a maximum of 0.2 Ah at full demand. Under normal conditions, these systems can provide protection for 8-12 weeks without recharging the battery. Remember that this system must have constant connection to the battery. Often the battery supply to the system is connected to a battery switching device causing the operator to inadvertently shut off the system while docked.

An impressed current system is more expensive to install than sacrificial anodes but, considering its low maintenance requirements and the superior protection it provides, the long term cost may be lower.

PROPELLERS

The propeller is the final link between the boat's drive system and the water. A perfectly maintained engine and hull are useless if the propeller is the wrong type, is damaged or is deteriorated. Although propeller selection for a specific application is beyond the scope of this manual, the following provides the basic information needed to make an informed decision. The professional at a reputable marine dealership is the best source for a propeller recommendation.

How a Propeller Works

As the curved blades of a propeller rotate through the water, a high-pressure area forms on one side of the blade and a low-pressure area forms on the other side of the blade (**Figure 12**). The propeller moves toward the low-pressure area, carrying the boat with it.

Propeller Parts

Although a propeller is usually a one-piece unit, it is made of several different parts (**Figure 13**). Variations in the design of these parts make different propellers suitable for different applications.

The blade tip is the point of the blade furthest from the center of the propeller hub or propeller shaft bore. The blade tip separates the leading edge from the trailing edge.

The leading edge is the edge of the blade nearest the boat. During forward operation, this is the area of the blade that first cuts through the water.

The trailing edge is the surface of the blade furthest from the boat. During reverse opera-

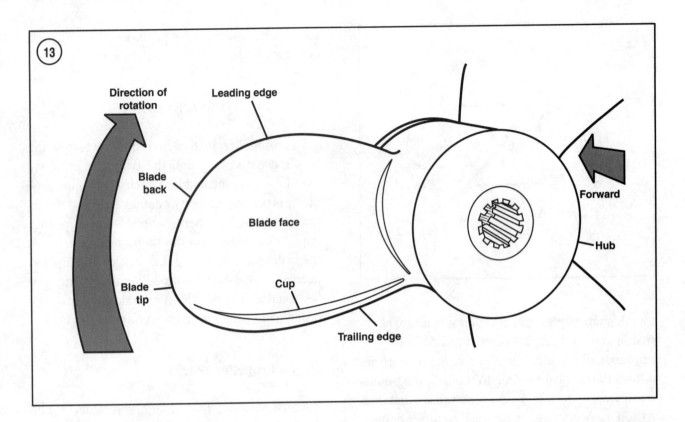

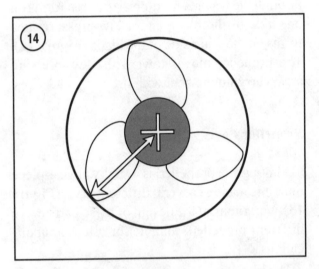

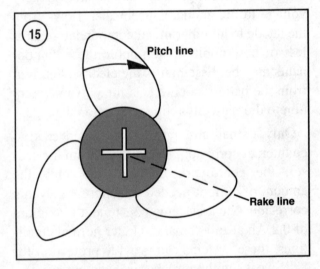

tion, this is the area of the blade that first cuts through the water.

The blade face is the surface of the blade that faces away from the boat. During forward operation, high-pressure forms on this side of the blade.

The blade back is the surface of the blade that faces toward the boat. During forward gear operation, low-pressure forms on this side of the blade.

The cup is a small curve or lip on the trailing edge of the blade. Cupped propeller blades generally perform better than non-cupped propeller blades.

The hub is the center portion of the propeller. It connects the blades to the propeller shaft. On most drive systems, engine exhaust is routed through the hub; in this case, the hub is made up of an outer and inner portion, connected by ribs.

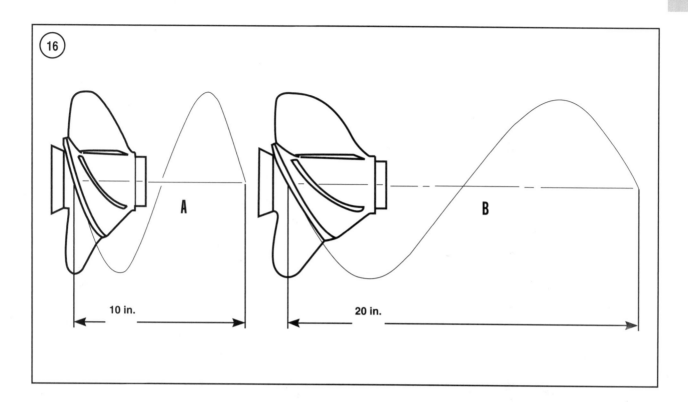

The diffuser ring is used on though- hub exhaust models to prevent exhaust gasses from entering the blade area.

Propeller Design

Changes in length, angle, thickness and material of propeller parts make different propellers suitable for different applications.

Diameter

Propeller diameter is the distance from the center of the hub to the blade tip, multiplied by two. Essentially it is the diameter of the circle formed by the blade tips during propeller rotation (**Figure 14**).

Pitch and rake

Propeller pitch and rake describe the placement of the blades in relation to the hub (**Figure 15**).

Pitch describes the theoretical distance the propeller would travel in one revolution. In A, **Figure 16**, the propeller would travel 10 inches in one revolution. In B, **Figure 16**, the propeller would travel 20 inches in one revolution. This distance is only theoretical; during operation, the propeller achieves only 75-85% of its pitch. Slip rate describes the difference in actual travel relative to the pitch. Lighter, faster boats typically achieve a lower slip rate than heavier, slower boats.

Propeller blades can be constructed with constant pitch (**Figure 17**) or progressive pitch (**Figure 18**). On a progressive propeller, the pitch starts low at the leading edge and increases toward the trailing edge. The propeller pitch specification is the average of the pitch across the entire blade. Propellers with progressive pitch usually provide better overall performance than constant pitch propellers.

Blade rake is specified in degrees and is measured along a line from the center of the hub to the blade tip. A blade that is perpendicular to the

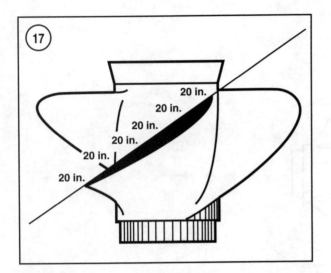

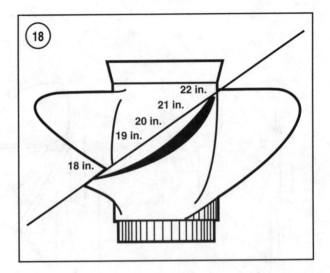

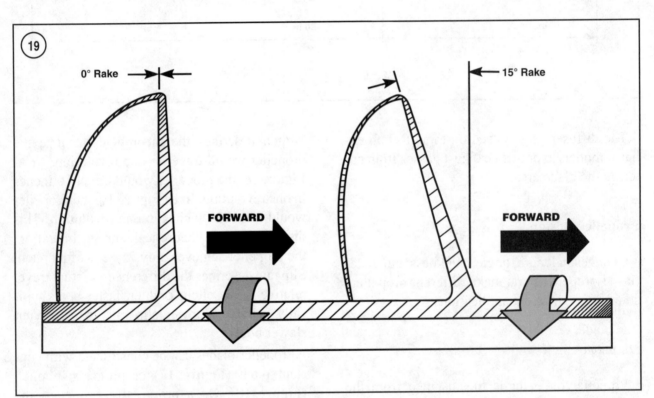

hub (**Figure 19**) has 0° rake. A blade that is angled from perpendicular (**Figure 19**) has a rake expressed by its difference from perpendicular. Most propellers have rakes ranging from 0-20°. Lighter faster boats generally perform better with propeller with a greater amount of rake. Heavier, slower boats generally perform better using a propeller with less rake.

Blade thickness

Blade thickness is not uniform at all points along the blade. For efficiency, blades are as thin a possible at all points while retaining enough strength to move the boat. Blades are thicker where they meet the hub and thinner at the blade tips (**Figure 20**). This is necessary to

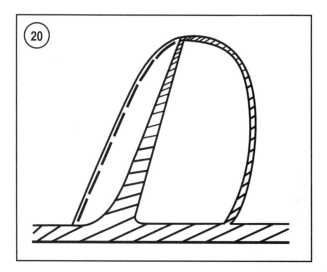

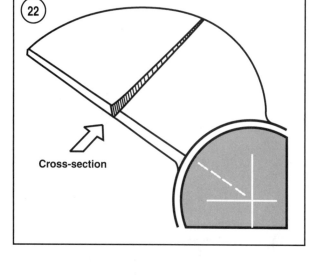

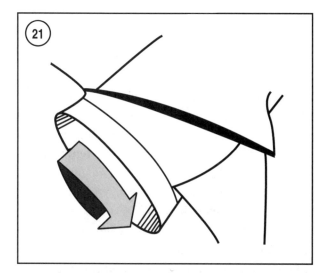

shaped cross-section (**Figure 22**). The leading edge is very thin and the blade thickness increases toward the trailing edge, where it is thickest. If a propeller such as this is run totally submerged, it is very inefficient.

Number of blades

The number of blades used on a propeller is a compromise between efficiency and vibration. A one-bladed propeller would the most efficient, but it would create an unacceptable amount of vibration. As blades are added, efficiency decreases, but so does vibration. Most propellers have three or four blades, representing the most practical trade-off between efficiency and vibration.

Material

Propeller materials are chosen for strength, corrosion resistance and economy. Stainless steel, aluminum, plastic and bronze are the most commonly used materials. Bronze is quite strong but rather expensive. Stainless steel is more common than bronze because of its combination of strength and lower cost. Aluminum alloy and plastic materials are the least expensive

support the heavier loads at the hub section of the blade. Overall blade thickness is dependent on the strength of the material used.

When cut along a line from the leading edge to the trailing edge in the central portion of the blade (**Figure 21**), the propeller blade resembles and airplane wing. The blade face, where high-pressure exists during forward rotation, is almost flat. The blade back, where low-pressure exists during forward rotation, is curved, with the thinnest portions at the edges and the thickest portion at the center.

Propellers that run only partially submerged, as in racing applications, may have a wedge

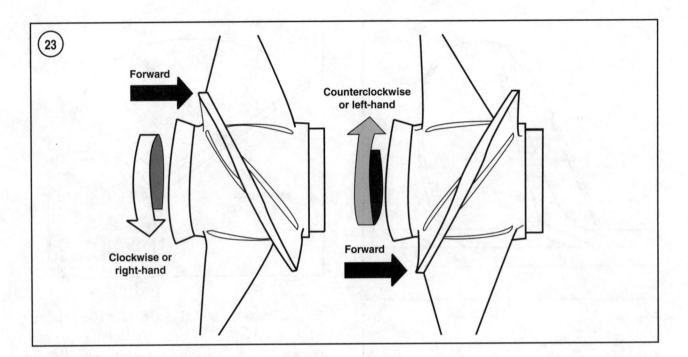

but usually lack the strength of stainless steel. Plastic propellers are more suited for lower horsepower applications.

Direction of rotation

Propellers are made for both right-hand and left hand rotations although right-hand is the most commonly used. As viewed from the rear of the boat while in forward gear, a right-hand propeller turns clockwise and a left-hand propeller turns counterclockwise. Off the boat, the direction of rotation is determined by observing the angle of the blades (**Figure 23**). A right-hand propeller's blade slant from the upper left to the lower right; a left-hand propeller's blades are opposite.

Cavitation and Ventilation

Cavitation and ventilation are *not* interchangeable terms; they refer to two distinct problems encountered during propeller operation.

To help understand cavitation, consider the relationship between pressure and the boiling point of water. At sea level, water boils at 212° F (100° C). As pressure increases, such as within an engine cooling system, the boiling point of the water increases—it boils at a temperature higher than 212° F (100° C). The opposite is also true. As pressure decreases, water boils at a temperature lower than 212° F (100° C). It the pressure drops low enough, water will boil at normal room temperature.

During normal propeller operation, low pressure forms on the blade back. Normally the pressure does not drop low enough for boiling to occur. However, poor propeller design, damaged blades or using the wrong propeller can cause unusually low pressure on the blade surface (**Figure 24**). If the pressure drops low enough, boiling occurs and bubbles form on the blade surfaces. As the boiling water moves to a higher pressure area of the blade, the boiling ceases and the bubbles collapse. The collapsing bubbles release energy that erodes the surface of the propeller blade.

Corroded surfaces, physical damage or even marine growth combined with high-speed operation can cause low pressure and cavitation on gearcase surfaces. In such cases, low pressure

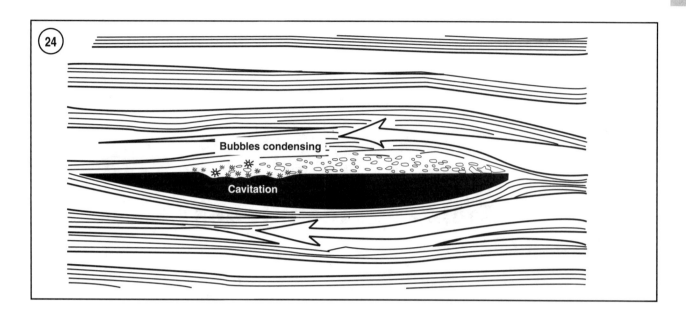

Bubbles condensing

Cavitation

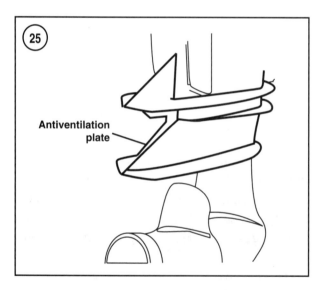

Antiventilation plate

forms as water flows over a protrusion or rough surface. The boiling water forms bubbles that collapse as they move to a higher pressure area toward the rear of the surface imperfection.

This entire process of pressure drop, boiling and bubble collapse is called *cavitation*. The ensuing damage is called *cavitation burn*. Cavitation is caused by a decrease in pressure, not an increase in temperature.

Ventilation is not as complex a process as cavitation. Ventilation refers to air entering the blade area, either from above the water surface or from a though-hub exhaust system. As the blades meet the air, the propeller momentarily looses it bite with the water and subsequently loses most of its thrust. An added complication is that the propeller and engine over-rev, causing very low pressure on the blade back and massive cavitation.

Most marine drive systems have a plate (**Figure 25**) above the propeller designed to prevent surface air from entering the blade area. This plate is correctly called an *anti-ventilation plate*, although it is often incorrectly called an *anticavitation plate*.

Most propellers have a flared section at the rear of the propeller called a diffuser ring. This feature forms a barrier, and extends the exhaust passage far enough aft to prevent the exhaust gases from ventilating the propeller.

A close fit of the propeller to the gearcase is necessary to keep exhaust gasses from exiting and ventilating the propeller. Using the wrong propeller attaching hardware can position the propeller too far aft, preventing a close fit. The wrong hardware can also allow the propeller to rub heavily against the gearcase, causing rapid wear to both components. Wear or damage to these surfaces will allow the propeller to ventilate.

Chapter Two

Tools and Techniques

This chapter describes the common tools required for marine engine repair and troubleshooting. Techniques that make the work easier and more effective are also described. Some of the procedures in this book require special skills or expertise; in some cases it is better to entrust the job to a specialist or qualified dealership.

SAFETY FIRST

Professional mechanics can work for years and never suffer a serious injury. Avoiding injury is as simple as following a few rules and using common sense. Ignoring the rules can and often does lead to physical injury and/or damaged equipment.

1. Never use gasoline as a cleaning solvent.

2. Never smoke or use a torch near flammable liquids, such as cleaning solvent. Dirty or solvent soaked shop towels are extremely flammable. If working in a garage, remember that most home gas appliances have pilot lights.

3. Never smoke or use a torch in an area where a battery is being charged. Highly explosive hydrogen gas is formed during the charging process.

4. Use the proper size wrench to avoid damaged fasteners and bodily injury.

5. If loosening a tight or stuck fastener, consider what could happen if the wrench slips. Protect yourself accordingly.

6. Keep the work area clean, uncluttered and well lighted.

7. Wear safety goggles while using any type of tool. This is especially important when drilling, grinding or using a cold chisel.

8. Never use worn or damaged tools.

9. Keep a Coast Guard approved fire extinguisher handy. Ensure it is rated for gasoline (Class B) and electrical (Class C) fires.

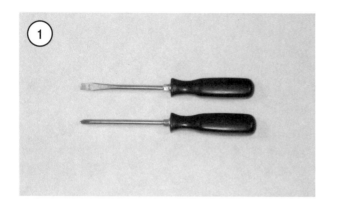

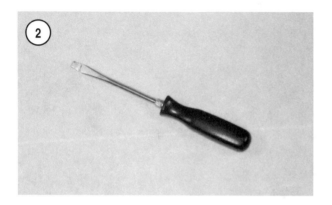

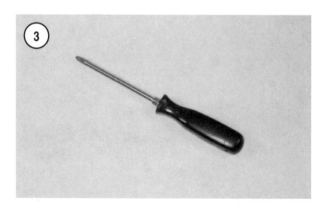

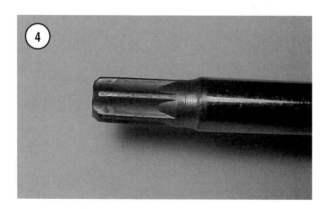

BASIC HAND TOOLS

2

A number of tools are required to maintain and repair a marine engine. Most of these tools are also used for home and automobile repair. Some tools are made especially for working on marine engines; these tools can be purchased from a marine dealership. Having the required tools always makes the job easier and more effective.

Keep the tools clean and in a suitable box. Keep them organized with related tools stored together. After using a tool, wipe it clean using a shop towel.

The following tools are required to perform virtually any repair job. Each tool is described and the recommended size given for starting a tool collection. Additional tools and some duplication may be added as you become more familiar with the equipment. You may need all U.S. standard tools, all metric size tools or a mixture of both.

Screwdrivers

A screwdriver (**Figure 1**) is a very basic tool, but if used improperly can do more damage than good. The slot on a screw has a definite dimension and shape. Always select a screwdriver that conforms to the shape of the screw. Use a small screwdriver for small screws and a large one for large screws or the screw head will be damaged.

Three types of screwdrivers are commonly required: a slotted (flat-blade) screwdriver (**Figure 2**), Phillips screwdriver (**Figure 3**) and Torx screwdriver (**Figure 4**).

Screwdrivers are available in sets, which often include an assortment of slotted Phillips and Torx blades. If you buy them individually, buy at least the following:

    a. Slotted screwdriver—5/16 × 6 in. blade.

    b. Slotted screwdriver—3/8 × 12 in. blade.

    c. Phillips screwdriver—No. 2 tip, 6 in. blade.

d. Phillips screwdriver—No. 3 tip, 6 in. blade.

e. Torx screwdriver—T15 tip, 6 in. blade.

f. Torx screwdriver—T20 tip, 6 in. blade.

g. Torx screwdriver—T25 tip, 6 in. blade.

Use screwdrivers only for driving screws. Never use a screwdriver for prying or chiseling. Do not attempt to remove a Phillips, Torx or Allen head screw with a slotted screwdriver; you can damage the screw head so that even the proper tool is unable to remove it.

Keep the tip of a slotted screwdriver in good condition. Carefully grind the tip to the proper size and taper if it is worn or damaged. The sides of the blade must be parallel and the blade tip must be flat. Replace a Phillips or Torx screwdriver if its tip is worn or damaged.

Pliers

Pliers come in a wide range of types and sizes. Pliers are useful for cutting, gripping, bending and crimping. Never use pliers to cut hardened objects or turn bolts or nuts. **Figure 5** shows several types of pliers.

Each type of pliers has a specialized function. General-purpose pliers are mainly used for gripping and bending. Locking pliers are used for gripping objects very tightly, like a vise. Use needlenose pliers to grip or bend small objects. Adjustable or slip-joint pliers (**Figure 6**) can be adjusted to grip various sized objects; the jaws remain parallel for gripping objects such as pipe or tubing. There are many more types of pliers. The ones described here are the most common.

Box-end and Open-end Wrenches

Box-end and open-end wrenches (**Figure 7**) are available in sets in a variety of sizes. The number stamped near the end of the wrench refers to the distance between two parallel flats on the hex head bolt or nut.

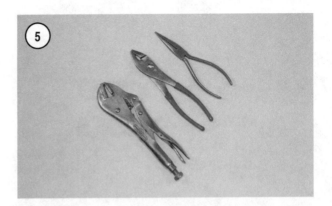

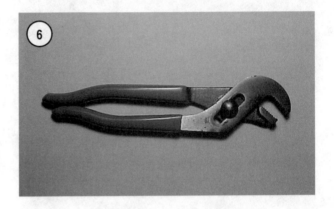

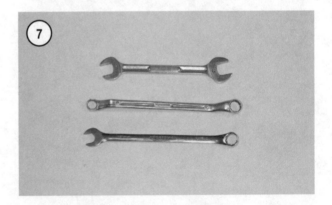

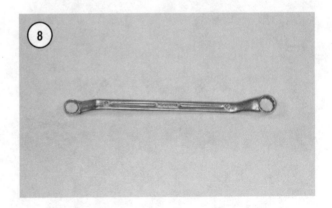

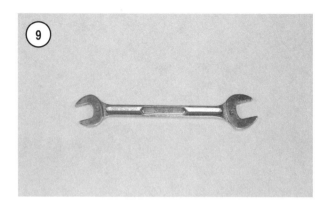

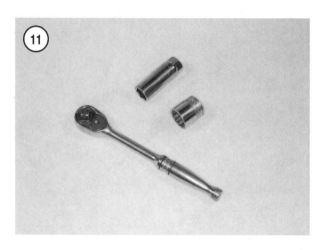

Box-end wrenches (**Figure 8**) provide a better grip on the nut and are stronger than open end wrenches. An open-end wrench (**Figure 9**) grips the nut on only two flats. Unless it fits well, it may slip and round off the points on the nut. A box-end wrench grips all six flats. Box-end wrenches are available with six-point or 12 point openings. The six-point opening provides

superior holding power; the 12-point allow a shorter swing if working in tight quarters.

Use an open-end wrench if a box-end wrench cannot be positioned over the nut or bolt. To prevent damage to the fastener, avoid using and open-end wrench if a large amount of tightening or loosening toque is required.

A combination wrench has both a box-end and open- end. Both ends are the same size.

Adjustable Wrenches

An adjustable wrench (**Figure 10**) can be adjusted to fit virtually any nut or bolt head. However, it can loosen and slip from the nut or bolt, causing damage to the nut and possible physical injury. Use an adjustable wrench only if a proper size open-end or box-end wrench is not available. Avoid using an adjustable wrench if a large amount of tightening or loosening torque is required.

Adjustable wrenches come in sized ranging from 4-18 in. overall length. A 6 or 8 in. size is recommended as an all-purpose wrench.

Socket Wrenches

A socket wrench (**Figure 11**) is generally faster, safer and more convenient to use than a common wrench. Sockets, which attach to a suitable handle, are available with six-point or 12-point openings and use 1/4, 3/8, and 1/2 in. drive sizes. The drive size corresponds to the square hole that mates with the ratchet or flex handle.

Torque Wrench

A torque wrench (**Figure 12**) is used with a socket to measure how tight a nut or bolt is installed. They come in a wide price range and in 1/4, 3/8, and 1/2 in. drive sizes. The drive size corresponds to the square hole that mates with the socket.

A typical 1/4 in. drive torque wrench measures in in.-lb. increments, and has a range of 20-150 in.-lb. (2.2-17 Nm,). A typical 3/8 or ½ in. torque measures in ft.-lb. increments, and has a range of 10-150 ft.-lb. (14-203 Nm.).

Impact Driver

An impact driver (**Figure 13**) makes removal of tight fasteners easy and reduces damage to bolts and screws. Interchangeable bits allow use on a variety of fasteners.

Snap Ring Pliers

Snap ring pliers are required to remove snap rings. Snap ring pliers (**Figure 14**) usually come with different size tips; many designs can be switched to handle internal or external snap rings.

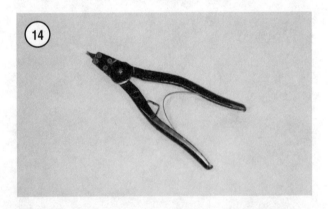

Hammers

Various types of hammers (**Figure 15**) are available to accommodate a number of applications. Use a ball-peen hammer to strike another tool, such as a punch or chisel. Use a soft-face hammer to strike a metal object without damaging it.

Never use a metal-faced hammer on engine and drive system components as severe damage will occur. You can always produce the same amount of force with a soft-faced hammer.

Always wear eye protection when using hammers. Make sure the hammer is in good condition and that the handle is not cracked. Select the correct hammer for the job and always strike the object squarely. Do not use the handle or the side of the hammer head to strike an object.

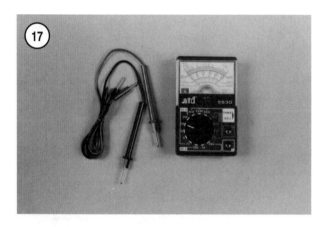

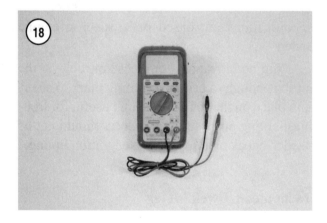

Feeler Gauges

This tool has either flat or wire measuring gauges (**Figure 16**). Use wire gauges to measure spark plug gap; use flat gauges for other measurements. A nonmagnetic (brass) gauge may be specified if working around magnetized components.

Other Special Tools

Many of the maintenance and repair procedures require special tools. Most of the necessary tools are available from a marine dealership or from tool suppliers. Instructions for their use and the manufacture's part number are included in the appropriate chapter.

Purchase the required tools from a local marine dealership or tool supplier. A qualified machinist, often at a lower price, can make some tools locally. Many marine dealerships and rental outlets will rent some of the required tools. Avoid using makeshift tools. Their use may result in damaged parts that cost far more than the recommended tool.

TEST EQUIPMENT

This section describes equipment used to perform testing, adjustments and measurements on marine engines. Most of these tools are available from a local marine dealership or automotive parts store.

Multimeter

This instrument is invaluable for electrical troubleshooting and service. It combines a voltmeter, ohmmeter and an ammeter in one unit. It is often called a VOM.

Two types of mutimeter are available, analog and digital. Analog meters (**Figure 17**) have a moving needle with marked bands on the meter face indicating the volt, ohm and amperage scales. An analog meter must be calibrated each time the scale is changed.

A digital meter (**Figure 18**) is ideally suited for electrical troubleshooting because it is easy to read and more accurate than an analog meter. Most models are auto-ranging, have automatic polarity compensation and internal overload protection circuits.

Either type of meter is suitable for most electrical testing described in this manual. An analog meter is better suited for testing pulsing voltage signals such as those produced by the ignition system. A digital meter is better suited for testing very low resistance or voltage reading (less than 1 volt or 1 ohm). The test procedure will indicate if a specific type of meter is required.

The ignition system produces electrical pulses that are too short in duration for accurate measurement with a using a conventional multimeter. Use a meter with peak-volt reading capability to test the ignition system. This type of meter captures the peak voltage reached during an electrical pulse.

Scale selection, meter specifications and test connections vary by the manufacturer and model of the meter. Thoroughly read the instructions supplied with the meter before performing any test. The meter and certain electrical components on the engine can be damaged if tested incorrectly. Have the test performed by a qualified professional if you are unfamiliar with the testing or general meter usage. The expense to replace damaged equipment can far exceed the cost of having the test performed by a professional.

Strobe Timing Light

This instrument is necessary for dynamic tuning (setting ignition timing while the engine is running). By flashing a light at the precise instant the spark plug fires, the position of the timing mark can be seen. The flashing light makes a moving mark appear to stand still next to a stationary mark.

Timing lights (**Figure 19**) range from inexpensive models with a neon bulb to expensive models with a xenon bulb, built in tachometer and timing advance compensator. A built in tachometer is very useful as most ignition timing

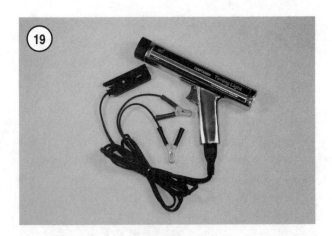

specifications are based on a specific engine speed.

A timing advance compensator delays the strobe enough to bring the timing mark to a certain place on the scale. Although useful for troubleshooting purposes, this feature should not be used to check or adjust the base ignition timing.

Tachometer/Dwell Meter

A portable tachometer (**Figure 20**) is needed to tune and test most marine engines. Ignition timing and carburetor adjustments must be performed at a specified engine speed. Tachometers are available with either an analog or digital display.

The fuel/air mixture must be adjusted with the engine running at idle speed. If using an analog

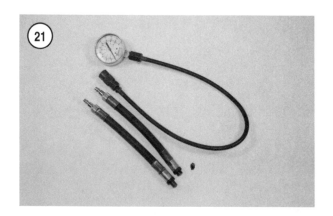

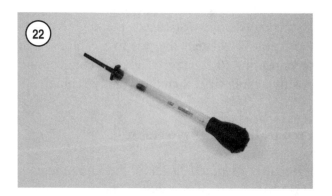

vide accurate measurement at all speeds without the need to change the range or scale. Many of these use an inductive pickup to receive the signal from the ignition system.

A dwell meter is often incorporated into the tachometer to allow testing and/or adjustments to engines with a breaker point ignition system.

Compression Gauge

This tool (**Figure 21**) measures the amount of pressure created in the combustion chamber during the compression stroke. Compression indicates the general engine condition making it one of the most useful troubleshooting tools.

The easiest type to use has screw-in adapters that fit the spark plug holes. Rubber tipped, press-in type gauges are also available. This type must be held firmly in the spark plug hole to prevent leakage and inaccurate test results..

Hydrometer

Use a hydrometer to measure specific gravity in the battery. Specific gravity is the density of the battery electrolyte as compared to pure water and indicates the battery's state of charge. Choose a hydrometer (**Figure 22**) with automatic temperature compensation; otherwise the electrolyte temperature must be measured during charging to determine the actual specific gravity.

Precision Measuring Tools

Various tools are required to make precision measurements. A dial indicator (**Figure 23**), for example, is used to determine piston position in the cylinder, runout and end play of shafts and assemblies. It is also used to measure free movement between the gear teeth (backlash) in the drive unit.

tachometer, choose one with a low range of 0-1000 rpm or 0-2000 rpm range and a high range of 0-6000 rpm. The high range setting is needed for testing purposes but lacks the accuracy needed at lower speeds. At lower speeds the meter must be capable of detecting changes of 25 rpm or less.

Digital tachometers are generally easier to use than most analog type tachometers. They pro-

Vernier calipers (**Figure 24**), micrometers (**Figure 25**) and other precision tools are used to measure the size of parts, such as the piston.

Precision measuring equipment must be stored, handled and used carefully or it will not remain accurate.

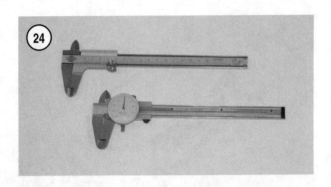

SERVICE HINTS

Most of the service procedures in this manual are straightforward and can be performed by anyone reasonably handy with tools. It is suggested, however, that you consider your skills and available tools and equipment before attempting a repair involving major disassembly of the engine or drive unit.

Some operations, for example, require the use of a press. Other operations require precision measurement. Have the procedure or measurements performed by a professional if you do not have access to the correct equipment or are unfamiliar with its use.

Special Battery Precautions

Disconnecting or connecting the battery can create a spike or surge of current throughout the electrical system. This spike or surge can damage certain components of the charging system. Always verify the ignition switch is in the OFF position before connecting or disconnecting the battery or changing the selection on a battery switch.

Always disconnect both battery cables and remove the battery from the boat for charging. If the battery cables are connected, the charger may induce a damaging spike or surge of current into the electrical system. During charging, batteries produce explosive and corrosive gasses. These gases can cause corrosion in the battery compartment and creates an extremely hazardous condition.

Disconnect the cables from the battery prior to testing, adjusting or repairing many of the systems or components on the engine. This is nec-

essary for safety, to prevent damage to test equipment and to ensure accurate testing or adjustment. Always disconnect the negative battery cable first, then the positive cable. When reconnecting the battery, always connect the positive cable first, then the negative cable.

Preparation for Disassembly

Repairs go much faster if the equipment is clean before you begin work. There are special cleaners such as Gunk or Bel-Ray Degreaser, for cleaning the engine and related components. Just spray or brush on the cleaning solution, let it stand, then rinse with a garden hose.

Use pressurized water to remove marine growth and corrosion or mineral deposits from external components such as the gearcase, drive shaft housing and clamp brackets. Avoid directing pressurized water directly as seals or gaskets; pressurized water can flow past seal and gasket surfaces and contaminate lubricating fluids.

> *WARNING*
> *Never use gasoline as a cleaning agent. It presents an extreme fire hazard. Always work in a well-ventilated area if using cleaning solvent. Keep a coast Guard approved fire extinguisher, rated for gasoline fires, readily accessible in the work area.*

Much of the labor charged for a job performed at a dealership is usually for removal and disas-

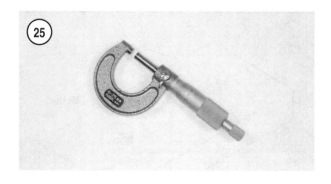

sembly of other parts to access defective parts or assemblies. It is frequently possible to perform most of the disassembly then take the defective part or assembly to the dealership for repair.

If you decide to perform the job yourself, read the appropriate section in this manual, in its entirety. Study the illustrations and text until you fully understand what is involved to complete the job. Make arrangements to purchase or rent all required special tools and equipment before starting.

Disassembly Precautions

During disassembly, keep a few general precautions in mind. Force is rarely needed to get things apart. If parts fit tightly, such as a bearing on a shaft, there is usually a tool designed to separate them. Never use a screwdriver to separate parts with a machined mating surface, such as the cylinder head or manifold. The surfaces will be damaged and leak.

Make diagrams or take instant photographs wherever similar-appearing parts are found. Often, disassembled parts are left for several days or longer before resuming work. You may not remember where everything came from, or carefully arranged parts may become disturbed.

Cover all openings after removing parts to keep contamination or other parts from entering.

Tag all similar internal parts for location and mounting direction. Reinstall all internal components in the same location and mounting direction as removed. Record the thickness and mounting location of any shims as they are removed. Place small bolts and parts in plastic sandwich bags. Seal and label the bags with masking tape.

Tag all wires, hoses and connections and make a sketch of the routing. Never rely on memory alone; it may be several days or longer before you resume work.

Protect all painted surfaces from physical damage. Never allow gasoline or cleaning solvent on these surfaces.

Assembly Precautions

No parts, except those assembled with a press fit, require unusual force during assembly. If a part is hard to remove or install, find out why before proceeding.

When assembling parts, start all fasteners, then tighten evenly in an alternating or crossing pattern unless a specific tightening sequence or procedure is given.

When assembling parts, be sure all shims, spacers and washers are installed in the same position and location as removed.

Whenever a rotating part butts against a stationary part, look for a shim or washer. Use new gaskets, seals and O-rings if there is any doubt about the conditions of the used ones. Unless otherwise specified, a thin coating of oil on gaskets may help them seal more effectively. Use heavy grease to hold small parts in place if they tend to fall out during assembly.

Use emery cloth and oil to remove high spots from piston surfaces. Use a dull screwdriver to remove carbon deposits from the cylinder head, ports and piston crown. *Do not* scratch or gouge these surfaces. Wipe the surfaces clean with a *clean* shop towel when finished.

If the carburetor must be repaired, completely disassemble it and soak all metal parts in a commercial carburetor cleaner. Never soak gaskets and rubber or plastic parts in these cleaners.

Clean rubber or plastic parts in warm soapy water. Never use a wire to clean jets and small passages because they are easily damaged. Use compressed air to blow debris from all passages in the carburetor body.

Take your time and do the job right. Break-in procedure for a newly rebuilt engine or drive is the same as for a new one. Use the recommended break-in oil and follow the instructions provided in the appropriate chapter.

SPECIAL TIPS

Because of the extreme demands placed on marine equipment, several points must be kept in mind when performing service and repair. The following are general suggestions that may improve the overall life of the machine and help avoid costly failure.

1. Unless otherwise specified, apply a threadlocking compound, such as Loctite Threadlocker, to all bolts and nuts, even if secured with a lockwasher. Use only the specified grade of threadlocking compound. A screw or bolt lost from an engine cover or bearing retainer could easily cause serious and expensive damage before the loss is noticed. When applying threadlocking compound, use only enough to lightly coat the threads. If too much is used, it can work its way down the threads and contaminate seals or bearings.

2. If self-locking fasteners are used, replace them with new ones. Do not install standard fasteners in place of self-locking ones.

3. Use caution when using air tools to remove stainless steel nuts or bolts. The heat generated during rapid spinning easily damages the threads of stainless steel fasteners. To prevent thread damage, apply penetrating oil as a cooling agent and loosen or tighten them slowly.

4. Use a wide chisel to straighten the tab of a fold-over type lockwasher. Such a tool provides a better contact surface than a screwdriver or pry bar, making straightening easier. During installa-

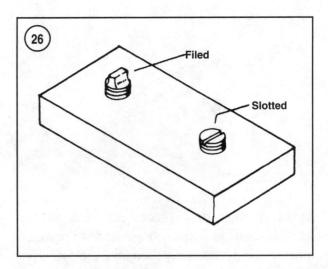

tion, use a new fold-over type lockwasher. If a new lockwasher is not available, fold over a tab on the washer that has not been previously used. Reusing the same tab may cause the washer to break, resulting in a loss of locking ability and a loose piece of metal adrift in the engine. When folding the tab into position, carefully pry it toward the flat on the bolt or nut. Use a pair or plies to bend the tab against the fastener. Do not use a punch and hammer to drive the tab into position. The resulting fold may be too sharp, weakening the washer and increasing its chance of failure.

5. Use only the specified replacement parts if replacing a missing or damaged bolt, screw or nut. Many fasteners are specially hardened for the application.

6. Install only the specified gaskets. Unless specified otherwise, install them without sealant. Many gaskets are made with a material that swells when it contacts oil. Gasket sealer prevents them from swelling as intended and can result in oil leakage. Most gaskets must be a specific thickness. Installing a gasket that is too thin or too thick in a critical area could cause expensive damage.

7. Make sure all shims and washers are reinstalled in the same location and position. Whenever a rotating part contacts a stationary part, look for a shim or washer.

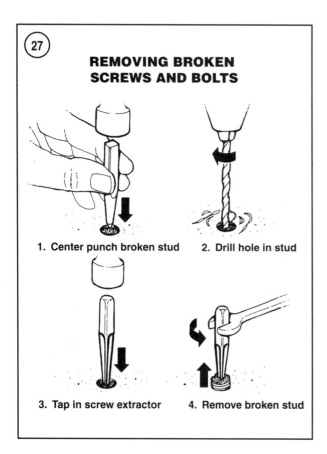

**REMOVING BROKEN
SCREWS AND BOLTS**

1. Center punch broken stud

2. Drill hole in stud

3. Tap in screw extractor

4. Remove broken stud

MECHANIC'S TECHNIQUES

Marine engines are subjected to conditions very different from most engines. They are repeatedly subjected to a corrosive environment followed by periods of non-use for weeks or longer. Such use invites corrosion damage to fasteners, causing difficulty or breakage during removal. This section provides information that is useful for removing stuck or broken fasteners and repairing damaged threads.

Removing Stuck Fasteners

When a nut or bolt corrodes and cannot be removed, several methods may be used to loosen it. First, apply penetrating oil, such as Liquid Wrench or WD-40. Apply it liberally to the threads and allow it to penetrate for 10-15 minutes. Tap the fastener several times with a small

hammer; however, do not hit it hard enough to cause damage. Reapply the penetrating oil if necessary.

For stuck screws, apply penetrating oil as described, then insert a screwdriver in the slot. Tap the top of the screwdriver with a hammer. This looses the corrosion in the threads allowing it to turn. If the screw head is too damaged to use a screwdriver, grip the head with locking pliers and twist the screw from the assembly.

A Phillips, Allen or Torx screwdriver may start to slip in the screw during removal. If slippage occurs, stop immediately and apply a dab of course valve lapping compound onto the tip of the screwdriver. Valve lapping compound or a special screw removal compound is available from most hardware and automotive parts stores. Insert the driver into the screw and apply downward pressure while turning. The gritty material in the compound improves the grip on the screw, allowing more rotational force before slippage occurs. Keep the compound away from any other engine components. It is very abrasive and can cause rapid wear if applied onto moving or sliding surfaces.

Avoid applying heat unless specifically instructed because it may melt, warp or remove the temper from parts.

Removing Broken Bolts or Screws

The head of bolt or screw may unexpectedly twist off during removal. Several methods are available for removing the remaining portion of the bolt or screw.

If a large portion of the bolt or screw projects out, try gripping it with locking pliers. If the projecting portion is too small, file it to fit a wrench or cut a slot in it to fit a screwdriver (**Figure 26**). If the head breaks off flush or cannot be turned with a screwdriver or wrench, use a screw extractor (**Figure 27**). To do this, center punch the remaining portion of the screw or bolt. Select the proper size of extractor for the size of the fastener. Using the drill size specified on the extractor, drill a hole into the fastener. Do not drill deeper than the remaining fastener. Carefully tap the extractor into the hole and back the remnant out using a wrench on the extractor.

Remedying Stripped Threads

Occasionally, threads are stripped through carelessness or impact damage. Often the threads can be repaired by running a tap (for internal threads on nuts) or die (for external threads on bolts) through threads (**Figure 28**).

To clean or repair spark plug threads, use a spark plug tap. If an internal thread is damaged, it may be necessary to install a Helicoil or some other type of thread insert. Follow the manufacturer's instructions when installing their insert.

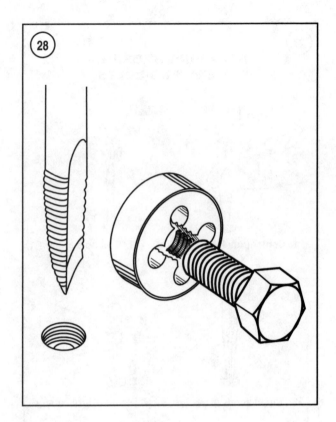

Chapter Three

Troubleshooting

Troubleshooting is a relatively simple matter when it is done logically. The first step in any troubleshooting procedure is to define the symptoms as closely as possible and then localize the problem. Subsequent steps involve testing and analyzing those areas which could cause the symptoms. A haphazard approach may eventually solve the problem, but it can be very costly in terms of wasted time and unnecessary parts replacement.

Proper lubrication, maintenance and periodic tune-ups as described in Chapter Four will reduce the necessity for troubleshooting. Even with the best of care, however, an outboard motor is prone to problems which will require troubleshooting.

This chapter contains brief descriptions of each operating system and troubleshooting procedures to be used. **Tables 1-3** present typical starting, ignition and fuel system problems with their probable causes and

solutions. **Tables 1-19** are at the end of the chapter.

OPERATING REQUIREMENTS

Every outboard motor requires 3 basic things to run properly: an uninterrupted supply of fuel and air in the correct proportions, proper ignition at the right time and adequate compression. If any of these are lacking, the motor will not run.

The electrical system is the weakest link in the chain. More problems result from electrical malfunctions than from any other source. Keep this in mind before you blame the fuel system and start making unnecessary carburetor adjustments.

If a motor has been sitting for any length of time and refuses to start, check the condition of the battery first to make sure it has an adequate charge, then look to the fuel delivery system. This includes the gas tank, fuel pump, fuel lines and carburetor(s). Rust may have formed in the tank, obstructing fuel flow. Gasoline deposits may have gummed up carburetor jets and air passages. Gasoline tends to lose its potency after standing for long periods. Condensation may contaminate it with water. Drain the old gas and try starting with a fresh tankful.

STARTING SYSTEM

Description

An electric starter motor (**Figure 1**) is optional on Suzuki DT 9.9-DT 50 outboards and standard on DT 60-DT 140 models. The motor is mounted vertically on the engine. When battery current is supplied to the starter motor, its pinion gear is thrust upward to engage the teeth on the engine flywheel. Once the engine starts, the pinion gear disengages from the flywheel. This is similar to the method used in cranking an automotive engine.

The electric starting system requires a fully charged battery to provide the large amount of current required to operate the starter motor. The battery may be charged externally or by a lighting coil on the magneto stator base which keeps the battery charged while the engine is running.

The starting circuit consists of the battery, a key ignition or push-button starter switch, an interlock switch, a stop switch, the starter motor, starter relay and connecting wiring.

The starter relay carries the heavy electrical current to the motor. See **Figure 2**. Depressing the starter switch or turning the key ignition switch to the START position allows current to flow through the relay coil. The relay contacts close and allow current to flow from the battery through the relay to the starter motor.

An interlock switch in all electric starting circuits prevents current flow to the starter motor if the shift mechanism is not in

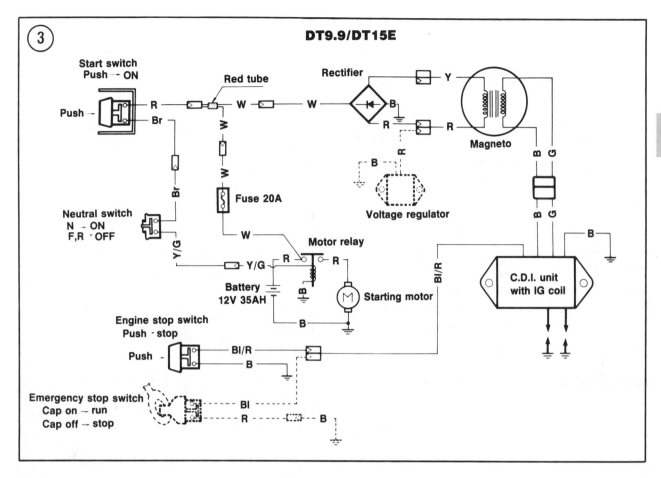

NEUTRAL. Most Suzuki models sold in the United States have an NSI circuit (Neutral Start Interlock) which prevents ignition unless the shift mechanism is in NEUTRAL. Models without the NSI circuit have a mechanical interlock in the rewind starter. This interlock device is connected to the interlock switch by a cable.

The stop switch shorts out the stator charge coil on all models except the DT 40, DT 115 and DT 140. These models incorporate a low voltage stop circuit which prevents a high voltage leak when the voltage is diverted to ground. **Figure 3** is a schematic of a typical Suzuki electrical system showing the starting and stop circuits.

CAUTION
Do not operate an electric starter motor continuously for more than 10 seconds.

Allow the motor to cool for at least 2 minutes between attempts to start the engine.

Troubleshooting

Refer to **Table 1** at the end of the chapter. Before troubleshooting the starting circuit, make sure that:

a. The battery is fully charged.

b. Battery cables are the proper size and length. Replace cables that are undersize or relocate the battery to shorten the distance between battery and starter relay.

c. The shift mechanism is in NEUTRAL and the emergency switch cap is properly installed on remote control models.

d. All electrical connections are clean and tight.

e. The wiring harness is in good condition, with no worn or frayed insulation or loose harness sockets.

f. The electrical circuit fuse is in good condition.

g. The fuel system is filled with an adequate supply of fresh gasoline that has been properly mixed with Suzuki CCI 50:1 Outboard Oil. See Chapter Four.

Troubleshooting is intended only to isolate a malfunction to a certain component. If further bench testing is necessary, remove the suspected component and have it tested by an authorized service center. Refer to Chapter Seven for component removal and installation procedures.

Starter Relay
Continuity Test

1. Disconnect the yellow/green and black starter relay leads.

2. Connect an ohmmeter between the 2 leads. See **Figure 4** (typical). If the meter does not read 3.2-3.8 ohms, replace the starter relay. See Chapter Seven.

Neutral Start Interlock
Switch Continuity Test

1. Disconnect the yellow/green and brown interlock switch leads.

2. Connect an ohmmeter between the 2 leads. See **Figure 5** (typical). There should be continuity with the shift lever in NEUTRAL and no continuity when the shift lever is moved to FORWARD or REVERSE.

3. If there is no continuity with the shift lever in NEUTRAL, manually depress the interlock switch plunger. If there is still no continuity, replace the switch.

4. If continuity is shown in Step 3, turn the switch adjusting bolt until the switch performs as described in Step 2.

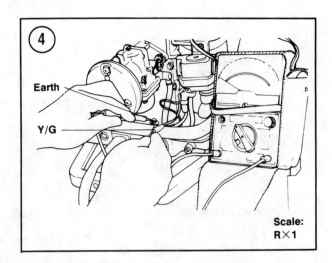

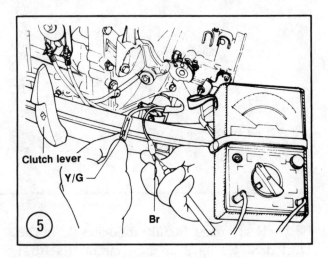

Push Button Start Switch
Continuity Test

1. Disconnect the red and black start button leads.

2. Connect an ohmmeter between the 2 leads. See **Figure 6** (typical). There should be no continuity.

3. Depress the start button. The meter should show continuity.

4. If the switch does not perform as described in Step 2 and Step 3, replace it.

Key Ignition Switch
Continuity Test

Test the key switch with an ohmmeter or self-powered test lamp. If there is not

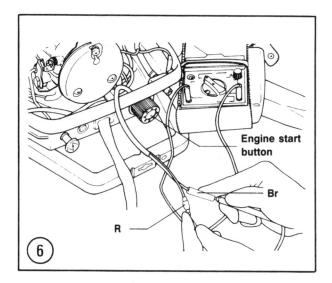

Engine start button

Br

R

⑥

⑦

IGNITION SWITCH CONTACT CHART

	B	G	W	B/W	Br	O
CHOKE				○		○
START			○	○	○	
ON			○	○		
OFF	○	○				

B : Black   W : White
Br : Brown   B/W : Black/White
G : Green   O : Orange

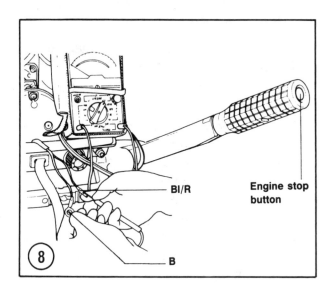

Bl/R

Engine stop button

⑧ B

continuity in each position as shown in **Figure 7**, replace the switch.

Stop Switch
Continuity Test

1. Disconnect the black and blue/red stop switch leads.
2. Connect an ohmmeter between the 2 leads. See **Figure 8** (typical). There should be no continuity.
3. Depress the stop switch. The meter should show continuity.
4. If the switch does not perform as described in Step 2 and Step 3, replace it.

LIGHTING SYSTEM

The AC lighting system consists of a lighting coil mounted on the magneto base assembly and permanent magnets located within the flywheel rim. The system provides alternating current to operate accessories such as boat lights only when the engine is running. Poor connections, defective wiring insulation or the use of too many accessories are major causes of AC lighting system problems.

The AC lighting system can be converted to a battery charging system by installing a rectifier (with fuse) to convert the AC lighting voltage to DC battery charging voltage.

To check the lighting coil resistance, see *Battery Charging Coil Resistance Test* in this chapter.

CHARGING SYSTEM

Description

The standard 7 amp charging system consists of a lighting or battery charging coil mounted on the magneto base assembly, permanent magnets located within the flywheel rim, a rectifier to change alternating current (AC) to direct current (DC), the battery, a 20 amp fuse and connecting wiring.

3

The system delivers 30 watts (DT 3.5) or 80 watts (all others) at 12 volts. **Figure 9** is a schematic of a typical Suzuki charging system.

The standard charging system can be converted to an optional 15 amp system by replacing the rectifier with a combination rectifier/voltage regulator. This optional system produces 200 watts at 12 volts and is recommended as a means of preventing battery overcharging during long periods of continuous use.

A malfunction in the charging system generally causes the battery to remain undercharged. Since the battery charging coil is protected by its location underneath the flywheel, it is more likely that the battery, rectifier, fuse or connecting wiring will cause problems. The following conditions will cause rectifier damage:

    a. Battery leads reversed.
    b. Running the engine with the battery leads disconnected.
    c. A broken wire or loose connection resulting in an open circuit.

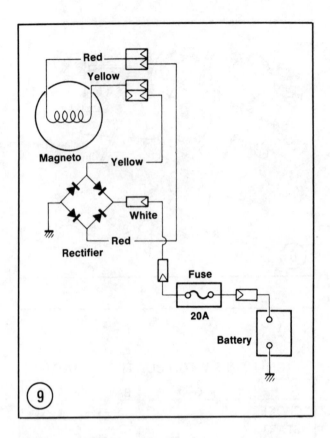

Troubleshooting

Before performing a battery charging coil or rectifier test, visually check the following.
1. Make sure the battery cables are properly connected. If polarity is reversed, check for a damaged rectifier.

NOTE
A damaged rectifier will generally have a discolored or a burned appearance.

2. Carefully inspect all wiring between the magneto base and battery for worn or cracked insulation and corroded or loose connections. Replace wiring or clean and tighten connections as required.
3. Check battery condition. Clean and recharge as required.

Battery Charging Coil Output Test

CAUTION
The engine must be provided with an adequate supply of water while performing this procedure. Install a flushing device, place the engine in a test tank or perform the step with the boat in the water.

1. Make sure the battery is fully charged.
2. Remove the engine cover.
3. Connect a tachometer according to manufacturer's instructions.
4. Start the engine and warm to normal operating temperature.
5. Connect an ammeter between the battery and the fuse. See **Figure 10**.
6. Gradually increase engine speed to approximately 5,000 rpm and note the ammeter reading. If it is not at least 6 amps (standard) or 14 amps (optional), replace the battery charging coil.

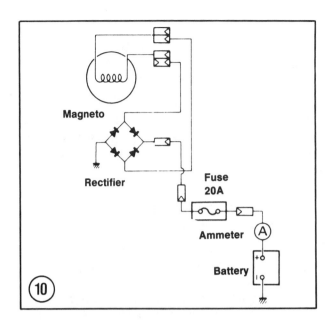

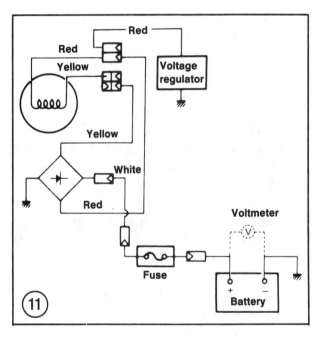

Battery Charging Coil Resistance Test

1. Remove the engine cover.

NOTE
On some models, one coil lead may be red or yellow/red instead of yellow as specified in Step 2. On DT 25 (1983-on), DT 30 and DT 40 models, the leads must be disconnected inside the junction box.

2. Disconnect the 2 yellow lighting or battery charging coil leads at their bullet connectors.
3. Connect an ohmmeter between the 2 disconnected leads.
4. Compare the reading to the specifications given in **Table 4**. If not within specifications, replace the lighting or battery charging coil.

Rectifier Test

1. Remove the engine cover.
2. Disconnect the red, white, yellow and black rectifier leads.
3. Connect a self-powered test lamp between the yellow and white leads, then reverse the test lamp connections. The lamp should light in one direction but not in the other.
4. Repeat Step 3 to test the red and white, black and red and yellow and black leads.
5. If the lamp does not perform as described at any one of the diode connections, replace the rectifier.

Voltage Regulator Test

CAUTION
The engine must be provided with an adequate supply of water while performing this procedure. Install a flushing device, place the engine in a test tank or perform the step with the boat in the water.

1. Make sure the battery is fully charged.
2. Remove the engine cover.
3. Connect a tachometer according to manufacturer's instructions.
4. Start the engine and warm to normal operating temperature.
5. Connect a voltmeter across the battery terminals. See **Figure 11**.
6. Gradually increase engine speed to approximately 5,000 rpm and note the voltmeter reading. If it is not 14-15 volts, replace the voltage regulator.

IGNITION SYSTEM

The wiring harness used between the ignition switch and engine is adequate to handle the electrical needs of the outboard. It will *not* handle the electrical needs of accessories. Whenever an accessory is added, run new wiring between the battery and accessory, installing a separate fuse panel on the instrument panel.

If the ignition switch requires replacement, *never* install an automotive-type switch. A marine-type switch must always be used.

Description

Variations of two different ignition systems have been used on Suzuki outboards since 1977. See Chapter Seven for a full description. For the purposes of troubleshooting, the ignition systems can be divided into 2 basic types:
1. A flywheel magneto breaker-point ignition.
2. A flywheel magneto capacitor discharge ignition called the Suzuki Pointless Electronic Ignition or PEI.

General troubleshooting procedures are provided in **Table 2**.

Precautions

Several precautions should be strictly observed to avoid damage to the ignition system.
1. Do not reverse the battery connections. This reverses polarity and can damage the rectifier or CDI unit on PEI ignitions.
2. Do not "spark" the battery terminals with the battery cable connections to check polarity.
3. Do not disconnect the battery cables with the engine running.
4. Do not crank engine if the CDI unit is not grounded to engine.

5. Do not touch or disconnect any ignition components when the engine is running, while the ignition switch is ON or while the battery cables are connected.
6. If you must run an engine that has a CDI ignition system without the battery connected to the harness, disconnect the stator base rectifier leads and tape them separately.

Troubleshooting Preparation (All Ignition Systems)

> *NOTE*
> *To test the wiring harness for poor solder connections in Step 1, bend the molded rubber connector while checking each wire for resistance.*

1. Check the wiring harness and all plug-in connections to make sure that all terminals are free of corrosion, all connectors are tight and the wiring insulation is in good condition.
2. Check all electrical components that are grounded to the engine for a good ground.
3. Make sure that all ground wires are properly connected and that the connections are clean and tight.
4. Check remainder of the wiring for disconnected wires and short or open circuits.
5. Make sure there is an adequate supply of fresh and properly mixed fuel available to the engine.
6. Check the battery condition (if so equipped). Clean terminals and recharge battery, if necessary.
7. Check spark plug cable routing. Make sure the cables are properly connected to their respective spark plugs.
8. Remove all spark plugs, keeping them in order. Check the condition of each plug. See Chapter Four.
9. Reconnect the proper plug cable to one plug. Lay the plug against the cylinder head so its base makes a good connection and turn the engine over. If there is no spark or only a

weak one, check for loose connections at the coil and battery. Repeat the check with each remaining plug. If all external wiring connections are good, the problem is most likely in the ignition system.

BREAKER-POINT IGNITION COMPONENT TESTING

An ignition analyzer should be used for accurate testing of the breaker points, condenser(s), stator coil and ignition coil(s). Suzuki recommends the use of its Electro-tester (part No. 09900-28106) and pocket tester (part No. 09900-25002). A Merc-O-Tronic ignition analyzer can also be used. These can be purchased through your Suzuki dealer. Each analyzer includes detailed instructions for component testing as well as complete component specifications according to engine model and year of manufacture. The procedures given here are general in nature to acquaint you with component testing. Refer to the instructions provided with the particular analyzer to be used for the exact procedure.

Ohmmeter readings should be made when the engine is cold. Readings taken on a hot engine will show increased resistance caused by engine heat and result in unnecessary parts replacement without solving the basic problem.

Breaker Point Test

1. Remove the flywheel. See Chapter Eight.
2. Disconnect the breaker point leads from the stator base.
3. Connect one analyzer test lead to the breaker arm. Connect the other test lead to the breaker point screw terminal.
4. Set the analyzer controls according to manufacturer's instructions.
5. If the breaker points are good, the analyzer needle will rest in the OK segment.

6. If the analyzer needle does not fall within the specified segment on the scale, clean the points with alcohol and recheck the analyzer leads to make sure that the connections are tight before discarding the points. The low current present in this test makes clean points and proper connections very important.

Condenser Tests

1. Remove the flywheel. See Chapter Eight.
2. Disconnect the condenser lead from the breaker point set.
3. Connect one analyzer test lead to the condenser lead. Connect the other test lead to the stator base.

> *WARNING*
> *High voltage is involved in a condenser leakage test. Handle the analyzer leads carefully and turn the analyzer switch to DISCHARGE before disconnecting the leads from the condenser.*

4. Set the analyzer controls according to manufacturer's instructions and check the condenser for leakage, resistance and capacity.
5. Compare the results in Step 4 with the specifications provided by the analyzer manufacturer. Replace the condenser if it fails any of the 3 tests.

Stator Coil Test (DT 2)

This test checks the primary and secondary coils for circuit continuity.
1. Remove the flywheel. See Chapter Eight.
2. Disconnect the black primary ignition coil lead at the bullet connector.
3. Disconnect the secondary coil lead at the spark plug.
4. Connect an ohmmeter between the primary coil lead and a good engine ground. Set the ohmmeter on the low ohms scale. The meter should show a resistance of 0.09-1.22 ohms.

3

5. Connect the ohmmeter between the secondary coil lead and a good engine ground. Set the ohmmeter on the high ohms scale. The ohmmeter should show a resistance of 5,200-6,900 ohms.

6. If the resistance values are not as specified in Step 4 and Step 5, replace the ignition coil. See Chapter Seven.

Stator Coil Test (All Others)

1. Remove the flywheel. See Chapter Eight.
2. Disconnect the stator coil lead at the bullet connector.
3. Connect an ohmmeter between the stator coil lead and a good engine ground. See **Figure 12**. Set the ohmmeter on the low ohms scale. If the meter does not show a resistance of 1.26-1.54 ohms, replace the stator coil.

Ignition Coil Power and Leakage Tests

> *WARNING*
> *All coil tests should be performed on a wooden or insulated bench top to prevent shock hazards or leakage.*

The ignition coil must be removed from the system before testing. See Chapter Seven.

1. Connect an ignition analyzer according to manufacturer's instructions.
2. Check the coil for power and leakage according to the analyzer manufacturer's instructions. Compare the results to the specifications provided with the analyzer. Replace the coil if it fails either of the tests. See Chapter Seven.

Ignition Coil Resistance Test (Except DT 2)

The ignition coil must be removed from the system before testing. See Chapter Seven.

1. Connect an ohmmeter between the coil terminals as shown in **Figure 13**. Compare the reading to specifications (**Table 5**).

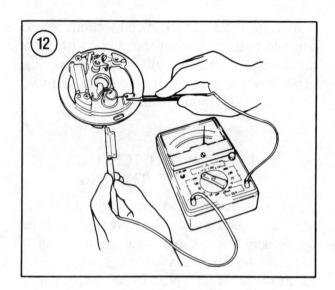

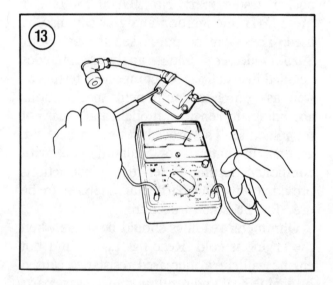

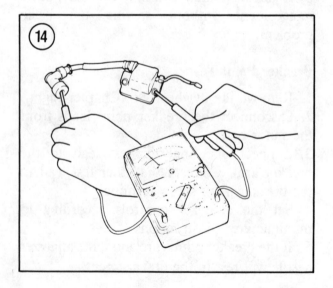

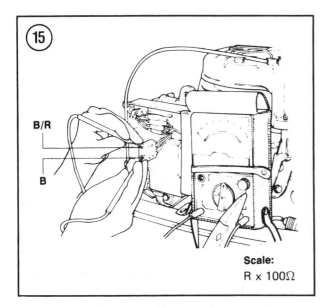

B/R

B

Scale:
R x 100Ω

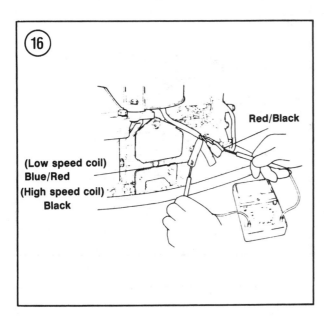

Red/Black

(Low speed coil)
Blue/Red
(High speed coil)
Black

2. Connect the ohmmeter between the coil terminal and spark plug lead as shown in **Figure 14**. Compare the reading to specifications (**Table 5**).

3. Replace the coil if it does not meet specifications in Step 1 or Step 2.

PEI IGNITION COMPONENT TESTING

Ohmmeter readings should be made when the engine is cold. Readings taken on a hot engine will show increased resistance caused by engine heat and result in unnecessary parts replacement without solving the basic problem.

The following procedures and specifications represent all of the service information provided by Suzuki. If a model is not mentioned, Suzuki does not provide the information.

3

Charge Coil Resistance Test

1. Remove the engine cover.

NOTE
The charge coil leads on DT 25 (1983-on), DT 30, DT 40 (independent ignition) and DT 50-DT 140 models are located inside the junction box. See **Figure 15**.

2. Disconnect the charge coil leads as follows:
   a. DT 5, DT 6, DT 8, DT 25 (1983-on) and DT 30—Black/red and black leads.
   b. DT 9.9 (1977-1982), DT 16 and DT 65—Blue/red and black leads.
   c. DT 9.9 (1983-on), DT 15 and DT 50—Green and black leads.
   d. DT 20, DT 25 (1977-1982) and DT 50M—Blue/red, black and red/black leads.
   e. DT 40—Blue/red and black (independent ignition) or blue/red and gray (simultaneous ignition) leads.
   f. DT 75-DT 140—Black/red and red/white leads.

3A. DT 20, DT 25 (1977-1982) and DT 50M—Connect an ohmmeter between the blue/red and black/red leads to check the low-speed coil, then move the test lead from the blue/red to the black lead to check the high-speed coil. See **Figure 16**. Replace the low-speed or high-speed coil if it is not within specifications (**Table 6**). See Chapter Seven.

3B. All others—Connect an ohmmeter between the disconnected leads. See **Figure 15** or **Figure 17**. Replace the charge coil if the reading is not within specifications (**Table 6**). See Chapter Seven.

Trigger Coil Resistance Test

1. Remove the engine cover.

> *NOTE*
> *The trigger coil(s) on DT 25 (1983-on), DT 30, DT 40 (independent ignition) and DT 50-DT 140 models are tested at the same junction box connector as the charge coil. See **Figure 15**.*

2. Disconnect the trigger coil leads as follows:
   a. DT 5, DT 6, DT 8, DT 65—Red/white and black leads.
   b. DT 25 (1983-on) and DT 30—Black/white and black leads.
   c. DT 40 (independent ignition), DT 50—Gray, pink and black leads.
   d. DT 75-DT 140—Green, pink, yellow/red and white/red leads.

> *NOTE*
> *The connector on DT 40, DT 50 and DT 75-DT 140 models contains separate terminals for each trigger coil. Perform Step 3 on each set of terminals to test both trigger coils.*

3. Connect an ohmmeter between the disconnected leads. Replace the trigger coil if the reading is not within specifications (**Table 7**). See Chapter Seven.

Ignition Coil Resistance Test

DT 5-16 and 1983-on DT 25-30 models use a combined secondary coil and CDI unit. The primary coil circuit is incorporated in the CDI unit and cannot be checked with this test.

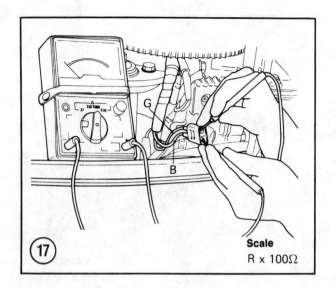

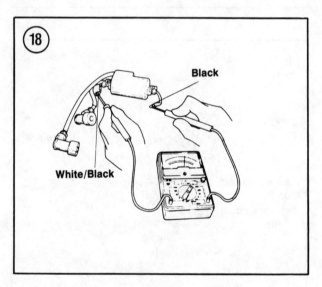

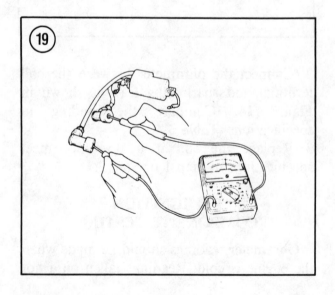

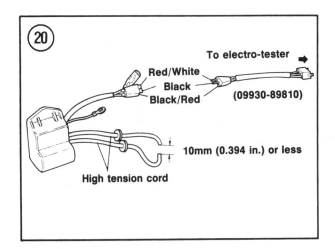

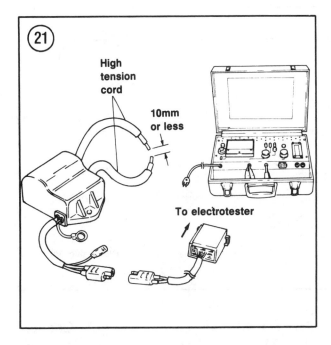

DT 20, DT 25 (1977-1982) and DT 40 (simultaneous ignition) use a single secondary coil with 2 spark plug leads.

All other models use separate secondary coils.

1. Remove the engine cover.

2A. DT 5-16 and 1983-on DT 25-30 models—Disconnect the spark plug leads.

2B. All others—Remove the coil(s) from the engine. See Chapter Seven.

3. Connect an ohmmeter between the primary and ground leads. See **Figure 18** (simultaneous ignition). Note the reading.

4A. DT 40 (independent ignition) and DT 50-DT 140 models—Connect an ohmmeter between the ground lead and spark plug wire. Note the reading.

4B. All others—Connect an ohmmeter between the 2 spark plug leads (**Figure 19**). Note the reading.

5. Compare the readings obtained in Step 3 and Step 4 with specifications (**Table 5**). Replace the coil if not within specifications.

CDI Unit Output Test (DT 5, DT 6, DT 8)

This test requires the use of a Suzuki Electro-tester (part No. 09900-28106) and CDI test cord. See **Table 8**.

1. Remove the engine cover.

2. Remove the CDI unit. See Chapter Seven.

3. Connect the CDI test cord to the Electro-tester.

4. Connect the CDI test cord to the CDI leads as shown in **Figure 20**.

5. Position the 2 spark plug leads as shown in **Figure 20** with a 0.394 in. (10 mm) gap between the ends of the leads.

6. Turn the tester switch ON. A spark should jump the gap between the spark plug leads at the same time the tester is turned on. If it does not, replace the CDI unit.

CDI Unit Output Test (DT 9.9-DT 30)

This test requires the use of a Suzuki Electro-tester (part No. 09900-28106) and CDI test cord. See **Table 8**.

1. Remove the engine cover.

2. Remove the CDI unit. See Chapter Seven.

3. Connect the CDI test cord to the Electro-tester.

4. Connect the CDI test cord to the CDI leads as shown in **Figure 21**.

5. Position the 2 spark plug leads as shown in **Figure 21** with a 0.394 in. (10 mm) gap between the ends of the leads.

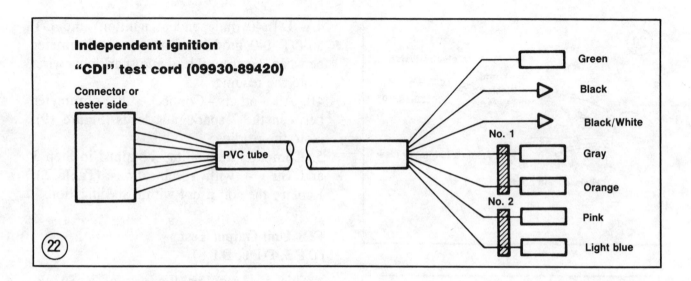

Independent ignition

"CDI" test cord (09930-89420)

Connector or tester side

PVC tube

No. 1 — Gray / Orange

No. 2 — Pink / Light blue

Green

Black

Black/White

Gray

Orange

Pink

Light blue

㉒

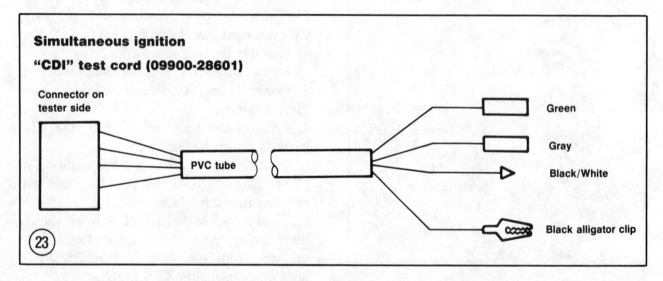

Simultaneous ignition

"CDI" test cord (09900-28601)

Connector on tester side

PVC tube

Green

Gray

Black/White

Black alligator clip

㉓

6. Turn the tester switch ON. A spark should jump the gap between the spark plug leads at the same time the tester is turned on. If it does not, replace the CDI unit.

CDI Unit Output Test (DT 40-DT 65)

This test requires the use of a Suzuki Electro-tester (part No. 09900-28106) and CDI test cord. See **Table 8**.
1. Remove the engine cover.
2. Remove the CDI unit. See Chapter Seven.
3. Connect the CDI test cord to the Electro-tester.

4A. DT 40 (Independent ignition)—Connect the CDI test cord to the CDI leads as shown in **Figure 22**. The gray and orange leads are connected to test cylinder No. 1, then the test cord is connected to the pink and light blue leads to test cylinder No. 2.
4B. DT 40 (simultaneous ignition)—Connect the CDI test cord to the CDI leads as shown in **Figure 23**.
4C. All others—Connect the CDI test cord to the CDI leads as shown in **Figure 24**.
5. Turn the tester switch ON. The neon tube in the tester should light at the same time the tester is turned on. If it does not, replace the CDI unit.

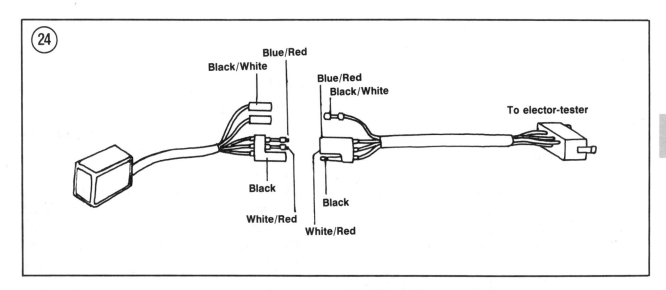

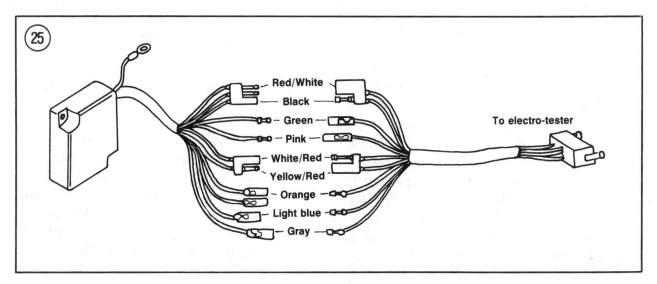

6. DT 40 (independent ignition)—Reconnect the test cord as described in Step 4A to check the No. 2 cylinder, then repeat Step 5.

**CDI Unit Output Test
(DT 75-DT 85)**

This test requires the use of a Suzuki Electro-tester (part No. 09900-28106) and CDI test cord. See **Table 8** and **Figure 25**.
1. Remove the engine cover.
2. Remove the CDI unit. See Chapter Seven.
3. Connect the CDI test cord to the Electro-tester.

4. Connect the red/white, black, green and orange CDI unit leads to the CDI test cord to check the No. 1 cylinder.
5. Turn the tester switch ON. The neon tube in the tester should light at the same time the tester is turned on.
6. Disconnect the green and orange CDI unit leads from the CDI test cord, connect the pink and light blue leads to check the No. 2 cylinder, then repeat Step 5.
7. Disconnect the pink and light blue CDI unit leads from the CDI test cord, connect the yellow/red, white/red and gray leads to check the No. 3 cylinder, then repeat Step 5.

8. If the neon tube does not light when the tester is turned on in Steps 5-7, replace the CDI unit.

CDI Unit Output Test (DT 115-DT 140)

This test requires the use of a Suzuki Electro-tester (part No. 09900-28106) and CDI test cord. See **Table 8** and **Figure 25**.
1. Remove the engine cover.
2. Remove the CDI unit. See Chapter Seven.
3. Connect the CDI test cord to the Electro-tester.
4. Connect the red/white, red/black, white/black, brown, green, orange and black CDI unit leads to the CDI test cord to check the No. 1 cylinder.
5. Turn the tester switch ON. The neon tube in the tester should light at the same time the tester is turned on.
6. Disconnect the red/white, brown, green and orange CDI unit leads from the CDI test cord, connect the pink and light blue leads to check the No. 2 cylinder, then repeat Step 5.
7. Disconnect the pink and light blue CDI unit leads from the CDI test cord, connect the yellow/red and gray leads to check the No. 3 cylinder, then repeat Step 5.
8. Disconnect the yellow/red and gray CDI unit leads from the CDI test cord, connect the white/red and light green leads to check the No. 4 cylinder, then repeat Step 5.
9. If the neon tube does not light when the tester is turned on in Steps 5-8, replace the CDI unit.

CDI Unit Resistance Test (DT 5, DT 6 and DT 8)

1. Remove the engine cover.
2. Remove the CDI unit. See Chapter Seven.
3. Connect an ohmmeter between the CDI unit leads as specified in **Table 9**. Compare the meter readings for each connection to

Table 9. Replace the CDI unit if any reading is not as specified.

CDI Unit Resistance Test (DT 9.9, DT 15 and DT 16)

This test checks the CDI unit and NSI circuit.
1. Remove the engine cover.
2. Remove the CDI unit. See Chapter Seven.
3. Connect an ohmmeter between the CDI unit leads as specified in **Table 10** (1977-1982 DT 9.9 and DT 16) or **Table 11** (1983-on DT 9.9 and DT 15). Replace the CDI unit if any reading is not as specified.

CDI Unit Resistance Test (DT 20, 1977-1982 DT 25, DT 40)

This test checks the CDI unit and NSI circuit.
1. Remove the engine cover.
2. Remove the CDI unit. See Chapter Seven.
3. Connect an ohmmeter between the CDI unit leads as specified in **Table 12** (DT 20, 1977-1982 DT 25), **Table 13** (DT 40 with independent ignition) or **Table 14** (DT 40 with simultaneous ignition). Replace the CDI unit if any reading is not as specified.

CDI Unit Resistance Test (DT 50M)

1. Remove the engine cover.
2. Remove the CDI unit. See Chapter Seven.
3. Connect an ohmmeter between the CDI unit leads as specified in **Table 15**. Replace the CDI unit if any reading is not as specified.

CDI Unit Resistance Test (DT 50, DT 60, DT 65)

1. Remove the engine cover.
2. Remove the CDI unit. See Chapter Seven.
3. Connect an ohmmeter between the CDI unit leads as specified in **Table 16** (DT 50-DT

60) or **Table 17** (DT 65). Replace the CDI unit if any reading is not as specified.

CDI Unit Resistance Test (DT 75-DT 140)

1. Remove the engine cover.
2. Remove the CDI unit. See Chapter Seven.
3. Connect an ohmmeter between the CDI unit leads as specified in **Table 18** (DT 75-DT 85) or **Table 19** (DT 115-DT 140). Replace the CDI unit if any reading is not as specified.

FUEL SYSTEM

Many outboard owners automatically assume that the carburetor is at fault when the engine does not run properly. While fuel system problems are not uncommon, carburetor adjustment is seldom the answer. In many cases, adjusting the carburetor only compounds the problem by making the engine run worse.

Fuel system troubleshooting should start at the gas tank and work through the system,

reserving the carburetor(s) as the final point. The majority of fuel system problems result from an empty fuel tank, sour fuel, a plugged fuel filter or a malfunctioning fuel pump. **Table 3** provides a series of symptoms and causes that can be useful in localizing fuel system problems. Chapter Six contains inspection and overhaul procedures for fuel system components. Chapter Twelve contains inspection and service procedures for oil injection system components.

Troubleshooting

As a first step, check the fuel flow. Remove the fuel tank cap and look into the tank. If there is fuel present, disconnect and ground the spark plug lead(s) as a safety precaution. Disconnect the fuel line at the carburetor (**Figure 26**, typical) and place it in a suitable container to catch any discharged fuel. See if gas flows freely from the line when the primer bulb is squeezed.

If there is no fuel flow from the line:
 a. The fuel petcock may be shut off or blocked by rust or foreign matter.
 b. The fuel line may be stopped up or kinked.
 c. A primer bulb check valve may be defective.
 d. The fuel pump may be defective.

If a good fuel flow is present, crank the engine 10-12 times to check fuel pump operation. A pump that is operating satisfactorily will deliver a good, constant flow of fuel from the line. If the amount of flow varies from pulse to pulse, the fuel pump is probably failing.

Carburetor chokes can also present problems. A choke that sticks open will show up as a hard starting problem; one that sticks closed will result in a flooding condition.

During a hot engine shut-down, the fuel bowl temperature can rise above 200°, causing the fuel inside to boil. While marine carburetors are vented to atmosphere to prevent this problem, there is a possibility that some fuel will percolate over the high-speed nozzle.

A leaking inlet needle and seat or a defective float will allow an excessive amount of fuel into the intake manifold. Pressure in the fuel line after the engine is shut down forces fuel past the leaking needle and seat. This raises the fuel bowl level, allowing fuel to overflow into the manifold.

Excessive fuel consumption may not necessarily mean an engine or fuel system problem. Marine growth on the boat's hull, a bent or otherwise damaged propeller or a fuel line leak can cause an increase in fuel consumption. These areas should all be checked *before* blaming the carburetor.

ENGINE TEMPERATURE AND OVERHEATING

Proper engine temperature is critical to good engine operation. An engine that runs too hot will be damaged internally. One that operates too cool will not run smoothly or efficiently.

A variety of problems can cause engine overheating. Some of the most commonly encountered are a defective thermostat, a low output or defective water pump, damaged or mispositioned water passage restrictors or even engine flashing in the cylinder head casting water discharge passage that was not removed during manufacture.

Troubleshooting

Engine temperature can be checked with the use of Markal Thermomelt Stiks available at your local marine dealer. This heat-sensitive stick looks like a large crayon (**Figure 27**) and will melt on contact with a metal surface at a specific temperature.

Two thermomelt sticks are required to properly check a Suzuki outboard: a 125° F

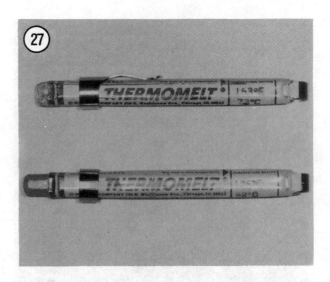

(52° C) stick and a 163° F (73° C) stick. The stick should not be applied to the center of the cylinder head, as this area may normally run hotter than 163° F.

The test is most efficient when carried out on a motor operating on a boat in the water. If necessary to perform the test using a test tank, run the engine at 3,000 rpm for a minimum of 5 minutes to assure that it is at operating temperature. Make sure inlet water temperature is below 80° F (26° C) and perform the test as follows.

1. Mark the cylinder water jacket with each stick. The mark will appear similar to a chalk mark. Make sure sufficient material is applied to the metal surface.

2. With the engine at operating temperature and running at idle in FORWARD gear, the 125° F stick mark should melt. If it does not melt on thermostat-equipped models (DT 25-DT 140), the thermostat is stuck open and the engine is running cold.

3. With the engine at operating temperature and running at full throttle in FORWARD gear, the 163° F stick mark should not melt. If it does, the power head is overheating. Look for a defective water pump or a clogged or leaking cooling system. On thermostat-equipped models (DT 25-DT 140), the thermostat may be stuck closed.

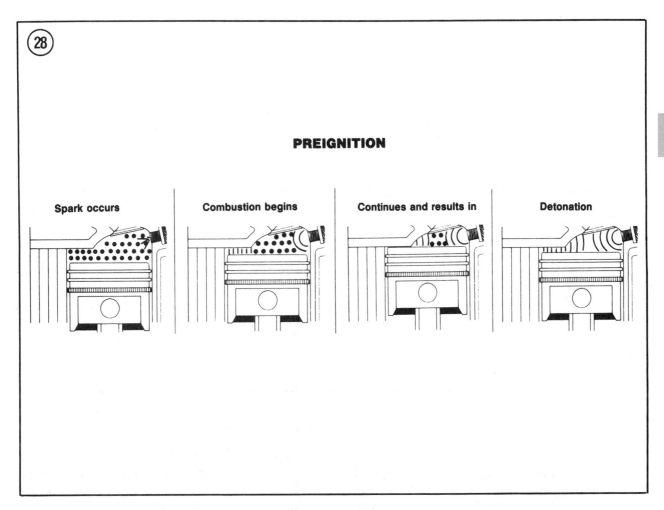

PREIGNITION

| Spark occurs | Combustion begins | Continues and results in | Detonation |

3

ENGINE

Engine problems are generally symptoms of something wrong in another system, such as ignition, fuel or starting. If properly maintained and serviced, the engine should experience no problems other than those caused by age and wear.

Overheating and Lack of Lubrication

Overheating and lack of lubrication cause the majority of engine mechanical problems. Outboard motors create a great deal of heat and are not designed to operate at a standstill for any length of time. Using a spark plug of the wrong heat range can burn a piston. Incorrect ignition timing, a defective water pump or thermostat, a propeller that is too large (over-propping) or an excessively lean fuel mixture can also cause the engine to overheat.

Preignition

Preignition is the premature burning of fuel and is caused by hot spots in the combustion chamber (**Figure 28**). The fuel actually ignites before it is supposed to. Glowing deposits in the combustion chamber, inadequate cooling or overheated spark plugs can all cause preignition. This is first noticed in the form of a power loss but will eventually result in extensive damage to the internal parts of the engine because of higher combustion chamber temperatures.

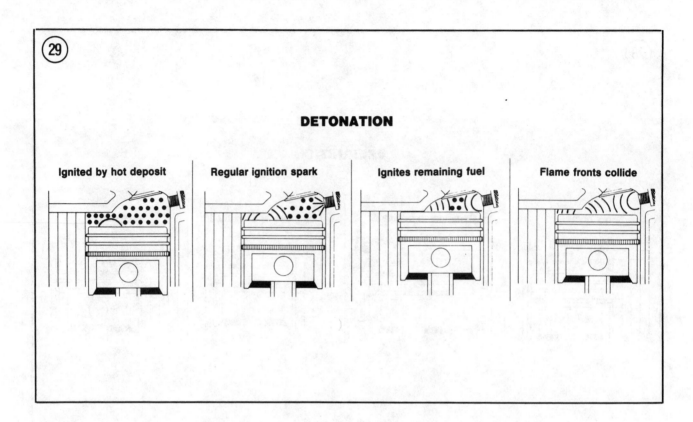

DETONATION

| Ignited by hot deposit | Regular ignition spark | Ignites remaining fuel | Flame fronts collide |

Detonation

Commonly called "spark knock" or "fuel knock," detonation is the violent explosion of fuel in the combustion chamber prior to the proper time of combustion (**Figure 29**). Severe damage can result. Use of low octane gasoline is a common cause of detonation.

Even when high octane gasoline is used, detonation can still occur if the engine is improperly timed. Other causes are over-advanced ignition timing, lean fuel mixture at or near full throttle, inadequate engine cooling, cross-firing of spark plugs, excessive accumulation of deposits on piston and combustion chamber or the use of a prop that is too large (over-propping).

Since outboard motors are noisy, engine knock or detonation is likely to go unnoticed by owners, especially at high engine rpm when wind noise is also present. Such inaudible detonation, as it is called, is usually the cause when engine damage occurs for no apparent reason.

Poor Idling

A poor idle can be caused by improper carburetor adjustment, incorrect timing or ignition system malfunctions. Check the gas cap vent for an obstruction.

Misfiring

Misfiring can result from a weak spark or a dirty spark plug. Check for fuel contamination. If misfiring occurs only under heavy load, as when accelerating, it is usually caused by a defective spark plug. Run the motor at night to check for spark leaks along the plug wire and under spark plug cap or use a spark leak tester.

> *WARNING*
> *Do not run engine in a dark garage to check for spark leak. There is considerable danger of carbon monoxide poisoning.*

Water Leakage in Cylinder

The fastest and easiest way to check for water leakage in a cylinder is to check the spark plugs. Water will clean a spark plug. If one of the 2 plugs on a multi-cylinder engine is clean and the other is dirty, there is most likely a water leak in the cylinder with the clean plug.

To remove all doubt, install a dirty plug in each cylinder. Run the engine in a test tank or on the boat in water for 5-10 minutes. Shut the engine off and remove the plugs. If one plug is clean and the other dirty (or if both plugs are clean), a water leak in the cylinder(s) is the problem.

Flat Spots

If the engine seems to die momentarily when the throttle is opened and then recovers, check for a dirty main jet in the carburetor, water in the fuel or an excessively lean mixture.

Power Loss

Several factors can cause a lack of power and speed. Look for air leaks in the fuel line or fuel pump, a clogged fuel filter or a choke/throttle valve that does not operate properly. Check ignition timing.

A piston or cylinder that is galling, incorrect piston clearance or a worn/sticky piston ring may be responsible. Look for loose bolts, defective gaskets or leaking machined mating surfaces on the cylinder head, cylinder or crankcase. Also check the crankcase oil seal; if worn, it can allow gas to leak between cylinders.

Piston Seizure

This is caused by one or more pistons with incorrect bore clearances, piston rings with an improper end gap, the use of an oil-fuel mixture containing less than 1 part oil to 50 parts of gasoline or an oil of poor quality, a spark plug of the wrong heat range or incorrect ignition timing. Overheating from any cause may result in piston seizure.

Excessive Vibration

Excessive vibration may be caused by loose motor mounts, worn bearings or a generally poor running motor.

Engine Noises

Experience is needed to diagnose accurately in this area. Noises are difficult to differentiate and even harder to describe. Deep knocking noises usually mean main bearing failure. A slapping noise generally comes from a loose piston. A light knocking noise during acceleration may be a bad connecting rod bearing. Pinging should be corrected immediately or damage to the piston will result. A compression leak at the head-to-cylinder joint will sound like a rapid on-off squeal.

3

Tables are on the following pages.

Table 1 STARTER TROUBLESHOOTING

Trouble	Cause	Remedy
Pinion does not move when starter is turned on	Blown fuse Pinion rusted to armature shaft Series coil or shunt broken or shorted Loose switch connections Rusted or dirty plunger	Replace fuse. Remove, clean or replace as required. Replace coil or shunt. Tighten connections Clean plunger.
Pinion meshes with ring gear but starter does not run	Worn brushes or brush springs touching armature Dirty or burned commutator Defective armature field coil Worn or rusted armature shaft bearing	Replace brushes or brush springs. Clean or replace as required. Replace armature. Replace bearing.
Starter motor runs at full speed before pinion meshes with ring gear	Worn pinion sleeve Pinion does not stop in correct position	Replace sleeve. Replace pinion.
Pinion meshes with gear and motor starts but engine does not crank	Defective overrunning clutch	Replace overrunning clutch
Starter motor does not stop when turned off after engine has started	Rusted or dirty plunger	Clean or replace plunger
Starter motor has low no-speed and high-current draw	Armature may be dragging on pole shoes from bent shaft, worn bearings or loose pole shoes Tight or dirty bearings	Replace shaft or bearings and/or tighten pole shoes. Loosen or clean bearings.
High current draw with no armature rotation	A direct ground switch, @ terminal or @ brushes or field connections Frozen shaft bearings which prevent armature from rotating	Replace defective parts. Loosen, clean or replace bearings.

(continued)

3

Table 1 STARTER TROUBLESHOOTING (continued)

Trouble	Cause	Remedy
Starter motor has grounded armature or field winding	Current passes through armature first, then to ground field windings	Disconnect grounded leads, then locate any abnormal grounds in starter motor.
Starter motor fails to operate and draws no current and/or high resistance	Open circuit in fields or armature, @ connections or brushes or between brushes and commutator	Repair or adjust broken or weak brush springs, worn brushes, high insulation between commutator bars or a dirty, gummy or oily commutator.
High resistance in starter motor	Low no-load speed and a low-current draw and low developed torque	Close "open" field winding on unit which has 2 or 3 circuits in starter motor (unit in which current divides as it enters, taking 2 or 3 parallel paths).
High free speed and high current draw	Shorted fields in starter motor	Install new fields and check for improved performance (fields normally have very low resistance, thus it is difficult to detect shorted fields, since difference in current draw between normal starter motor field windings would not be very great).
Excessive voltage drop	Cables too small	Install larger cables to accomodate high current draw.
High circuit resistance	Dirty connections	Clean connections.
Starter motor has grounded armature or field winding	Field and/or armature is burned or lead is thrown out of commutator due to excess leakage	Raise grounded brushes from commutator and insulate them with cardboard. Use Magneto Analyzer (part No. C-91-25213) (Selector No. 3) and test points to check between insulated terminal or starter motor and starter motor frame (remove ground connection of shunt coils on motors with this feature). If analyzer shows resistance (meter needle moves to right), there is a ground. Raise other brushes from armature and check armature and fields separately to locate ground.

(continued)

Table 1 STARTER TROUBLESHOOTING (continued)

Trouble	Cause	Remedy
Starter does not operate	Run-down battery	Check battery with hydrometer. If reading is below 1.230, recharge or replace battery.
	Poor contact @ terminals	Remove terminal clamps. Scrape terminals and clamps clean and tighten bolts securely.
	Wiring or key switch	Coat with sealer to protect against further corrosion.
	Starter solenoid	Check for resistance between: (a) positive (+) terminal of battery and large input terminal of starter solenoid, (b) large wire @ top of starter motor and negative (-) terminal of battery and (c) small terminal of starter solenoid and positive battery terminal. Key switch must be in START position. Repair all defective parts.
	Starter motor	With a fully charged battery, connect a negative (-) jumper wire to upper terminal on side of starter motor and a positive jumper to large lower terminal of starter motor. If motor still does not operate, remove for overhaul or replacement.
Starter turns over too slowly	Low battery or poor contact @ battery terminal	See "Starter does not operate."
	Poor contact @ starter solenoid or starter motor	Check all terminals for looseness and tighten all nuts securely.
	Starter mechanism	Disconnect positive (+) battery terminal. Rotate pinion gear in disengaged position. Pinion gear and motor should run freely by hand. If motor does not turn over easily, clean starter and replace all defective parts.
	Starter motor	See "Starter does not operate."
Starter spins freely but does not engage engine	Low battery or poor contact @ battery terminal	See "Starter does not operate."
	Poor contact @ starter solenoid or starter motor	See "Starter does not operate."
	Dirty or corroded pinion drive	Clean thoroughly and lubricate the spline underneath the pinion with Suzuki water-resistant grease (part No. 99000-25170).

(continued)

Table 1 STARTER TROUBLESHOOTING (continued)

Trouble	Cause	Remedy
Starter does not engage freely	Pinion or flywheel gear	Inspect mating gears for excessive wear. Replace all defective parts.
	Small anti-drift spring	If drive pinion interferes with flywheel gear after engine has started, inspect anti-drift spring located under pinion gear. Replace all defective parts. NOTE: If drive pinion tends to stay engaged in flywheel gear when starter motor is in idle position, start motor @ 1/4 throttle to allow starter pinion gear to release flywheel ring gear instantly.
Starter keeps on spinning after key is turned ON	Key not fully returned	Check that key has returned to normal ON position from START position. Replace switch if key constantly stays in START position.
	Starter solenoid	Inspect starter solenoid to see if contacts have become stuck in closed position. If starter does not stop running with small yellow lead disconnected from starter solenoid, replace starter solenoid.
	Wiring or key switch	Inspect all wires for defects. Open remote control box and inspect wiring @ switches. Repair or replace all defective parts.
Wires overheat	Battery terminals improperly connected	Check that negative marking on harness matches that of battery. If battery is connected improperly, red wire to rectifier will overheat.
	Short circuit in wiring system	Inspect all connections and wires for looseness or defects. Open remote control box and inspect wiring @ switches.
	Short circuit in choke solenoid	Repair or replace all defective parts. Check for high resistance. If blue choke wire heats rapidly when choke is used, choke solenoid may have internal short. Replace if defective.
	Short circuit in starter solenoid	If yellow starter solenoid lead overheats, there may be internal short (resistance) in starter solenoid. Replace if defective.
	Low battery voltage	Battery voltage is checked with an ampere-volt tester when battery is under a starting load. Battery must be recharged if it registers under 9.5 volts. If battery is below specified hydrometer reading of 1.230, it will not turn engine fast enough to start it.

3

Table 2 IGNITION TROUBLESHOOTING

Symptom	Probable cause
Engine won't start, but fuel and spark are good	Defective or dirty spark plugs Spark plug gap set too wide Improper spark timing Shorted "kill" or stop button Air leaks into fuel pump Broken piston ring(s) Cylinder head, crankcase or cylinder sealing faulty Worn crankcase oil seal
Engine misfires @ idle	Incorrect spark plug gap Defective, dirty or loose spark plugs Spark plugs of incorrect heat range Cracked distributor cap Leaking or broken high tension wires Weak armature magnets Defective coil or condenser Defective ignition switch Spark timing out of adjustment
Engine misfires at high speed	See "Engine misfires @ idle." Coil breaks down Coil shorts through insulation Spark plug gap too wide Wrong type spark plugs Too much spark advance
Engine backfires through exhaust	Cracked spark plug insulator Carbon path in distributor cap Improper timing Crossed spark plug wires
Engine backfires through carburetor	Improper ignition timing
Engine preignition	Spark advanced too far Incorrect type spark plug Burned spark plug electrodes
Engine noises (knocking at power head)	Spark advanced too far
Ignition coil fails	Extremely high voltage Moisture formation Excessive heat from engine
Spark plugs burn and foul	Incorrect type plug Fuel mixture too rich Inferior grade of gasoline Overheated engine Excessive carbon in combustion chambers
Ignition causing high fuel consumption	Incorrect spark timing Leaking high tension wires Incorrect spark plug gap Fouled spark plugs Incorrect spark advance Weak ignition coil Preignition

Table 3 FUEL SYSTEM TROUBLESHOOTING

Symptom	Probable cause
No fuel @ carburetor	No gas in tank
	Air vent in gas cap not open
	Air vent in gas cap clogged
	Fuel tank sitting on fuel line
	Fuel line fittings not properly connected to engine or fuel tank
	Air leak @ fuel connection
	Fuel pickup clogged
	Defective fuel pump
Flooding @ carburetor	Choke out of adjustment
	High float level
	Float stuck
	Excessive fuel pump pressure
	Float saturated beyond buoyancy
Rough operation	Dirt or water in fuel
	Reed valve open or broken
	Incorrect fuel level in carburetor bowl
	Carburetor loose @ mounting flange
	Throttle shutter not closing completely
	Throttle shutter valve installed incorrectly
	Carburetor backdraft jets plugged
	(if so equipped)
Carburetor spit-back @ idle	Chipped or broken reed valve(s)
Engine misfires @ high speed	Dirty carburetor
	Lean carburetor adjustment
	Restriction in fuel system
	Low fuel pump pressure
Engine backfires	Poor quality fuel
	Air-fuel mixture too rich or too lean
	Improperly adjusted carburetor
Engine preignition	Excessive oil in fuel
	Inferior grade of gasoline
	Lean carburetor mixture
Spark plugs burn and foul	Fuel mixture too rich
	Inferior grade of gasoline
High gas consumption:	
Flooding or leaking	Cracked carburetor casting
	Leaks @ line connections
	Defective carburetor bowl gasket
	High float level
	Plugged vent hole in cover
	Loose needle and seat
	Defective needle valve seat gasket
	Worn needle valve and seat
	Foreign matter clogging needle valve
	Worn float pin or bracket
	Float binding in bowl
	High fuel pump pressure

(continued)

Table 3 FUEL SYSTEM TROUBLESHOOTING (continued)

Symptom	Probable cause
Overrich mixture	Choke lever stuck
	High float level
	High fuel pump pressure
Abnormal speeds	Carburetor out of adjustment
	Too much oil in fuel

Table 4 LIGHTING/BATTERY CHARGING COIL RESISTANCE SPECIFICATIONS

Model	Ohms
DT 2, DT 4.5	Not available
DT 3.5	1.31-1.60
DT 5-9	0.37-0.45
DT 9.9	
1977-1982	0.38-0.46
1983-on	0.18-0.26
DT 15	0.18-0.26
DT 16	0.38-0.46
DT 20	0.43-0.53
DT 25	
1977-1982	0.43-0.53
1983-on	0.24-0.36
DT 30	0.24-0.36
DT 40	0.33-0.41
DT 50	0.33-0.41
DT 50M	0.41-0.50
DT 60-DT 65	0.33-0.41
DT 75-DT 140	
Standard (80 watts)	0.54-0.66
Optional (200 watts)	0.36-0.44

Table 5 IGNITION COIL RESISTANCE SPECIFICATIONS

Model	Primary (ohms)	Secondary (ohms)
DT 2	0.9-1.22	5,200-6,900
DT 3.5	0.87-1.17	5,020-6,790
DT 4.5	Not available	
DT 5, DT 6, DT 8		
Breaker-point ignition	0.87-1.17	5,000-6,000
PEI		1,350-1,830
DT 7.5, DT 9	Slightly over 1 ohm	Several kiloohms
DT 9.9		
1977-1982		2,130-2,880
1983-on		2,000-3,000
DT 15		2,000-3,000
DT 16		2,130-2,880
DT 20	0.28-0.38	2,975-4,025
DT 25		
1977-1982	0.28-0.38	2,975-4,025
1983-on		2,140-3,260
DT 30		2,140-3,260
DT 40		
Independent ignition	0.87-1.17	5,020-6,790
Simultaneous ignition	0.08-0.10	3,000-4,000
DT 50M		
1977-1982	0.28-0.38	2,980-4,030
1983-on	0.87-1.17	5,020-6,790
DT 50-DT 60	0.87-1.17	5,020-6,790
DT 65	0.76-1.04	2,980-4,030
DT 75	0.21-0.29	5,020-6,790
DT 85-DT 140		
1979-1982	0.21-0.29	2,130-2,880
1983-on	0.21-0.29	5,020-6,790

3

Table 6 CHARGE COIL RESISTANCE SPECIFICATIONS

Model	Ohms
DT 2, DT 3.5, DT 4.5	Not available
DT 7.5, DT 9	Not available
DT 5, DT 6, DT 8	255-315
DT 9.9	
1977-1982	135-165
1983-on	240-306
DT 15	240-306
DT 16	135-165
DT 20, 1977-1982 DT 25	
Low-speed coil	122-149
High-speed coil	1.62-1.98
1983-on, DT 25 DT 30	102-154
DT 40	
Independent ignition	225-275
Simultaneous ignition	135-165

(continued)

Table 6 CHARGE COIL RESISTANCE SPECIFICATIONS (continued)

Model	Ohms
DT 50M	
High-speed coil	1.62-1.98
Low-speed coil	122-149
DT 50-DT 60	225-275
DT 65	135-165
DT 75-DT 140	
High-speed coil	114-140
Low-speed coil	680-831

Table 7 TRIGGER COIL RESISTANCE SPECIFICATIONS

Model	Ohms
DT 5, DT 6, DT 8	20.5-25.1
1983-on DT 25, DT 30	27.9-41.9
DT 40 (independent ignition)	180-220
DT 50-DT 60	180-220
DT 65	7.29-8.91
DT 75-DT 140	320-391

Table 8 CDI UNIT TEST CORDS

Model	Year	Part No.
DT 5, DT 8	1981-on	09930-89811
DT 6		Not available
DT 9.9, DT 16	1980-1982	09900-28610
DT 9.9/15	1983-on	09930-89310
DT 20/25	1977-1982	09900-28612
DT 25/30	1983-on	09930-89610
DT 40	All	09930-89421
DT 50M	All	09900-28612
DT 50	1977-1979	09900-28612
DT 50/60	1980-on	09930-89421
DT 65	1978	09900-28612
DT 65	1979-on	09900-28614
DT 75/85	All	09930-89510
DT 115/140	All	09930-89410

Table 9 CDI UNIT RESISTANCE TEST (DT 5, DT 6, AND DT 8)*

Connect positive tester lead to:	Connect negative tester lead to:					
	Black/red	Red/white	Black	Blue	No. 1 plug lead	No. 2 plug lead
Black/red		X	O	O	O	O
Red/white	O		O	O	O	O
Black	DEF	X		O	O	O
Blue	X	X	X		O	O
No. 1 plug Lead	O	O	O	O		1,590
No. 2 plug Lead	O	O	O	O	1,590	O

* Use R×100 scale. X = a reading of less than 100K ohms. O = a reading of more than 100K ohms. DEF = meter needle deflects and returns to its original position. Other numbers indicate specified reading in ohms.

Table 10 CDI AND NSI UNIT RESISTANCE TEST (1977-1982 DT 9.9; DT 16)

Connect positive tester lead to:	Connect negative tester lead to:[1]			
	Blue/red	Green	Brown	Yellow/green
Blue/red		X	O	DEF
Green	O		O	DEF
Brown	X	X		DEF
Yellow/green	DEF	DEF	O	

Connect positive tester lead to:	Connect negative tester lead to:[2]			
	Green	Black	No. 1 plug lead	No. 2 plug lead
Green		X	O	O
Black	DEF		O	O
No. 1 plug lead	O	O		2,200-2,900
No. 2 plug lead	O	O	2,200-2,900	

1. Use R×100 scale. X = a reading of less than 200 ohms. O = a reading of more than 200 ohms. DEF = meter needle deflects and returns to its original position.
2. Use R×100 scale. X = a reading of less than 100 ohms. O = a reading of more than 100 ohms. DEF = meter needle deflection and return to its original position. Other numbers indicate specified reading in ohms.

Table 11 CDI UNIT RESISTANCE TEST (1983-ON DT 9.9, DT 15)*

Connect positive tester lead to:	Connect negative tester lead to:				
	Green	Black	Blue/ red	No. 1 Plug lead	No. 2 Plug lead
Green		X	O	O	O
Black	DEF		O	O	O
Blue/red	X	X		O	O
No. 1 plug lead	O	O	O		2,500
No. 2 plug lead	O	O	O	2,500	

* Use R×100 scale. X = a reading of less than 100K ohms. O = a reading of more than 100K ohms. DEF = meter needle deflects and returns to its original position. Other numbers indicate specified reading in ohms.

Table 12 CDI AND NSI UNIT RESISTANCE TEST (DT 20, 1977-1982 DT 25)

Connect positive tester lead to:	Connect negative tester lead to:[1]				
	Green	Blue/ red	Red/ black	Black	White/ black
Green		O	O	O	O
Blue/red	DEF		O	X	X
Red/black	DEF	O		X	X
Black	DEF	O	O		X
White/black	DEF	O	O	DEF	

Connect positive tester lead to:	Connect negative tester lead to:[2]			
	Blue/ red	Green	Brown	Yellow/ green
Blue/red		X	O	DEF
Green	O		O	DEF
Brown	X	X		DEF
Yellow/green	DEF	DEF	O	

1. Use R×100 scale. X = a reading of less than 100K ohms. O = a reading of more than 100K ohms. DEF = meter needle deflects and returns to its original position.
2. Use R×100 scale. X = a reading of less than 200K ohms. O = a reading of more than 200K ohms. DEF = meter needle deflects and returns to its original position.

Table 13 CDI AND NSI UNIT RESISTANCE TEST (DT 40, INDEPENDENT IGNITION)

Connect positive tester lead to:	Connect negative tester lead to:[1]							
	Green	Gray	Pink	Black	Blue/red	Orange	Lt. blue	Black/white
Green		X	X	X	O	DEF	DEF	DEF
Gray	O		O	O	O	O	O	O
Pink	O	O		O	O	O	O	O
Black	DEF	X	X		X	DEF	DEF	DEF
Blue/red	O	O	O	O		O	O	O
Orange	O	O	O	O	O		O	O
Lt. blue	O	O	O	O	O	O		O
Black/white	X	X	X	X	O	X	X	

Connect positive tester lead to:	Connect negative tester lead to:[2]			
	Blue/red	Green	Brown	Yellow/green
Blue/red		X	O	DEF
Green	O		O	DEF
Brown	X	X		DEF
Yellow/green	DEF	DEF	O	

1. Use R×100 scale. X = a reading of less than 100K ohms. O = a reading of more than 100K ohms. DEF = meter needle deflects and returns to its original position.
2. Use R×100 scale. X = a reading of less than 200K ohms. O = a reading of more than 200K ohms. DEF = meter needle deflects and returns to its original position.

Table 14 CDI UNIT RESISTANCE TEST (DT 40, SIMULTANEOUS IGNITION)*

Connect positive tester lead to:	Connect negative tester lead to:				
	Green	Gray	Black/white	Blue/red	Black
Green		X	O	O	X
Gray	DEF		X	O	X
Black/white	DEF	DEF		O	DEF
Blue/red	X	O	O		O
Black	DEF	X	X	O	

* Use R×100 scale. X = a reading of less than 100K ohms. O = a reading of more than 100K ohms. DEF = meter needle deflects and returns to its original position.

3

Table 15 CDI UNIT RESISTANCE TEST (DT 50M)

Connect positive tester lead to:	Connect negative tester lead to:[1]				
	Blue/red(2)	Red/black	Black	White/black	Blue/red
Blue/red[2]		O	X	X	X
Red/black	DEF		X	X	X
Black	DEF	O		X	X
White/black	DEF	O	DEF		DEF
Blue/red	X	O	X	X	

1. Use R×100 scale. X = a reading of less than 100K ohms. O = a reading of more than 100K ohms. DEF = meter needle deflects and returns to its original position.
2. Large connector.

Table 16 CDI UNIT RESISTANCE TEST (DT 50 AND DT 60)*

Connect positive tester lead to:	Connect negative tester lead to:							
	Green	Gray	Pink	Black	Blue/red	Orange	Lt. blue	Black white
Green		X	X	X	O	DEF	DEF	DEF
Gray	O		O	O	O	O	O	O
Pink	O	O		O	O	O	O	O
Black	DEF	X	X		X	DEF	DEF	DEF
Blue/red	O	O	O	O		O	O	O
Orange	O	O	O	O	O		O	O
Lt. blue	O	O	O	O	O	O		O
Black/white	X	X	X	X	O	X	X	

* Use R×100 scale. X = a reading of less than 100K ohms. O = a reading of more than 100K ohms. DEF = meter needle deflects and returns to its original position.

Table 17 CDI UNIT RESISTANCE TEST (DT 65)*

Connect positive tester lead to:	Connect negative tester lead to:				
	Blue/ red	White/ red	Black	Blue/ red	Black/ white
Blue/red		X	X	X	X
White/red	O		O	O	O
Black	DEF	X		DEF	X
Blue/red	X	X	X		X
Black/white	DEF	DEF	DEF	DEF	

* Use R×100 scale. X = a reading of less than 100K ohms. O = a reading of more than 100K ohms. DEF = meter needle deflects and returns to its original position.

Table 18 CDI UNIT RESISTANCE TEST (DT 75 AND DT 85)*

Connect positive tester lead to:	Connect negative tester lead to:				
	Black/ red	Red/ white	Black	Green	Pink
Black/red		X	X	X	X
Red/white	O		O	O	O
Black	O	O		X	X
Green	O	O	X		X
Pink	O	O	O	O	
White/red	O	O	X	X	X
Yellow/red	O	O	X	X	X
Orange	DEF	DEF	DEF	O	O
Lt. blue	DEF	DEF	DEF	O	O
Gray	DEF	DEF	DEF	O	O
Black/white	X	X	X	X	X

Connect positive tester lead to:	Connect negative tester lead to:					
	White/ red	Yellow/ red	Orange	Lt. blue	Gray	Black/ white
Black/red	X	X	O	O	O	X
Red/white	O	O	O	O	O	O
Black	X	X	DEF	DEF	DEF	O

(continued)

3

Table 18 CDI UNIT RESISTANCE TEST (DT 75 AND DT 85)* (continued)

Connect positive tester lead to:	Connect negative tester lead to:					
	White/red	Yellow/red	Orange	Lt. blue	Gray	Black/white
Green	X	X	DEF	DEF	DEF	O
Pink	O	O	O	O	O	O
White/red		X	DEF	DEF	DEF	O
Yellow/red	X		DEF	DEF	DEF	O
Orange	DEF	DEF		O	O	DEF
Lt. blue	DEF	DEF	O		O	DEF
Gray	DEF	DEF	O	O		DEF
Black/white	X	X	DEF	DEF	DEF	

* Use R×100 scale. X = a reading of less than 100K ohms. O = a reading of more than 100K ohms.
DEF = meter needle deflects and returns to its original position.

Table 19 CDI UNIT RESISTANCE TEST (DT 115 AND DT 140)*

Connect positive tester lead to:	Connect negative tester lead to:						
	Black/red	Red/white	White/black	Brown	Green	Pink	Yellow/red
Black/red		X	O	O	O	O	O
Red/white	O		O	X	O	O	O
White/black	O	O		X	O	O	O
Brown	O	X	O		O	O	O
Green	O	X	O	X		O	O
Pink	O	X	O	X	O		O
Yellow/red	O	X	O	X	O	O	
Orange	O	X	O	X	X	O	O
Lt. blue	O	X	O	X	O	X	O
Gray	O	X	O	X	O	O	X
Lt. green	O	X	O	X	O	O	O
Black/white	O	O	O	O	X	X	X
Black	O	X	O	X	X	X	X

(continued)

Table 19 CDI UNIT RESISTANCE TEST (DT 115 AND DT 140)* (continued)

Connect positive tester lead to:	Connect negative tester lead to:						
	White/red	Orange	Lt. blue	Gray	Lt. Green	Black/white	Black
Black/red	O	O	O	O	O	O	X
Red/white	O	O	O	O	O	X	X
White/black	O	O	O	O	O	O	X
Brown	O	O	O	O	O	X	X
Green	O	O	O	O	O	X	X
Pink	O	O	O	O	O	X	X
Yellow/red	O	O	O	O	O	X	X
White/red		O	O	O	O	X	X
Orange	O		O	O	O	X	X
Lt. blue	O	O		O	O	X	X
Gray	O	O	O		O	X	X
Lt. green	X	O	O	O		X	X
Black/white	X	O	O	O	O		X
Black	X	O	O	O	O	X	

* Use R×100 scale. X = a reading of less than 100K ohms. O = a reading of more than 100K ohms.

3

Chapter Four

Lubrication, Maintenance and Tune-up

The modern outboard motor delivers more power and performance than ever before, with higher compression ratios, new and improved electrical systems and other design advances. Proper lubrication, maintenance and tune-ups have thus become increasingly important as ways in which you can maintain a high level of performance, extend engine life and extract the maximum economy of operation.

You can do your own lubrication, maintenance and tune-ups if you follow the correct procedures and use common sense. The following information is based on recommendations from Suzuki that will help you keep your outboard motor operating at its peak performance level.

Table 1 provides a complete model history. **Tables 1-6** are at the end of the chapter.

LUBRICATION

Proper Fuel Selection

Two-stroke engines are lubricated by mixing oil with the fuel. The various components of the engine are thus lubricated as the fuel-oil mixture passes through the crankcase and cylinders. Since outboard fuel serves the dual function of producing ignition and distributing the lubrication, the use of low-octane marine white gasoline should be avoided. Such gasoline also has a tendency to cause ring sticking and port plugging.

All Suzuki outboards will use any gasoline with a minimum posted pump octane rating of 85 that works satisfactorily in an automotive engine. Lead-free gasoline is preferable to leaded gasoline, as it offers longer spark plug life.

Sour Fuel

Fuel should not be stored for more than 60 days (under ideal conditions). Gasoline forms gum and varnish deposits as it ages. Such fuel will cause starting problems. A good grade of gasoline stabilizer and conditioner additive may be used to prevent gum and varnish formation during storage or prolonged periods of non-use but it is always better to drain the tank in such cases. Always use fresh gasoline when mixing fuel for your outboard.

Gasohol

Some gasolines sold for marine use now contain alcohol, although this fact may not be advertised. A mixture of 10 percent ethyl alcohol and 90 percent unleaded gasoline is called gasohol. While Suzuki does *not* recommend gasohol for use in its outboards, testing to date has found that it causes no major deterioration of the fuel system or its component parts when consumed immediately after purchase.

Fuels with an alcohol content tend to slowly absorb moisture from the air. When the moisture content of the fuel reaches approximately one percent, it combines with the alcohol and separates from the fuel. This separation does not normally occur when gasohol is used in an automobile, as the tank is generally emptied within a few days after filling it.

The problem does occur in marine use, however, because boats often remain idle between start-ups for days or even weeks. This length of time permits separation to take place. The alcohol-water mixture settles at the bottom of the fuel tank. Since outboard motors will not run on this mixture, it is necessary to drain the fuel tank, flush out the fuel system with clean gasoline and then remove, clean and reinstall the spark plugs before the engine can be started.

Continued use of fuels containing alcohol can "melt" the fuel level indicator lens in portable fuel tanks. Many late-model replacement tanks now contain an alcohol-resistant lens.

The major danger of using gasohol in an outboard motor is that a shot of the water-alcohol mix may be picked up and sent to one of the carburetors of a multicylinder engine. Since this mixture contains no oil, it will wash oil off the bore of any cylinder it enters. The other carburetor receiving good fuel-oil mixture will keep the engine running while the cylinder receiving the water-alcohol mixture can suffer internal damage.

The problem of unlabeled gasohol has become so prevalent around the United States that Miller Tools (32615 Park Lane, Garden City, MI 48135) now offers an Alcohol Detection Kit (part No. C-4846) so that owners and mechanics can determine the quality of fuel being used.

The kit cannot differentiate between types of alcohol (ethanol, methanol, etc.) nor is it considered to be absolutely accurate from a scientific standpoint, but it is accurate enough to determine whether or not there is sufficient alcohol in the fuel to cause the user to take precautions.

Recommended Fuel Mixture

Oil injection is used with 1980-on DT 85-DT 140, 1983-on DT 60-DT 75 and 1984 DT 40-DT 50 engines. A mechanical pump driven by the crankshaft (**Figure 1**) automatically injects oil into the intake manifold at a variable ratio from approximately 120:1 at idle to 50:1 at full throttle. A sensor monitoring the injection system sounds when the oil tank requires replenishment. To replenish the system, lift the lid on the engine cover. Reach inside, remove the oil tank cap and pour in a can of Suzuki CCI 50:1 Outboard Oil. See Chapter

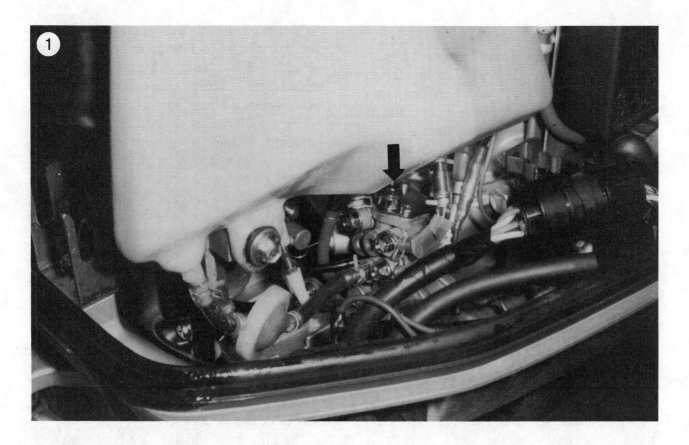

Twelve for system operation and service procedures.

With all other Suzuki engines covered in this manual, use the specified gasoline and mix with Suzuki CCI 50:1 Outboard Oil in the following ratios:

> *CAUTION*
> *Do not, under any circumstances, use multigrade or other high detergent automotive oils or oils containing metallic additives. Such oils are harmful to 2-stroke engines. Since they do not mix properly with gasoline, do not burn as 2-cycle oils do and leave an ash residue, their use may result in piston scoring, bearing failure or other engine damage.*

a. During the break-in period, thoroughly mix 26 ounces of Suzuki CCC 50:1 Outboard Oil with each 5 7/8 gallons of gasoline in your 6 gallon Suzuki fuel tank (or 17 ounces with each 3 7/8 gallons in a 4 gallon tank). This provides the recommended 30:1 mixture.

b. After engine break-in, mix 16 ounces with each 5 7/8 gallons of gasoline in your 6 gallon Suzuki fuel tank (or 10 ounces with each 3 7/8 gallons in a 4 gallon tank). This provides a 50:1 mixture.

c. Operation in Canada requires mixing 16 U.S. ounces of Suzuki CCC 50:1 Outboard Oil to each 4.9 Imperial gallons of gasoline in your 6 gallon Suzuki fuel tank (or 10 U.S. ounces with each 3.2 Imperial gallons in a 4 gallon tank).

> *CAUTION*
> *There are a number of oil products on the market which specify use at 100:1. They are **not** BIA TC-W approved and should **not** be used.*

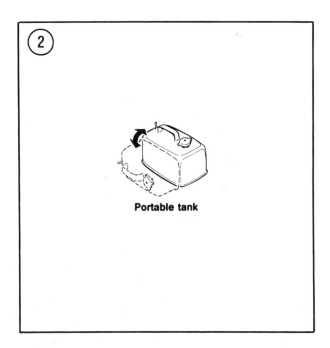

Portable tank

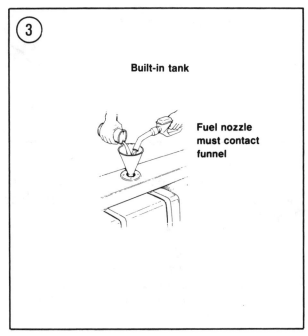

Built-in tank

**Fuel nozzle
must contact
funnel**

If Suzuki CCC 50:1 Outboard Oil is not available, any high-quality 2-stroke oil intended for outboard use may be substituted provided the oil meets BIA rating TC-W and specifies so on the container. Follow the manufacturer's mixing instructions on the container but do not exceed a 50:1 ratio (30:1 during break-in).

Correct Fuel Mixing

Mix the fuel and oil outdoors or in a well-ventilated indoor location. Mix the fuel directly in the remote tank.

> *WARNING*
> *Gasoline is an extreme fire hazard. Never use gasoline near heat, sparks or flame. Do not smoke while mixing fuel.*

Using less than the specified amount of oil can result in insufficient lubrication and serious engine damage. Using more oil than specified causes spark plug fouling, erratic carburetion, excessive smoking and rapid carbon accumulation which can cause preignition.

Cleanliness is of prime importance. Even a very small particle of dirt can cause carburetion problems. Always use fresh gasoline. Gum and varnish deposits tend to form in gasoline stored in a tank for any length of time. Use of sour fuel can result in carburetor problems and spark plug fouling.

Above 32° F (10° C)

Measure the required amounts of gasoline and Suzuki CCC 50:1 Outboard Oil accurately. Pour the specified amount of oil into the portable tank and add one-half of the gasoline to be mixed. Install the tank filler cap and mix the fuel by tipping the tank on its side and back to an upright position several times. See **Figure 2**. Remove the tank cap and add the balance of the gasoline, then mix again.

If a built-in tank is used, insert a large metal filter funnel in the tank filler neck. Slowly pour the Suzuki CCC 50:1 Outboard Oil into the funnel at the same time the tank is being filled with gasoline. See **Figure 3**.

Below 32° F (0° C)

Measure the required amounts of gasoline and Suzuki CCC 50:1 Outboard Oil accurately. Pour about one gallon of gasoline in the tank and then add the required amount of oil. Install the tank filler cap and shake the tank to thoroughly mix the fuel and oil. Remove the cap and add the balance of the gasoline.

If a built-in tank is used, insert a large metal filter funnel in the tank filler neck. Mix the required amount of Suzuki CCC 50:1 Outboard Oil with one gallon of gasoline in a separate container. Slowly pour the mixture into the funnel at the same time the tank is being filled with gasoline.

Consistent Fuel Mixtures

The carburetor idle adjustment is sensitive to fuel mixture variations which result from the use of different oils and gasolines or from inaccurate measuring and mixing. This may require readjustment of the idle needle. To prevent the necessity for constant readjustment of the carburetor from one batch of fuel to the next, always be consistent. Prepare each batch of fuel exactly the same as previous ones.

Pre-mixed fuels sold at some marinas are not recommended for use in Suzuki outboards, since the quality and consistency of pre-mixed fuels can vary greatly. The possibility of engine damage resulting from use of an incorrect fuel mixture outweighs the convenience offered by pre-mixed fuel.

Gearcase Lubrication

Change the gearcase lubricant after the first 10 hours of operation and replace at 50 hour intervals or at least once per season. Use Suzuki Outboard Motor Gear Oil. If this is

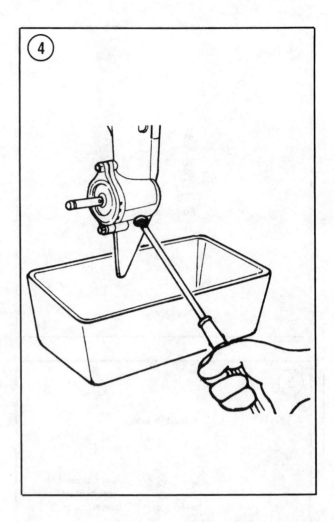

not available, use a high quality non-corrosive E.P. 90 outboard gear lubricant.

CAUTION
Do not use regular automotive grease in the gearcase. Its expansion and foam characteristics are not suitable for marine use.

Gearcase Lubricant Check

To assure a correct level check, the engine must be in the upright position and not run for at least 2 hours before performing this procedure. Refer to **Figure 4** (2 hp) or **Figure 5** (all others) as required.

1. Remove the engine cover and disconnect the spark plug lead(s) as a safety precaution to prevent accidental starting of the engine.

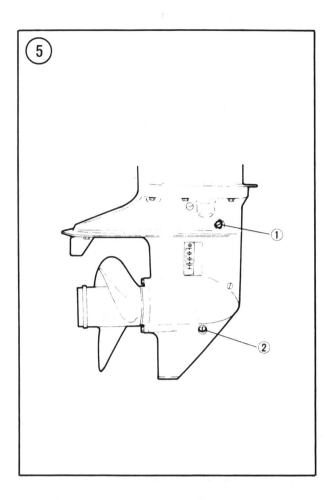

2. Locate and loosen (but do not remove) the gearcase drain plug (2, **Figure 5**) or fill/drain plug (2 hp). Allow a small amount of lubricant to drain. If there is water in the gearcase, it will drain before the lubricant. Retighten the plug securely.

3. If water is noted in Step 2, retighten the plug securely and pressure test the gearcase to determine if a seal has failed or if the water is simply condensation in the gearcase. See Chapter Nine.

4. Remove the vent plug (1, **Figure 5**) on DT 3.5-DT 140 models. Do not lose the accompanying washer. The lubricant should be level with the bottom of the vent plug hole.

CAUTION
Never lubricate the gearcase without first removing the vent plug, as the injected lubricant displaces air which

must be allowed to escape. The gearcase cannot be completely filled otherwise.

5. If the lubricant level is low, remove the drain plug on DT 3.5-DT 140 hp models. See 2, **Figure 5**.

NOTE
On 2 hp gearcases, the lubricant will flow out of the drain hole when the gearcase is full.

6. Inject lubricant into the fill/drain hole (**Figure 4**) or drain hole (2, **Figure 5**) until excess fluid flows out the vent plug hole.

7. Install the fill/drain plug on 2 hp models. Install the vent plug, then the drain plug on DT 3.5-DT 140 hp models. Be sure the washers are in place under the head of each, so that water will not leak past the threads into the housing.

8. Wipe any excess lubricant off the gearcase exterior.

9. On DT 3.5-DT 140 hp models, remove the vent plug and washer (1, **Figure 5**). Let gearcase stand upright for a minimum of 1/2 hour, then recheck the lubricant level. Top up if necessary, then reinstall vent plug and washer.

Gearcase Lubricant Change

Refer to **Figure 4** or **Figure 5** for this procedure.

1. Remove the engine cover and disconnect the spark plug lead(s) as a safety precaution to prevent accidental starting of the engine.

2. Place a container under the fill/drain (**Figure 4**) or drain plug (2, **Figure 5**) and remove it. Remove the vent plug on DT 3.5-DT 140 hp models (1, **Figure 5**). Drain the lubricant from the gearcase.

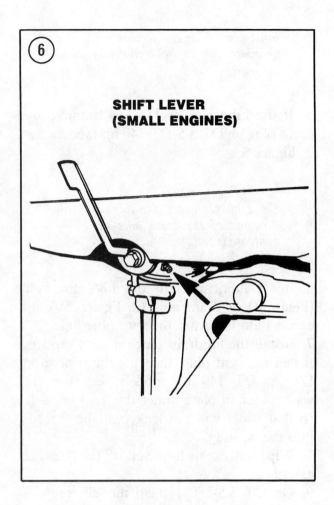

⑥ SHIFT LEVER (SMALL ENGINES)

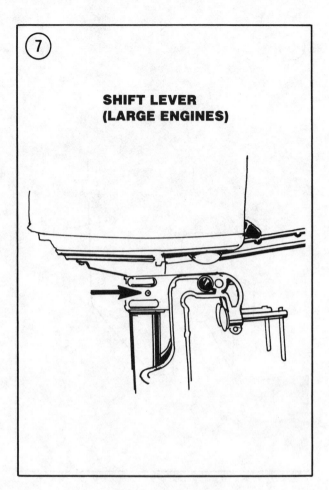

⑦ SHIFT LEVER (LARGE ENGINES)

NOTE
If the lubricant is creamy in color or metallic particles are found in Step 3, remove and disassemble the gearcase to determine and correct the cause of the problem.

3. Wipe a small amount of lubricant on a finger and rub the finger and thumb together. Check for the presence of metallic particles in the lubricant. Note the color of the lubricant. A white or creamy color indicates water in the lubricant. Check the drain container for signs of water separation from the lubricant.

4. Perform Steps 6-9 of *Gearcase Lubricant Check* in this chapter.

Other Lubrication Points

Refer to **Figures 6-11** (typical) and **Table 2** for other lubricant points and frequency of

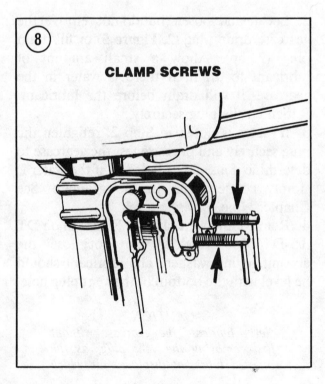

⑧ CLAMP SCREWS

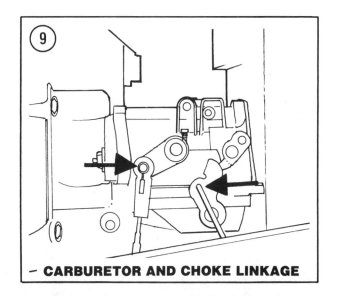

— CARBURETOR AND CHOKE LINKAGE

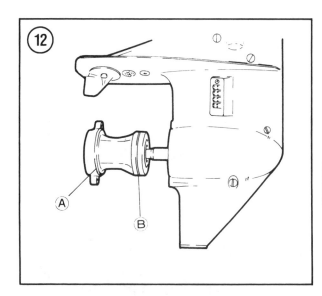

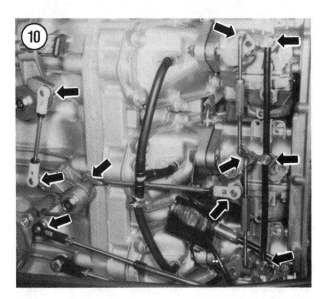

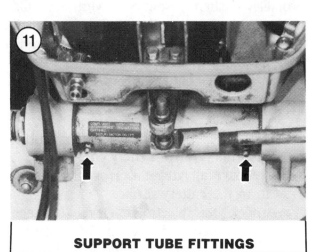

SUPPORT TUBE FITTINGS

lubrication. Use water-resistant grease for all grease fittings and Suzuki Outboard Motor Gear Oil for topping up or changing the gearcase lubricant.

In addition to these lubrication points, some motors may also have grease fittings provided at critical points where bearing surfaces are not externally exposed. These fittings should be lubricated at least each season with an automotive type grease gun and water-resistant grease.

CAUTION
When lubricating the steering cable on models so equipped, make sure its core is fully retracted into the cable housing. Lubricating the cable while extended can cause a hydraulic lock to occur.

Salt Water Corrosion of Gearcase Bearing Cage or Spool

Salt water corrosion that is allowed to build up unchecked can eventually split the gearcase and destroy the lower unit. If the motor is used in salt water, remove the propeller shaft bearing housing (**Figure 12**, typical) at least once a year after the initial 10-hour inspection. Clean all corrosive deposits and dried-up lubricant from each end of the housing.

Install new O-rings on the bearing housing and wipe the outer diameter of the housing at A and B, **Figure 12** with Suzuki water-resistant grease. Apply a thin coat of Suzuki silicone seal to the gearcase and bearing housing mating surfaces and install the housing. Lubricate the propeller shaft splines with Suzuki water-resistant grease and reinstall the propeller.

STORAGE

The major consideration in preparing an outboard motor for storage is to protect it from rust, corrosion and dirt. Suzuki recommends the following procedure.

1. Remove the engine cover.
2. Operate the motor in a test tank or attach a flush device (**Figure 13**). Start the engine and run at fast idle until warmed up.
3. Shift the engine into NEUTRAL. Disconnect the fuel line and run the engine at fast idle while pouring about 2 ounces of Suzuki CCI 50:1 Outboard Oil into the carburetor air intake until the engine stalls out.
4. Remove spark plug(s) as described in this chapter. Pour about one ounce of Suzuki CCI 50:1 Outboard Oil into each spark plug hole. Slowly rotate flywheel by hand several times to distribute the oil throughout the cylinder(s). Reinstall spark plugs.
5. Service the fuel tank filter as follows:
   a. Disconnect the fuel line at the tank adapter.
   b. Unthread and remove the tank adapter.
   c. Remove the hose clamp holding the filter screen to the pick-up end of the adapter.
   d. Remove the screen, rinse it in clean benzine and blow low-pressure compressed air through the screen in the direction of the plastic collar.
   e. Reinstall filter screen to the tank adapter. Thread adapter in place and connect the fuel line.

6. Service the engine fuel filter as described in this chapter.
7. Drain and refill gearcase as described in this chapter. Check condition of vent, fill or fill/drain plug gaskets. Replace as required.
8. Refer to **Figures 6-11** and **Table 2** as appropriate and lubricate motor at all specified points. See **Table 3** for recommended lubricants.
9. Clean the motor, including all accessible power head parts. Coat with a good marine-type wax. Install the engine cover.
10. Remove the propeller and lubricate propeller shaft splines with Suzuki water-resistant grease. Reinstall the propeller.
11. Store the motor upright in a dry and well-ventilated area.
12. Service the battery (if so equipped) as follows:

   a. Disconnect the negative battery cable, then the positive battery cable.
   b. Remove all grease, corrosion and dirt from the battery surface.
   c. Check the electrolyte level in each battery cell and top up with distilled water, if necessary. Fluid level in each

cell should not be higher than 3/16 in. above the perforated baffles.

d. Lubricate the terminal bolts with grease or petroleum jelly.

CAUTION
A discharged battery can be damaged by freezing.

e. With the battery in a fully charged condition (specific gravity 1.260-1.275), store in a dry place where the temperature will not drop below freezing.

f. Recharge the battery every 45 days or whenever the specific gravity drops below 1.230. Before charging, cover the plates with distilled water, but not more than 3/16 in. above the perforated baffles. The charge rate should not exceed 6 amps. Stop charging when the specific gravity reaches 1.260 at 80° F (27° C).

g. Before placing the battery back into service after storage, remove the excess grease from the terminals, leaving a small amount on. Install battery in a fully charged state.

COMPLETE SUBMERSION

An outboard motor which has been lost overboard should be recovered as quickly as possible. If the motor was running when submerged, disassemble and clean it immediately—any delay will result in rust and corrosion of internal components once it has been removed from the water. If the motor was not running and appears to be undamaged mechanically with no abrasive dirt or silt inside, take the following emergency steps immediately.

1. Wash the outside of the motor with clean water to remove weeds, mud and other debris.

2. Remove the engine cover.

3. If recovered from salt water, flush motor completely with fresh water.

4. Remove the spark plug(s) as described in this chapter.

CAUTION
Do not force the motor if it does not turn over freely by hand in Step 5. This may be an indication of internal damage such as a bent connecting rod or broken piston.

5. Drain as much water as possible from the power head by placing the motor in a horizontal position. Manually rotate the flywheel with the spark plug hole(s) facing downward.

6. Dry and reinstall the spark plugs.

7. Dry all ignition components.

8. Drain the fuel lines and carburetor(s).

9. On models with an integral fuel tank, drain the tank and flush with fresh gasoline until all water has been removed.

CAUTION
If there is a possibility that sand may have entered the power head, do not try to start the motor or severe internal damage may occur.

10. Try starting the motor with a fresh fuel source. If motor will start, let it run at least one hour to eliminate any water remaining inside.

CAUTION
If it is not possible to disassemble and clean the motor immediately in Step 11, resubmerge the power head in water to prevent rust and corrosion formation until such time as it can be properly serviced.

11. If the motor will not start in Step 10, try to diagnose the cause as fuel, electrical or mechanical and correct the problem. If the engine cannot be started within 2 hours,

disassemble, clean and oil all parts thoroughly as soon as possible.

ANTI-CORROSION MAINTENANCE

1. Flush the cooling system with fresh water as described in this chapter after each time motor is used in salt water. Wash exterior with fresh water.
2. Dry exterior of motor and apply primer over any paint nicks and scratches. Use only Suzuki touch-up paints available at your dealer. Do not use paints containing mercury or copper. Do not paint sacrificial anodes.
3. Spray power head and all electrical connections with a good quality corrosion and rust preventative.
4. Check sacrifical anodes. Replace any that are less than half their original size.
5. Lubricate more frequently than specified in **Table 2**. If used consistently in salt water, reduce lubrication intervals by one-half.

ENGINE FLUSHING

Periodic engine flushing will prevent salt or silt deposits from accumulating in the water passageways. This procedure should also be performed whenever an outboard motor is operated in salt water or polluted water.

Keep the engine in an upright position during and after flushing. This prevents water from passing into the power head through the drive shaft housing and exhaust ports during the flushing procedure. It also eliminates the possibility of residual water being trapped in the drive shaft housing or other passageways.

1. Attach a flushing device according to manufacturer's instructions.
2. Connect a garden hose between a water tap and the flushing device.
3. Open the water tap partially—do not use full pressure.
4. Shift into NEUTRAL, then start engine. Keep engine speed at idle speed.

5. Adjust water flow so that there is a slight loss of water around the rubber cups of the flushing device. See **Figure 13**.
6. Check the engine to make sure that water is being discharged from the "tell-tale" nozzle. If it is not, stop the engine immediately and determine the cause of the problem.

CAUTION
*Flush the engine for at least 5 minutes
if used in salt water.*

7. Flush engine until discharged water is clear. Stop engine.
8. Close water tap and remove flushing device from gearcase.

TUNE-UP

A tune-up consists of a series of inspections, adjustments and parts replacements to compensate for normal wear and deterioration of outboard engine components. Regular tune-ups are important for power, performance and economy. Suzuki recommends that its outboards be serviced every 6 months or 50 hours of operation, whichever comes first. If subjected to limited use, the engine should be tuned at least once a year.

Since proper outboard engine operation depends upon a number of interrelated system functions, a tune-up consisting of only one or two corrections will seldom give lasting results. For best results, a thorough and systematic procedure of analysis and correction is necessary.

Prior to performing a tune-up, it is a good idea to flush the engine as described in this chapter and check for satisfactory water pump operation.

The tune-up sequence recommended by Suzuki includes the following:

    a. Compression check.
    b. Spark plug service.

(14)

c. Gearcase and water pump check.
d. Fuel system service.
e. Ignition system service.
f. Battery, starter and relay/solenoid check (if so equipped).
g. Wiring harness check.
h. Timing, synchronization and adjustment.
i. Performance test (on boat).

Anytime the fuel or ignition systems are adjusted or defective parts replaced, the engine timing, synchronization and adjustment *must* be checked. These procedures are described in Chapter Five. Perform the timing, synchronization and adjustment procedure for your engine *before* running the performance test.

Compression Check

An accurate cylinder compression check gives a good idea of the condition of the basic working parts of the engine. It is also an important first step in any tune-up, as an engine with low or unequal compression between cylinders *cannot* be satisfactorily

tuned. Any compression problem discovered during this check must be corrected before continuing with the tune-up procedure.

1. With the engine warm, disconnect the spark plug wire(s) and remove the plug(s) as described in this chapter.
2. Ground the spark plug wire(s) to the engine to disable the ignition system.
3. Connect the compression tester to the top spark plug hole according to manufacturer's instructions (**Figure 14**).
4. With the throttle set to the wide-open position, crank the engine through at least 4 compression strokes. Record the gauge reading.
5. Repeat Step 3 and Step 4 on each cylinder of multicylinder engines.

The actual readings are not as important as the differences in readings when interpreting the results. A variation of more than 10-15 psi between 2 cylinders indicates a problem with the lower reading cylinder, such as worn or sticking piston rings or scored pistons or cylinders. In such cases, pour a tablespoon of engine oil into the suspect cylinder and repeat Step 3 and Step 4. If the compression is raised significantly (by 10 psi in an older engine), the rings are worn and should be replaced.

Many outboard engines are plagued by hard starting and generally poor running for which there seems to be no good cause. Carburetion and ignition check out satisfactorily and a compression test may show that everything is well in the engine's upper end. With everything apparently pointing to a sound engine, owners focus on the propeller as the cause of the problem and start swapping props, often with disastrous results.

What a compression test does *not* show is lack of primary compression. In a 2-stroke engine, the crankcase must be alternately under high pressure and low pressure. After the piston closes the intake port, further downward movement of the piston causes the entrapped mixture to be pressurized so that it can rush quickly into the cylinder when the scavenging ports are opened. Upward piston movement creates a lower pressure in the crankcase, enabling fuel-air mixture to pass in from the carburetor.

When the crankshaft seals or case gaskets leak, the crankcase cannot hold pressure and proper engine operation becomes impossible. Any other source of leakage, such as defective cylinder base gaskets or a porous or cracked crankcase casting, will result in the same conditions.

If the power head shows signs of overheating (discolored or scorched paint) but the compression test turns up nothing abnormal, check the cylinder(s) visually through the transfer ports for possible scoring. A cylinder can be slightly scored and still deliver a relatively good compression reading. In such a case, it is also a good idea to double-check the water pump operation as a possible cause for overheating.

Spark Plugs

Suzuki outboards are equipped with NGK spark plugs selected for average use conditions. Under adverse use conditions, the recommended spark plug may foul or overheat. In such cases, check the ignition and carburetion systems to make sure they are operating correctly. If no defect is found, replace the spark plug with one of a hotter or colder heat range as required. **Table 4** contains the recommended spark plugs for all models covered in this book. **Table 5** provides a cross-reference for use when NGK spark plugs are not available.

Spark Plug Wires

Metal-shielded spark plug caps were installed on some 1977-1978 DT 9.9-DT 25 and DT 50-DT 65 models. The metal shields are responsible for erratic engine operation, causing such intermittent malfunctions as firing on only one cylinder, no power at low speed or shutting the engine down when it is shifted into gear.

To correct such problems, pry the metal shield halves apart, then remove and discard them. The plug caps can also be replaced by part No. 33510-41111.

Spark Plug Removal

CAUTION
Whenever the spark plugs are removed, dirt around them can fall into the plug holes. This can cause engine damage that is expensive to repair.

1. Blow out any foreign matter from around the spark plugs with compressed air. Use a compressor if you have one. If you do not, use a can of compressed inert gas, available from photo stores.
2. Disconnect the spark plug wires by twisting the wire boot back and forth on the plug insulator while pulling outward. Pulling on the wire instead of the boot may cause internal damage to the wire.
3. Remove the plugs with an appropriate size spark plug socket or box end wrench. Keep the plugs in order so you know which cylinder they came from.
4. Examine each spark plug. Compare its condition with **Figure 15**. Spark plug condition indicates engine condition and can warn of developing trouble.
5. Check each plug for make and heat range. All should be of the same make and number or heat range.
6. Suzuki recommends the plugs be cleaned and reused if in good condition; however, such plugs seldom last very long. New plugs are inexpensive and far more reliable.

4

SPARK PLUG ANALYSIS
(CONVENTIONAL GAP SPARK PLUGS)

⑮

A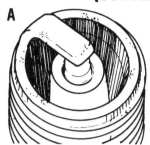

B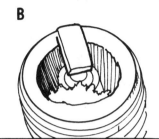

C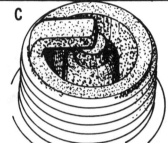

D

E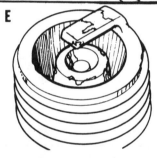

F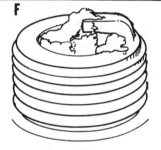

A. **Normal**—Light tan to gray color of insulator indicates correct heat range. Few deposits are present and the electrodes are not burned.

B. **Core bridging**—These defects are caused by excessive combustion chamber deposits striking and adhering to the firing end of the plug. In this case, they wedge or fuse between the electrode and core nose. They originate from the piston and cylinder head surfaces. Deposits are formed by one or more of the following:
   a. Excessive carbon in cylinder.
   b. Use of non-recommended oils.
   c. Immediate high-speed operation after prolonged trolling.
   d. Improper fuel-oil ratio.

C. **Wet fouling**—Damp or wet, black carbon coating over entire firing end of plug. Forms sludge in some engines. Caused by one or more of the following:
   a. Spark plug heat range too cold.
   b. Prolonged trolling.
   c. Low-speed carburetor adjustment too rich.

   d. Improper fuel-oil ratio.
   e. Induction manifold bleed-off passage obstructed.
   f. Worn or defective breaker points.

D. **Gap bridging**—Similar to core bridging, except the combustion particles are wedged or fused between the electrodes. Causes are the same.

E. **Overheating**—Badly worn electrodes and premature gap wear are indicative of this problem, along with a gray or white "blistered" appearance on the insulator. Caused by one or more of the following:
   a. Spark plug heat range too hot.
   b. Incorrect propeller usage, causing engine to lug.
   c. Worn or defective water pump.
   d. Restricted water intake or restriction somewhere in the cooling system.

F. **Ash deposits or lead fouling**—Ash deposits are light brown to white in color and result from use of fuel or oil additives. Lead fouling produces a yellowish brown discoloration and can be avoided by using unleaded fuels.

Spark Plug Gapping

New or cleaned plugs should be carefully gapped to ensure a reliable, consistent spark. Use a special spark plug tool with a wire gauge. See **Figure 16** for one common type.

1. Remove the plugs and gaskets from the boxes. Install the gaskets.

NOTE
Some plug brands may have small end pieces that must be screwed on before the plugs can be used.

2. Insert the appropriate size round feeler between the electrodes. See **Table 4**. If the gap is correct, there will be a slight drag as the wire is pulled through. If there is no drag or if the wire will not pull through, bend the side electrode with the gapping tool (**Figure 17**) to change the gap. Remeasure with the wire gauge.

CAUTION
Never try to close the electrode gap by tapping the spark plug on a solid surface. This can damage the plug internally. Always use the gapping and adjusting tool to open or close the gap.

Spark Plug Installation

Improper installation of spark plugs is one of the most common causes of poor spark plug performance in outboard engines. The gasket on the plug must be fully compressed against a clean plug seat in order for heat transfer to take place effectively. This requires close attention to proper tightening during installation.

1. Inspect the spark plug hole threads and clean them with a thread chaser (**Figure 18**). Wipe cylinder head seats clean before installing the new plugs.

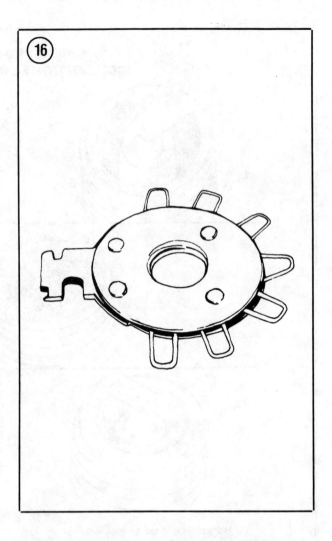

2. Screw each plug in by hand until it seats. Very little effort is required. If force is necessary, the plug is cross-threaded. Unscrew it and try again.

3. Tighten the spark plugs. If you have a torque wrench, tighten to 10-15 ft.-lb. If not, seat the plug finger-tight on the gasket, then tighten an additional 1/4 turn with a wrench.

4. Inspect each spark plug wire before reconnecting it to its cylinder. If insulation is damaged or deteriorated, install a new plug wire. Push wire boot onto plug terminal and make sure it seats fully.

Gearcase and Water Pump Check

A faulty water pump or one that performs below specifications can result in extensive

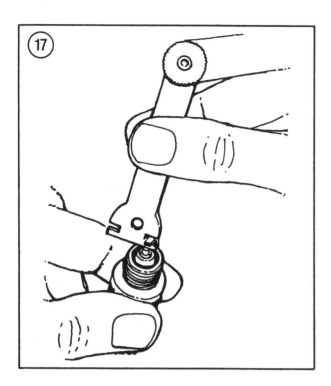

engine damage. Thus, it is a good idea to replace the water pump impeller, seals and gaskets once a year or whenever the gearcase is removed for service. See Chapter Nine.

Fuel System Service

The clearance between the carburetor and choke shutter should not be greater than 0.015 in. when the choke is closed or a hard starting condition will result. When changing from one brand of gasoline to another, it may be necessary to readjust the carburetor idle mixture needle slightly (1/4 turn) to accommodate variations in volatility.

Fuel Lines

1. Visually check all fuel lines for kinks, leaks, deterioration or other damage.

2. Disconnect fuel lines and blow out with compressed air to dislodge any contamination or foreign material.

3. Reinstall the fuel lines.

Engine Fuel Filter Service

DT 2 models have an integral fuel tank and utilize gravity fuel feed instead of a fuel pump. A filter screen is attached to the fuel line fitting on the bottom of the tank. A filter screen is also installed in the carburetor inlet fuel fitting.

Other models may use one of the following:
 a. An inline filter.
 b. A canister filter.
 c. A fuel pump filter screen.

> *WARNING*
> *Suzuki recommends the use of gasoline as a cleaning solvent in the following procedures. Work in a well-ventilated area away from any source of ignition. Keep a fire extinguisher handy.*

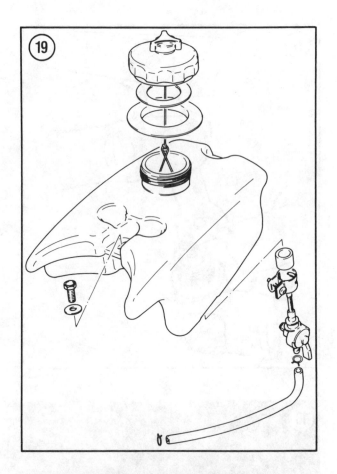

Integral tank filter

Refer to **Figure 19** for this procedure.

1. Remove the fuel tank, if necessary, to provide working room. See Chapter Six.

2. Loosen the fuel petcock clamp. Remove the petcock from the hose.

3. Remove the filter screen from the petcock.

4. Clean the screen in gasoline. If excessively dirty or contaminated with water, discard and install a new screen.

5. Installation is the reverse of removal.

Inline filter

1. Slide each hose retaining clamp off the filter nipple with a pair of pliers and disconnect the hoses from the filter. See **Figure 20**.

2. Clean the filter assembly in gasoline. If excessively dirty or contaminated with water, discard and install a new filter.

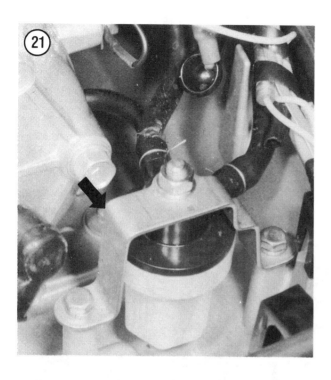

3. Reinstall the hoses on the filter nipples. Make sure embossed arrow on filter points in the direction of fuel flow.

4. Slide the retaining clamps on each hose over the nipple to assure a leak-free connection.

5. Check fuel filter installation for leakage by priming fuel system with fuel line primer bulb.

Canister filter

Refer to **Figure 21** for this procedure.

1. Unscrew and remove the filter canister from the adapter.

2. Remove the filter element from the canister.

3. Clean the filter element in gasoline. If excessively dirty or contaminated with water, discard and install a new element.

4. Reinstall the element in the canister. Fit the O-ring and gasket in position, then thread canister on adapter and tighten securely.

5. Check fuel filter installation for leakage by priming fuel system with fuel line primer bulb.

Fuel pump filter

1. Remove the bolt in the center of the fuel pump cover. Remove the cover and O-ring or gasket.

2. Remove the filter screen from the fuel pump body.

3. Clean the filter screen in gasoline. If excessively dirty or contaminated with water, discard and install a new screen.

4. Installation is the reverse of removal. Use a new pump cover O-ring or gasket.

5. Check filter screen installation for leakage by priming fuel system with fuel line primer bulb.

Fuel Pump

The fuel pump does not generally require service during a tune-up. However, if the engine has more than 100 hours on it since the fuel pump was last serviced, it is a good idea to remove and disassemble the pump, inspect each part carefully for wear or damage and reassemble it with a new diaphragm. See Chapter Six.

Fuel pump diaphragms are fragile and one that is defective often produces symptoms that are diagnosed as an ignition system problem. A common malfunction results from a tiny pinhole or crack in the diaphragm caused by an engine backfire. This defect allows gasoline to enter the crankcase and wet-foul the spark plug at idle speed, causing hard starting and engine stall at low rpm. The problem disappears at higher speeds, as fuel quantity is limited. Since the plug is not fouled by excess fuel at higher speeds, it fires normally.

Pressure test

NOTE
Fuel pump pressure cannot be tested on integral fuel pump carburetors.

Tee a fuel pressure gauge into the line between the carburetor and fuel pump. Loosen the fuel tank vent cap to relieve any pressure in the system. With the engine in a test tank or on the boat in the water, the fuel pump pressure should be at least 2.5 psi at 4,500 rpm. If not, rebuild the fuel pump with a new diaphragm and gaskets. See Chapter Six.

**Breaker Point Ignition
System Service**

The condition and gap of the breaker points will greatly affect engine operation. Burned or badly oxidized points will allow little or no current to pass. A gap that is too narrow will not allow the coil to build up sufficient voltage and will result in a weak spark. An excessive point gap will allow the points to open before the primary current reaches its maximum.

While slightly pitted points can be dressed with a file, this should be done only as a temporary measure, as the points may arc after filing. Oxidized, dirty or oily points can be cleaned with alcohol but new points are inexpensive and always preferable for efficient engine operation.

The condenser absorbs the surge of high voltage from the coil and prevents current from arcing across the points when they open. Condensers can be tested as described in Chapter Three, but are also inexpensive and should be replaced as a matter of course whenever new breaker points are installed.

NOTE
Breaker points must be adjusted correctly. An error in gap of 0.0015 in. will change engine timing by as much as one degree.

All breaker point sets are installed on the stator base under the flywheel and are set to

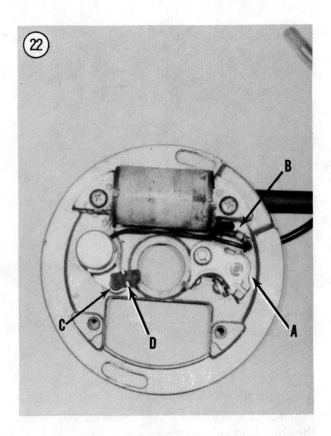

0.012-0.016 in. regardless of model. After establishing the breaker point gap, ignition timing should be checked. See Chapter Five.

CAUTION
Always rotate the crankshaft in a clockwise direction in the following procedures. If rotated more than 180° in a counterclockwise direction, the water pump impeller may be damaged.

Breaker Point Replacement

Refer to **Figure 22** (typical) for this procedure.
1. Disconnect the negative battery cable, if so equipped.
2. Remove the engine cover.
3. Remove the flywheel. See Chapter Eight.
4. Remove the screw holding the breaker point set to the stator base (A, **Figure 22**).
5. Disconnect the coil and condenser leads (B, **Figure 22**) at the breaker point set. Remove the breaker point set.

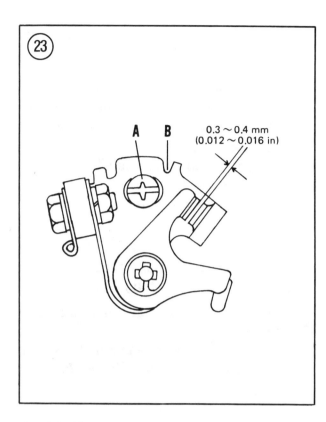

A B   0.3 ~ 0.4 mm
(0.012 ~ 0.016 in)

6. Remove the screw holding the condenser to the stator base (C, **Figure 22**). Remove the condenser.

7. Install a new breaker point set on the stator base. Make sure the pivot point on the bottom of the point set engages the hole in the stator base. Install but do not tighten the hold-down screw.

8. Install a new condenser on the stator base and tighten attaching screw securely, then connect the coil and condenser leads to the breaker point set.

9. Repeat Steps 4-8 to replace the other point set and condenser on 2-cylinder engines.

CAUTION
Do not over-lubricate the breaker cam in Step 10. Excessive lubrication will cause premature point set failure.

10A. If equipped with a felt lubrication wick (D, **Figure 22**), squeeze the wick to see if it is dry. If dry, lubricate with 1-2 drops of 30W engine oil.

10B. If no felt wick is used, lightly lubricate the breaker cam with cam grease.

11. Adjust the breaker point gap(s) as described in this chapter.

12. Reverse Steps 1-3 to complete installation.

Breaker Point Adjustment (1-cylinder Engine)

The following procedure is used when new breaker points have been installed. Slots are provided in the flywheel rotor for checking and adjusting the point gap without flywheel rotor removal.

1. Install the flywheel nut on the crankshaft and rotate the stator base to the wide-open throttle position.

2. Place a wrench on the flywheel nut and rotate the crankshaft clockwise until the breaker point rubbing block rests on a high point on the cam (the points will be wide open).

3. Loosen the point set hold-down screw (A, **Figure 23**). Insert a screwdriver in the adjusting notch (B, **Figure 23**) and move the point set base to obtain a gap of 0.012-0.016 in. when measured with a flat feeler gauge. The gap is correct when the feeler gauge offers a slight drag as it is slipped between the points. When the gap is correct, tighten the hold-down screw securely and recheck the point gap.

Breaker Point Adjustment (2-cylinder Engine)

1. If the breaker points have been replaced, install the flywheel (without starter cup) on the crankshaft. If point gap is being adjusted without replacing the breaker set, remove the starter cup from the flywheel.

2A. DT 4.5, DT 5 and DT 8—Rotate the flywheel clockwise until the cylinder housing timing mark aligns with the No. 1 cylinder timing mark (T1) on the flywheel. See A, **Figure 24**.

2B. DT 7.5 and DT 9—Rotate the flywheel clockwise until the magneto housing timing mark aligns with the "U" mark on the flywheel. See B, **Figure 24**.

3. Check the No. 1 cylinder point gap with a flat feeler gauge. If it is not 0.012-0.016 in., loosen the point set hold-down screw (A, **Figure 23**). Insert a screwdriver in the adjusting notch (B, **Figure 23**) and move the point set base to obtain the specified gap. The gap is correct when the feeler gauge offers a slight drag as it is slipped between the points. When the gap is correct, tighten the hold-down screw securely and recheck the point gap.

4A. DT 4.5, DT 5 and DT 9—Rotate the flywheel clockwise until the cylinder housing timing mark aligns with the No. 2 cylinder timing mark (T2) on the flywheel. See A, **Figure 24**.

4B. DT 7.5 and DT 9—Rotate the flywheel clockwise until the magneto housing timing mark aligns with the "L" mark on the flywheel. See B, **Figure 24**.

5. Repeat Step 3 to check and adjust the No. 2 cylinder point gap.

6. Reinstall the starter cup.

**Battery and Starter Motor Check
(Electric Start Models Only)**

1. Check the battery's state of charge. See Chapter Seven.

2. Connect a voltmeter between the starter motor positive terminal (**Figure 25**) and ground.

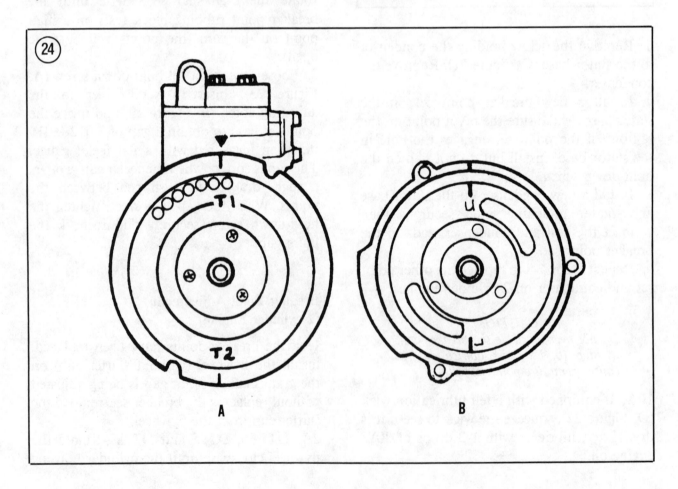

3. Turn ignition switch to START and check voltmeter scale.

4A. If voltage exceeds 9.5 volts and the starter motor does not operate, replace the motor.

4B. If voltage is less than 9.5 volts, recheck battery and connections. Charge battery, if necessary, and repeat procedure.

Starter Relay Resistance Check (Electric Start Models Only)

The starter relay is attached to the starter motor housing. Refer to **Figure 26** (typical) for this procedure.

1. Disconnect the negative battery cable.
2. Locate the black relay ground connection.
3. Disconnect the yellow/green lead between the relay and neutral start interlock switch.

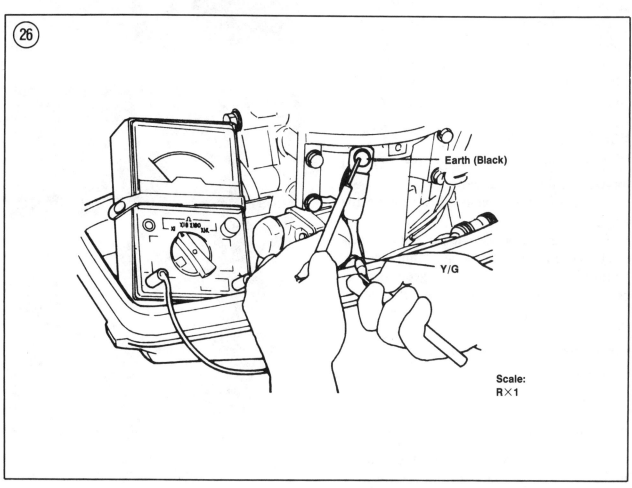

Earth (Black)

Y/G

Scale:
R×1

4. Connect an ohmmeter between the relay ground connection and the yellow/green relay lead.

5. If the meter does not read 3.2-3.8 ohms on the R×1 scale, replace the relay.

6. Reconnect the yellow/green lead and negative battery cable.

Choke Solenoid Resistance Check
(DT 30-DT 140 Electric
Start Models Only)

The choke solenoid is located on the starboard side of the engine. It may be positioned at the base of the choke linkage (**Figure 27**) or at the top of the linkage (**Figure 28**).

1. Disconnect the orange choke solenoid lead at the bullet connector.

2. Connect an ohmmeter between the orange solenoid lead and a good engine ground.

3. If the reading obtained in Step 2 is not within specifications (**Table 6**), replace the choke solenoid.

Wiring Harness Check

1. Check the wiring harness for signs of frayed or chafed insulation.

2. Check for loose connections between the wires and terminal ends.

3. If the harness is suspected of contributing to electrical malfunctions, check all wires for continuity and resistance between harness connection and terminal end. Repair or replace as required.

Engine Synchronization and
Adjustment

See Chapter Five.

Performance Test (On Boat)

Before performance testing the engine, make sure that the boat bottom is cleaned of

all marine growth and that there is no evidence of a "hook" or "rocker" (**Figure 29**) on the bottom. Any of these conditions will reduce performance considerably.

The boat should be performance tested with an average load and with the motor tilted at an angle that will allow the boat to ride on an even keel. If equipped with an adjustable trim tab, it should be properly adjusted to allow the boat to steer in either direction with equal ease.

Check engine rpm at full throttle. If not within the maximum rpm range for the motor as specified in Chapter Five, check the propeller pitch. A high pitch propeller will reduce rpm while a lower pitch prop will increase it.

Readjust the idle mixture and speed under actual operating conditions as required to obtain the best low-speed engine performance.

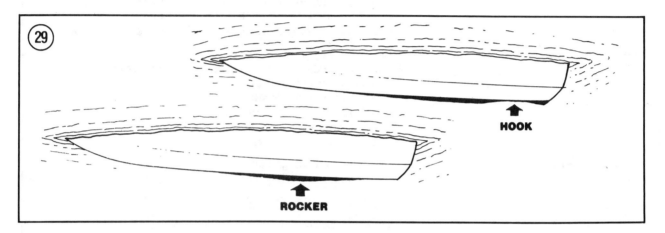

Table 1 MODEL HISTORY

	1977	1978	1979	1980	1981	1982	1983	1984
DT 2	X	X	X	X	X	X	X	X
DT 3.5			X	X	X	X	X	X
DT 4.5	X							
DT 5		X	X	X	X	X	X	
DT 6								X
DT 7.5	X	X	X					
DT 8				X	X	X	X	X
DT 9	X	X	X					
DT 9.9	X	X	X	X	X	X	X	X
DT 15							X	X
DT 16	X	X	X	X	X	X		
DT 20	X	X	X	X				
DT 25	X	X	X	X	X	X	X	X
DT 30							X	X
DT 40				X	X	X	X	X
DT 50/50M	X	X	X	X	X	X	X	X
DT 60							X	X
DT 65		X	X	X	X	X		
DT 75							X	X
DT 85			X	X	X	X	X	X
DT 115					X	X	X	X
DT 140					X	X	X	X

Table 2 MAINTENANCE SCHEDULE*

At first 10 hours	• Change gearcase lubricant
Every 10 hours	• Retighten bolts and nuts • Check wire harness connections • Check idle speed (DT 2-DT 16) • Check and adjust carburetors (DT 20-DT 140) • Check propeller for damage • Lubricate propeller shaft splines • Check fuel lines for leakage • Check intake manifold hose for deterioration • Lubricate steering handle • Check neutral start interlock switch operation • Check emergency switch operation (if so equipped) • Check and adjust remote control linkage (if so equipped) • Check engine key and choke operation (if so equipped) • Check starter button and choke operation (if so equipped)
Every 50 hours	• Clean and regap spark plugs • Decarbonize the piston(s), cylinder and cylinder head • Change gearcase lubricant • Check fuel strainer or filter • Check steering handle preload • Check starter rope condition • Check tilt mechanism preload
Every 100 hours	• Check and adjust ignition timing • Check water pump impeller
Every week	• Check oil injection lines (if so equipped)
Every month	• Lubricate carburetor and choke linkage • Lubricate clamp screws
Every 3 months	• Lubricate swivel bracket • Lubricate support tube • Lubricate shift lever
Once each season	• Change starter rope • Check fuel tank condition • Replace water pump impeller

* Not all items apply to all engines. Perform only those pertaining to your engine.

Table 3 RECOMMENDED LUBRICANTS

Type	Part No.
Water-resistant grease	99000-25170
Outboard Motor Gear Oil	99000-22540
Suzuki CCI 50:1 Outboard Oil	99105-00153
Super Grease "A"	99000-25010
Silicone Seal	99000-31120
Bond No. 4	99000-31030
Cemedine 366E	99000-31090
Thread Lock 1342	99000-32050
Thread Lock Super 1333B	99000-32020
DEXRON automatic transmission fluid	—

4

Table 4 RECOMMENDED SPARK PLUGS

	NGK part No.	Gap (in.)
DT 2	B5HS, BR5HS	0.028
DT 3.5		
1979-1981	BPR6HS	0.028-0.031
1982-on	BP6HS	0.024-0.028
DT 4.5	B6HS	0.028
DT 5		
1978-1980	BPR6HS	0.028
1981-on	BP6HS	0.036
DT 6	BP6HS	0.036
DT 7.5	B6HS	0.028
DT 8		
1980	BPR6HS	0.028
1981-on	BP6HS	0.036
DT 9	B6HS	0.028
DT 9.9		
1977-1982	B6HS	0.028
1983-on	BR7HS-10	0.040
DT 15	BR7HS-10	0.040
DT 16		
1977-1981	BR7HS	0.028
1982	B7HS	0.028
DT 20	B7HS	0.028
DT 25		
1977-1982	B7HS	0.028
1983-on	BR7HS-10	0.040
DT 30	BR7HS-10	0.040
DT 40		
1980-1983	BR8HS	0.036
1984	B8HS	0.036
DT 50		
1977-1983	B8HS	0.036
1984	B8HS-10	0.040
DT 60, DT 65	B8HS-10	0.040
DT 75-DT 140	B8HS	0.036

Table 5 SPARK PLUG CROSS-REFERENCE CHART*

NGK	Champion	AC
B4HS, BR5HS	L81, L88A	44F, 44FF
B6HS, BR6HS	L9J, QL7J, RL7J	42F, 42FF
BP6HS, BPR6HS	RL12Y, RL87Y, L66Y	42FS, 43FS, R43FS
B7HS, BR7HS	L5, L7J	M42FF, S42FR
BR7HS-10	—	—
B8HS, BR8HS	L4J, RL4J, L78, RL78	S41FR, S40FR, M41FF

* The cross-referenced spark plugs are not exact replacements for original plug heat range and should be used only as a temporary replacement.

Table 6 CHOKE SOLENOID RESISTANCE SPECIFICATIONS

Model	Ohms
DT 30	4.1-4.5
DT 40	
1980-1982	3.6-4.0
1983-on	4.1-4.5
DT 50-DT 85	4.1-4.5
DT 115-DT 140	
1981-1982	2.9-3.3
1983-on	4.1-4.5

Chapter Five

Timing, Synchronization and Adjustment

If an engine is to deliver its maximum efficiency and peak performance, the ignition must be timed and the carburetor operation synchronized with the ignition. This procedure is the final step of a tune-up. It must also be performed whenever the fuel or ignition systems are serviced or adjusted.

Procedures for timing, synchronization and adjustment on Suzuki outboards differ according to model and ignition system. This chapter is divided into self-contained sections dealing with particular models/ignition systems for fast and easy reference. Each section specifies the appropriate procedure and sequence to be followed and provides the necessary tune-up data. Read the general information at the beginning of the chapter and then select the section pertaining to your outboard.

Tables 1-3 are at the end of the chapter.

ENGINE TIMING AND SYNCHRONIZATION

As engine rpm increases, the ignition system must fire the spark plug(s) more rapidly. Proper ignition timing synchronizes the spark plug firing with engine speed.

As engine speed increases, the carburetor must provide an increased amount of fuel for combustion. Synchronizing is the process of timing the carburetor operation to the ignition (and thereby the engine speed).

Engines equipped with a breaker point ignition are static-timed in 1 of 2 ways:

a. By measuring the amount of piston travel relative to breaker point opening and closing.

b. By aligning a set of timing marks to correspond with the breaker point opening.

Correct timing thus depends upon a correct breaker point gap setting. If the breaker point gap is correct, but piston travel or timing mark alignment is incorrect, the magneto stator position is readjusted as required.

Synchronization is automatic on models with a breaker point ignition once the point gap and piston travel or timing mark alignment are correct.

Engines equipped with the Suzuki PEI (CDI ignition) are static-timed by aligning timing marks on the throttle cam or stopper with marks on the flywheel. Initial timing and timing advance are both set in this manner, then timing is checked with a timing light.

On all models with the Suzuki PEI ignition (except the DT 20, DT 25 (1977-1982) and DT 50M), the magneto stator base is mechanically linked to the throttle. As the throttle is opened, the ignition timing is advanced. Timing advance is checked with a timing light.

The DT 20, 1977-1982 DT 25 and DT 50M models use a fixed magneto stator base, with timing advanced electrically according to engine speed. Timing advance can be checked with a timing light.

Required Equipment

Static timing of an engine with a breaker point ignition requires the use of a timing gauge (dial indicator) and timing tester (ohmmeter or self-powered test lamp) to set ignition timing properly.

Dynamic engine timing uses a stroboscopic timing light connected to the No. 1 spark plug wire. See **Figure 1**. As the engine is cranked or operated, the light flashes each time the spark plug fires. When the light is pointed at the moving flywheel, the mark on the flywheel appears to stand still. The flywheel mark should align with the stationary timing mark on the engine.

A tachometer connected to the engine is used to determine engine speed during idle and high-speed adjustments.

CAUTION
Never operate the engine without water circulating through the gearcase to the engine. This will damage the water pump and the gearcase and can cause engine damage.

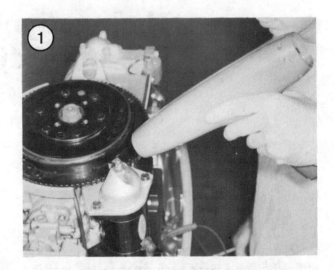

Some form of water supply is required whenever the engine is operated during the procedure. The use of a test tank and test wheel is the most convenient method. While the procedure may be carried out with the boat in the water, checking engine timing while speeding across open water is neither easy nor safe.

Suzuki recommends that a test wheel (**Figure 2**) be substituted for the propeller to put a load on the propeller shaft and prevent

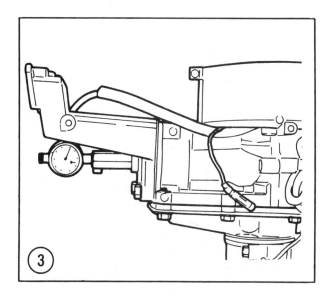

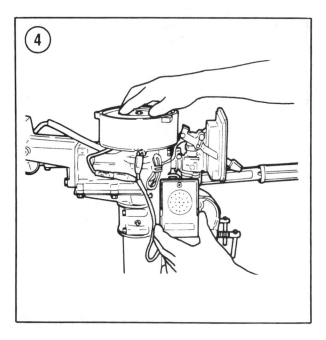

engine damage from excessive rpm. Test wheel recommendations provided by Suzuki are given in **Table 1**.

Timing Adjustment (DT 2 and DT 3.5)

1. Remove the engine cover(s).
2. Remove the fuel tank. See Chapter Six.
3. Remove the rewind starter. See Chapter Ten.
4. Check and adjust breaker point gap as required. See Chapter Four.
5. Disconnect the black stator lead at the bullet connector.
6. Remove the spark plug. See Chapter Seven.
7. Install timing gauge (part No. 09931-00112) or a suitable dial indicator in spark plug hole. See **Figure 3** (typical).
8. Rotate flywheel clockwise until timing gauge shows that the piston has reached top dead center (TDC). This is the point at which the indicator needle reverses its direction of movement as the flywheel is rotated.
9. Reset timing gauge indicator to zero.
10. Connect the timing tester (part No. 09900-27003) between the disconnected stator lead and a good engine ground. See **Figure 4** (typical).

> *NOTE*
> *If an ohmmeter or test lamp is used instead of the timing tester, the meter needle will deflect or the lamp will light in Step 11.*

11. Slowly rotate the flywheel rotor counterclockwise until the timing tester buzzes, indicating that the points have closed.
12. Check the timing gauge to determine the amount of piston travel. If the reading is 0.032 in. (DT 2) or 0.099 in. (DT 3.5), the timing is properly adjusted.
13. If the timing gauge does not read as specified in Step 12, remove the flywheel rotor. See Chapter Eight.

5

14. Loosen the stator base screws (A, **Figure 5**). Rotate the stator clockwise (to retard) or counterclockwise (to advance) as required to bring the piston travel into specifications. Temporarily reinstall the flywheel rotor and repeat Step 11 and Step 12 to check piston travel. Repeat this step until the piston travel is correct.

15. When piston travel is correct, tighten stator base screws securely. Remove all test equipment and reinstall the flywheel rotor, rewind starter, fuel tank and engine cover(s).

Timing Adjustment
(DT 4.5, DT 5 and DT 8 with
Breaker Point Ignition)

The cylinder housing has a stationary timing mark. The flywheel rotor has a set of timing marks for each cylinder. See T1, **Figure 6** (No. 1 cylinder) and T2, **Figure 6** (No. 2 cylinder).

1. Remove the engine cover.
2. Disconnect the spark plug leads.
3. Remove the rewind starter. See Chapter Ten.
4. Disconnect the stator coil leads at the bullet connectors.
5. Connect an ohmmeter between the red stator lead and a good engine ground.
6. Slowly rotate the flywheel rotor clockwise until the meter needle starts to deflect, indicating that the No. 1 cylinder breaker points have started to open. The timing mark on the cylinder housing should align with the No. 1 cylinder timing mark on the flywheel rotor.
7. If the marks do not align as specified in Step 6, loosen the stator base screws and rotate the stator until the marks align. Tighten the stator base screws and readjust the breaker point gap.
8. Connect the ohmmeter between the blue stator lead and a good engine ground.

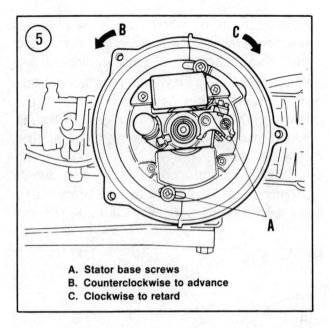

A. Stator base screws
B. Counterclockwise to advance
C. Clockwise to retard

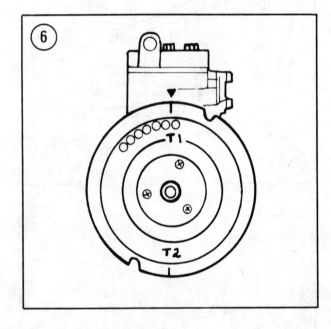

9. Rotate the flywheel rotor 180° counterclockwise while watching the meter needle. When the needle starts to deflect (indicating that the No. 2 cylinder breaker points have started to open), the timing mark on the cylinder housing should align with the No. 2 cylinder timing mark on the flywheel rotor.

10. If the marks do not align as specified in Step 9, loosen the stator base screws and

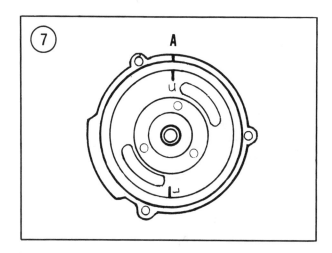

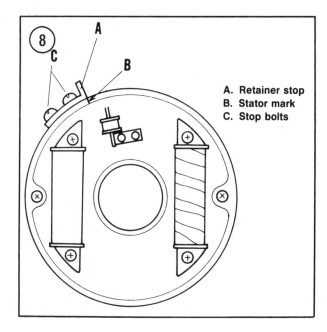

A. Retainer stop
B. Stator mark
C. Stop bolts

3. Remove the rewind starter. See Chapter Ten.

4. Disconnect the stator coil leads at the bullet connectors.

5. Connect an ohmmeter between the red stator lead and a good engine ground.

6. Slowly rotate the flywheel rotor clockwise until the meter needle starts to deflect, indicating that the No. 1 cylinder breaker points have started to open. The timing mark on the magneto housing should align with the No. 1 cylinder timing mark on the flywheel rotor (U, **Figure 7**).

7. If the marks do not align as specified in Step 6, loosen the stator base screws and rotate the stator until the marks align. Tighten the stator base screws and readjust the breaker point gap (Chapter Four).

8. Connect the ohmmeter between the blue stator lead and a good engine ground.

9. Rotate the flywheel rotor 180° counterclockwise while watching the meter needle. When the needle starts to deflect (indicating that the No. 2 cylinder breaker points have started to open), the timing mark on the magneto housing should align with the No. 2 cylinder timing mark on the flywheel rotor (L, **Figure 7**).

10. If the marks do not align as specified in Step 9, loosen the stator base screws and rotate the stator until the marks align. Tighten the stator base screws and readjust the breaker point gap (Chapter Four).

rotate the stator until the marks align. Tighten the stator base screws and readjust the breaker point gap (Chapter Four).

Timing Adjustment
(DT 7.5 and DT 9)

The magneto housing has a stationary timing mark. The flywheel rotor has a set of timing marks for each cylinder. See U, **Figure 7** (No. 1 cylinder) and L, **Figure 7** (No. 2 cylinder).

1. Remove the engine cover.

2. Disconnect the spark plug leads.

Static Timing Adjustment
(DT 5, DT 6 and DT 8 with PEI)

1. Remove the engine cover.

2. Rotate the twist grip to the closed throttle position.

3. Loosen the retainer stop screws. Align the end of the retainer stop with the flywheel timing mark and tighten the stop screws. See **Figure 8**. This sets ignition timing to TDC ±2°.

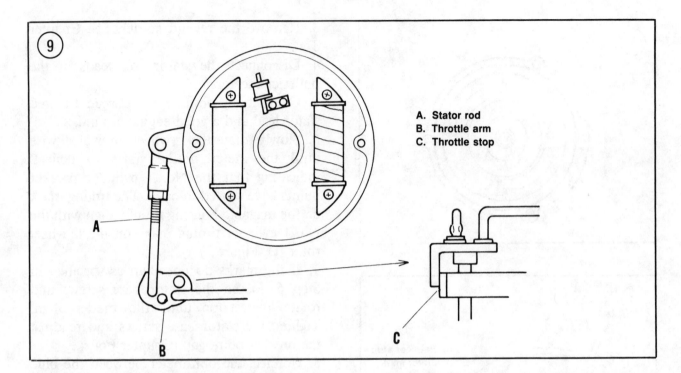

A. Stator rod
B. Throttle arm
C. Throttle stop

4. Rotate the twist grip to the wide-open throttle position. The throttle arm should just contact the throttle stop.

5. If throttle arm adjustment is necessary, disconnect the stator rod from the stator base. Loosen the connector locknut and rotate the connector to adjust the stator rod to the proper length. Reconnect stator rod to stator base. See **Figure 9**. This sets maximum advance to 25 ±2°.

6. Open and close the throttle with the twist grip. The flywheel mark and retainer stop should align with the throttle closed. The throttle arm should just touch its stop with the throttle open.

Dynamic Timing Check
(DT 5, DT 6 and DT 8 with PEI)

The engine should be in a test tank or on the boat in the water for this procedure.

1. Remove the engine cover.

2. Connect a timing light according to manufacturer's instructions.

3. Start the engine and allow it to warm up for approximately 5 minutes.

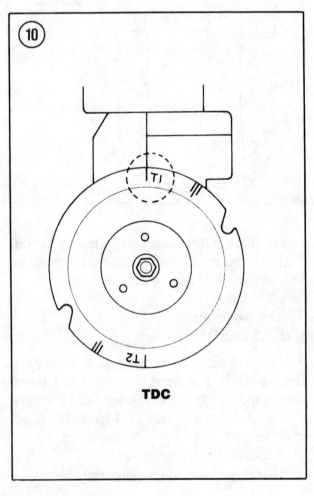

TDC

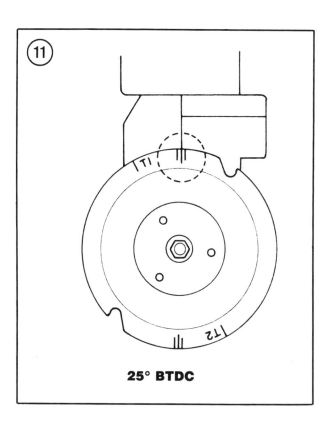

25° BTDC

4. With the engine idling in NEUTRAL, point the timing light at the cylinder case center line. It should align with the flywheel timing mark. See **Figure 10**.

5. Repeat Step 4 with the engine in NEUTRAL and the throttle wide open. The cylinder case center line should align with one of the series of 3 flywheel marks shown in **Figure 11**.

6. If the timing marks do not align as specified in Step 4 or Step 5, repeat the *Static Timing Adjustment* in this chapter.

5

Static Timing Adjustment
(1977-1982 DT 9.9 and DT 16)

1. Remove the engine cover.

2. Rotate the twist grip to the closed throttle position.

3. Loosen the retainer stop screws (A, **Figure 12**). Align the end of the retainer stop with

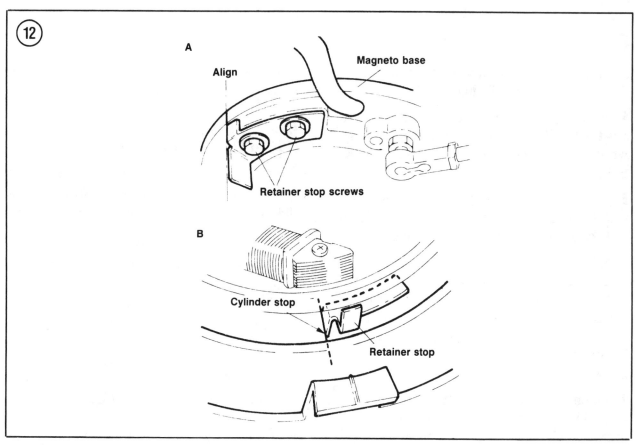

A

Align

Magneto base

Retainer stop screws

B

Cylinder stop

Retainer stop

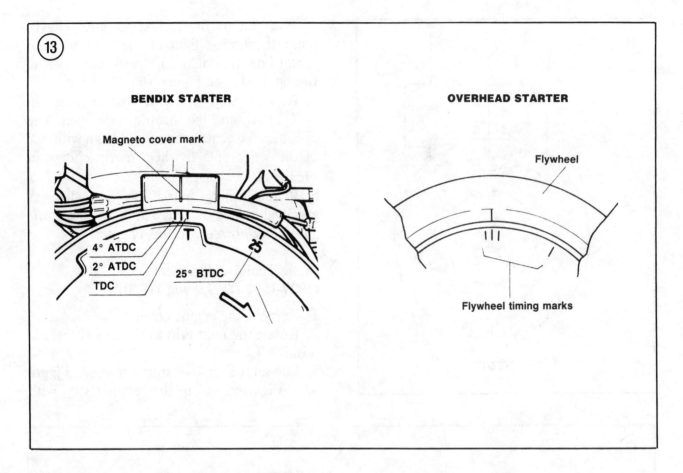

the magneto base timing mark and tighten the stop screws. See B, **Figure 12**.

4. Rotate the flywheel until the retainer stop hits the boss in the center of the cylinder case. At this point, ignition timing is 2° ATDC ±2°.

5. Rotate the twist grip to the wide open throttle position. The retainer stop should just contact the stop on the side of the magneto cover.

6. If adjustment is necessary, disconnect the stator link from the stator base. Loosen the connector locknut and rotate the connector to adjust the link to the proper length. Reconnect stator link to stator base. This sets maximum advance to 25°.

7. Open and close the throttle with the twist grip. The retainer stop and magneto base mark should align with the throttle closed.

The retainer stop should just touch the magneto cover stop with the throttle open.

Dynamic Timing Check
(1977-1982 DT 9.9 and DT 16)

The engine should be in a test tank or on the boat in the water for this procedure. Note that the timing marks differ in appearance according to starter type. See **Figure 13**.

1. Remove the engine cover.

2. Connect a timing light according to manufacturer's instructions.

3. Start the engine and allow it to warm up for approximately 5 minutes.

4. With the engine idling in NEUTRAL, point the timing light at the magneto cover timing mark. It should align with one of the 3 flywheel timing marks. See **Figure 13**.

5. Repeat Step 4 with the engine in NEUTRAL and the throttle wide open. The

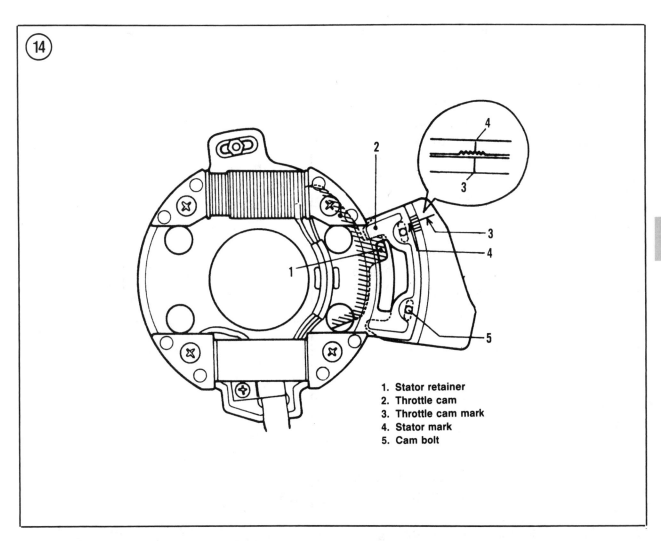

1. Stator retainer
2. Throttle cam
3. Throttle cam mark
4. Stator mark
5. Cam bolt

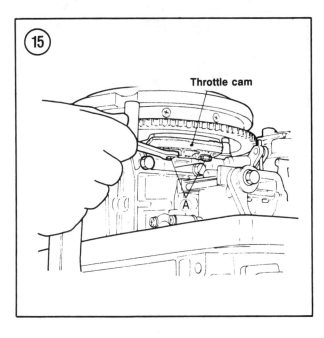

Throttle cam

single flywheel timing mark should align with the magneto case timing mark.

6. If the timing marks do not align as specified in Step 4 or Step 5, repeat the *Static Timing Adjustment* in this chapter.

**Static Timing Adjustment
(1983-on DT 9.9 and DT 15)**

1. Remove the engine cover.

2. Rotate the twist grip to the closed throttle position.

3. Rotate the stator until the retainer stop contacts the throttle cam. See **Figure 14**.

4. If the cam and stator timing marks do not align, loosen the throttle cam bolts (**Figure 15**).

5. Reposition the throttle cam as required to align the cam and stator timing marks, then tighten the cam bolts. See **Figure 16**. At this point, ignition timing is 2° ATDC ±2°.

6. Rotate the twist grip to the wide-open throttle position. The magneto stop should just contact the throttle cam stop screw (DT 9.9) or throttle cam (DT 15). Maximum advance is 18.5° BTDC ±2° (DT 9.9) or 25° BTDC ±2° (DT 15) at 5,000 rpm.

7. Open and close the throttle with the twist grip. The cam and stator timing marks should align with the throttle closed. The magneto stop should just touch the throttle cam stop screw (DT 9.9) or throttle cam (DT 15) with the throttle wide open.

Dynamic Timing Check
(1983-on DT 9.9 and DT 15)

The engine should be in a test tank or on the boat in the water for this procedure.

1. Remove the engine cover.

2. Connect a timing light according to manufacturer's instructions.

3. Start the engine and allow it to warm up for approximately 5 minutes.

4. With the engine idling in NEUTRAL, point the timing light at the rewind starter cover timing mark. It should align with the 2° ATDC (±2°) timing mark on the flywheel. See A, **Figure 17**.

5. Repeat Step 4 with the engine in NEUTRAL and the throttle wide open. The rewind starter cover timing mark should align with the 18.5° BTDC (±2°) mark on DT 9.9 engines or the 25° BTDC (±2°) mark on DT 15 engines. See B, **Figure 17**.

6. If the timing marks do not align as specified in Step 4 or Step 5, repeat the *Static Timing Adjustment* in this chapter.

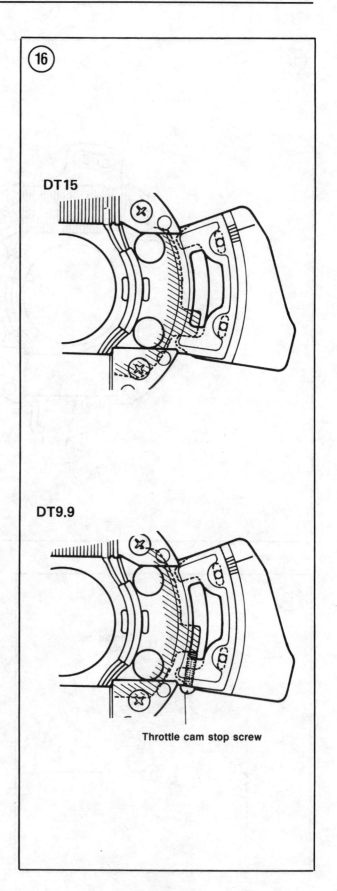

16

DT15

DT9.9

Throttle cam stop screw

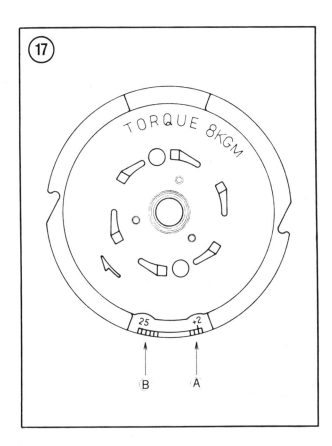

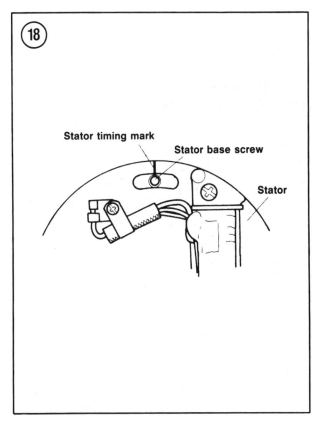

Static Timing Adjustment
(DT 20, 1977-1982 DT 25 and DT 50M)

Maximum advance does not have to be set on these models. Advance is electrically controlled.

1. Remove the engine cover.
2. Remove the flywheel. See Chapter Eight.
3. Loosen the stator mounting screws.
4. Position the stamped mark on the stator in the center of the mounting screw (**Figure 18**) and tighten the screw securely. This sets ignition timing to 2° ATDC ± 2° at 1,000 rpm (DT 20 and 1977-1982 DT 50M) or 8° BTDC at 1,000 rpm (DT 25M).

Dynamic Timing Check
(DT 20, 1977-1982 DT 25 and DT 50M)

The engine should be in a test tank or on the boat in the water for this procedure.

1. Remove the engine cover.
2. Connect a timing light and tachometer according to manufacturer's instructions.
3. Start the engine and allow it to warm up for approximately 5 minutes.
4A. DT 20 and 1977-1982 DT 25—Run the engine at 1,000 rpm in NEUTRAL and point the timing light at the magneto housing timing mark. It should align with the center of the 3 timing marks on the flywheel. See **Figure 19**.

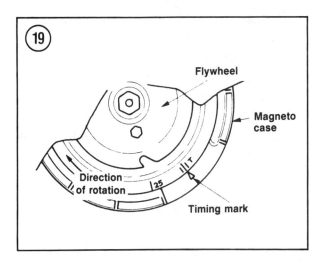

5

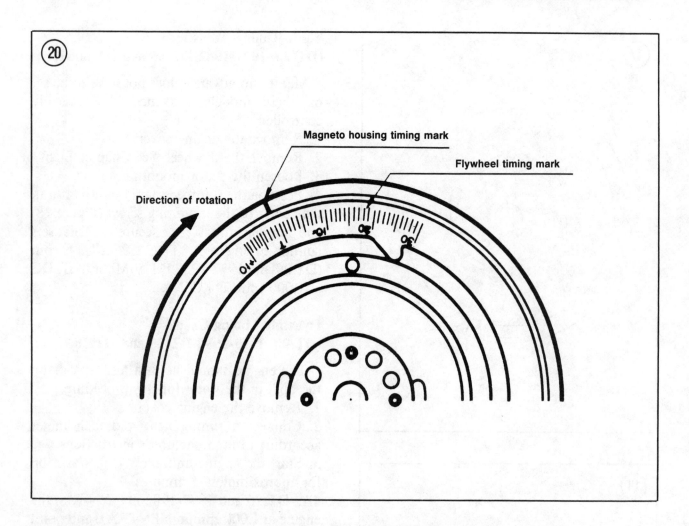

Magneto housing timing mark

Flywheel timing mark

Direction of rotation

4B. DT 50M—Run the engine at 1,000 rpm in NEUTRAL and point the timing light at the magneto housing timing mark. It should align with the 8° BTDC mark on the flywheel timing scale. See **Figure 20**.

5. Repeat / Step 4 with the engine in NEUTRAL and the throttle wide open:

   a. DT 20 and 1977-1982 DT 25—The magneto housing timing mark should align with the single (25° BTDC) timing mark on the flywheel. See **Figure 19**.

   b. DT 50M—The magneto housing timing mark should align with the 25° BTDC mark on the flywheel timing scale. See **Figure 20**.

6. If the timing marks do not align as specified in Step 4 or Step 5, repeat the *Static Timing Adjustment* in this chapter.

Throttle Adjustment (DT 20 and 1977-1982 DT 25)

1. Remove the engine cover.

2. Rotate the twist grip to place the throttle lever arm in a vertical position.

3. Loosen the cable adjusting nuts, rotate the cable adjuster counterclockwise until the throttle cables are tight and tighten the adjusting nuts.

4. Disconnect the throttle rod at the pivot ball.

5. Rotate the twist grip to the wide-open throttle position.

6. Loosen the throttle rod adjusting nut and adjust the rod length to provide 0.078-0.118 in. throttle arm clearance when the rod is reconnected. Tighten adjusting nut.

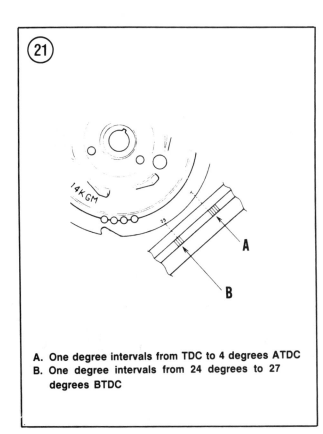

A. One degree intervals from TDC to 4 degrees ATDC
B. One degree intervals from 24 degrees to 27 degrees BTDC

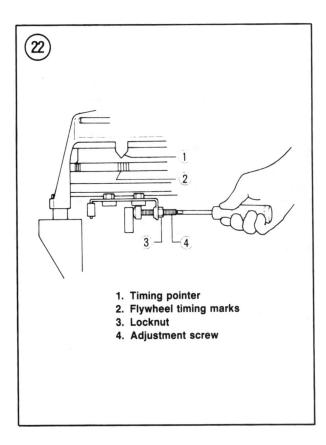

1. Timing pointer
2. Flywheel timing marks
3. Locknut
4. Adjustment screw

7. Reconnect throttle rod to pivot ball. Rotate twist grip to a closed throttle position and check throttle arm clearance. If not within specifications in Step 6, repeat Steps 4-6.

Dynamic Timing Adjustment (1983-on DT 25 and DT 30)

The engine should be in a test tank or on the boat in the water for this procedure.

1. Remove the engine cover.

2. Connect a timing light and tachometer according to manufacturer's instructions.

3. Start the engine and allow it to warm up for approximately 5 minutes.

4. Run the engine at 1,000 rpm in NEUTRAL and point the timing light at the rewind starter timing pointer. It should align with one of the marks (preferably the center mark) in the series of 5 flywheel timing marks. See A, **Figure 21**.

5. If the timing pointer does not align as specified in Step 4, shut the engine off. Loosen the adjusting screw locknut and turn the screw clockwise to advance or counterclockwise to retard the timing. See **Figure 22**.

6. Restart the engine and repeat Step 4. If the timing pointer and marks now align, shut the engine off and tighten the locknut. If they still are not in alignment, repeat adjustment of the screw as required.

7. Repeat Step 4 with the engine in NEUTRAL and the throttle wide open. The timing pointer should align with the 25 degree BTDC mark on the flywheel. See B, **Figure 21**.

8. If the timing pointer does not align as specified in Step 7, shut the engine off and proceed as follows:

   a. Disconnect the stator rod from the stator base.

5

b. Loosen the connector locknut and rotate the connector to adjust the stator rod to the proper length.

c. Reconnect the stator rod to the stator base.

d. Start the engine and repeat Step 7.

e. If the timing pointer and mark now align, shut the engine off and tighten the connector locknut.

f. If the pointer and mark still do not align, repeat this step as required.

Dynamic Timing Adjustment (DT 40)

The engine should be in a test tank or on the boat in the water for this procedure.

1. Remove the engine cover.

2. Connect a timing light and tachometer according to manufacturer's instructions.

3. Start the engine and allow it to warm up for approximately 5 minutes.

4. Run the engine at 1,000 rpm in NEUTRAL and point the timing light at the rewind starter timing pointer (**Figure 23**). It should align with the 6 degree ATDC (independent ignition) or 2 degree ATDC (simultaneous ignition) mark on the flywheel.

5. If the timing pointer does not align as specified in Step 4, shut the engine off. Loosen the retainer stop bolts and position the right side of the retainer against the stop. See **Figure 24**. Tighten the stop bolts.

6. Restart the engine and repeat Step 4. If the timing pointer still does not align with the correct timing mark, repeat Step 5 as required.

7. Run the engine at 1,000 rpm in NEUTRAL. Point the timing light at the rewind starter timing pointer and move the retainer manually until it rests against the stop (**Figure 25**). The timing pointer should align with the 27 degree BTDC mark on the flywheel.

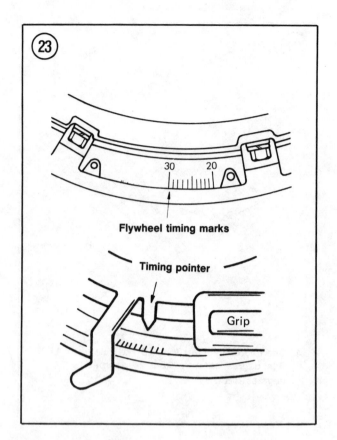

Flywheel timing marks

Timing pointer

Grip

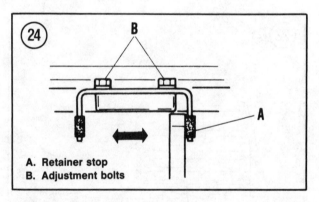

A. Retainer stop
B. Adjustment bolts

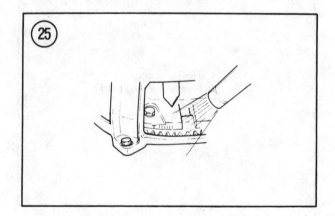

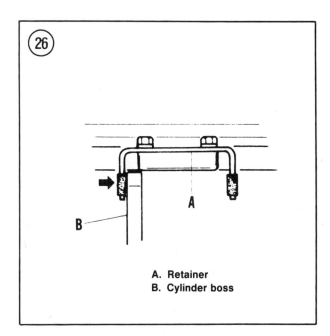

A. Retainer
B. Cylinder boss

8. If the timing pointer does not align as specified in Step 7, shut the engine off. Loosen the retainer stop bolts and position the left side of the retainer against the stop. See **Figure 26**. Tighten the stop bolts.

9. Restart the engine and repeat Step 7. If the timing pointer still does not align with the correct timing mark, repeat Step 8 as required.

5

Timing Adjustment (DT 50 and DT 65)

NOTE
This procedure does not cover the DT 50M; that model appears in a separate heading in this chapter.

The engine should be in a test tank or on the boat in the water for this adjustment. Refer to **Figure 27** for this procedure.

1. Remove the engine cover.

2. Connect a timing light and tachometer according to manufacturer's instructions.

3. Rotate the throttle lever clockwise until it touches the throttle stop.

4. If the timing marks on the magneto stator and timer base do not align, loosen the spark advance lever nut and shorten or lengthen the spark advance link as required until the marks align, then retighten the nut. This sets maximum advance at 25° BTDC.

5. Start the engine and run at 1,000 rpm in NEUTRAL. Point the timing light at the starter cap timing mark (**Figure 27**). It should align with the 4 degree ATDC mark (DT 50) or 3 degree ATDC mark (DT 65) on the flywheel.

6. If the timing marks do not align as specified in Step 5, loosen the throttle adjustment screw locknut and turn the adjustment screw as required to align the marks.

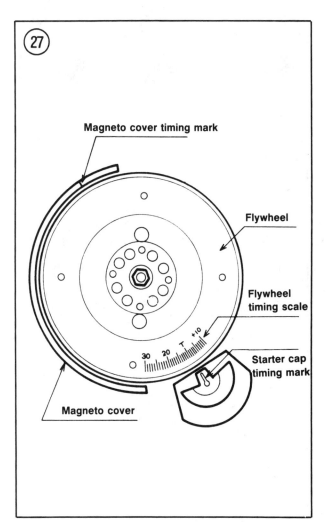

Magneto cover timing mark

Flywheel

Flywheel timing scale

Starter cap timing mark

Magneto cover

NOTE
*Maximum advance was set to 25°
BTDC in Step 4. When checked at
1,000 rpm in Step 7, there should be a
time lag of 2.5° BTDC, resulting in a
reading of 27.5° BTDC at 1,000 rpm.*

7. With the engine running at 1,000 rpm in NEUTRAL, rotate the throttle to the wide-open position. Point the timing light at the starter cap timing mark (**Figure 27**). It should align with the 27.5 degree BTDC mark on the flywheel.

8. If the timing marks do not align as specified in Step 7, repeat Step 6.

Dynamic Timing Adjustment
(DT 75 and DT 85)

The engine should be in a test tank or on the boat in the water for this adjustment.

1. Remove the engine cover.

2. Connect a timing light and tachometer according to manufacturer's instructions.

3. Start and run the engine until it reaches operating temperature (about 5 minutes).

4. Adjust the carburetor throttle stop screw to bring engine rpm to 1,000 rpm.

5. Move the spark advance lever to the closed throttle position (full retard). See **Figure 28**.

6. Point the timing light at the starter bracket timing mark (**Figure 29**). It should align with the 7 degree ATDC mark on the flywheel at 650 rpm.

7. If the timing marks do not align as specified in Step 6, loosen the throttle adjustment screw locknut and turn the adjustment screw as required to align the marks.

8. With the engine running at 1,000 rpm in NEUTRAL, move the spark advance lever to the wide-open throttle position (**Figure 30**).

NOTE
*Maximum advance is specified as 21.5°
BTDC at 5,000 rpm. When checked at*

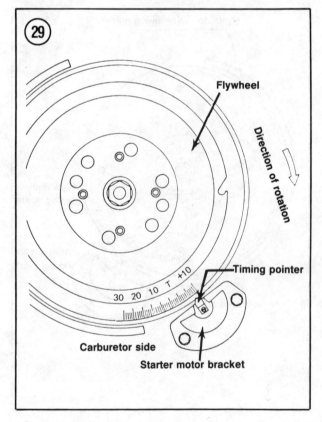

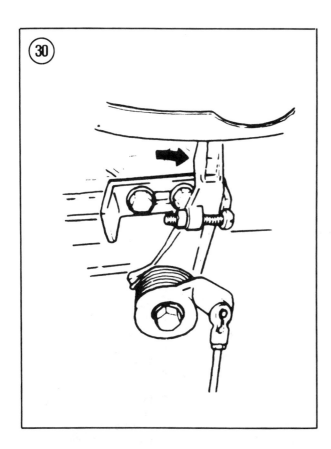

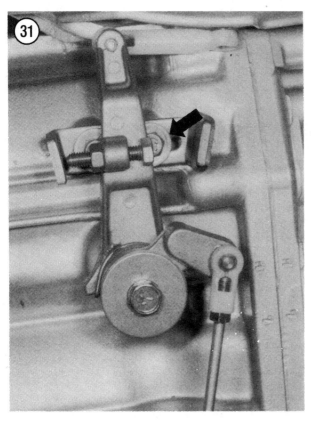

1,000 rpm in Step 10, there should be a time lag of 1.5° BTDC, resulting in a reading of 23° BTDC.

9. Point the timing light at the starter bracket timing mark (**Figure 29**). It should align with the 23 degree BTDC mark on the flywheel.

10. If the timing marks do not align as specified in Step 9, shut the engine off. Loosen the 2 bolts on the spark advance stop behind the spark advance lever (**Figure 31**).

11. Restart the engine and repeat Step 8 and Step 9. Move the spark advance stop as required to align the timing marks, then carefully tighten the bolts.

Static Timing Adjustment (DT 115 and DT 140)

These engines must be static-timed whenever components have been replaced. Timing should be checked during a tune-up with the *Dynamic Timing Adjustment* in this chapter. Refer to **Figure 32** for this procedure.

1. Remove the engine cover.

2. Disconnect the throttle and shift lever cables.

3. Move the throttle lever against the wide-open throttle stop and hold in that position.

4. Check the 25° BTDC timing mark on the timer base. It should align with the timing mark stamped on the cylinder housing.

5. If the timing marks do not align as specified in Step 4, proceed as follows:

    a. Disconnect the link between the throttle and spark advance levers (**Figure 33**).

    b. Loosen the connector locknuts and rotate the connectors to lengthen or shorten the link as required.

    c. Reconnect the link and repeat Step 3 and Step 4.

    d. Repeat this step as required until the timing marks align.

    e. Tighten the connector locknuts.

5

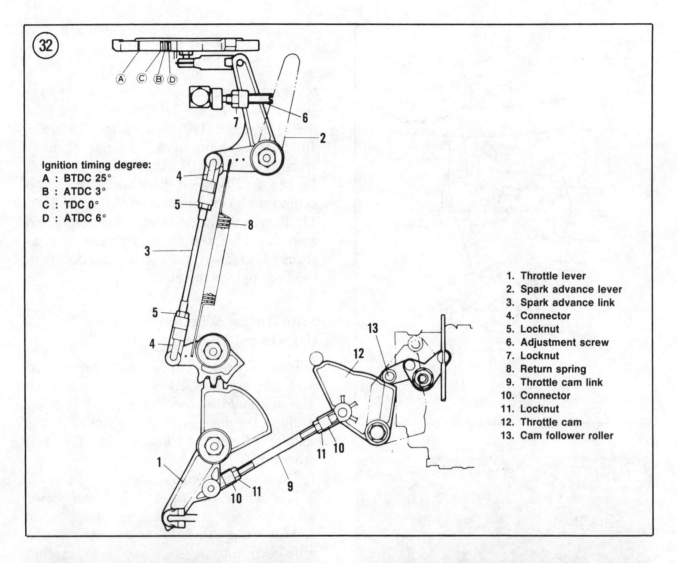

(32)

Ignition timing degree:
A : BTDC 25°
B : ATDC 3°
C : TDC 0°
D : ATDC 6°

1. Throttle lever
2. Spark advance lever
3. Spark advance link
4. Connector
5. Locknut
6. Adjustment screw
7. Locknut
8. Return spring
9. Throttle cam link
10. Connector
11. Locknut
12. Throttle cam
13. Cam follower roller

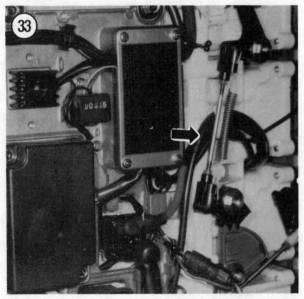

(33)

(34)

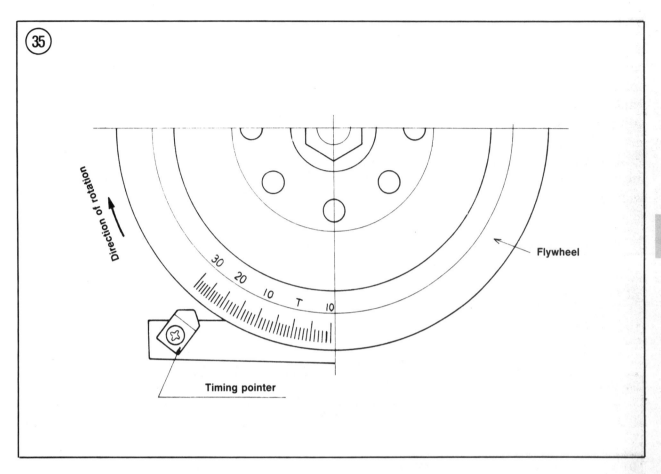

Direction of rotation

Flywheel

Timing pointer

5

6. Loosen the locknut on the throttle cam adjustment screw.

7. Rotate the throttle lever counterclockwise as far as possible without stretching the return spring. Hold throttle lever in this position and turn throttle cam adjustment screw as required until the 3 degree ATDC mark on the timer base aligns with the cylinder housing timing mark. Tighten the locknut.

8. Rotate the throttle lever until the TDC mark on the timer base aligns with the cylinder housing timing mark. Hold throttle lever in this position.

9. Loosen the throttle lever link locknuts and rotate the connectors as required until the throttle cam mark aligns with the center of the carburetor cam follower roller. See **Figure 34**. Tighten the locknuts.

10. Rotate the throttle lever several times to make sure that it moves freely. There should

be at least 0.118 in. clearance between the wire harness clamp and return spring.

11. Reconnect the shift and throttle cables.

12. Perform the *Dynamic Timing Adjustment* described in this chapter.

Dynamic Timing Adjustment
(DT 115 and DT 140)

The engine should be in a test tank or on the boat in the water for this adjustment.

1. Remove the engine cover.

2. Connect a timing light and tachometer according to manufacturer's instructions.

3. Start and run the engine until it reaches operating temperature (about 5 minutes).

4. With the engine idling in NEUTRAL, move the remote control lever to the fully closed throttle position.

5. Point the timing light at the timing pointer (**Figure 35**). It should align with the 6 degree

ATDC mark on the flywheel at 900 rpm or less.

6. If the timing marks do not align as specified in Step 5, loosen the throttle adjustment screw locknut and turn the adjustment screw as required to align the marks.

7. Disconnect the throttle cam link and move the remote control lever to the wide-open throttle position.

NOTE
Maximum advance is specified as 23° BTDC ±1 degree at 5,000 rpm. When

checked at 2,000 rpm in Step 8, there should be a time lag of 2° BTDC, resulting in a reading of 25° BTDC.

8. Point the timing light at the timing pointer (**Figure 35**). It should align with the 25 degree BTDC mark on the flywheel.

9. If the timing marks do not align as specified in Step 8, loosen the throttle stop screw locknut and adjust the stop screw as required to align the marks. Tighten the locknut.

10. Once maximum advance timing is correct, connect the throttle cam link.

Table 1 TEST WHEEL RECOMMENDATIONS*

Model	Test wheel	Minimum rpm
1982		
DT 2	79970	4,350
DT 3.5	79820	4,900
DT 5	79810	4,800
DT 8	79810	5,100
DT 9.9	79941	4,700
DT 9.9P	79320	4,700
DT 16	79941	5,300
DT 16P	79320	5,300
DT 25	79951	5,500
DT 25P	79310	5,500
DT 40	79410	5,300
DT 50	79980	4,900
DT 65	79980	5,000
DT 85	79510	5,100
DT 115, DT 140	79420	5,100
1983		
DT 2	79970	4,350
DT 3.5	79821	4,900
DT 5	79810	4,800
DT 8	79810	5,100
DT 9.9/9.9E	79840	5,000
DT 15/15E	79840	5,200
DT 25	79830	5,100
DT 30/30E	79830	5,200
DT 40	79410	5,300
(continued)		

Table 1 TEST WHEEL RECOMMENDATIONS* (continued)

Model	Test wheel	Minimum rpm
1983		
DT 40E	79410	5,000
DT 50	79980	4,900
DT 60	79980	5,000
DT 75TC	79510	5,000
DT 85TC	79510	5,100
DT 115TC	79410	5,100
DT 140TC	79410	5,100

* These are the only recommendations provided by Suzuki.

5

Table 2 ENGINE SPECIFICATIONS

Model	Displacement cu. in. (cc)	Bore×stroke	Maximum operating range (rpm)
DT 2	3.1 (50)	1.61×1.49 in.	4,200-4,800
DT 3.5			
1979-1982	4.3 (70)	1.81×1.65 in.	4,800-5,000
1983-on	4.3 (70)	1.81×1.65 in.	4,800-5,300
D 4.5	Not available		
DT 5			
1978-1982	10.1 (165)	1.97×1.65 in.	5,200-5,700
1983-on	6.9 (113)	1.69×1.54 in.	4,800-5,500
DT 6	10.1 (165)	1.97×1.65 in.	4,500-5,500
DT 7.5	10.1 (165)	1.97×1.65 in.	5,200-5,800
DT 8	10.1 (165)	1.97×1.65 in.	5,200-5,700
DT 9	10.1 (165)	1.97×1.65 in.	5,200-5,800
DT 9.9			
1977-1982	15.62 (256)	2.21×2.05 in.	4,500-5,500
1983-on	17.3 (284)	2.31×2.04 in.	4,500-5,300
DT 15	17.3 (284)	2.31×2.04 in.	4,700-5,500
DT 16			
1977-1981	17.3 (284)	2.32×2.05 in.	5,200-5,700
1982	15.62 (256)	2.21×2.05 in.	4,800-5,500
DT 20	24.16 (396)	2.52×2.42 in.	5,200-5,700
DT 25			
1977-1982	27.28 (447)	2.68×2.42 in.	4,800-5,500
1983-on	30.5 (499)	2.80×2.48 in.	4,800-5,500
DT 30	30.5 (499)	2.80×2.48 in.	4,800-5,500
DT 40			
1977-1983	37.7 (617)	3.09×2.68 in.	4,800-5,500
1984	42.5 (696)	3.09×2.78 in.	4,800-5,300
DT 50			
1980-1982	44.12 (723)	3.15×2.83 in.	4,800-5,500
1984	48.7 (798)	3.29×2.82 in.	4,800-5,300
DT 60, DT 65	48.7 (798)	3.29×2.82 in.	4,800-5,500
DT 75, DT 85	73.04 (1,197)	3.29×2.82 in.	4,800-5,300
DT 115, DT 140	108.2 (1,773)	3.29×3.14 in.	4,800-5,500

Table 3 IGNITION TIMING

Model	Maximum retard @ 1,000 rpm	Maximum advance @ 5,000 rpm
DT 25		
1983-on	2° ATDC	25° BTDC
1977-1982	TDC	25° BTDC
DT 30	2° ATDC	25° BTDC
DT 40	6° ATDC	25° BTDC
DT 50	4° ATDC	25° BTDC
DT 50M	8° BTDC	25° BTDC
DT 60	4° ATDC	21.5° BTDC
DT 65	3° ATDC	25° BTDC
DT 75	7° ATDC	21.5° BTDC
DT 85		
1979-1982	7° ATDC	21.5° BTDC
1983-on	3° ATDC	23° BTDC
DT 115, DT 140	3° ATDC	23° BTDC

Chapter Six

Fuel System

This chapter contains removal, overhaul, installation and adjustment procedures for fuel pumps, carburetors, reed valves, fuel tanks and connecting lines. **Tables 1-3** are at the end of the chapter.

FUEL PUMP

All DT 2 outboards have an integral fuel tank that uses a gravity flow fuel system; they require no fuel pump.

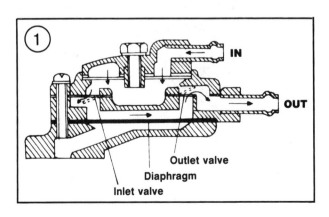

The diaphragm-type fuel pump used on DT 3.5-DT 140 models operates by crankcase pressure. Pressure pulsations created by movement of the pistons reach the fuel pump through a passageway between the crankcase and pump.

Upward piston motion creates a low pressure on the pump diaphragm. This low pressure opens the inlet check valve in the pump, drawing fuel from the line into the pump. At the same time, the low pressure draws the air-fuel mixture from the carburetor into the crankcase.

Downward piston motion creates a high pressure on the pump diaphragm. This pressure closes the inlet check valve and opens the outlet check valve, forcing the fuel into the carburetor and drawing the air-fuel mixture from the crankcase into the cylinder for combustion. **Figure 1** shows the operational sequence of a typical Suzuki fuel pump.

Since this type of fuel pump cannot create sufficient pressure to draw fuel from the tank during cranking, fuel is transferred to the carburetor for starting by operating the primer bulb installed in the fuel line.

Suzuki outboards use either a self-contained, remote fuel pump mounted on the power head or a combination fuel pump and carburetor. Pump design is extremely simple and reliable in operation. Diaphragm failures are the most common problem, although the use of dirty or improper fuel-oil mixtures can cause check valve problems.

Remote Fuel Pump Removal/Installation

Refer to **Figure 2** or **Figure 3** (typical) for this procedure.

1. Compress the fuel line fitting clamp with hose clamp pliers, slide the clamp off the

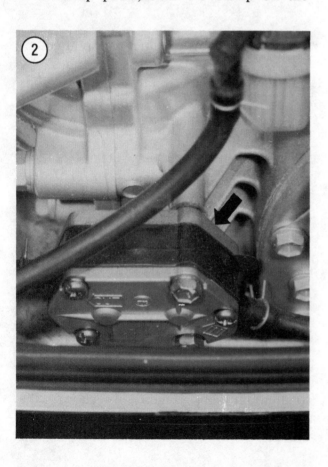

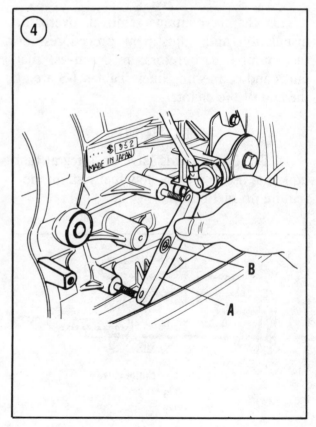

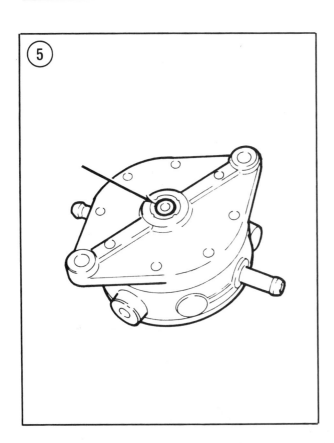

fitting and disconnect the fuel line at the pump. Repeat this step to disconnect the remaining fuel line(s) from the pump. Plug the lines to prevent leakage.

2. Remove the screws holding the fuel pump assembly to the power head. Remove the fuel pump.

3. Remove the fuel pump insulator, if so equipped. See **Figure 4**.

4. Clean all gasket residue from the engine mounting pad. Work carefully to avoid gouging or damaging the mounting surface.

5. Installation is the reverse of removal. Use a new mounting gasket. If equipped with an insulator (A, **Figure 4**), install a new O-ring in the insulator (B, **Figure 4**) and fuel pump body (**Figure 5**).

Carburetor Fuel Pump
Removal/Installation

Refer to **Figure 6** for this procedure.

6

1. Disconnect the fuel line at the inlet cover. Plug the line to prevent leakage.
2. Remove the 4 screws holding the fuel pump components to the side of the carburetor.
3. Remove the pump cover, gaskets, diaphragms and pump body as an assembly.
4. Installation is the reverse of removal.

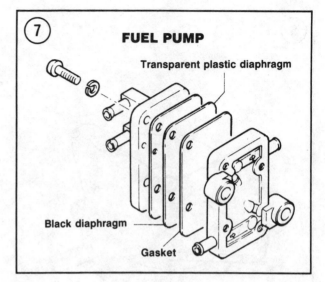

Remote Fuel Pump
Disassembly/Assembly

Refer to **Figure 7** and **Figure 8** (typical) for this procedure.

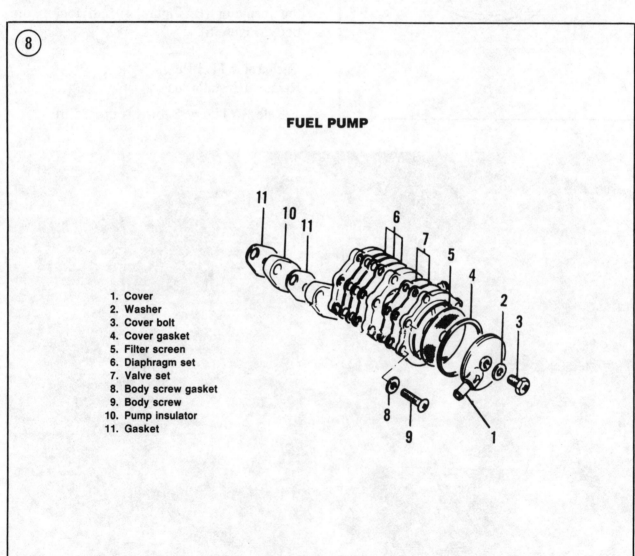

1. Cover
2. Washer
3. Cover bolt
4. Cover gasket
5. Filter screen
6. Diaphragm set
7. Valve set
8. Body screw gasket
9. Body screw
10. Pump insulator
11. Gasket

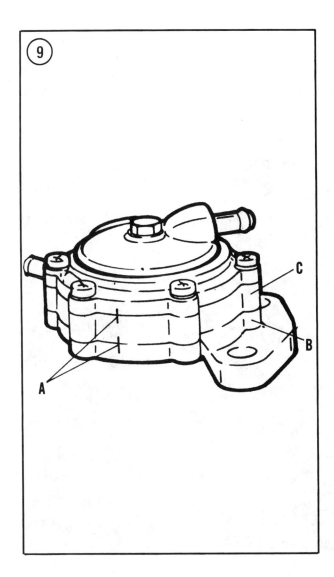

Carburetor Fuel Pump
Disassembly/Assembly

1. Separate the pump cover, diaphragm and valve assembly and fuel pump body. Peel gaskets from cover and body and discard.
2. Assemble components with new gaskets in reverse of order given in Step 1.

Cleaning and Inspection
(All Models)

1. Clean all metal parts in solvent and blow dry with compressed air.
2. Hold diaphragm up to a strong light source and check for pin holes, breaks or excessive stretching. Replace if any defects are found.
3. Check condition of fuel pump reeds or check valve diaphragm. Install new reeds or diaphragm if there are signs of warpage, tension or curling of the reeds or check valve ends.
4. Check pump body and cover condition. Replace pump body or cover as required if cracks or rough gasket mating surfaces are found.

1. Etch a match mark across the side of the pump to provide an alignment reference for the upper and lower halves. See **Figure 9**.
2. Separate the pump halves. Remove and discard all gaskets.
3. Remove the check valves. Some pumps use a flap-type check valve diaphragm; others use metal reed-type valves secured by a small bolt and nut.
4. Remove the diaphragm or diaphragm set.
5. Assembly is the reverse of disassembly. Refer to **Figure 7** or **Figure 8** for gasket and diaphragm positioning. Align etch marks made in Step 1 (see **Figure 9**) and tighten pump body screws securely.

CARBURETOR
REMOVAL/INSTALLATION

Suzuki outboards use a variety of Mikuni carburetors. All operate essentially the same, but housing shape and design varies slightly according to engine size.

All carburetors use a fixed main jet and require no high-speed adjustment. Poor fuel quality or use in high-altitude areas may make rejetting necessary. See your Suzuki dealer for jet recommendations.

When removing and installing a carburetor, make sure that the mounting nuts

(**Figure 10**) are securely tightened. A carburetor that is loose will cause a lean-running condition.

Before removing and disassembling any carburetor, be sure you have the correct overhaul kit, the proper tools and a sufficient quantity of fresh cleaning solvent.

DT 2 Models

1. Remove the right and left engine covers (**Figure 11**).

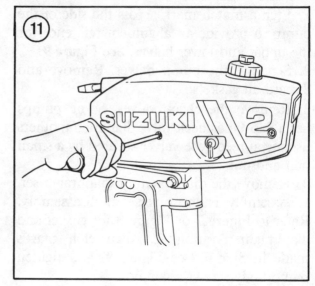

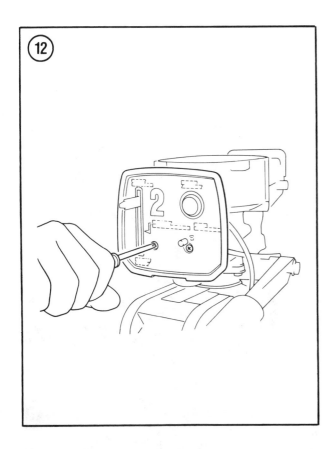

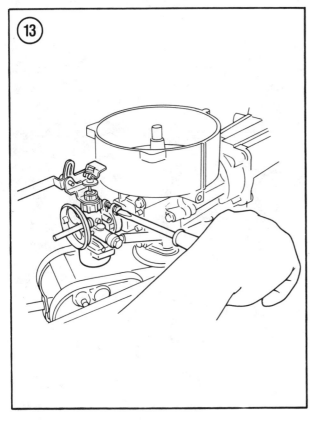

6

2. Loosen the choke knob setscrew. Remove the knob from the control panel.

3. Remove the throttle lever knob.

4. Remove the 2 screws holding the control panel to the carburetor (**Figure 12**).

5. Slide fuel line clamp from carburetor fuel fitting with hose clamp pliers and disconnect the fuel line at the carburetor. Plug the line to prevent leakage.

6. Loosen the clamp screw holding the carburetor to the crankcase. See **Figure 13**. Remove the carburetor.

7. Remove and discard the O-ring inside the carburetor throat.

8. Installation is the reverse of removal. Install a new O-ring in the carburetor throat. Tighten the clamp screw securely to prevent an air leak.

All Other Models

1. Remove the engine cover.

2. Remove the air silencer and gasket, if so equipped. See **Figure 14** (typical).

3. Slide fuel line clamp from carburetor fuel fitting with hose clamp pliers and disconnect the fuel line at each carburetor to be removed. See **Figure 15** (typical). Plug the line(s) to prevent leakage.

4. Disconnect the throttle and choke linkage at each carburetor to be removed. See **Figure 16** (typical).

5. Remove the choke rod knob, if so equipped.

6A. Clamp screw attachment—Loosen the clamp screw holding the carburetor to the intake manifold. See **Figure 13**. Remove the carburetor. Remove and discard the O-ring inside the carburetor throat.

6B. Hex nut attachment—Remove the 2 hex nuts holding the carburetor to the intake manifold. See **Figure 10**. Remove the carburetor from the manifold, pulling the choke rod (if so equipped) through the lower support grommet. Remove and discard the carburetor gasket.

7. Installation is the reverse of removal. Use a new mounting gasket or install a new O-ring in the carburetor throat as required. Tighten the hex nuts or clamp screw securely to prevent an air leak. Adjust the carburetor as described in this chapter.

CARBURETOR OVERHAUL/ADJUSTMENT

Work slowly and carefully, follow the disassembly procedures and refer to the exploded drawing of your carburetor when necessary. When referring to the exploded drawing, note that not all carburetors will use all of the components shown.

Do not apply excessive force at any time.

It is not necessary to disassemble the carburetor linkage or remove the throttle cam

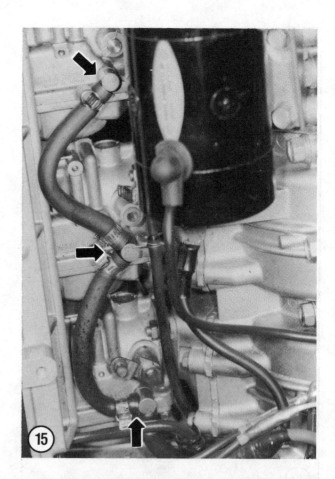

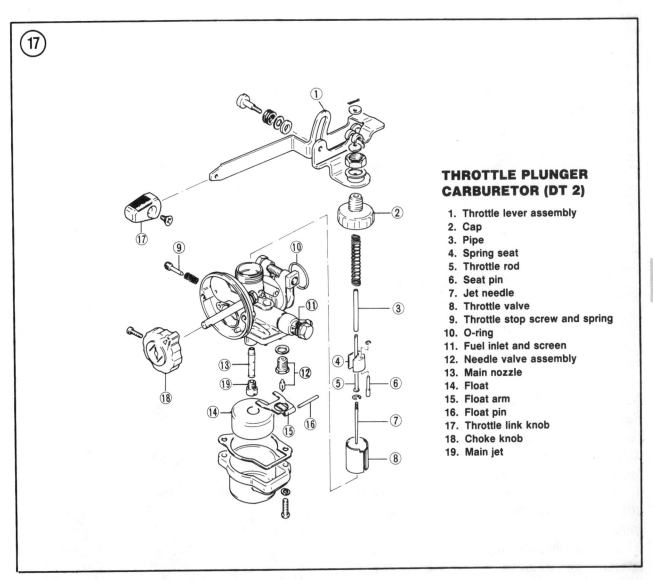

THROTTLE PLUNGER CARBURETOR (DT 2)

1. Throttle lever assembly
2. Cap
3. Pipe
4. Spring seat
5. Throttle rod
6. Seat pin
7. Jet needle
8. Throttle valve
9. Throttle stop screw and spring
10. O-ring
11. Fuel inlet and screen
12. Needle valve assembly
13. Main nozzle
14. Float
15. Float arm
16. Float pin
17. Throttle link knob
18. Choke knob
19. Main jet

6

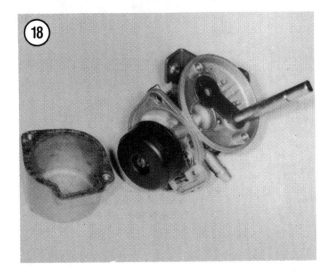

or other external components. Remove the throttle or choke plate only if it is damaged or binds. Carburetor specifications are provided in **Table 1**.

THROTTLE PLUNGER CARBURETOR (DT 2)

Overhaul

Refer to **Figure 17** for this procedure.

1. Remove fuel bowl attaching screws. Separate fuel bowl from carburetor body (**Figure 18**). Remove and discard the fuel bowl gasket.

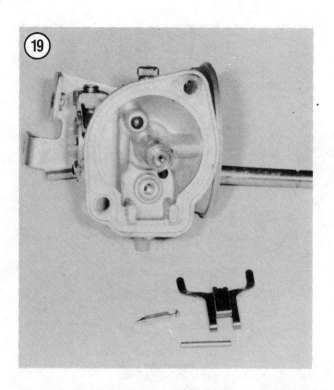

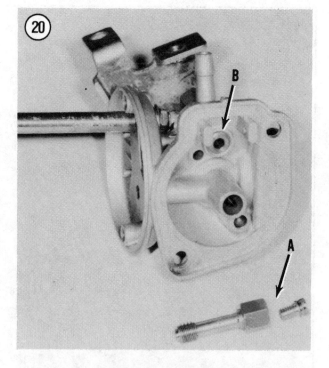

2. Remove float hinge pin from float arm. Remove float arm and needle valve from fuel bowl. See **Figure 19**.

3. Remove main nozzle and main jet assembly (A, **Figure 20**).

4. Remove needle seat and gasket (B, **Figure 20**) with a wide-blade screwdriver. Discard gasket.

5. Loosen throttle stop screw and unscrew retainer cap. Remove cap with bracket and throttle valve assembly (**Figure 21**).

6. Disconnect throttle plunger from needle valve. Remove valve, retainer and spring. Make sure the tiny E-clip is intact on jet needle valve. See **Figure 22**.

7. Lightly seat throttle stop screw, counting the number of turns required for reinstallation reference. Back screw out and remove from carburetor with spring (**Figure 23**).

8. Remove fuel inlet fitting and filter screen.

9. Clean and inspect all parts as described in this chapter.

10. Assembly is the reverse of disassembly, plus the following:

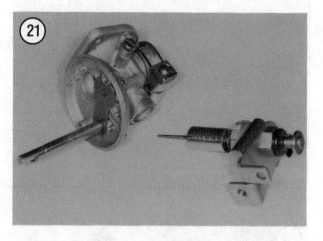

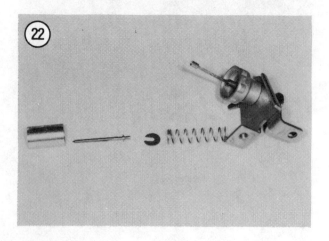

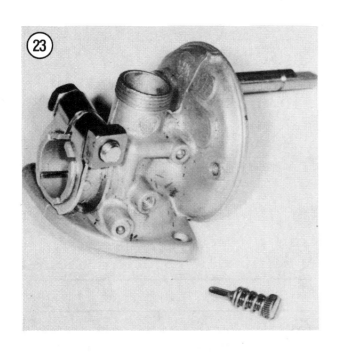

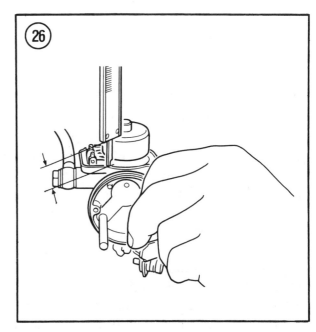

6

a. Install throttle stop screw and spring. Lightly seat screw, then back out the number of turns noted during removal.
b. Reassemble throttle valve assembly. Jet needle retainer should be positioned with slot aligned as shown in **Figure 24**.
c. Install throttle lever post in throttle valve with anchor in pocket at bottom of valve body. See **Figure 25**.
d. Check float adjustment as described in this chapter.

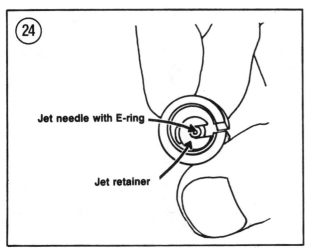

Float Adjustment

1. Invert carburetor body and lower float until adjusting tab just touches inlet needle. Hold float in this position and measure the distance between the carburetor body (without gasket) and the bottom of the float, as shown in **Figure 26**.

> *CAUTION*
> *Bend the float adjustment arm or tang carefully when adjustment is required—do **not** press down on the float. Downward pressure on the float will press the inlet needle tip into its seat and can damage the tip surface.*

2. If float level is not within specifications (**Table 1**), adjust float by bending the adjusting tab (**Figure 27**) as required.

Mid-range Jet Needle Adjustment

The position of the E-ring on the jet needle determines the proper low- and medium-speed range mixture. See **Figure 28**. The standard setting (the 3rd groove from the top) should be suitable for most operating conditions.

If a too-rich or too-lean condition results from extreme changes in elevation, temperature or humidity, the E-ring position can be changed. The closer the E-ring is installed to the top of the needle, the leaner the mixture. Remember that it is always preferable to run a slightly richer mixture than one that is too lean.

Idle Speed Adjustment

The engine should be installed in a test tank or on the boat in the water for this procedure.

1. Remove the engine cover.

2. Check and adjust ignition timing. See Chapter Five.

3. Connect a tachometer according to manufacturer's instructions.

4. Start the engine and run for 5-10 minutes to bring it to normal operating temperature.

5. Shift the engine into FORWARD.

6. If idle speed is not 800-900 rpm, adjust the throttle stop screw (A, **Figure 29**) as required to bring idle speed within specifications.

THROTTLE PLUNGER
CARBURETOR
(DT 7.5 AND DT 9)

Overhaul

Refer to **Figure 30** (DT 7.5) or **Figure 31** (DT 9) for this procedure.

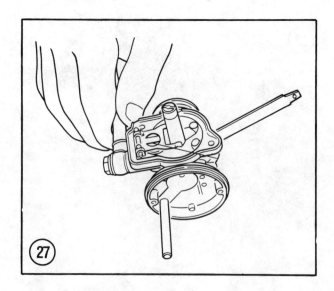

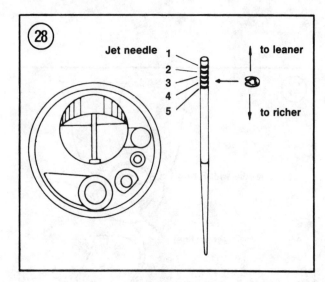

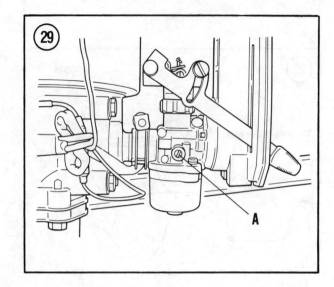

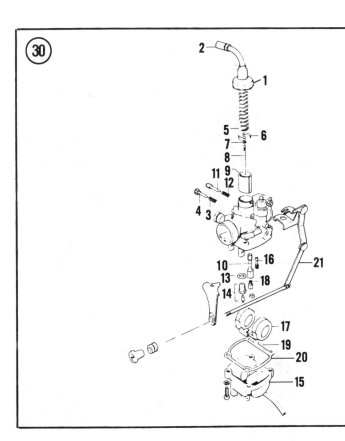

THROTTLE PLUNGER CARBURETOR (DT 7.5)

1. Cap
2. Cable adjuster
3. Throttle stop screw spring
4. Throttle stop screw
5. Throttle valve spring
6. Spring seat
7. Jet retainer
8. Jet needle
9. Throttle valve
10. Main nozzle
11. Pilot (idle) air screw
12. Pilot (idle) air screw spring
13. Needle valve seat gasket
14. Needle valve and seat
15. Float bowl
16. Pilot (idle) jet
17. Float
18. Main jet
19. Gasket
20. Hinge pin
21. Choke lever assembly

6

THROTTLE PLUNGER CARBURETOR (DT 9)

1. Cap
2. Throttle rod
3. Throttle stop screw spring
4. Throttle stop screw
5. Throttle valve spring
6. Spring seat
7. Jet retainer
8. Jet needle
9. Throttle valve
10. Main nozzle
11. Pilot (idle) air screw
12. Pilot (idle) air screw spring
13. Needle valve seat gasket
14. Needle valve and seat
15. Cup gasket
16. Pilot (idle) jet
17. Cup
18. Main jet
19. Hinge pin
20. Float
21. Gasket
22. Choke lever assembly

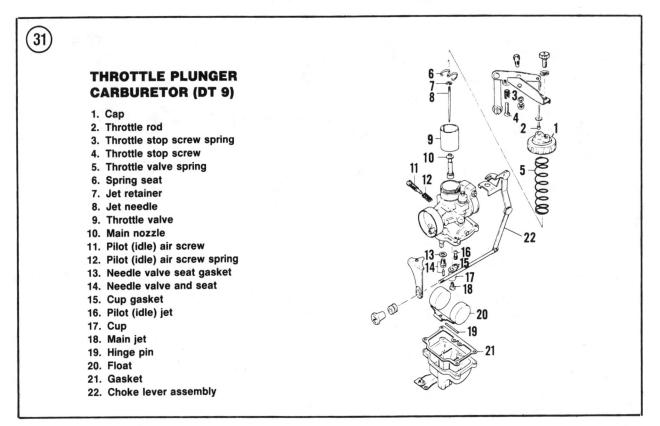

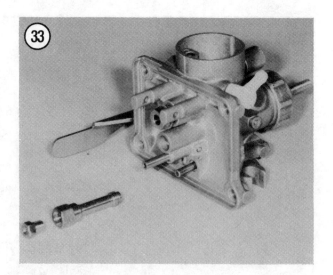

1. Remove fuel bowl attaching screws. Separate fuel bowl from carburetor body. See **Figure 32**. Remove and discard fuel bowl gasket.

2. Remove float hinge pin. Remove float assembly and inlet seat needle from fuel bowl.

3. Remove main jet and needle nozzle (**Figure 33**).

4. Remove inlet needle seat and gasket (**Figure 34**) with a jet remover or a wide-blade screwdriver. Discard the gasket.

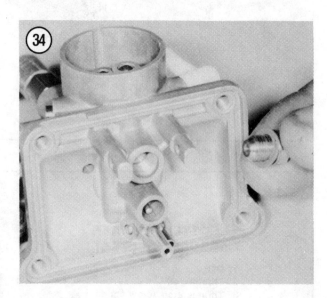

5. Unscrew and remove the carburetor mixing chamber top cover.

6. Remove throttle valve spring, seat and throttle valve assembly from carburetor.

7. Disassemble throttle valve assembly as shown in **Figure 35**.

8. Remove choke plunger assembly. See **Figure 36** (typical).

9. Lightly seat pilot (idle) air screw, counting the number of turns required for reinstallation reference. Back screw out and remove from carburetor with spring.

10. On DT 7.5 models, repeat Step 9 to remove the throttle stop screw.

11. Clean and inspect all parts as described in this chapter.

12. Assembly is the reverse of disassembly, plus the following:

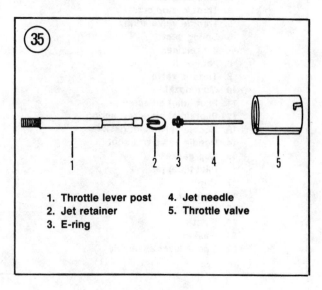

1. Throttle lever post   4. Jet needle
2. Jet retainer   5. Throttle valve
3. E-ring

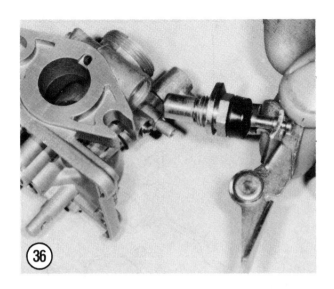

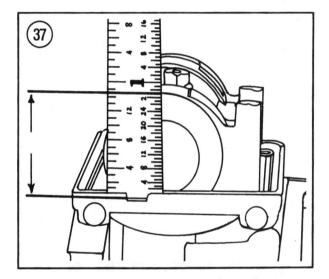

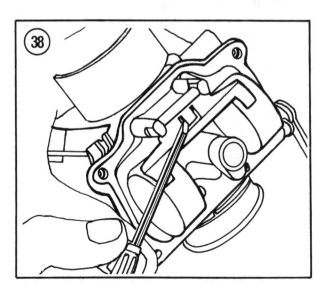

a. Install pilot (idle) air and throttle stop screws with their springs. Lightly seat each screw, then back out the number of turns noted during removal.

b. Reassemble throttle valve assembly. Jet needle retainer should be positioned with slot aligned as shown in **Figure 24**.

c. Install throttle lever post in throttle valve with anchor in pocket at bottom of valve body. See **Figure 25**.

d. Check float adjustment as described in this chapter.

Float Adjustment

1. Invert carburetor body and lower float until adjusting tab just touches inlet needle. Hold float in this position and measure the distance between the carburetor body (without gasket) and the bottom of the float, as shown in **Figure 37**.

> *CAUTION*
> *Bend the float adjustment arm or tang carefully when adjustment is required—do **not** press down on the float. Downward pressure on the float will press the inlet needle tip into its seat and can damage the tip surface.*

2. If float level is not within specifications (**Table 1**), adjust float by bending the adjusting tab (**Figure 38**) as required.

Mid-range Jet Needle Adjustment

The position of the E-ring on the jet needle determines the proper low- and medium-speed range mixture. See **Figure 28**. The standard setting (the 3rd groove from the top) should be suitable for most operating conditions.

If a too-rich or too-lean condition results from extreme changes in elevation, temperature or humidity, the E-ring position can be changed. The closer the E-ring is installed to the top of the needle, the leaner the mixture. Remember that it is always preferable to run a slightly richer mixture than one that is too lean.

Idle Speed Adjustment

The engine should be installed in a test tank or on the boat in the water for this procedure.

1. Remove the propeller. See Chapter Nine.
2. Remove the engine cover.
3. Check and adjust ignition timing. See Chapter Five.
4. Connect a tachometer according to manufacturer's instructions.
5. Lightly seat the pilot (idle) air screw, then back it out one full turn.
6. Start the engine and run for 5-10 minutes to bring it to normal operating temperature.
7. Shift the engine into FORWARD.

> *NOTE*
> *The throttle stop screw is located on the DT 7.5 carburetor mixing chamber. On the DT 9, the screw is under the throttle lever arm.*

8. If idle speed is not 700-850 rpm, adjust the throttle stop screw as required to bring idle speed within specifications.

CENTERBOWL CARBURETOR (DT 3.5-DT 16)

Overhaul

Several variations of this carburetor design have been used on Suzuki DT 3.5-DT 16 outboards. All operate essentially the same, varying primarily in calibration and linkage design.

The needle valve seat is not serviceable. If worn or damaged, the entire carburetor must be replaced.

Refer to **Figure 39** (typical) for this procedure.

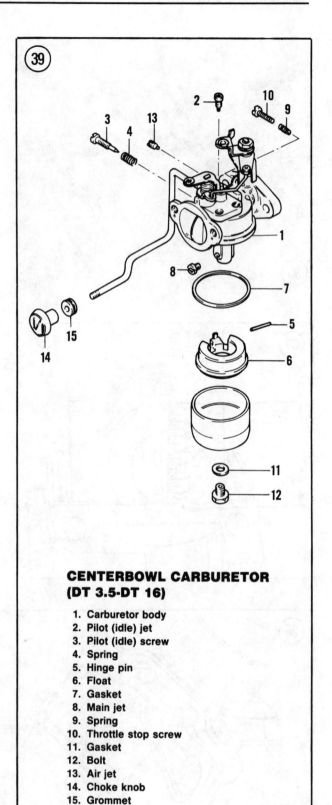

CENTERBOWL CARBURETOR (DT 3.5-DT 16)

1. Carburetor body
2. Pilot (idle) jet
3. Pilot (idle) screw
4. Spring
5. Hinge pin
6. Float
7. Gasket
8. Main jet
9. Spring
10. Throttle stop screw
11. Gasket
12. Bolt
13. Air jet
14. Choke knob
15. Grommet

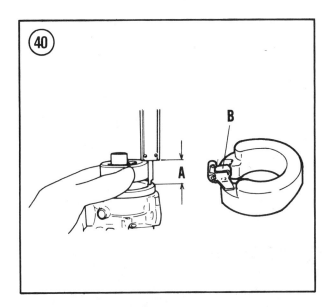

1. Remove the hex head bolt and washer from the float bowl. Remove the float bowl and O-ring from the fuel bowl. Discard the O-ring.

2. Slide the float hinge pin to one side and remove the float and pin assembly from the carburetor.

CAUTION
The inlet needle is permanently installed in the valve seat on some models. Do not try to remove needle individually in Step 3 unless it comes out easily.

3. Remove the inlet needle.

4. Remove the main jet with a jet remover or wide-blade screwdriver.

5. Remove the pilot (idle) jet with a suitable removal tool.

6. Remove the air jet with a suitable removal tool.

7. Lightly seat the pilot (idle) screw, counting the number of turns required for reinstallation reference. Back screw out and remove from carburetor with spring.

8. Clean and inspect all parts as described in this chapter.

9. Assembly is the reverse of disassembly, plus the following:

a. Install pilot (idle) screw and spring. Lightly seat screw, then back out the number of turns noted during removal.

b. Check float adjustment as described in this chapter.

Float Adjustment

Floats supplied on 1978-1981 carburetors are non-adjustable. Replacement floats available from Suzuki dealers are adjustable.

1. Invert carburetor body and lower float until adjusting tab just touches inlet needle. Measure the distance between the carburetor body (without gasket) and the bottom of the float, as shown in A, **Figure 40**.

CAUTION
*Bend the float adjustment arm or tang carefully when adjustment is required—do **not** press down on the float. Downward pressure on the float will press the inlet needle tip into its seat and can damage the tip surface.*

2A. 1978-1981 models (factory-supplied float)—If float level is not within specifications (**Table 1**), replace the float.

2B. All others—If float level is not within specifications (**Table 1**), adjust float by bending the adjusting tab (B, **Figure 40**) as required.

Idle Speed Adjustment

The engine should be installed in a test tank or on the boat in the water for this procedure.

1. Remove the engine cover.

2. Check and adjust ignition timing. See Chapter Five.

3. Connect a tachometer according to manufacturer's instructions.

4. Start the engine and run for 5-10 minutes to bring it to normal operating temperature.

5. Lightly seat the pilot (idle) air screw, then back it out gradually until the engine speed

stops increasing. See **Figure 41** for typical variations in air screw location.

6. Shift the engine into FORWARD.

7. If idle speed is not 900-1,000 rpm (DT 3.5) or 600-650 rpm (all others), adjust the throttle stop screw as required to bring idle speed within specifications. See **Figure 42** for typical variations in throttle stop screw location.

8. DT 3.5—Check slack in throttle cable at carburetor bracket. If greater than 0.04 in., loosen jam nut and adjust slack to specifications.

INTEGRAL FUEL PUMP CARBURETOR (1983-ON DT 9.9 AND DT 15)

Refer to **Figure 43** for this procedure.

1. Remove the fuel pump components as described in this chapter (**Figure 44**).

2. Remove the hex head bolt and washer from the float bowl. Remove the float bowl and O-ring from the fuel bowl. Discard the O-ring.

3. Slide the float hinge pin to one side and remove the float and pin assembly from the carburetor.

> *NOTE*
> *The needle valve seat is permanently installed. If valve seat is damaged, replace the carburetor body.*

4. Remove the inlet needle.

5. Remove the main jet with a jet remover or wide-blade screwdriver.

6. Remove the pilot (idle) jet with a suitable removal tool.

7. Lightly seat the pilot (idle) screw, counting the number of turns required for reinstallation reference. Back screw out and remove from carburetor with spring.

8. Clean and inspect all parts as described in this chapter.

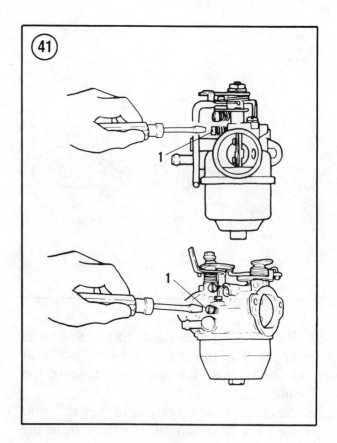

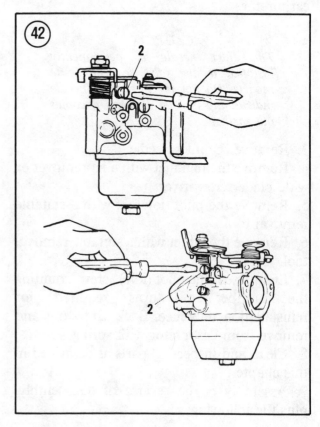

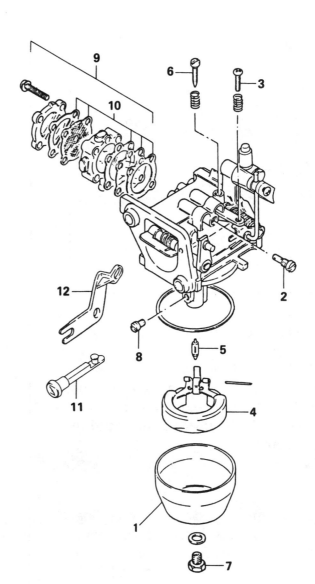

43

INTEGRAL FUEL PUMP CARBURETOR

1. Float bowl
2. Pilot (idle) jet
3. Throttle stop screw
4. Float
5. Inlet needle
6. Pilot (idle) screw
7. Bolt
8. Main jet
9. Fuel pump assembly
10. Valve and diaphragm set
11. Choke lever knob
12. Choke lever

6

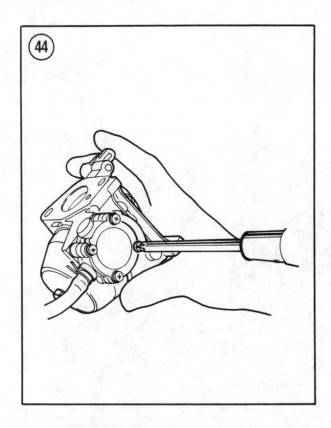

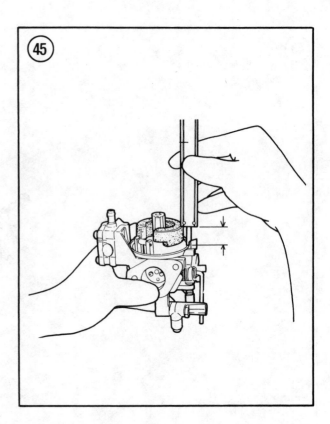

9. Assembly is the reverse of disassembly, plus the following:

   a. Install pilot (idle) screw and spring. Lightly seat screw, then back out the number of turns noted during removal.

   b. Check float adjustment as described in this chapter.

Float Adjustment

1. Invert carburetor body and lower float until adjusting tab just touches inlet needle. Hold float in this position and measure the distance between the carburetor body (without gasket) and the bottom of the float, as shown in **Figure 45**.

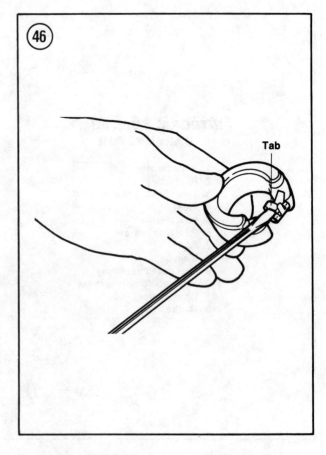

> *CAUTION*
> *Bend the float adjustment arm or tang carefully when adjustment is required—do **not** press down on the float. Downward pressure on the float will press the inlet needle tip into its seat and can damage the tip surface.*

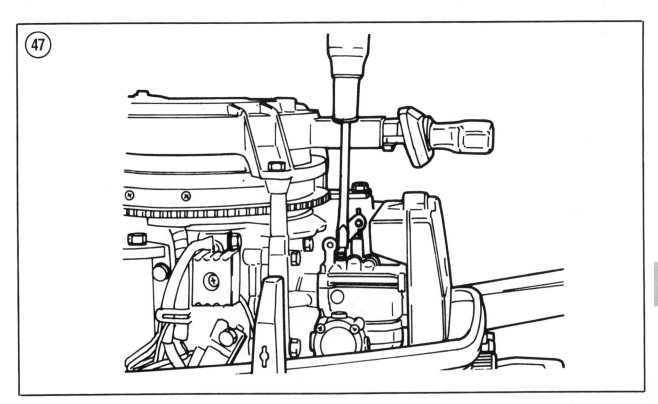

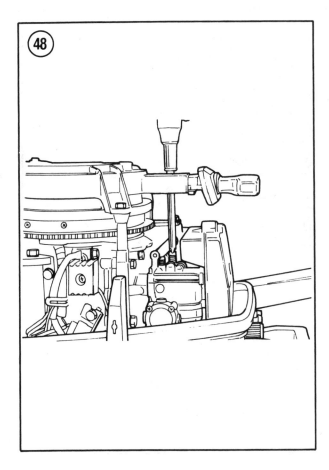

2. If float level is not within specifications (**Table 1**), adjust float by bending the adjusting tab (**Figure 46**) as required.

Idle Speed Adjustment

The engine should be installed in a test tank or on the boat in the water for this procedure.

1. Remove the engine cover.

2. Check and adjust ignition timing. See Chapter Five.

3. Connect a tachometer according to manufacturer's instructions.

4. Start the engine and run for 5-10 minutes to bring it to normal operating temperature.

5. Lightly seat the pilot (idle) air screw, then back it out 1 1/4-1 3/4 turns. See **Figure 47**.

6. Shift the engine into FORWARD.

7. Rotate the throttle lever to the closed position (full retard).

8. If idle speed is not 600-650 rpm, adjust the throttle stop screw (**Figure 48**) as required to bring idle speed within specifications.

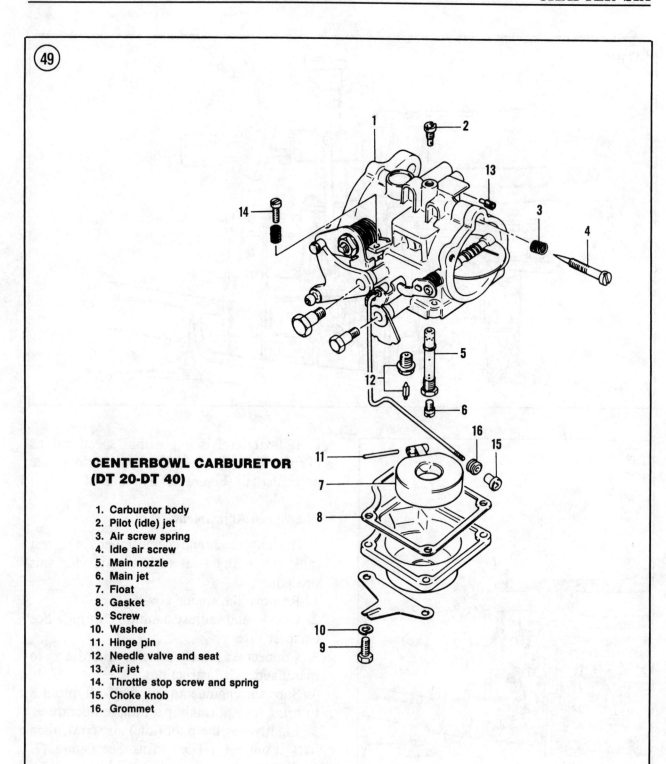

④⑨

**CENTERBOWL CARBURETOR
(DT 20-DT 40)**

1. Carburetor body
2. Pilot (idle) jet
3. Air screw spring
4. Idle air screw
5. Main nozzle
6. Main jet
7. Float
8. Gasket
9. Screw
10. Washer
11. Hinge pin
12. Needle valve and seat
13. Air jet
14. Throttle stop screw and spring
15. Choke knob
16. Grommet

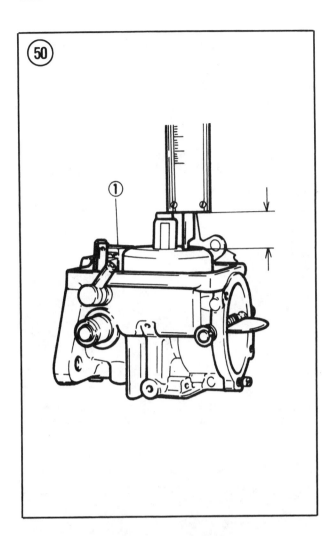

3. Remove the inlet needle. Remove the needle valve seat with an appropriate size socket wrench.

4. Remove the main jet and nozzle with a jet remover or wide-blade screwdriver. Remove and discard the nozzle O-ring.

5. Remove the pilot (idle) jet with a suitable removal tool.

6. Remove the air jet (if so equipped) with a suitable removal tool.

7. Lightly seat the pilot (idle) air screw, counting the number of turns required for reinstallation reference. Back screw out and remove from carburetor with spring.

8. Clean and inspect all parts as described in this chapter.

9. Assembly is the reverse of disassembly, plus the following:

    a. Install pilot (idle) screw and spring. Lightly seat screw, then back out the number of turns noted during removal.

    b. Check float adjustment as described in this chapter.

CENTERBOWL CARBURETOR
(DT 20-DT 140)

Overhaul

Several variations of this carburetor design have been used on Suzuki DT 20-DT 140 outboards. All operate essentially the same, varying primarily in calibration and linkage connections. Refer to **Figure 49** (typical) for this procedure.

1. Remove the float bowl attaching screws. Remove the float bowl and gasket from the fuel bowl. Discard the gasket.

2. Slide the float hinge pin to one side and remove the float and pin assembly from the carburetor.

Float Adjustment

1. Invert carburetor body and lower float until adjusting tab just touches inlet needle. Hold float in this position and measure the distance between the carburetor body (without gasket) and the bottom of the float, as shown in **Figure 50**.

CAUTION
*Bend the float adjustment arm or tang carefully when adjustment is required—do **not** press down on the float. Downward pressure on the float will press the inlet needle tip into its seat and can damage the tip surface.*

2. If float level is not within specifications (**Table 1**), adjust float by bending the adjusting tab (1, **Figure 50**) as required.

Idle Speed Adjustment

The engine should be installed in a test tank or on the boat in the water for this procedure.

1. Remove the engine cover.

2. Check and adjust ignition timing. See Chapter Five.

3. Connect a tachometer according to manufacturer's instructions.

4. Start the engine and run for 5-10 minutes to bring it to normal operating temperature.

5. Lightly seat the pilot (idle) air screw. Refer to **Table 2** and back it out the number of turns specified.

6. Shift the engine into FORWARD.

7A. DT 20-DT 40—If idle speed is not 650-700 rpm (DT 40) or 600-650 rpm (all

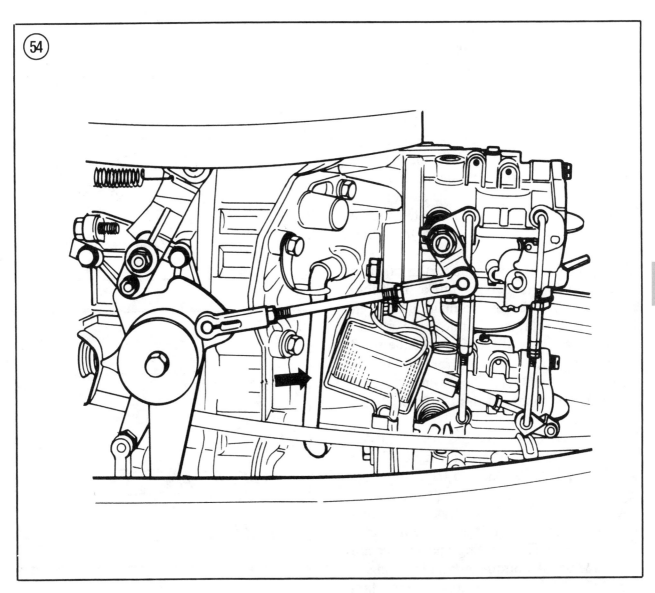

others), adjust the throttle stop screw (A, **Figure 51**) as required to bring the idle speed within specifications.

NOTE
Do not adjust the throttle stop screws to make the adjustment in Step 7B.

7B. If idle speed is not 650-700 rpm (DT 50-DT 65) or 600-700 rpm (DT 75-DT 140), loosen the throttle speed bolt locknut and adjust the bolt as required to bring idle speed within specifications. See **Figure 52** or **Figure 53** (typical). When idle speed is correct, tighten locknut.

Carburetor Balancing

Carburetors on DT 50-DT 85 engines should be balanced whenever they are installed after servicing. This procedure requires the use of a carburetor balancer (part No. 09913-13121) and tachometer.

1. Disconnect the intake manifold line (**Figure 54**) at the top carburetor. Plug the line to prevent leakage.

2. Connect the left carburetor balancer line to the intake manifold fitting. See **Figure 55**.

3. Start the engine and run at 1,000 rpm.

4. Turn the air screw at the bottom of the balancer tube which is connected to the engine (**Figure 56**) until the steel ball inside the tube rests on the center line (**Figure 57**).

5A. DT 50-DT 65—Disconnect the balancer line at the top carburetor intake manifold fitting and connect the second balancer line in its place. Repeat Step 4 until the steel ball in the second balancer tube rests on the center line.

5B. DT 77-DT 85—Disconnect the balancer line at the top carburetor intake manifold fitting. Remove the intake manifold line at the center carburetor. Connect the second balancer line in its place. Connect the third balancer line to the top carburetor intake manifold fitting. Repeat Step 4 until the steel balls in the second and third balancer tubes rest on the center line.

6. Once a balancer tube has been adjusted for each carburetor, shut the engine off and connect the balancer lines to the carburetors as follows.

    a. DT 50-DT 65—Connect the first balancer tube to the top carburetor intake manifold fitting and the second tube to the bottom carburetor fitting.

    b. DT 75-DT 85—Connect the first balancer tube to the top carburetor intake manifold fitting. Connect the second tube to the center carburetor fitting. Connect the third tube to the bottom carburetor fitting.

7. Restart the engine and run at 1,000 rpm. Make sure the steel ball in the top balancer tube rests on the center line (the others will not).

8A. DT 50-DT 65—Loosen the throttle rod locknut, rotate the throttle rod until the steel ball in the second balancer tube rests on the center line and tighten the locknut. See **Figure 58**.

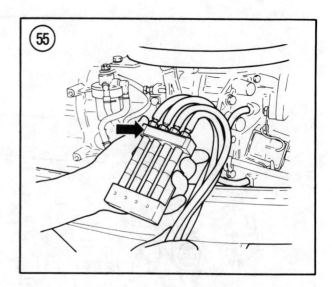

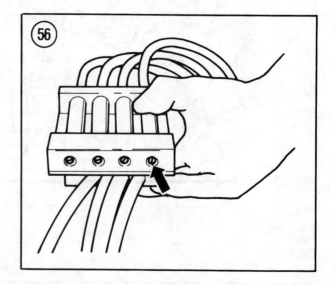

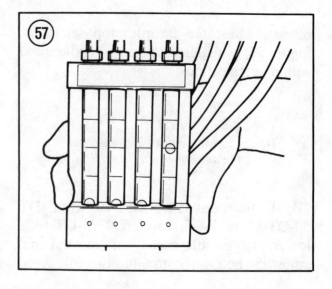

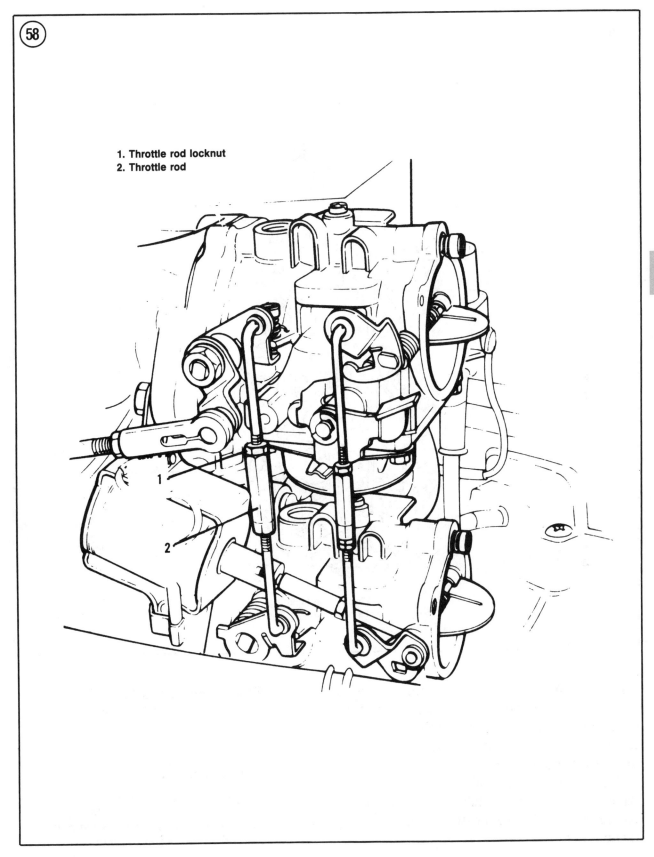

58

1. Throttle rod locknut
2. Throttle rod

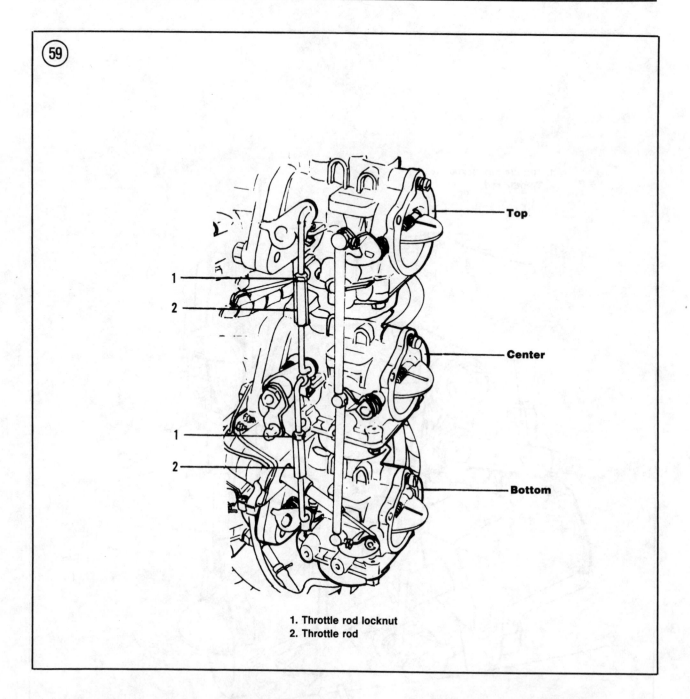

1. Throttle rod locknut
2. Throttle rod

8B. DT 75-DT 85—Loosen the throttle rod locknuts, rotate the throttle rods until the steel ball in the second and third balancer tubes rests on the center line, then tighten the locknuts. See **Figure 59**.

9. Shut the engine off. Disconnect the balancer from the intake manifold and reconnect the intake hose(s). Remove the tachometer.

CARBURETOR CLEANING AND INSPECTION

WARNING
Suzuki recommends the use of gasoline as a cleaning solvent in the following procedures. Work in a well-ventilated area away from any source of ignition. Keep a fire extinguisher handy.

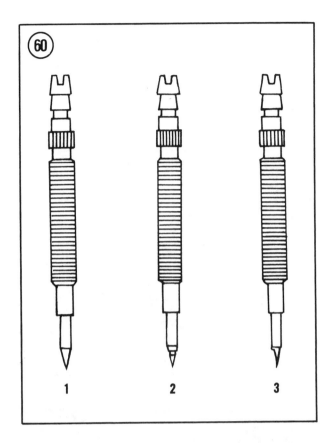

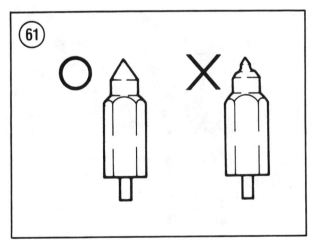

Wipe the carburetor casting and linkage with a cloth moistened in solvent to remove any contamination and operating film. Clean the carburetor castings with fresh gasoline or an aerosol solvent and a brush. Do not submerge them in a hot tank or carburetor cleaner. A sealing compound is used to eliminate porosity problems. Submersion in a hot tank or carburetor cleaner will remove this sealing compound.

Spray the gasoline or cleaner on the casting and scrub off any gum or varnish with a small bristle brush. Spray the cleaner through the casting metering passages. Never clean passages with a wire or drill as you may enlarge the passage and change the carburetor calibration.

Blow castings dry with low-pressure (25 psi or less) compressed air. The use of higher pressures can damage the sealing compound.

Check the float for fuel absorption. Check the float arm for wear in the hinge pin and needle valve contact areas. Replace as required.

Check the pilot (idle) air screw tip for grooving, nicks or scratches. **Figure 60** shows a good screw tip (1), a screw tip damaged from excessive pressure when seating (2) and one with wear on one side caused by vibration resulting from the use of a damaged propeller (3).

Check the inlet needle tip (seat surface) for grooving, nicks or scratches. See **Figure 61**. Replace idle needle if tip is damaged.

Check the inlet needle seat for grooving, nicks or scratches. If defects are noted, replace needle seat if serviceable. On DT 3.5-DT 16 centerbowl and integral fuel pump models, replace the carburetor body.

Check the throttle and choke shafts for excessive wear or play. The throttle and choke valves must move freely without binding. Replace carburetor if any of these defects are noted.

Clean all gasket residue from mating surfaces and remove any nicks, scratches or slight distortion with a surface plate and emery cloth.

REED VALVE ASSEMBLY

The reed valve assembly is mounted between the intake manifold and crankcase

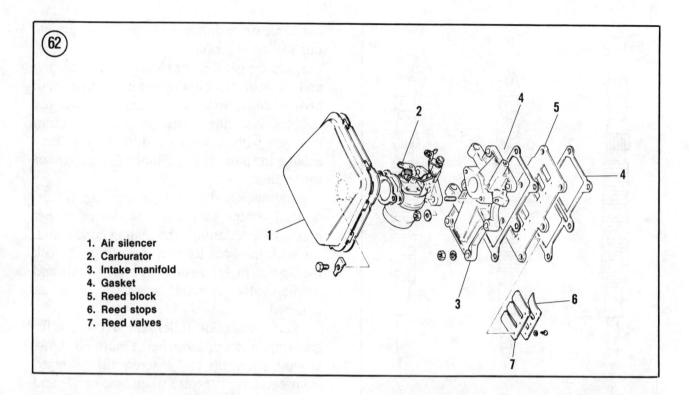

1. Air silencer
2. Carburator
3. Intake manifold
4. Gasket
5. Reed block
6. Reed stops
7. Reed valves

on DT 3.5-DT 140 engines. See **Figure 62**. On DT 2 models, the reed valve assembly is an integral part of the front crankcase half (**Figure 63**).

Reed valves control the passage of air-fuel mixture into the crankcase by opening and closing as crankcase pressure changes. When crankcase pressure is high, the reeds maintain contact with the reed plate to which they are attached. As crankcase pressure drops on the compression stroke, the reeds move away from the plate and allow air-fuel mixture to pass. Reed travel is limited by the reed stop. As crankcase pressure increases, the reeds return to the reed plate.

Figure 64 (DT 9.9 and 16) and **Figure 65** (DT 40) show typical reed valve arrangements.

Removal/Installation (DT 2)

The reed valves are attached to the inside of the front crankcase half on this model. Access to the reed valves for inspection and

service requires that the engine be removed and the crankcase separated. See Chapter Eight.

Removal/Installation (All Others)

1. Remove the carburetor as described in this chapter.

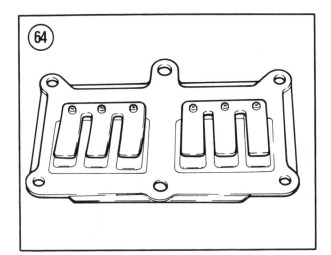

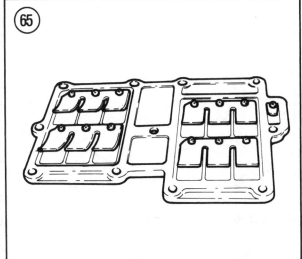

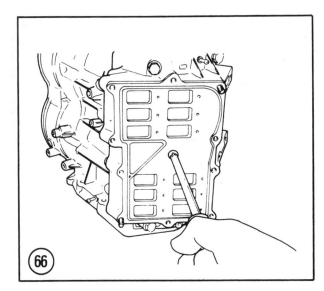

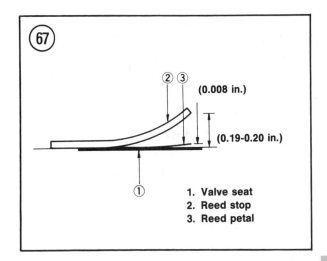

1. Valve seat
2. Reed stop
3. Reed petal

2. Disconnect any hoses connected to the intake manifold.

NOTE
*On some models, the reed valve assembly is secured to the crankcase by one or more separate fasteners. With this design, the intake manifold must be removed first, then the reed valve assembly fastener(s) removed before the assembly and gasket can be removed. See **Figure 66**.*

3. Remove the screws holding the intake manifold to the crankcase cover. Remove the intake manifold, gasket, reed valve assembly and gasket from the crankcase. Discard the gaskets.

4. Clean all mating surfaces of gasket or sealant residue.

5. Installation is the reverse of removal. Use new gaskets and make sure that reed assembly faces crankcase.

Inspection

Refer to **Figure 67** for this procedure.

1. Check reeds for cracking or other damage. Replace if any defects are noted.

2. Reeds should lie flat on the valve seat with no preload. To check flatness, gently push each reed petal out. Constant resistance should be felt with no audible noise.

3. Check the clearance between the reed and the valve seat with a flat feeler gauge. If greater than 0.008 in., replace the reed set as described in this chapter.

4. Measure the distance between the reed stop and valve seat and compare to **Table 3**. If not within specifications, check the valve seat for warpage and replace as required. If valve seat is not warped, replace the reed stop assembly as described in this chapter.

Reed and Reed Stop Replacement

1. Remove the screws holding the reed stop and reeds to the valve seat (**Figure 68**).

2. Remove the reed stop and reeds.

3. Place a new reed on the valve seat and check for flatness.

4. Center the reed over the valve seat openings.

5. Wipe reed stop screw threads with Thread Lock 1342. Install reed stop and tighten screws securely.

6. Check reed tension and opening. See *Inspection* in this chapter.

FUEL TANK

The DT 2 and DT 3.5 models have an integral fuel tank. The DT 2 transports fuel from the tank to the carburetor by gravity feed.

Since the DT 3.5 can also be operated from a remote fuel tank, it has a fuel pump installed between the integral tank and carburetor. See **Figure 69**. When running the engine on its integral tank, the fuel petcock should be in a horizontal position. To run the engine on a remote tank, connect the remote tank line to the fuel line socket and turn the integral tank petcock to a vertical position.

Removal/Installation
(DT 2)

1. Remove the right and left engine covers.

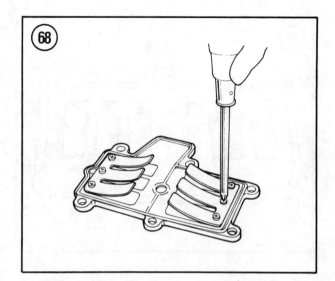

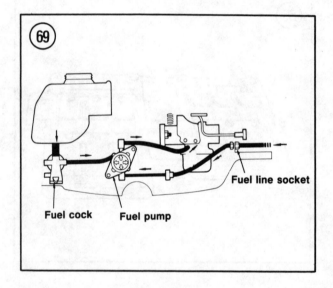

Fuel cock   Fuel pump   Fuel line socket

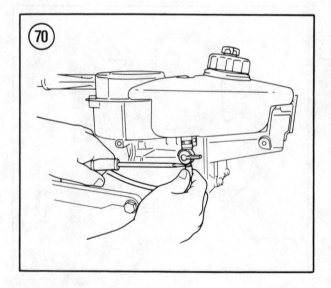

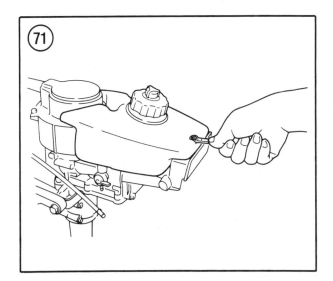

2. Make sure the fuel petcock lever is in the OFF or S position, then disconnect the fuel line at the petcock. See **Figure 70**. Plug the end of the line to prevent leakage.

3. Remove the front and rear screws holding the fuel tank to the support plate (**Figure 71**).

4. Remove the tank and petcock assembly from the engine.

5. If petcock removal is required, loosen the hose clamp and pull the petcock and hose from the fuel tank. See **Figure 72**.

6. Installation is the reverse of removal.

Removal/Installation (DT 3.5)

1. Remove the engine cover.

2. Make sure the fuel petcock lever is in the OFF or B position, then disconnect the fuel line at the petcock. See **Figure 69**. Plug the end of the line to prevent leakage.

3. Remove the bolts holding the fuel tank to the engine (**Figure 73**). Remove the fuel tank.

4. Installation is the reverse of removal.

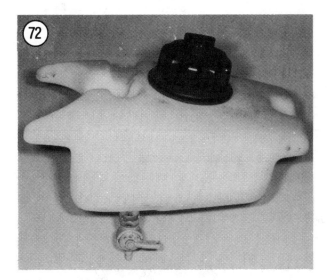

Portable Fuel Tank

Suzuki offers 2 types of portable or remote fuel tanks. **Figure 74** (recreational) and **Figure 75** (commercial) show the components of each fuel tank, including the primer bulb assembly.

When some oils are mixed with gasoline and stored in a warm place, a bacterial substance will form. This colorless substance covers the fuel pickup, restricting flow through the fuel system. Bacterial formation can be prevented by using a good quality fuel conditioner on a regular basis. If present, bacteria can be removed with a good marine engine cleaner.

To remove any dirt or water that may have entered the tank during refilling and to prevent the build-up of gum and varnish, clean the inside of the tank once each season

6

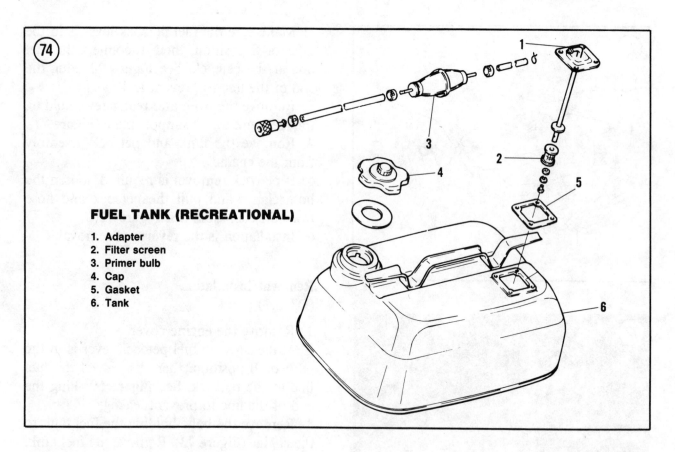

(74)

FUEL TANK (RECREATIONAL)

1. Adapter
2. Filter screen
3. Primer bulb
4. Cap
5. Gasket
6. Tank

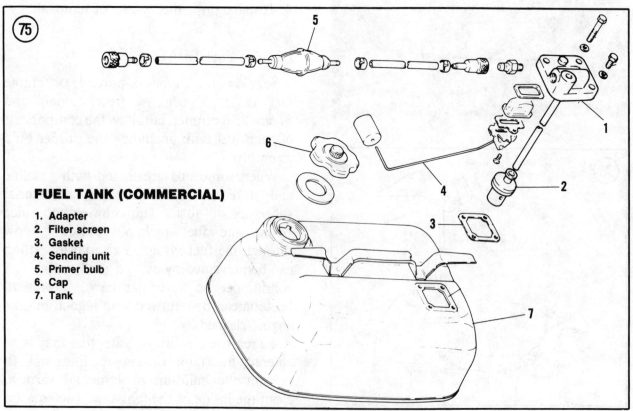

(75)

FUEL TANK (COMMERCIAL)

1. Adapter
2. Filter screen
3. Gasket
4. Sending unit
5. Primer bulb
6. Cap
7. Tank

by flushing with clean lead-free gasoline or kerosene.

Check the inside and outside of the tank for signs of rust, leakage or corrosion. Replace as required. Do not attempt to patch the tank with automotive fuel tank repair materials. Portable marine fuel tanks are subject to

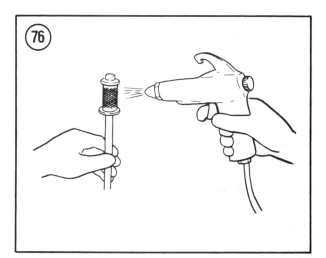

much greater pressure and vacuum conditions.

To check the fuel tank adapter filter screen for possible restrictions, remove the adapter and inspect the hose and screen for damage. Clean the screen with solvent, then blow low-pressure compressed air through the screen to remove any particles. See **Figure 76**.

FUEL LINE AND PRIMER BULB

When priming the engine, the primer bulb should gradually become firm. If it does not become firm or if it stays firm even when disconnected, the check valve inside the primer bulb is malfunctioning.

The line should be checked periodically for cracks, breaks, restrictions and chafing. The bulb should be checked periodically for proper operation. Make sure all fuel line connections are tight and securely clamped.

6

Table 1 CARBURETOR SPECIFICATIONS*

DT 2	
Type	VM-11-10
Main jet	No. 95
Jet needle	
1977-1981	3E6-4
1983-on	3E6-3
Needle jet	2.0
Float level	0.75-0.83 in.
Idle speed	800-900 rpm in gear
DT 3.5	
Type	BV18-15
Main jet	No. 90
Pilot (idle) jet	No. 15
Pilot (idle) outlet	1.5 mm
Main air jet	1.8 mm
Float level	0.47-0.55 in.
Idle speed	900-1,000 rpm in gear

(continued)

Table 1 CARBURETOR SPECIFICATIONS* (continued)

DT 5
  Type   BV18-15
  Main jet
    1978-1979   No. 180
    1980-on   No. 100
  Pilot (idle) jet   No. 20
  Pilot (idle) outlet   2.0 mm
  Main air jet   1.8 mm
  Float level   0.51-0.59 in.
  Idle speed   600-650 rpm in gear

DT 6, DT 8
  Type   BV24-18
  Main jet
    Short shaft   No. 95
    Long shaft   No. 100
  Pilot (idle) jet   No. 50
  Pilot (idle) outlet   0.7 mm
  Main air jet   1.2 mm
  Float level   0.87-0.94 in.
  Idle speed   600-650 rpm in gear

DT 7.5
  Type   VM15SC
  Main jet   No. 180
  Jet needle   3J2-3
  Pilot (idle) jet   No. 20
  Pilot (idle) outlet   1.1 mm
  Starter jet   No. 50
  Float level   0.787 in.
  Idle speed   700-850 rpm in gear

DT 9
  Type   VM19SC
  Main jet   No. 145
  Jet needle   4N7-2
  Pilot (idle) jet   No. 40
  Pilot (idle) outlet   1.2 mm
  Starter jet   No. 50
  Float level   0.955 in.
  Idle speed   700-850 rpm in gear

DT 9.9 (1977-1982)
  Type   BV24-16
  Main jet
    1977-1979   No. 150
    1980-1982   No. 92.5
  Pilot (idle) jet   No. 55
  Pilot (idle) outlet   0.8 mm
  Air jet   1.2 mm
  Float level   0.73-0.81 in.
  Idle speed   600-650 rpm in gear

(continued)

Table 1 CARBURETOR SPECIFICATIONS* (continued)

DT 9.9 (1983-on)
Type   BV24-15
Main jet   No. 110
Main air jet   1.2 mm
Pilot (idle) jet   No. 52.5
Pilot (idle) air jet   1.4 mm
Float level   0.91-0.98 in.
Idle speed   600-650 rpm in gear

DT 15
Type   BV24-18
Main jet   No. 122.5
Main air jet   1.2 mm
Pilot (idle) jet   No. 57.5
Pilot (idle) air jet   1.2 mm
Float level   0.91-0.98 in.
Idle speed   600-650 rpm in gear

DT 16
Type   BV24-19
Main jet
  1977-1979   No. 117.5
  1980-on   No. 140
Pilot (idle) jet   No. 57.5
Pilot (idle) outlet   0.8 mm
Air jet   1.2 mm
Float level   0.73-0.81 in.
Idle speed   600-650 rpm in gear

DT 20
Type   BV28-22
Main jet
  1977-1978   No. 125
  1979-1980   No. 130
Pilot (idle) jet   No. 62.5
Pilot (idle) outlet   1.0 mm
Air jet   1.0 mm
Float level   0.41-0.49 in.
Idle speed   600-650 rpm in gear

DT 25 (1977-1982)
Type   BV32-28
Main jet
  1977-1979   No. 155
  1980-1982   No. 160
Pilot (idle) jet   No. 75
Pilot (idle) air jet   0.9 mm
Main air jet   1.0 mm
Float level   0.41-0.49 in.
Idle speed   600-650 rpm in gear

DT 25 (1983-on)
Type   BV32-24
Main jet   No. 142.5
Pilot (idle) jet   No. 90

(continued)

Table 1 CARBURETOR SPECIFICATIONS* (continued)

DT 25 (1983-on) (continued)

Pilot (idle) air jet	1.2 mm
Main air jet	1.4 mm
Float level	0.394-0.472 in.
Idle speed	650-700 rpm in gear

DT 30

Type	BV32-28
Main jet	No. 160
Pilot (idle) jet	No. 85
Pilot (idle) air jet	1.2 mm
Main air jet	1.4 mm
Float level	0.394-0.472 in.
Idle speed	650-700 rpm in gear

DT 40

Type	B40-32
Main jet	No. 200
Pilot (idle) jet	No. 80
Float level	0.66-0.74 in.
Idle speed	650-700 rpm in gear

DT 50, DT 50M

Type	B40-32
Main jet	No. 165
Pilot (idle) jet	No. 85
Pilot (idle) air jet	
1977-1982	1.5 mm
1983-on	1.2 mm
Main air jet	1.2 mm
Float level	0.65-0.73 in.
Idle speed	650-700 rpm in gear

DT 60

Type	B40-32
Main jet	No. 160
Pilot (idle) jet	No. 95
Pilot (idle) air jet	1.2 mm
Main air jet	1.2 mm
Float level	0.63-0.71 in.
Idle speed	650-700 rpm in gear

DT 65

Type	B32-28
Main jet	No. 167.5
Pilot (idle) jet	No. 67.5
Pilot (idle) air jet	1.5 mm
Main air jet	1.2 mm
Float level	0.65-0.73 in.
Idle speed	650-700 rpm in gear

DT 75

Type	B32-28
Main jet	No. 140
Pilot (idle) jet	No. 80
Pilot (idle) air jet	1.2 mm

(continued)

Table 1 CARBURETOR SPECIFICATIONS* (continued)

DT 75 (continued)	
Main air jet	1.2 mm
Float level	0.49-0.57 in.
Idle speed	600-700 rpm in gear
DT 85 (1979-1982)	
Type	B32-28
Main jet	No. 162.5
Pilot (idle) jet	No. 75
Pilot (idle) air jet	1.5 mm
Main air jet	1.2 mm
Float level	
1979	0.60-0.68 in.
1980-1982	0.63-0.71 in.
Idle speed	600-700 rpm in gear
DT 85 (1983-on)	
Type	B40-32
Main jet	
With standard shaft	No. 162.5
With ultralong shaft	No. 167.5
Pilot (idle) jet	No. 75
Pilot (idle) air jet	1.2 mm
Main air jet	1.2 mm
Float level	0.69-0.77 in.
Idle speed	600-700 rpm in gear
DT 115	
Type	B32-28
Main jet	No. 135
Pilot (idle) jet	
1981-1982	No. 80
1983-on	No. 75
Pilot (idle) air jet	
1981-1982	1.0 mm
1983-on	1.2 mm
Main air jet	
1981-1982	1.5 mm
1983-on	1.2 mm
Float level	0.41-0.49 in.
Idle speed	600-700 rpm in gear
DT 140	
Type	B40-32
Main jet	No. 160
Pilot (idle) jet	No. 80
Pilot (idle) air jet	1.2 mm
Main air jet	
1981-1982	1.5 mm
1983-on	1.2 mm
Float level	
1981-1982	0.61-0.69 in.
1983-on	0.67-0.75 in.
Idle speed	600-700 rpm in gear

* Suzuki does not provide specifications for the DT 4.5.

6

Table 2 IDLE AIR SCREW ADJUSTMENT

Model	Turns out from lightly seated position
DT 20	1-1 1/2
DT 25	
1977-1982	1 1/4-3/4
1983-on	3/4-1 1/4
DT 30	1 1/4-1 3/4
DT 40	
Independent ignition	1 3/4-2 1/4
Simultaneous ignition	1 7/8-2 3/8
DT 50, DT 65	1 3/4-2 1/4
DT 60	1 5/8-2 1/8
DT 75	1-1 1/2
DT 85	1 1/4-1 3/4
DT 115	1 1/2
DT 140	1 3/8

Table 3 REED STOP OPENING

Model	Opening (in.)
DT 2, DT 5, DT 6, DT 8	0.157
DT 3.5	0.19-0.20
DT 4.5	Not available
DT 7.5, DT 9	0.00-0.008
DT 9.9	
1977-1982	0.327
1983-on	0.09-0.10
DT 15	0.22-0.23
DT 16	0.327
DT 20	0.433
DT 25	
1977-1982	0.433
1983-on	0.24-0.25
DT 30	0.24-0.25
DT 40	0.390
DT 50/50M	
1983-on	0.30-0.31
1977-1982	0.30-0.32
DT 60, DT 75, DT 85	0.30-0.31
DT 65	0.30-0.32
DT 115, DT 140	0.31-0.33

Chapter Seven

Electrical Systems

This chapter provides service procedures for the battery, starter motor (if so equipped) and each ignition system used on Suzuki outboard motors. Wiring diagrams are included at the end of the book. **Tables 1-3** are at the end of the chapter.

BATTERY

Since batteries used in marine applications endure far more rigorous treatment than those used in an automotive charging system, they are constructed differently. Marine batteries have a thicker exterior case to cushion the plates inside during tight turns and rough weather. Thicker plates are also used, with each one individually fastened within the case to prevent premature failure. Spill-proof caps on the battery cells prevent electrolyte from spilling into the bilges.

Automotive batteries are not designed to be run down and recharged repeatedly. For this reason, they should *only* be used in an emergency situation when a suitable marine battery is not available.

Suzuki recommends that any battery used to crank DT 9.9-DT 40 motors have a minimum rating of 35 amp hours. DT 50-DT 140 motors requires a battery with a minimum rating of 70 amp hours.

> *CAUTION*
> *Sealed or maintenance-free batteries are **not** recommended for use with the unregulated charging systems used on Suzuki outboards. Excessive charging during continued high-speed operation will cause the electrolyte to boil, resulting in its loss. Since water cannot be added to such batteries, such overcharging will ruin the battery.*

Separate batteries may be used to provide power for any accessories such as lighting, fish finders, depth finder, etc. To determine the required capacity of such batteries, calculate the average discharge rate of the accessories and refer to **Table 1**.

Batteries may be wired in parallel to double the ampere hour capacity while maintaining a 12-volt system. See **Figure 1**. For

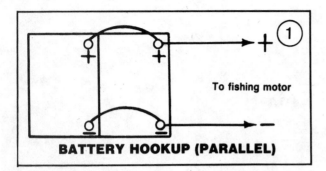

BATTERY HOOKUP (PARALLEL)

To fishing motor

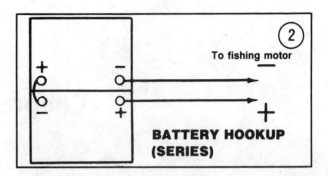

To fishing motor

BATTERY HOOKUP (SERIES)

accessories which require 24 volts, batteries may be wired in series (**Figure 2**) but only accessories specifically requiring 24 volts should be connected into the system. Whether wired in parallel or in series, charge the batteries individually.

Battery Installation in Aluminum Boats

If a battery is not properly secured and grounded when installed in an aluminum boat, it may contact the hull and short to ground. This will burn out remote control cables, tiller handle cables or wiring harnesses.

The following preventive steps should be taken when installing a battery in a metal boat.

1. Choose a location as far as practical from the fuel tank while providing access for maintenance.

2. Install the battery in a plastic battery box with cover and tie-down strap (**Figure 3**).

3. If a covered container is not used, cover the positive battery terminal with a non-conductive shield or boot (**Figure 4**).

4. Make sure the battery is secured inside the battery box and that the box is fastened in position with the tie-down strap.

Care and Inspection

1. Remove the battery container cover (**Figure 3**) or hold-down (**Figure 4**).

2. Disconnect the negative battery cable. Disconnect the positive battery cable.

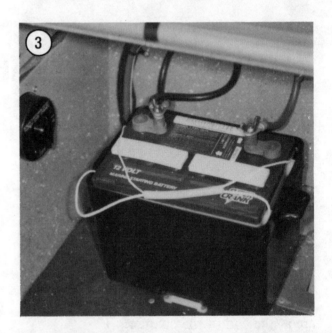

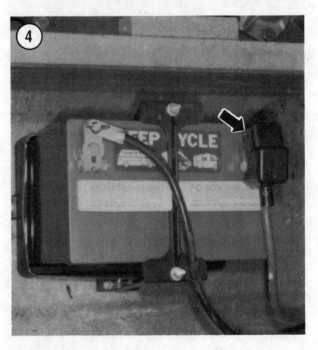

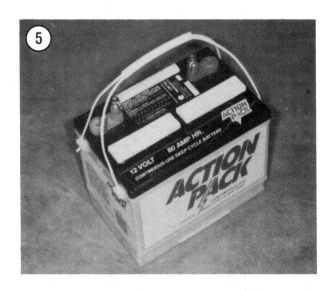

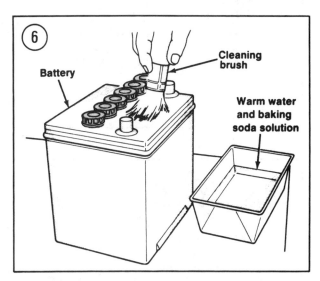

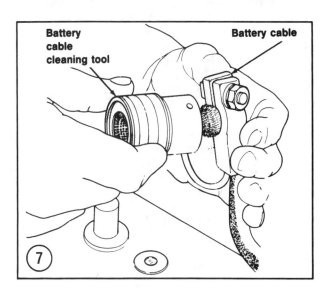

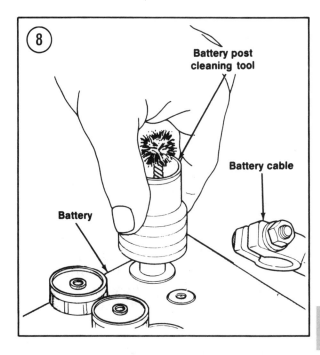

7

NOTE
*Some batteries have a built-in carry strap (**Figure 5**) for use in Step 3.*

3. Attach a battery carry strap to the terminal posts. Remove the battery from the battery tray or container.

4. Check the entire battery case for cracks.

5. Inspect the battery tray or container for corrosion and clean if necessary with a solution of baking soda and water.

NOTE
Keep cleaning solution out of the battery cells in Step 6 or the electrolyte will be seriously weakened.

6. Clean the top of the battery with a stiff bristle brush using the baking soda and water solution (**Figure 6**). Rinse the battery case with clear water and wipe dry with a clean cloth or paper towel.

7. Position the battery in the battery tray or container.

8. Clean the battery cable clamps with a stiff wire brush or one of the many tools made for this purpose (**Figure 7**). The same tool is used for cleaning the battery posts. See **Figure 8**.

9. Reconnect the positive battery cable, then the negative cable.

> *CAUTION*
> *Be sure the battery cables are connected to their proper terminals. Connecting the battery backwards will reverse the polarity and damage the rectifier.*

10. Tighten the battery connections and coat with a petroleum jelly such as Vaseline or a light mineral grease.

> *NOTE*
> *Do not overfill the battery cells in Step 11. The electrolyte expands due to heat from charging and will overflow if the level is more than 3/16 in. above the battery plates.*

11. Remove the filler caps and check the electrolyte level. Add distilled water, if necessary, to bring the level up to 3/16 in. above the plates in the battery case. See **Figure 9**.

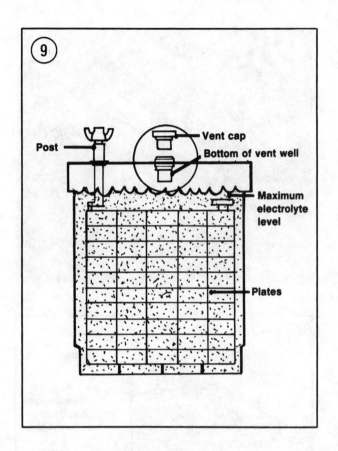

Testing

Hydrometer testing is the best way to check battery condition. Use a hydrometer with numbered graduations from 1.100-1.300 rather than one with just color-coded bands. To use the hydrometer, squeeze the rubber ball, insert the tip in a cell and release the ball (**Figure 10**).

> *NOTE*
> *Do not attempt to test a battery with a hydrometer immediately after adding water to the cells. Charge the battery for 15-20 minutes at a rate high enough to cause vigorous gassing and allow the water and electrolyte to mix thoroughly.*

Draw enough electrolyte to float the weighted float inside the hydrometer. When using a temperature-compensated hydro-

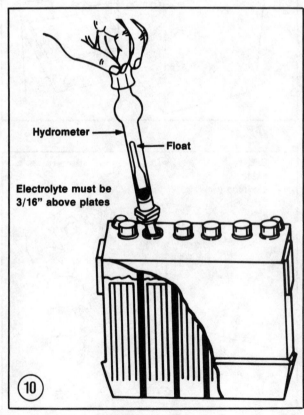

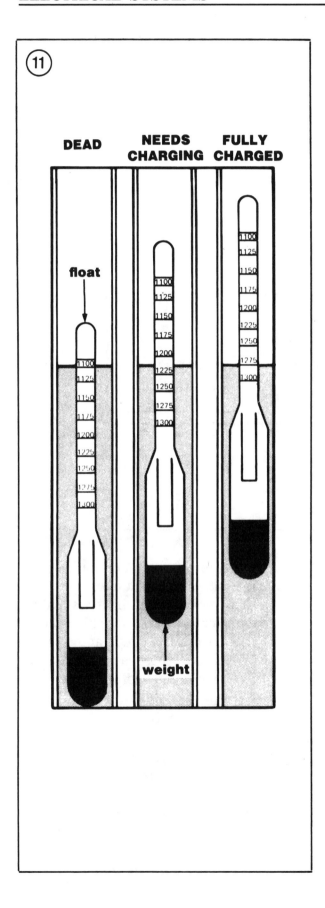

⑪

DEAD   NEEDS   FULLY
              CHARGING   CHARGED

float

weight

meter, release the electrolyte and repeat this process several times to make sure the thermometer has adjusted to the electrolyte temperature before taking the reading.

Hold the hydrometer vertically and note the number in line with the surface of the electrolyte (**Figure 11**). This is the specific gravity for the cell. Return the electrolyte to the cell from which it came.

The specific gravity of the electrolyte in each battery cell is an excellent indicator of that cell's condition. A fully charged cell will read 1.260 or more at 68° F (20° C). A cell that is 75 percent charged will read from 1.220-1.230 while one with a 50 percent charge reads from 1.170-1.180. If the cell tests below 1.120, the battery must be recharged and one that reads 1.100 or below is dead. Charging is also necessary if the specific gravity varies more than 0.050 from cell to cell.

NOTE
If a temperature-compensated hydrometer is not used, add 0.004 to the specific gravity reading for every 10° above 80° F (25° C). For every 10° below 80° F (25° C), subtract 0.004.

Storage

Wet cell batteries slowly discharge when stored. They discharge faster when warm than when cold. See **Table 2**. Before storing a battery for the season, clean the case with a solution of baking soda and water. Rinse with clear water and wipe dry. The battery should be fully charged (no change in specific gravity when 3 readings are taken 1 hour apart) and then stored in as cool and dry a place as possible.

Charging

A good state of charge should be maintained in batteries used for starting.

7

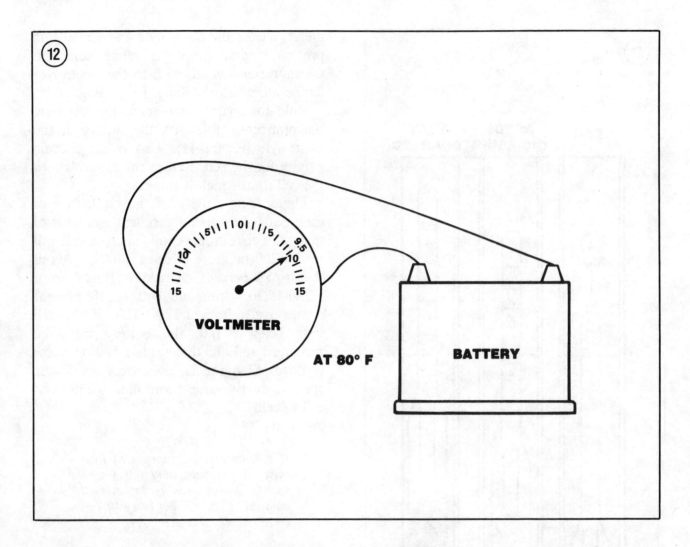

Check the battery with a voltmeter as shown in **Figure 12**. Any battery that cannot deliver at least 9.6 volts under a starting load should be recharged. If recharging does not bring it up to strength or if it does not hold the charge, replace the battery.

The battery does not have to be removed from the boat for charging, but it is a recommended safety procedure since a charging battery gives off highly explosive hydrogen gas. In many boats, the area around the battery is not well ventilated and the gas may remain in the area for hours after the charging process has been completed. Sparks or flames occuring near the battery can cause it to explode, spraying battery acid over a wide area.

For this reason, it is important that you observe the following precautions:

a. Do not smoke around batteries that are charging or have been recently charged.

b. Do not break a live circuit at the battery terminals and cause an electrical arc that can ignite the hydrogen gas.

Disconnect the negative battery cable first, then the positive cable. Make sure the electrolyte is fully topped up.

Connect the charger to the battery— negative to negative, positive to positive. If the charger output is variable, select a 4 amp setting. Set the voltage regulator to 12 volts and plug the charger in. If the battery is severely discharged, allow it to charge for at least 8 hours. Batteries that are not as badly

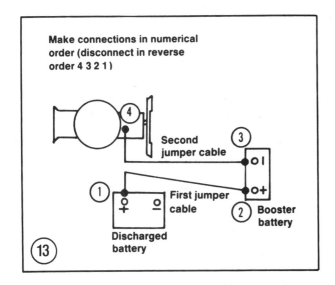

Make connections in numerical order (disconnect in reverse order 4 3 2 1)

Second jumper cable

First jumper cable

Discharged battery

Booster battery

13

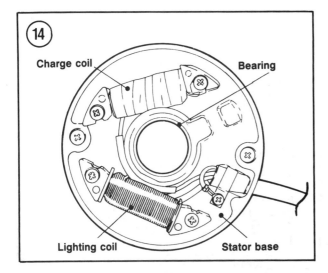

14

Charge coil

Bearing

Lighting coil

Stator base

discharged require less charging time. **Table 3** gives approximate charge rates for batteries used primarily for cranking. Check the charging progress with the hydrometer.

Jump Starting

If the battery becomes severely discharged, it is possible to start and run an engine by jump starting it from another battery. If the proper procedure is not followed, however, jump starting can be dangerous. Check the electrolyte level before jump starting any battery. If it is not visible or if it appears to be

frozen, do not attempt to jump start the battery.

WARNING
Use extreme caution when connecting a booster battery to one that is discharged to avoid personal injury or damage to the system.

1. Connect the jumper cables in the order and sequence shown in **Figure 13**.

WARNING
An electrical arc may occur when the final connection is made. This could cause an explosion if it occurs near the battery. For this reason, the final connection should be made to a good ground away from the battery and not to the battery itself.

2. Check that all jumper cables are out of the way of moving engine parts.
3. Start the engine. Once it starts, run it at a moderate speed.

CAUTION
Running the engine at wide-open throttle may cause damage to the electrical system.

4. Remove the jumper cables in the exact reverse order shown in **Figure 13**. Remove the cables at point 4, then 3, 2 and 1.

LIGHTING SYSTEM

An AC lighting system is standard on DT 7.5-DT 50 models and optional on DT 3.5-DT 6 models. This system is used to power lights used for boating or fishing at night. When the engine is running at approximately 4,500-5,000 rpm, the system will deliver 80 watts of 12 volt AC current.

The AC lighting system consists of an AC lighting coil on the magneto stator base (**Figure 14**), permanent magnets located in

7

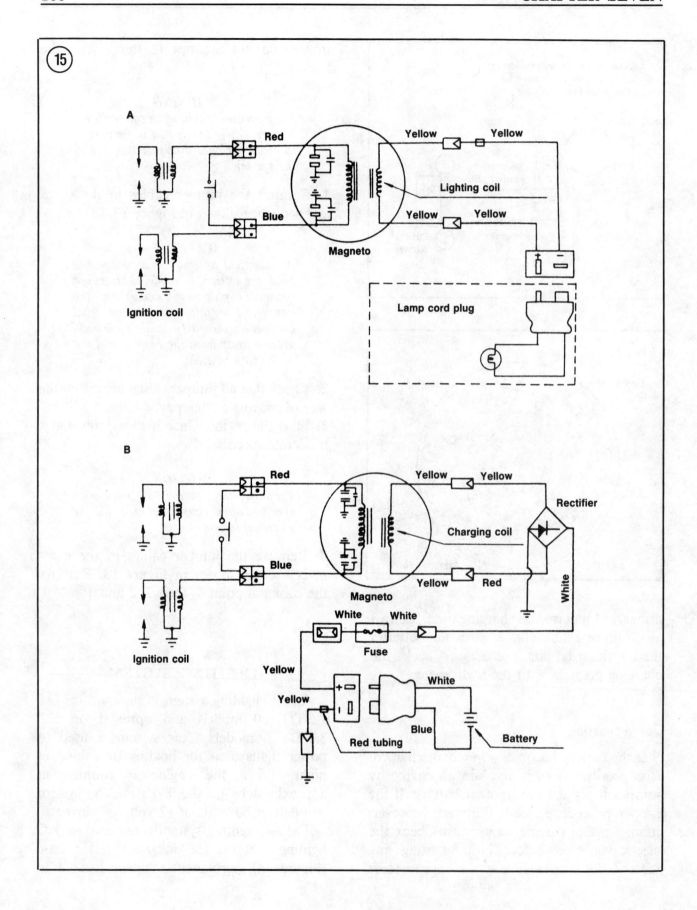

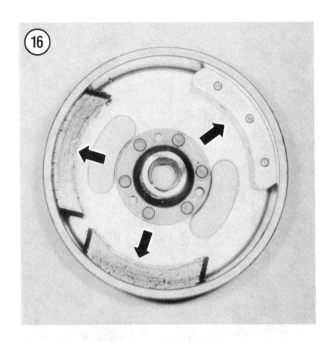

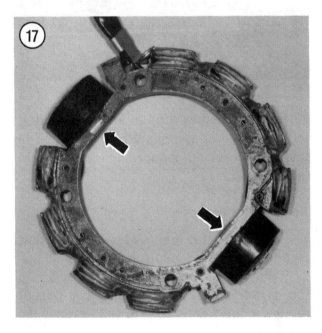

the flywheel rim and connecting wiring between the lighting coil and a plug-in socket.

Rotation of the flywheel magnets past the lighting coil creates alternating current. This current is sent to the plug-in socket installed on the engine cover to power accessories. **Figure 15** includes schematics of a typical AC lighting circuit and DC battery charging circuit.

Lighting Coil Replacement

Refer to **Figure 14** for this procedure.
1. Remove the engine cover.
2. Remove the flywheel. See Chapter Eight.

NOTE
One of the coil leads in Step 3 may be red or yellow/red instead of yellow as specified.

3. Disconnect the 2 yellow lighting coil leads at the quick-disconnect terminals (A, **Figure 15**).
4. Remove the lighting coil ground lead screw. Remove the 2 coil mounting screws. Remove the coil from the stator base.
5. Installation is the reverse of removal. Be sure to reconnect ground lead and route wires so they do not contact or interfere with any moving components.

BATTERY CHARGING SYSTEM

A battery charging system is standard on all electric start models and optional on DT 3.5 and larger manual models equipped with an AC lighting system.

The battery charging system on DT 3.5-DT 65 Suzuki outboards consists of the AC lighting coil, permanent magnets located in the flywheel rim (**Figure 16**), a rectifier, battery and connecting wiring with a 20 amp fuse. **Figure 15** contains a schematic of a typical battery charging system.

DT 75-DT 140 models with a standard 7 amp charging system use an alternator stator with 2 charge coils and 8 lighting coils (**Figure 17**), permanent magnets located in the flywheel rim (**Figure 16**), a rectifier and connecting wiring. The optional 15 amp system is similar except a rectifier/regulator unit is used in place of the standard rectifier.

7

NOTE
When used in a battery charging system, the AC lighting coil is referred to as a battery charging coil.

Rotation of the flywheel magnets past the AC lighting coil(s) creates alternating current. This current is sent to the rectifier (A, **Figure 18**) where it is converted into direct current and then supplied to the battery or electrical accessories through a fuse (B, **Figure 18**).

A malfunction in the battery charging system will result in an undercharged battery. Perform the following visual inspection to determine the cause of the problem. If the visual inspection proves satisfactory, test the lighting coil and rectifier. See Chapter Three.

1. Check the fuse in the line between the rectifier and battery (B, **Figure 18**).
2. Make sure that the battery cables are connected properly. The red cable must be connected to the positive battery terminal. If polarity is reversed, check for a damaged rectifier.
3. Inspect the battery terminals for loose or corroded connections. Tighten or clean as required.
4. Inspect the physical condition of the battery. Look for bulges or cracks in the case, leaking electrolyte or corrosion build-up.
5. Carefully check the wiring between the lighting coil and battery for signs of chafing, deterioration or other damage.
6. Check the circuit wiring for corroded, loose or disconnected connections. Clean, tighten or connect as required.
7. Determine if the electrical load on the battery from accessories is greater than the battery capacity.

Battery Charging Coil Replacement

See *Lighting Coil Replacement* in this chapter for DT 3.5-DT 65 engines. On DT

75-DT 140 engines with an alternator stator, the entire stator is replaced as described in this chapter if one or more lighting coils are defective.

Rectifier Replacement

1. Disconnect the red, white and yellow rectifier lead bullet connectors.
2. Remove the bolt holding the rectifier to the power head or electrical component mounting bracket (A, **Figure 18**). Remove the rectifier.
3. Remove the black rectifier ground lead screw. Disconnect the ground lead from the power head.
4. Installation is the reverse of removal.

ELECTRIC STARTING SYSTEMS

Outboards covered in this manual may use a rope-operated mechanical (rewind) starting system or an electric (starter motor) starting

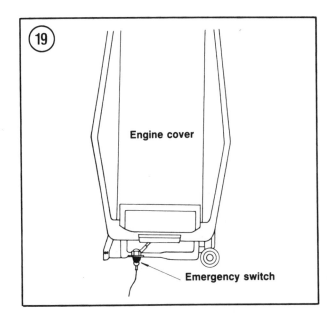

Engine cover

Emergency switch

An optional switch connected into the ignition system shuts the engine off in case of an emergency. Outboards equipped with a remote control have the emergency switch located on the remote box. On outboards using a steering handle, the switch is bracket-mounted on the lower engine cover (**Figure 19**).

Starting system operation and troubleshooting is described in Chapter Three.

STARTER MOTOR

Marine starter motors are very similar in design and operation to those found on automotive engines. They use an inertia-type drive in which external spiral splines on the armature shaft mate with internal splines on the drive assembly.

The starter motor produces very high torque but only for a brief period of time, due to heat buildup. Never operate the starter motor continuously for more than 10 seconds. Let the motor cool for at least 2 minutes before operating it again.

If the starter motor does not turn over, check the battery and all connecting wiring for loose or corroded connections. If this does not solve the problem, refer to Chapter Three. Except for brush replacement, service to the starter motor is limited to replacement with a new or rebuilt unit.

Starter Motor Removal/Installation (Attached Starter Relay)

1. Disconnect the negative battery cable.
2. Remove the engine cover.
3. Disconnect the yellow/green starter relay lead at its bullet connector. Remove the screw holding the black relay ground lead. See A and B, **Figure 20**.

system. Mechanical starters are covered in Chapter Ten.

The electric starting circuit consists of the battery, an ignition switch, neutral start switch, the starter motor, starter relay and connecting wiring. While control of the neutral start switch is a function of the ignition system on most engines, some engines may also have a mechanical starter interlock device to prevent starting in gear.

7

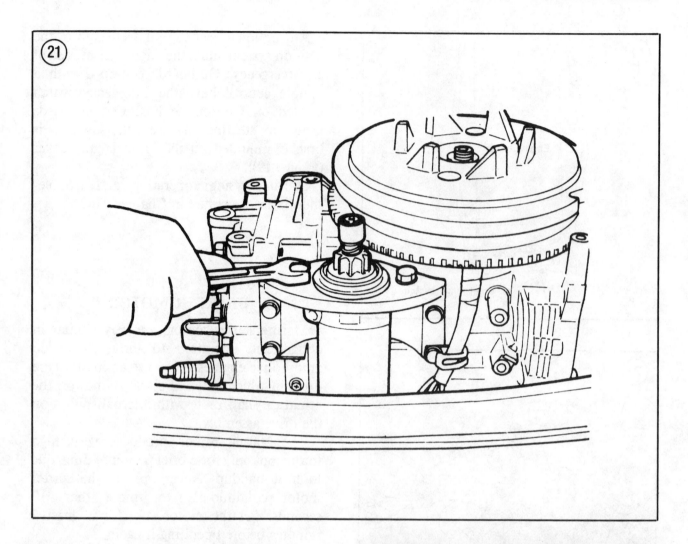

4. Disconnect the battery and starter cables from the relay terminals.

5. Remove the relay (**Figure 20**).

6. DT 40—Remove the clamp holding the starter motor to the base of the mounting bracket.

7. Remove the 2 mounting bolts holding the starter motor to its mounting bracket (**Figure 21**). Remove the starter motor.

8. Installation is the reverse of removal.

Starter Motor Removal/Installation (Remote Starter Relay)

1. Disconnect the negative battery cable.

2. Remove the engine cover.

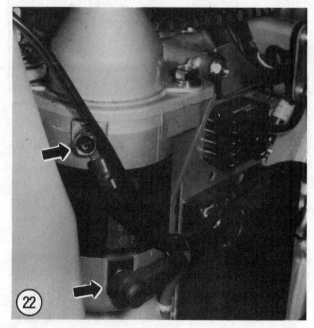

3. Disconnect the starter cables from their terminals. See **Figure 22** (typical).

4. Remove the clamp holding the starter motor to the base of the mounting bracket, if so equipped. See **Figure 23**.

5. Remove the 2 vertical mounting bolts holding the starter motor to its mounting bracket. See **Figure 24**.

6. Lower the starter motor from the mounting bracket and remove from the engine.

7. Installation is the reverse of removal.

Brush Replacement

7

Suzuki outboards use a variety of starter motors, manufactured primarily by Hitachi. Engines may use either a 2- or 4-brush starter design. See **Figure 25** for typical starter components. Always replace brushes in complete sets.

1. Remove the starter as described in this chapter.

2. Remove the 2 through-bolts from the starter.

3. Remove the end cap cover, circlip and thrust washer, if so equipped.

4. Lightly tap on end of starter drive with a rubber mallet until the lower end cap breaks free of starter housing. Remove end cap, taking care not to lose the brush springs.

5. Check brush spring tension by pulling spring back and releasing it. Replace the spring if it does not snap the brush firmly into position.

NOTE
If corrosion causes the brushes to stick during Step 6, replace the brush holder plate.

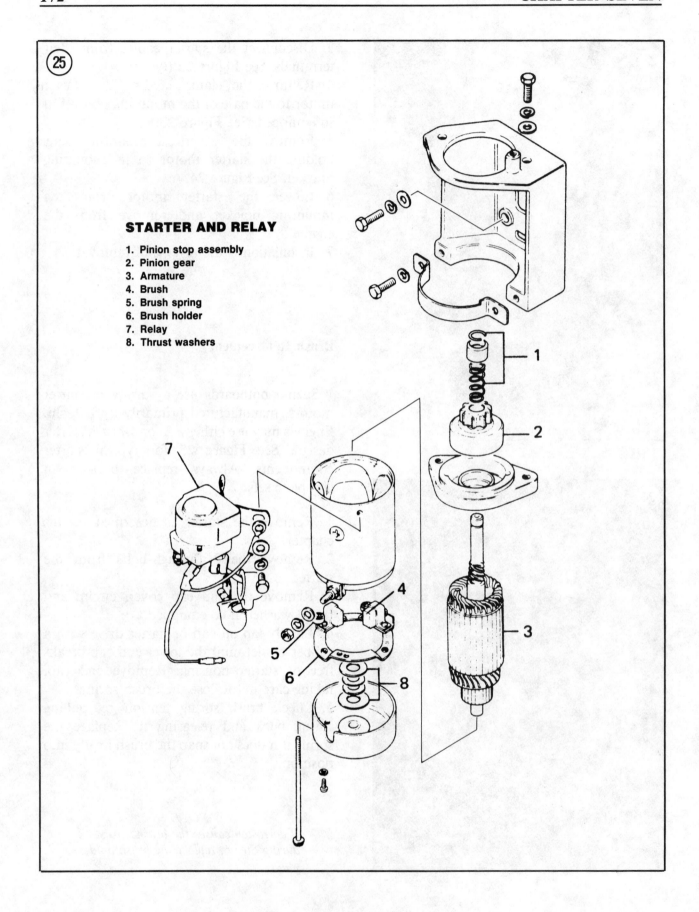

STARTER AND RELAY

1. Pinion stop assembly
2. Pinion gear
3. Armature
4. Brush
5. Brush spring
6. Brush holder
7. Relay
8. Thrust washers

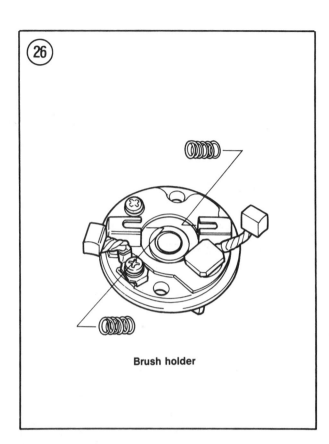

Brush holder

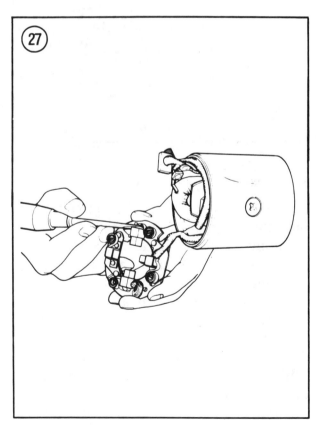

6. Remove the brushes and springs from the brush holder plate. See **Figure 26** or **Figure 27** (typical).

7. Inspect the brushes. Replace all brushes if any are pitted or oil-soaked. Replace brushes if worn to the following dimension or less:

   a. DT 9.9 and DT 15—0.177 in.

   b. 1983-on DT 30 and DT 40—0.354 in.

   c. DT 50—0.374 in.

   d. All others—0.453 in.

8. If brush holder is installed in end cap:

   a. Remove the positive terminal nut, insulators and O-ring. See **Figure 28** (typical).

   b. Remove the screws holding the brush holder to the end cap. See **Figure 29** (typical).

7

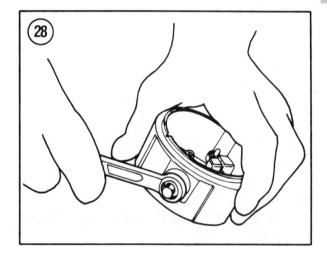

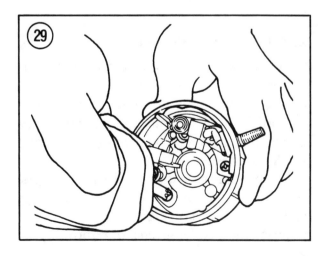

c. Remove the brush holder plate from the end cap.

9. Connect an ohmmeter between the negative and positive brush holders on the brush holder plate (**Figure 30**). Replace the brush holder plate if the meter shows continuity.

10. Install a new positive terminal and brush assembly to the brush holder, if used.

11. Install a new ground brush to the brush holder plate.

12. Fit the springs and brushes into their respective brush holders.

13. Coat end cap bushing bore with water-resistant grease.

14. Press the brushes into the holders and use a narrow strip of flexible metal or plastic as shown in **Figure 31** to keep them in place.

15. Fit brush holder or end cap (containing brush holder) in place, removing the temporary brush retainer as the brushes slip over the commutator.

16. If brush holder is separate from end cap, install end cap to starter frame.

17. Align end cap mark with center of positive terminal or end cap tab with starter frame notch, as appropriate.

18. Install through-bolts and tighten securely.

19. Install thrust washer, circlip and end cap cover, if so equipped.

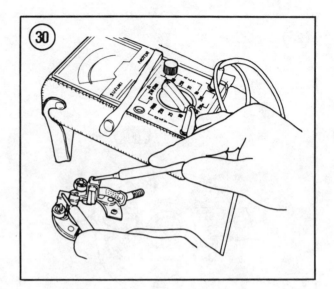

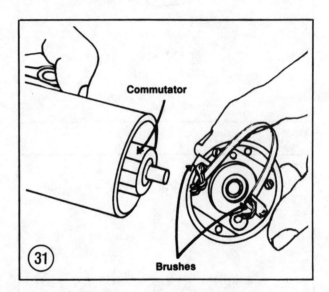

Commutator

Brushes

Starter Relay Replacement

1. Disconnect the negative battery cable.

2. Remove the engine cover.

3. Disconnect the yellow/green starter relay lead at its bullet connector. Remove the screw holding the black relay ground lead. See A and B, **Figure 20**.

4. Disconnect the battery and starter cables from the relay terminals.

5. Remove the relay (**Figure 20**).

6. Installation is the reverse of removal.

Interlock Switch Replacement

The interlock switch is mounted in different locations near the shift lever according to engine size and model year.

1. Disconnect the negative battery cable.

2. Remove the engine cover.

3. Disconnect the brown and yellow/green interlock switch lead wires at their bullet connectors.

4. Remove the mounting screws and washers. See **Figure 32** (typical). Remove the interlock switch.

5. Installation is the reverse of removal.

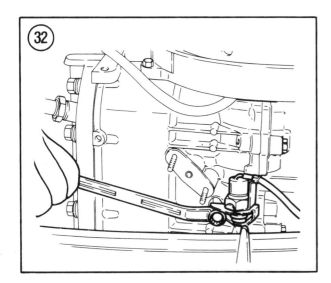

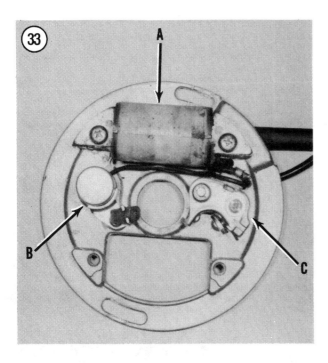

IGNITION SYSTEM

The outboards covered in this manual use one of the following ignition systems:

   a. Magneto breaker point.

   b. Independent magneto Pointless Electronic Ignition (PEI).

   c. Simultaneous magneto Pointless Electronic Ignition (PEI).

Refer to Chapter Three for troubleshooting and test procedures.

MAGNETO BREAKER POINT IGNITION

The DT 2 uses a magneto ignition with a combined primary/secondary ignition coil, a condenser and one set of breaker points.

The DT 3.5 uses a magneto ignition with separate primary and secondary ignition coils, a condenser and one set of breaker points.

Two-cylinder models use a magneto ignition with a single primary ignition coil feeding into 2 separate secondary coils. The primary ignition coil contains 2 sets of windings; one to control the No. 1 cylinder and the other (wound in the opposite direction) to control the No. 2 cylinder.

The primary ignition coil, condenser(s) and breaker point set(s) are mounted on the stator base under the flywheel. **Figure 33** shows the DT 2 stator base with primary/secondary ignition coil (A), condenser (B) and breaker point set (C).

The secondary coil(s) may be found on the port or starboard side of the power head, according to model design.

Troubleshooting and test procedures are given in Chapter Three.

Operation

As the flywheel rotates, magnets around its outer diameter create a current that flows through the closed breaker points. This flow of current through the coil primary winding builds a strong magnetic field. When the cam opens the No. 1 point set, the magnetic field collapses, inducing a high voltage (approximately 18,000 volts) in the coil secondary winding; this voltage is sent to the No. 1 spark plug. The condenser absorbs any residual current remaining in the primary windings. This eliminates arcing at the points and produces a stronger spark at the plug. The breaker points close and the flywheel

7

continues to rotate, duplicating the sequence in 2-cylinder engines for the No. 2 point set and ignition coil to fire the No. 2 spark plug.

Stator Base
Removal/Installation

1. Remove the engine cover.
2. DT 2-DT 3.5—Remove the fuel tank. See Chapter Six.
3. Remove the rewind starter assembly. See Chapter Ten.
4. Remove the flywheel. See Chapter Eight.
5. DT 2—Disconnect the spark plug lead from the spark plug.
6. Disconnect the stator lead wires at their bullet connectors.
7. Remove the screws holding the stator to the magneto housing (**Figure 34**). Remove the stator base.
8. Installation is the reverse of removal.

Breaker Point and
Condenser Replacement

See *Tune-up*, Chapter Four.

Primary Coil
Removal/Installation

1. Remove the stator base as described in this chapter.
2. Disconnect the coil lead wires at the breaker point set and ground.
3. DT 2—Remove the spark plug boot from the plug lead.
4. Remove the 2 screws holding the coil to the stator base.
5A. DT 2—Pull the spark plug lead through the stator base grommet and remove the coil.
5B. All others—Remove the coil from the stator base.
6. Installation is the reverse of removal. On DT 2 models, insert the spark plug lead through the stator base cutout before installing coil mounting screws.

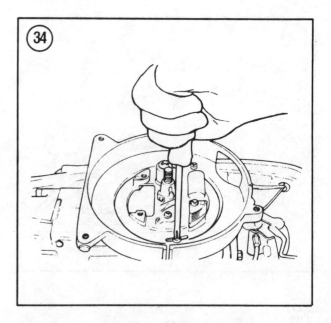

Secondary Coil Replacement

1. Remove the engine cover.
2. Disconnect the coil lead at the spark plug.
3. Disconnect the stator lead at the coil.
4. Remove the coil mounting bolts and washers (**Figure 35**). Remove the coil.
5. Installation is the reverse of removal.

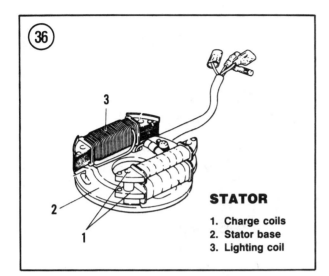

STATOR

1. Charge coils
2. Stator base
3. Lighting coil

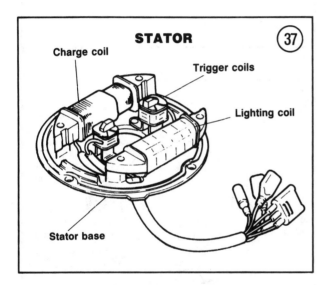

STATOR

Charge coil

Trigger coils

Lighting coil

Stator base

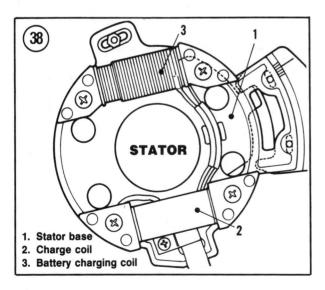

STATOR

1. Stator base
2. Charge coil
3. Battery charging coil

PEI IGNITION

The Suzuki PEI (Pointless Electronic Ignition) system is basically a magneto CDI (capacitor discharge ignition) system. Several variations have been used on the models covered in this manual:

a. DT 20, 1977-1982 DT 25 and DT 50M models have a simultaneous ignition which uses a single secondary coil (with 2 spark plug leads) and two charge coils with different output voltages. See **Figure 36**. The CDI unit combines the 2 different signal waves to electronically advance ignition timing when firing the spark plugs.

b. DT 40-DT 50 models with independent ignition use a single charge coil and 2 trigger coils which supply current to the CDI unit. See **Figure 37**. The CDI unit in turn triggers the 2 ignition coils to fire the spark plugs as required. Ignition advance is mechanical, with the stator base and throttle interlocked.

c. DT 40 and DT 60-DT 65 models with simultaneous ignition use a single charge coil which supplies current to the CDI unit. The CDI unit in turn fires the single secondary coil (with 2 spark plug leads). Ignition advance is mechanical, with the stator base and throttle interlocked.

d. 1980-on DT 9.9, DT 15 and DT 16 models use a single charge coil (**Figure 38**) which supplies current to a combined CDI unit and single secondary coil. Ignition advance is mechanical, with the stator base and throttle interlocked. The 1979 and earlier DT 9.9 and DT 16 models have a single charge coil and 2 trigger coils on a fixed stator base with electrical advance. The CDI unit and secondary ignition coil are separate components.

7

e. DT 5-8 and 1983-on DT 25-DT 30 models use a single charge coil and a trigger coil (**Figure 39**) which supplies current to a combined CDI unit and single secondary coil. Ignition advance is mechanical, with the stator base and throttle interlocked.

f. DT 75-DT 140 models use an alternator stator with 2 charge coils and 8 (3-cylinder) or 10 (4-cylinder) battery charging coils. **Figure 40** shows the 3-cylinder stator. An aluminum timer base underneath the stator contains 2 trigger coils enclosed in iron to help build up the magnetic field and prevent interference from external sources. With 3-cylinder engines, one trigger coil controls the No. 1 and No. 3 cylinders (**Figure 41**). The other trigger coil controls the No. 2 cylinder. On 4-cylinder engines, one trigger coil controls the No. 1 and No. 2 cylinders; the second trigger coil controls the No. 3 and No. 4 cylinders (**Figure 42**). Ignition advance is mechanical, with the timer base and throttle interlocked.

Ignition timing should be adjusted (Chapter Five) whenever a component is replaced.

Operation

The outer rim of the flywheel contains a series of magnets which create a magnetic field during rotation. This magnetic field cuts through the charge coil windings and produces an alternating current of positive and negative waveforms. This current is sent to the CDI unit where it is changed into direct current by an internal rectifier and stored in a capacitor.

On models without a trigger coil, the CDI capacitor is charged by positive waveforms. Negative waveforms cause an electronic switch in the CDI unit to close, discharging the stored voltage into the ignition coil where

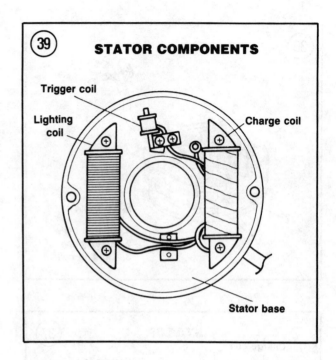

STATOR COMPONENTS

Trigger coil

Lighting coil

Charge coil

Stator base

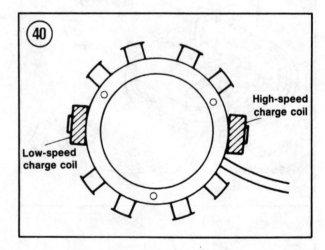

High-speed charge coil

Low-speed charge coil

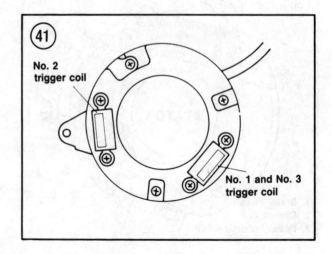

No. 2 trigger coil

No. 1 and No. 3 trigger coil

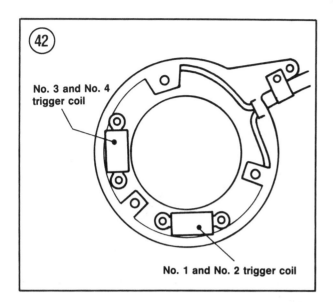

No. 3 and No. 4 trigger coil

No. 1 and No. 2 trigger coil

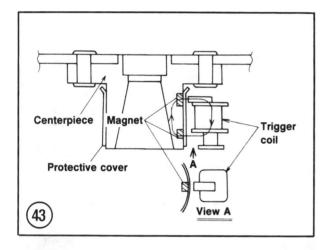

Centerpiece   Magnet

Protective cover

Trigger coil

View A

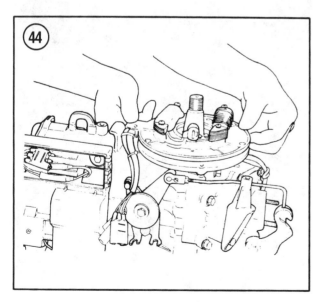

it is stepped up to a higher voltage and sent to the spark plugs.

On models with a trigger coil, the rotation of a timing magnet in the flywheel hub past the trigger coil on the stator base creates a magnetic field. See **Figure 43**. As the flywheel continues to rotate, this magnetic field collapses, inducing a small voltage pulse in the trigger coil. This pulse causes an electronic switch in the CDI module to close, discharging the stored voltage into the ignition coil where it is stepped up to a higher voltage and sent to the spark plugs.

Independent ignitions use a separate ignition coil to fire each cylinder; simultaneous ignitions use a single coil to fire both cylinders. The simultaneous ignition system is also called a "waste spark" system. When the piston in one cylinder is at TDC, the other is at BDTC. If both spark plugs fire at the same time, the spark in the cylinder with the piston at TDC is "used" while the spark in the other cylinder is "wasted."

Depressing the stop switch shorts the charge coil to ground and shuts the engine off. On some models, the charge coil is shorted to ground through a low voltage engine stop circuit to prevent a possible voltage leak.

Stator Base/Alternator Stator Removal/Installation

1. Disconnect the negative battery cable, if so equipped.
2. Remove the engine cover.
3. Remove the flywheel. See Chapter Eight.

NOTE
On DT 40-DT 140 models, the stator lead connections are housed in the junction box.

4. Disconnect the stator leads at their connectors.
5A. Stator base—Remove the screws holding the stator base to the upper oil seal housing. Remove the stator base (**Figure 44**).

5B. Alternator stator—Remove the screws holding the alternator stator to the timer base. Remove the alternator stator (**Figure 45**).

6. Installation is the reverse of removal.

Timer Base Removal/Installation (DT 75-DT 140)

1. Remove the alternator stator as described in this chapter.

2. Disconnect the timer base link from the spark advance lever.

3. Remove the junction box cover and disconnect the trigger coil leads.

4. Remove the timer base retaining screws (**Figure 46**). Remove the timer base.

5. Installation is the reverse of removal.

Charge Coil, Lighting Coil, Battery Charging Coil or Trigger Coil Replacement (Except DT 75-DT 140)

1. Remove the stator base as described in this chapter.

2. Remove the 2 screws holding the defective coil to the stator base.

3. Unwrap the tie straps or wiring harness cover to separate the stator leads. On some models, PVC tubing may have been used to form a wiring harness cover. If so, carefully slit the tubing to remove the coil lead(s).

4. Remove the defective coil from the stator base, pulling its lead(s) through the base cutout.

5. Installation is the reverse of removal. If PVC tubing was used for a wiring harness cover, secure the leads together with tie straps.

Charge Coil or Lighting/ Charging Coil Replacement (DT 75-DT 140)

The alternator stator is replaced as an assembly if any coil is defective.

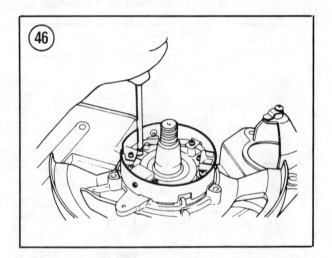

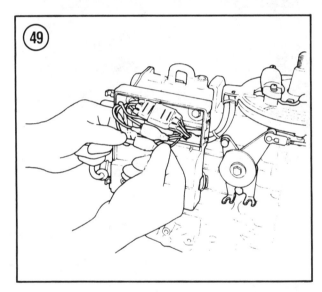

Trigger Coil Replacement (DT 75-DT 140)

See *Charge Coil, Lighting Coil, Battery Charging Coil or Trigger Coil Replacement* in this chapter.

Secondary Ignition Coil Replacement (Individual Unit)

1. Disconnect the negative battery cable, if so equipped.
2. Remove the engine cover.

3. Disconnect the coil primary leads at their bullet connectors. On DT 85-DT 140 models, the connections are inside the junction box (A, **Figure 47**).
4. Disconnect the coil secondary lead at the spark plug (B, **Figure 47**).
5. Remove the coil mounting screws and lockwashers (C, **Figure 47**). Remove the coil.
6. Installation is the reverse of removal. Be sure to reinstall the black ground lead under one of the coil mounting screws.

CDI Unit Removal/Installation (Individual Unit)

1. Disconnect the negative battery cable, if so equipped.
2. Remove the engine cover.
3. Disconnect the CDI unit leads at their bullet connectors. On DT 75-DT 140 models, the connections are inside the junction box (A, **Figure 47**).
4. Remove the CDI unit ground lead screw.
5. Remove the CDI unit mounting screw(s). See **Figure 48** (typical). Remove the CDI unit.
6. Installation is the reverse of removal.

CDI Unit/Secondary Coil Removal/Installation (Combined Unit)

1. Disconnect the negative battery cable, if so equipped.
2. Remove the engine cover.
3. Disconnect the secondary wires at the spark plugs.
4A. 1983-on DT 25-DT 30—Remove the junction box cover and disconnect the 3-wire, yellow and red lead wire connectors. See **Figure 49**.
4B. All others—Disconnect the CDI/coil leads at their bullet connectors.
5A. 1983-on DT 25-DT 30—Remove the 3 bolts holding the electric component assembly to the power head. See **Figure 50**.

7

5B. All others—Remove the screws holding the CDI/coil unit to the power head. See **Figure 51** (typical).

6. Remove the electric component assembly (1983-on DT 25-DT 30) or the CDI/coil unit (all others).

7. 1983-on DT 25-DT 30—From the rear of the electric component assembly, remove the

band holding the CDI/coil unit in place. Remove the CDI/coil unit from the component assembly.

8. Installation is the reverse of removal. Be sure to reinstall the black ground lead under one of the mounting screws.

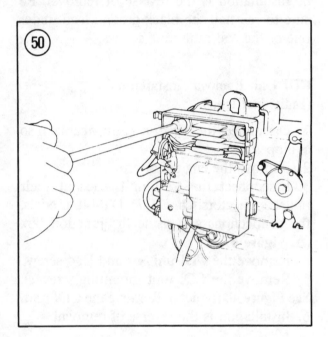

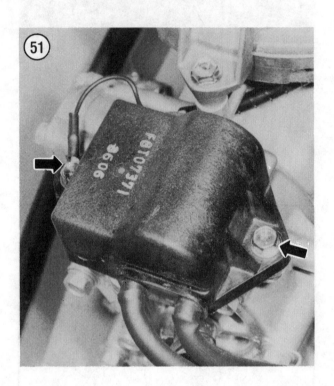

Table 1 BATTERY CAPACITY (HOURS)

Accessory draw	80 amp-hour battery provides continuous power for:	Approximate recharge time
5 amps	13.5 hours	16 hours
15 amps	3.5 hours	13 hours
25 amps	1.8 hours	12 hours
Accessory draw	105 amp-hour battery provides continuous power for:	Approximate recharge time
5 amps	15.8 hours	16 hours
15 amps	4.2 hours	13 hours
25 amps	2.4 hours	12 hours

Table 2 SELF-DISCHARGE RATE

Temperature	Approximate allowable self-discharge per day for first 10 days (specific gravity)
100° F (37.8° C)	0.0025 points
80° F (26.7° C)	0.0010 points
50° F (10.0° C)	0.0003 points

Table 3 TIGHTENING TORQUES

Fastener	in.-lb.	ft.-lb.
CDI unit mounting bolts	30-40	
Flywheel nut		
2A, 3.5, 8A		22-25
2B, air-cooled 5		29-36
4, water-cooled 5, 8B		30-35
9.9, 15C		55-60
15A, W15, 20, early 25, 28		50-57
Late 25		70-80
30,		110-125
40A, 40B, 40 Twin Carb		137
48		109
Standard bolts and nuts		
5 mm	30-47	
6 mm	52-82	
8 mm		10-15
10 mm		20-32
12 mm		25-35

7

Chapter Eight

Power Head

This chapter covers the basic repair of Suzuki outboard power heads. The procedures involved are similar from model to model, with minor differences. Some procedures require the use of special tools, which can be purchased from a dealer. Certain tools may also be fabricated by a machinist, often at substantial savings. Power head stands are available from specialty shops such as Bob Kerr's Marine Tool Co. (P.O. Box 1135, Winter Garden, FL 32787).

Work on the power head requires considerable mechanical ability. You should carefully consider your own capabilities before attempting any operation involving major disassembly of the engine.

Much of the labor charge for dealer repairs involves the removal and disassembly of other parts to reach the defective component. Even if you decide not to tackle the entire power head overhaul after studying the text and illustrations in this chapter, it can be cheaper to perform the preliminary

operations yourself and then take the power head to your dealer. Since many marine dealers have lengthy waiting lists for service (especially during the spring and summer season), this practice can reduce the time your unit is in the shop. If you have done much of the preliminary work, your repairs can be scheduled and performed much quicker.

Repairs go much faster and easier if your motor is clean before you begin work. There are special cleaners for washing the motor and related parts. Just spray or brush on the cleaning solution, let it stand, then rinse it away with a garden hose. Clean all oily or greasy parts with fresh solvent as you remove them.

WARNING
Never use gasoline as a cleaning agent. It presents an extreme fire hazard. Be sure to work in a well-ventilated area when using cleaning solvents. Keep a fire extinguisher rated for gasoline and oil fires nearby in case of emergency.

Once you have decided to do the job yourself, read this chapter thoroughly until you have a good idea of what is involved in completing the overhaul satisfactorily. Make arrangements to buy or rent any special tools necessary and obtain replacement parts before you start. It is frustrating and time-consuming to start an overhaul and then be unable to complete it because the necessary tools or parts are not at hand.

Before beginning the job, re-read Chapter Two of this manual. You will do a better job with this information fresh in your mind.

Remember that new engine break-in procedures should be followed after an engine has been overhauled. Refer to your owner's manual for specific instructions.

Since this chapter covers a large range of models over a lengthy time period, the procedures are somewhat generalized to accommodate all models. Where individual differences occur, they are specifically pointed out. The power heads shown in the accompanying pictures are current designs. While it is possible that the components shown in the pictures may not be identical with those being serviced, the step-by-step procedures may be used with all models covered in this manual.

Tables 1-3 are at the end of the chapter.

ENGINE SERIAL NUMBER

Suzuki outboards are identified by engine serial number and model number. These numbers are stamped on a plate riveted to the port side stern bracket or to the starboard side of the support plate.

This information identifies the outboard and indicates if there are unique parts or if internal changes have been made during the model run. The serial and model numbers should be used when ordering any replacement parts for your outboard.

FASTENERS AND TORQUE

Always replace a worn or damaged fastener with one of the same size, type and torque requirement.

Power head tightening torques are given in **Table 1**. Where a specification is not provided for a given bolt, use the standard bolt and nut torque according to fastener size.

To prevent cylinder head warpage on DT 2-DT 7.5 models, tighten the head bolts to 50 in.-lb.. Continue tightening in 25 in-lb. increments until the specified torque is reached. On DT 8-DT 140 models, tighten to 75 in.-lb. initially, then continue tightening in 50 in.-lb. increments until the specified torque is reached.

Other power head fasteners should be tightened in 2 steps. Tighten to 50 percent of the torque value in the first step, then to 100 percent in the second step.

Retighten the cylinder head bolts after the engine has been run for 15 minutes and allowed to cool. It is a good idea to retorque them again after 10 hours of operation.

To retighten the power head mounting fasteners properly, back them out one turn and then tighten to specifications.

When spark plugs are reinstalled after an overhaul, tighten to the specified torque. Warm the engine to normal operating temperature, let it cool down and retorque the plugs.

8

FLYWHEEL

**Removal/Installation
(DT 2-DT 20; 1977-1982 DT 25)**

1A. DT 2 and DT 3.5—Remove the fuel tank. See Chapter Six.

1B. All others—Remove the engine cover.

2. Disconnect the spark plug lead(s) to prevent accidental starting of the engine.

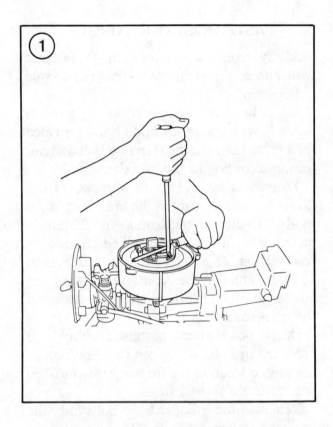

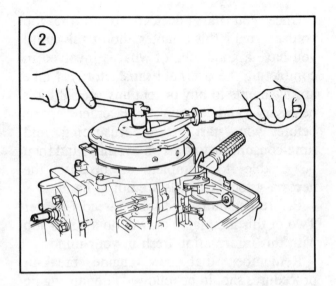

3. Remove the bolt holding the starter rewind cup, if so equipped. Remove the starter cup. **Figure 1** shows the DT 2.

4. Remove the overhead starter, if so equipped. See Chapter Ten.

5. Install flywheel holder (part No. 09930-40113 or equivalent) to hold the flywheel while loosening the flywheel nut. See **Figure 2** (DT 9.9 shown).

6. Remove the flywheel nut and install flywheel puller (part No. 09930-30713 or equivalent) to the flywheel with the puller bolts.

> *CAUTION*
> *Do not strike puller screw with excessive force in Step 7 or crankshaft and/or bearing damage may result.*

7. Hold puller body with puller handle and tighten center screw (**Figure 3**). If flywheel does not pop from the crankshaft taper, lightly tap the puller center screw with a brass hammer (**Figure 4**).

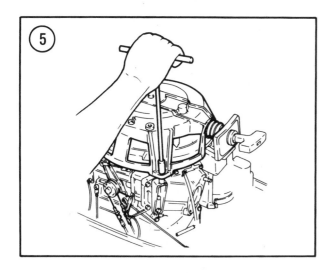

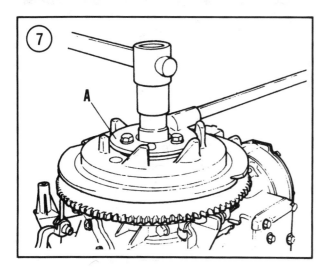

8. Remove puller from flywheel. Remove flywheel from crankshaft. Remove flywheel key from crankshaft if it does not come off with the flywheel.

9. Inspect flywheel carefully as described in this chapter.

10. Install flywheel key, flywheel, starter cup and bolt. Tighten flywheel nut to specifications (**Table 1**).

11A. DT 2-DT 3.5—Install the fuel tank. See Chapter Six.

11B. All others—Install the engine cover.

Removal/Installation
(1983-on DT 25, DT 30, DT 40)

Electric start models require the use of flywheel holder part No. 09930-49410. Manual start models require the use of flywheel holder part No. 09930-39520. Flywheel puller part No. 09930-39410 and puller bolts part No. 09930-39420 are used with both models.

1. Remove the engine cover.

2. Disconnect the negative battery cable or the spark plug leads to prevent accidental starting of the engine.

3. Remove the overhead starter (**Figure 5**). See Chapter Ten. Remove the bolt holding the starter cup, if so equipped. Remove the starter cup.

4. Electric start—Remove the starter motor and bracket (**Figure 6**). See Chapter Seven.

5. Install the appropriate flywheel holder and remove the flywheel nut. See **Figure 7** (manual start).

> *CAUTION*
> *Do not strike puller screw with excessive force in Step 6 or crankshaft and/or bearing damage may result.*

6. Install the puller to the flywheel with the puller bolts. Hold puller body with puller

handle and tighten center screw (**Figure 8**). If flywheel does not pop from the crankshaft taper, lightly tap the puller center screw with a brass hammer (**Figure 9**).

7. Remove puller from flywheel. Remove flywheel from crankshaft. Remove flywheel key from crankshaft if it does not come off with the flywheel.

8. Inspect flywheel carefully as described in this chapter.

9. Inspect crankshaft and flywheel tapers. They must be perfectly dry and free of oil. Swab tapered surfaces with solvent and blow dry with compressed air.

10. Install flywheel key with outer edge of key parallel to the crankshaft centerline.

11. Install the flywheel on the crankshaft.

12. Install flywheel nut and tighten to specifications (**Table 1**).

13. Reverse Steps 1-4 to complete installation.

Removal/Installation (DT 50-DT 140)

1. Remove the engine cover.

2. Disconnect the negative battery cable or the spark plug leads to prevent accidental starting of the engine.

3. Remove the engine hooks (**Figure 10**).

4. Install flywheel holder part No. 09930-49410 or equivalent in the engine hook attaching holes and remove the flywheel nut and washer. See **Figure 11**.

5. Remove the magneto insulator (**Figure 12**), if so equipped.

> *CAUTION*
> *Do not strike puller screw with excessive force in Step 6 or crankshaft and/or bearing damage may result.*

6. Install puller part No. 09930-39410 to the flywheel with the puller bolts. Hold flywheel with the flywheel holder and tighten the puller center screw (**Figure 13**). If flywheel

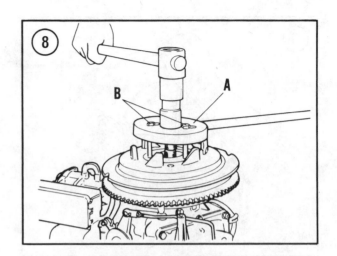

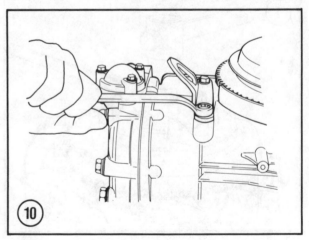

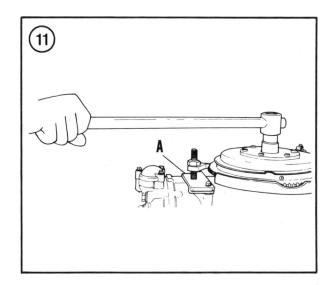

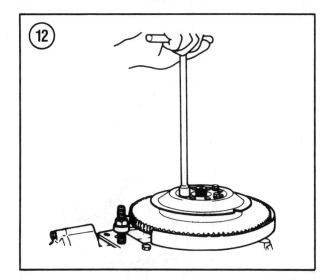

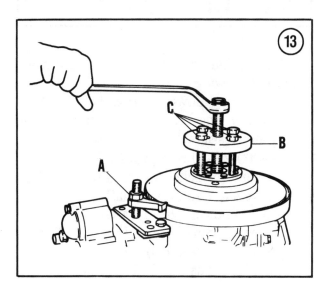

does not pop from the crankshaft taper, lightly tap the puller center screw with a brass hammer (**Figure 9**).

7. Remove puller from flywheel. Remove flywheel from crankshaft. Remove flywheel key from crankshaft if it does not come off with the flywheel.

8. Inspect flywheel carefully as described in this chapter.

9. Inspect crankshaft and flywheel tapers. They must be perfectly dry and free of oil. Swab tapered surfaces with solvent and blow dry with compressed air.

10. Install flywheel key with outer edge of key parallel to the crankshaft centerline.

11. Install the flywheel on the crankshaft.

12. Install the magneto insulator (**Figure 12**), if so equipped.

13. Install flywheel nut and tighten to specifications (**Table 1**).

14. Install the engine hooks (**Figure 10**).

15. Reconnect spark plug leads or negative battery cable. Install the engine cover.

Inspection

1. Check the flywheel carefully for cracks or breaks.

> *WARNING*
> *Cracked or chipped flywheel must be replaced. A damaged flywheel may fly apart at high rpm, throwing metal fragments over a large area. Do not attempt to repair a damaged flywheel.*

2. Check tapered bore of flywheel and crankshaft taper for signs of fretting or working.

3. On electric start models, check the flywheel teeth for signs of excessive wear or damage.

4. Check crankshaft and flywheel nut threads for wear or damage.

5. Replace flywheel, crankshaft and/or flywheel nut as required.

8

POWER HEAD

When removing any power head, it is a good idea to make a sketch or take an instant picture of the location, routing and positioning of electrical wiring, brackets and J-clamps for reassembly reference. Take notes as you remove wires, washers and engine grounds so they may be reinstalled in their correct position. Unless specified otherwise, install lockwashers on the engine side of the electrical lead to assure a good ground.

> *CAUTION*
> *After overhauling an oil-injected engine, the first 30 gallons (5 full tanks) of fuel used should be a 50:1 fuel-oil mixture (see Chapter Four)* **in addition** *to the lubricant supplied by the injection pump. Mark the power head oil tank level and make sure the injection system works properly (oil level diminishes) before switching over to plain gasoline at the end of the 30 gallon break-in period.*

Removal/Installation (DT 2)

1. Remove the starboard and port engine covers. See **Figure 14**.
2. Remove the fuel tank. See Chapter Six.
3. Remove the flywheel as described in this chapter.
4. Disconnect the spark plug lead.
5. Disconnect the 2 stator lead wires.
6. Remove the screws holding the stator (**Figure 15**). Remove the stator.
7. Remove the carburetor and fuel shut-off valve. See Chapter Six.
8. Remove the 6 bolts holding the power head to the drive shaft housing (**Figure 16**). Remove the power head.
9. Remove and discard the power head mounting gasket.
10. Clean the power head mounting and drive shaft housing gasket surfaces of all gasket residue.

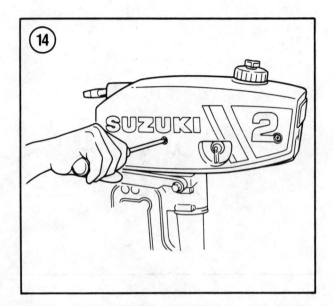

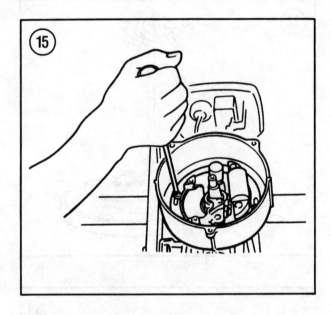

11. Installation is the reverse of removal, plus the following:
   a. Use a new power head gasket.
   b. Lightly coat drive shaft splines with water-resistant grease (part No. 99000-25610 or equivalent).
   c. Rotate propeller as required to align drive shaft and crankshaft splines.
   d. Coat power head attaching screw threads with Thread Lock 1342 (part No. 99000-32050) and tighten to specifications (**Table 1**).

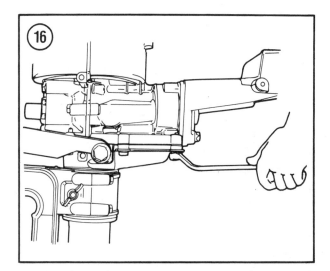

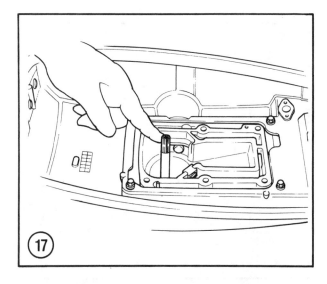

5. Remove the carburetor and fuel pump. See Chapter Six.

6. Disconnect the stator leads. Remove the ignition coil. See Chapter Seven.

7. Remove the flywheel as described in this chapter.

8. Remove the screws holding the stator to the power head. Remove the stator.

NOTE
At this point, there should be no linkage, ground leads or other electrical wiring connecting the power head to the support plate. Recheck to make sure that nothing will hamper power head removal.

9. Remove the 4 bolts and 2 nuts holding the power head to the drive shaft housing. Remove the power head and place on a clean workbench.

10. Remove and discard the power head mounting gasket.

11. Clean the power head mounting and drive shaft housing gasket surfaces of all gasket residue.

12. Installation is the reverse of removal, plus the following:

   a. Lightly coat the drive shaft splines with water-resistant grease (part No. 99000-25160 or equivalent). See **Figure 17**.

   b. Coat power head attaching screw threads with Silicone Seal (part No. 99000-31120) or equivalent.

   c. Tighten all fasteners to specifications (**Table 1**).

   d. Perform engine synchronization and linkage adjustments. See Chapter Five.

8

   e. Tighten all fasteners to specifications (**Table 1**).

   f. Perform engine synchronization and linkage adjustments. See Chapter Five.

**Removal/Installation
(DT 3.5, DT 4.5, DT 7.5 and DT 9)**

1. Remove the engine cover.

2. Disconnect the spark plug leads to prevent accidental starting of the engine.

3. DT 3.5—Remove the fuel tank. See Chapter Six.

4. Remove the overhead starter. See Chapter Ten.

**Removal/Installation
(DT 5, DT 6 and DT 8)**

1. Disconnect the negative battery cable, if so equipped.

2. Remove the engine cover.

3. Disconnect the spark plugs.

4. DT 8—Remove the carburetor silencer cover. See **Figure 18**.

5. Disconnect the fuel line at the carburetor and remove the choke knob.

6. Remove the carburetor, fuel pump and fuel filter. See Chapter Six.

7. Remove the CDI unit (if so equipped) and ignition coil(s). See Chapter Seven.

8. Remove the spool starter. See Chapter Ten.

9. Loosen the throttle cable locknuts (**Figure 19**) and remove the cable.

10. Remove the flywheel as described in this chapter.

11. Disconnect the stator leads. Remove the stator screws (**Figure 20**). Remove the stator.

12. Remove the 4 screws holding the upper oil seal housing to the power head (**Figure 21**).

NOTE
At this point, there should be no linkage, ground leads or other electrical wiring connecting the power head to the support plate. Recheck to make sure that nothing will hamper power head removal.

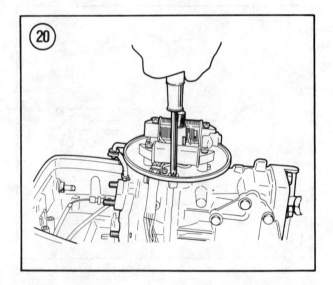

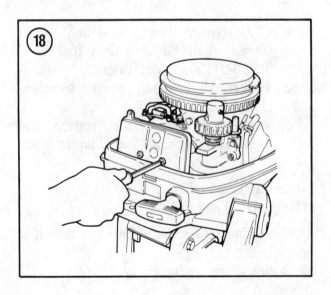

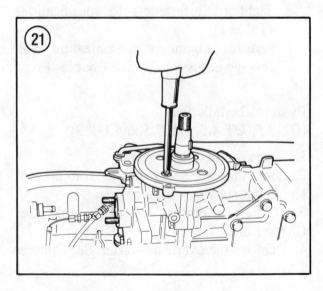

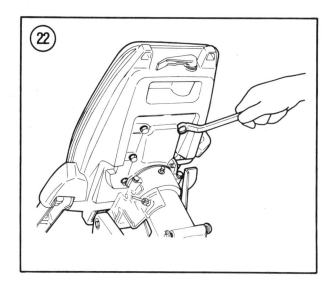

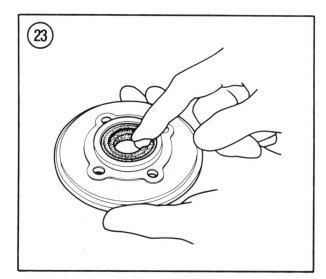

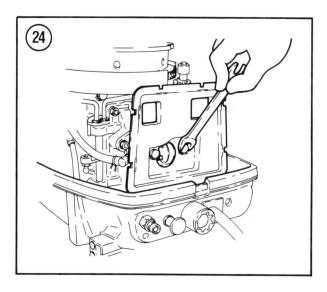

13. Remove the 6 bolts holding the power head to the drive shaft housing (**Figure 22**).

14. Lift the power head from the drive shaft housing and remove from the support plate. Place the power head on a clean workbench.

15. Clean all gasket residue from the power head mounting and drive shaft housing support plate surfaces.

16. Installation is the reverse of removal, plus the following:

  a. Use a new power head mounting gasket.
  b. Lightly coat the drive shaft splines with water-resistant grease (part No. 99000-25160 or equivalent).
  c. Rotate propeller as required to align crankshaft and drive shaft splines.
  d. Install a new upper oil seal housing seal with its lip facing the power head. Lubricate seal lips with Super Grease A (part No. 99000-25010). See **Figure 23**.
  e. Coat power head attaching screw threads with water-resistant grease or equivalent.
  f. Tighten all fasteners to specifications (**Table 1**).
  g. Perform engine synchronization and linkage adjustments. See Chapter Five.

Removal/Installation
(1977-1982 DT 9.9 and DT 16)

1. Remove the engine cover.

2. Electric start—Disconnect the negative battery cable.

3. Disconnect spark plug leads. Remove the spark plugs.

4. Remove the silencer cover and case. **Figure 24** shows the cover removed and the case being removed.

5. Disconnect the fuel line at the lower support. Remove the carburetor, fuel pump and fuel filter. See Chapter Six.

6. Remove the spool or overhead starter, as equipped. See Chapter Ten.

8

7. Disconnect all stator electrical leads. Remove the CDI unit (if so equipped) and the ignition coil(s).

8. Remove the rectifier and starter relay bracket (**Figure 25**).

9. Remove the starter, starter bracket and neutral interlock switch. See Chapter Seven.

10. Loosen the throttle cable locknuts and remove the cable assembly. See **Figure 26**.

11. Remove the flywheel as described in this chapter.

12. Remove the stator assembly from the magneto cover. Remove the bolts holding the magneto cover. Remove the magneto cover.

13. Remove the screws holding the upper oil seal housing to the power head (**Figure 27**). Remove the housing from the power head.

14. From underneath the drive shaft housing, disconnect the interlock rod from the clutch lever plate (**Figure 28**).

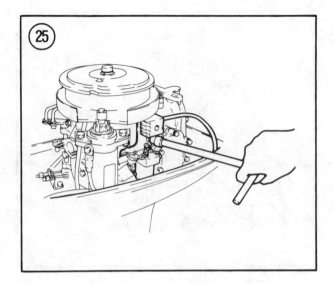

> *NOTE*
> *At this point, there should be no hoses, wires or linkage connecting the power head to the exhaust housing. Recheck this to make sure nothing will hamper power head removal.*

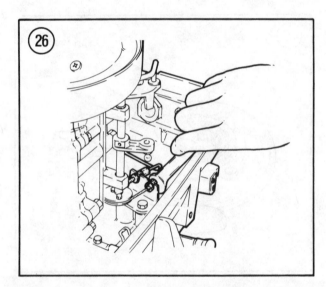

15. Remove the 6 bolts holding the drive shaft housing to the power head.

16. Remove the power head and place it on a clean workbench.

17. Clean all gasket residue from the power head and spacer plate surfaces.

18. Installation is the reverse of removal, plus the following:

    a. Use a new power head gasket.

    b. Lightly coat the drive shaft splines with water-resistant grease (part No. 99000-25160 or equivalent).

    c. Rotate propeller as required to align crankshaft and drive shaft splines.

    d. Install a new upper oil seal housing seal with the lip facing the power head.

    e. Lubricate seal lip with Suzuki Super Grease A (part No. 99000-25010).

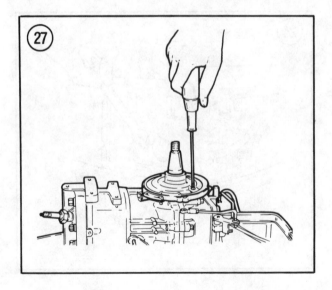

f. Coat power head attaching bolt threads with water-resistant grease.

g. Tighten all fasteners to specifications (**Table 1**).

h. Perform engine synchronization and linkage adjustments. See Chapter Five.

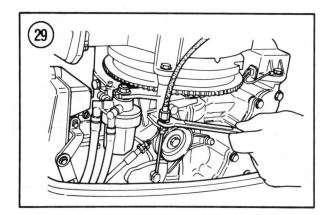

Removal/Installation (1983-on DT 9.9, DT 15, DT 20, 1977-1982 DT 25)

1. Remove the engine cover.

2. Electric start—Disconnect the negative battery cable.

3. Disconnect the spark plug leads. Remove the spark plugs.

4. Remove the overhead or spool starter assembly. See Chapter Ten.

5. Remove the flywheel as described in this chapter.

6. Electric start—Disconnect electrical leads at the following components and remove the components. See Chapter Seven:

   a. Neutral start switch.

   b. CDI unit.

   c. Rectifier (DT 9.9-DT 15) or electrical plate holder (DT 20-DT 25).

   d. Starter relay.

   e. Starter.

   f. Ignition coil(s).

7A. DT 9.9-DT 15—Loosen the neutral starter interlock locknut and disconnect the interlock cable from the throttle limiter (**Figure 29**).

7B. DT 20-DT 25—Disconnect the interlock rod (**Figure 30**).

8. Loosen the throttle cable locknuts and disconnect the cable from the control lever (**Figure 31**), if so equipped.

8

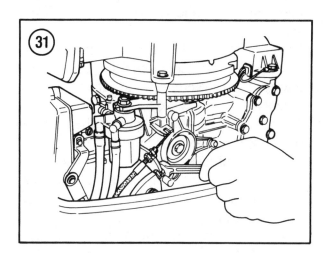

9. Remove the silencer cover and pull off the choke lever knob. Straighten the silencer case tabs (DT 20-DT 25) and remove the silencer case (all models).

10. Remove the flywheel as described in this chapter.

11. Disconnect the stator connector and remove the throttle control lever.

12. Remove the screws holding the stator to the power head. Remove the stator assembly.

13. DT 20-DT 25—Remove the screws holding the upper oil seal housing. Remove the housing.

14. Disconnect the fuel lines and remove the carburetor and fuel pump. See Chapter Six.

15. DT 9.9-DT 15—Remove the nut on the rear of the starter switch assembly and pull the switch from the lower support.

16. DT 9.9-DT 15—Remove the starter cable clamp and grommet. Pull the starter cable from the lower support.

NOTE
At this point, there should be no hoses, wires or linkage connecting the power head to the drive shaft housing. Recheck this to make sure nothing will hamper power head removal.

17. Remove the 6 bolts holding the power head to the drive shaft housing.

18. Remove the power head from the drive shaft housing and place it on a clean workbench.

19. DT 9.9-DT 15—Remove the 4 bolts holding the starter motor bracket to the power head. Remove the starter motor bracket.

20. DT 20-DT 25—Remove the exhaust tube from the base of the power head.

21. Clean all gasket residue from the power head and drive shaft engine holder surfaces.

22. Installation is the reverse of removal, plus the following:

    a. Use a new power head gasket.

    b. Lightly coat drive shaft splines with water-resistant grease (part No. 99000-25610 or equivalent).

    c. Make sure the locating dowels in the drive shaft support plate are in position.

    d. Rotate the propeller as required to align crankshaft and drive shaft splines.

    e. Coat DT 9.9-DT 15 power head attaching bolt threads with Silicone Seal (part No. 99000-31120) or equivalent.

    f. Coat DT 20-DT 25 power head attaching bolt threads with Thread Lock 1342 (part No. 99000-32050) or equivalent.

    g. Install a new upper oil seal housing seal with its lip facing the power head.

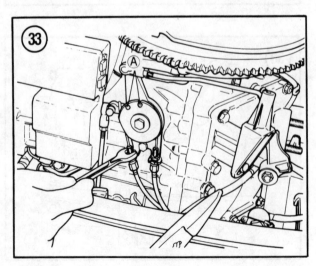

Lubricate seal lips with Super Grease A (part No. 99000-25010). See **Figure 23**.

h. Tighten all fasteners to specifications (**Table 1**).

i. Perform engine synchronization and linkage adjustments. See Chapter Five.

Removal/Installation (1983-on DT 25 and DT 30)

1. Disconnect the negative battery cable.

2. Remove the engine cover.

3. Remove the overhead starter assembly. See Chapter Ten.

4. Remove the carburetor silencer.

5. Remove the junction box cover. Disconnect all electrical leads. Remove the

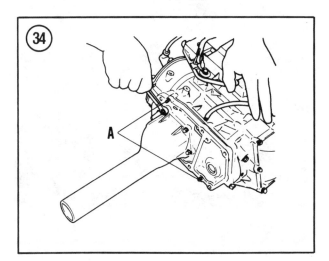

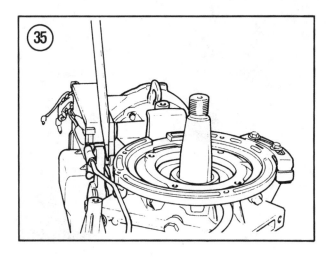

starter relay, starter motor and motor bracket. See Chapter Seven.

6. Remove the clamp holding the battery cable. Remove the battery cable grommet and pull the cable from the lower support.

7. Disconnect the fuel line connections and remove the carburetor. See Chapter Six.

8. Disconnect the throttle rod from the control lever. See **Figure 32**.

9. Loosen the throttle cable locknuts and pull the cable ends (A, **Figure 33**) from the control lever.

NOTE
At this point, there should be no hoses, wires or linkage connecting the power head to the drive shaft housing. Recheck this to make sure nothing will hamper power head removal.

10. Remove the 8 bolts holding the power head to the drive shaft housing.

11. Remove the power head from the drive shaft housing and place it on a clean workbench.

12. Remove the 5 bolts and 2 dowel pins (A, **Figure 34**) holding the exhaust tube and lower oil seal housing to the power head.

13. Clean all gasket residue from the power head and drive shaft housing surfaces.

14. Remove the fuel filter and fuel pump. See Chapter Six.

15. Remove the flywheel as described in this chapter.

16. Remove the screws holding the stator assembly to the power head. Remove the stator assembly.

17. Remove the 4 screws holding the stator retainer and upper oil seal housing. Disconnect the stator retainer-to-throttle control lever connector (**Figure 35**). Remove the assembly and discard the gasket.

18. Remove the electrical parts holder, throttle control lever, throttle cable stay, overhead starter brace and lubrication hose.

8

19. Installation is the reverse of removal, plus the following:

a. Install the lubrication hose with the check valve arrow pointing toward the top of the power head. See **Figure 36**.

b. Use a new power head gasket.

c. Install a new upper oil seal housing seal with its lip facing the power head. Lubricate seal lips with Super Grease A (part No. 99000-25030) or equivalent.

d. Install a new lower oil seal housing seal with its lip facing away from the power head. Lubricate seal lips with Silicone Seal (part No. 99000-31120) or equivalent.

e. Lightly coat the drive shaft splines with water-resistant grease (part No. 99000-25160) or equivalent.

f. Make sure the locating dowels in the drive shaft support plate are in position.

g. Rotate the propeller as required to align crankshaft and drive shaft splines.

h. Coat the power head attaching bolt threads with Silicone Seal (part No. 99000-31120 or equivalent).

i. Tighten all fasteners to specifications (**Table 1**).

j. Perform engine synchronization and linkage adjustments. See Chapter Five.

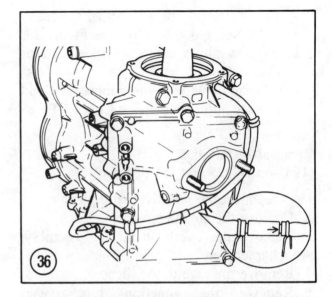

Removal/Installation (DT 40-DT 65)

1. Disconnect the negative battery cable.

2. Remove the engine cover.

3. Disconnect the spark plug leads. Remove the spark plugs.

4. Remove the carburetor silencer cover. Remove the silencer case, if so equipped.

5. Disconnect the throttle rod (**Figure 37**).

6. Disconnect the choke solenoid lead, if so equipped. Remove the choke knob.

7. Disconnect the carburetor lines. Disconnect the fuel line at the lower support

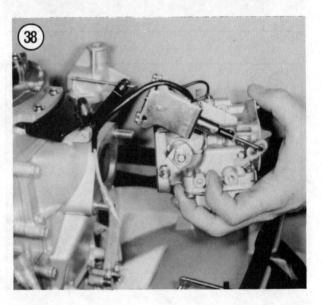

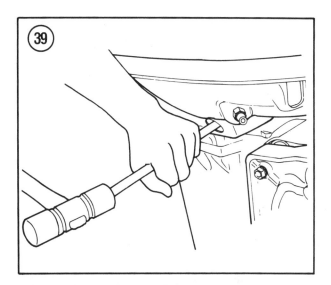

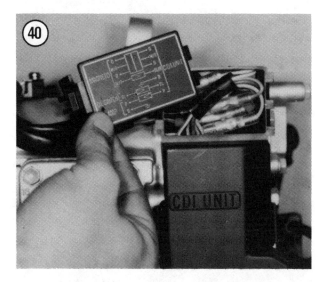

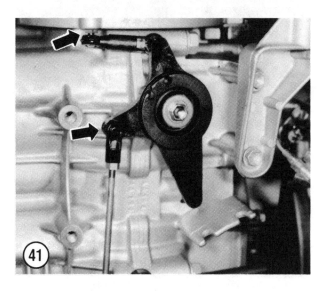

inlet. Remove the carburetor(s) and choke solenoid (**Figure 38**).

8. DT 50-DT 65—Remove the grommet on the starboard side of the drive shaft housing. Insert an appropriate size socket wrench and remove the clutch shaft nuts, then disconnect the clutch rod and shaft with a punch and hammer. See **Figure 39**.

9. Manual start—Remove the overhead starter assembly. See Chapter Ten.

10. If equipped with oil injection, remove the oil tank. See Chapter Twelve.

11. Disconnect the starter motor and relay leads. Remove the starter motor assembly. See Chapter Seven.

12. Remove the junction box cover (**Figure 40**) and disconnect all electrical leads.

13. Remove the ignition coil and CDI unit. Remove the electric parts holder, if so equipped.

14. If equipped with power trim, remove the power trim solenoids. See Chapter Eleven.

15. Remove the neutral start interlock switch.

16. Disconnect the throttle control link rods and remove the throttle lever. See **Figure 41**.

> *NOTE*
> *Steps 17-21 apply to DT 50-DT 65 models only. At this point, there should be no hoses, wires or linkage connecting the power head to the drive shaft housing. Recheck this to make sure nothing will hamper power head removal.*

17. DT 50-DT 65:
   a. Remove the 8 bolts and 1 nut holding the power head to the drive shaft housing.

> *WARNING*
> *If a hoist is not available for use in Step b, have an assistant help with power head removal to avoid possible serious personal injury.*

8

b. Attach a hoist to the engine hooks and remove the power head from the drive shaft housing.

c. Place the power head on a clean workbench.

d. Remove the fuel filter and fuel pump. See Chapter Six.

e. Remove the clutch link pin (**Figure 42**).

18. Remove the flywheel as described in this chapter.

19. Remove the screws holding the stator assembly to the power head. Remove the stator assembly (**Figure 43**).

20. Remove the upper oil seal housing (**Figure 44**).

21. Remove the spark advance lever and bracket (**Figure 45**). Remove the starter motor brackets.

NOTE
Step 22 and Step 23 apply to DT 40 models only. At this point, there should be no hoses, wires or linkage connecting the DT 40 power head to the drive shaft housing. Recheck this to make sure nothing will hamper power head removal.

22. DT-40:
   a. Loosen the clutch rod turnbuckle (**Figure 46**).
   b. Remove the bolts holding the power head to the drive shaft housing.
   c. Remove the power head from the drive shaft housing and place it on a clean workbench.
   d. Remove the fuel filter and fuel pump. See Chapter Six.
   e. Remove the starter motor bracket.

23. If equipped with oil injection, remove the oil pump and driven gear assembly. See Chapter Twelve.

24. Installation is the reverse of removal, plus the following:
   a. Use a new power head gasket.
   b. Install a new upper oil seal housing seal with its lip facing the power head.

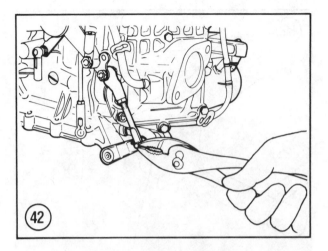

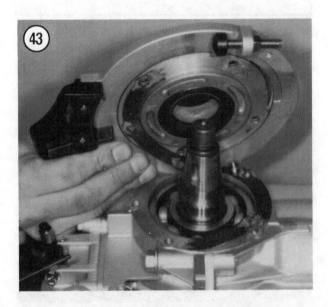

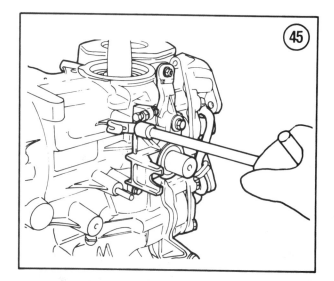

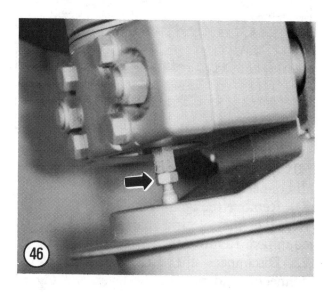

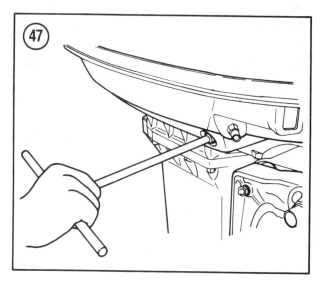

Lubricate seal lips with Super Grease A (part No. 99000-25030) or equivalent.

c. Fill the cavity between the lower oil seal and backup oil seal in the lower oil seal housing with water-resistant grease (part No. 99000-25160) or equivalent.

d. Lightly coat the drive shaft splines with water-resistant grease.

e. Make sure the locating dowels in the drive shaft support plate are in position, if so equipped.

f. Rotate the propeller as required to align crankshaft and drive shaft splines.

g. DT 40—Coat the power head attaching bolt threads with Thread Lock 1342 (part No. 99000-32050) or equivalent.

h. DT 50-DT 65—Coat the power head attaching bolt threads with Silicone Seal (part No. 99000-31120) or equivalent.

i. DT 50-DT 65—Coat the silencer cover bolt threads with Thread Lock 1342.

j. Tighten all fasteners to specifications (**Table 1**).

k. Perform engine synchronization and linkage adjustments. See Chapter Five.

**Removal/Installation
(DT 75-DT 85)**

1. Remove the engine top cover.

2. Remove the lower front and rear engine covers.

3. Disconnect the negative battery cable.

4. Remove the battery cable clamp, disconnect the cable grommet from the lower support housing and remove the cables.

5. Disconnect the spark plug leads. Remove the spark plugs.

6. Disconnect the fuel line at the lower support housing fuel inlet and remove the fuel filter. See Chapter Six.

7. Remove the grommet on the starboard side of the drive shaft housing. Insert an appropriate size socket wrench and remove the clutch shaft nuts (**Figure 47**), then

8

disconnect the clutch rod and shaft with a punch and hammer.

> *NOTE*
> *At this point, there should be no hoses, wires or linkage connecting the power head to the drive shaft housing. Recheck this to make sure nothing will hamper power head removal.*

8. Remove the 8 bolts and 1 nut holding the power head to the drive shaft housing.

> *WARNING*
> *If a hoist is not available for use in Step 9, have an assistant help with power head removal to avoid possible serious personal injury.*

9. Attach a hoist to the engine hooks and remove the power head from the drive shaft housing.

10. Check the power head base for alignment dowel pins. If any came off with the power head, remove and reinstall in the drive shaft housing mounting flange.

11. Place the power head on a clean workbench or suitable power head stand.

12. Remove the oil injection tank. See Chapter Twelve.

13. Remove the carburetor silencer cover, straighten the case lockwashers and remove the case. See **Figure 48**.

14. Disconnect the throttle and oil pump control rods.

15. Disconnect the orange choke solenoid lead. Remove the carburetors and solenoid. See Chapter Six.

16. Remove the fuel pump and insulator assembly. See Chapter Six.

17. Remove the power trim solenoids. See Chapter Eleven.

18. Remove the oil injection check valves, pump and driven gear retainer. See Chapter Twelve.

19. Remove the starter motor and relay. See Chapter Eight.

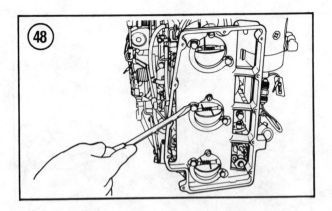

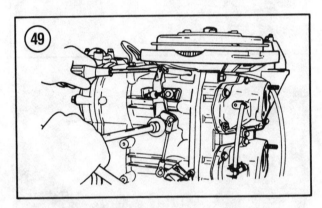

20. Remove the junction box cover and disconnect all electrical leads.

21. Remove the ignition coils and CDI unit. Remove the electric parts holder, if so equipped. Remove the wiring harness.

22. Disconnect the spark advance lever connector and remove the lever. See **Figure 49**.

23. Remove the throttle control lever and link.

24. Remove the spark advance adjustment plate.

25. Remove the clutch control arm (**Figure 50**).

26. Remove the flywheel as described in this chapter.

27. Remove the screws holding the stator assembly to the power head. Remove the stator assembly.

28. Remove the screws holding the timer base and sensor assembly. Remove the assembly.

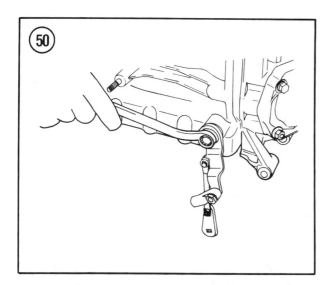

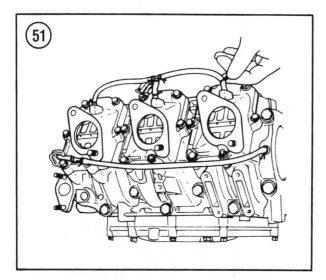

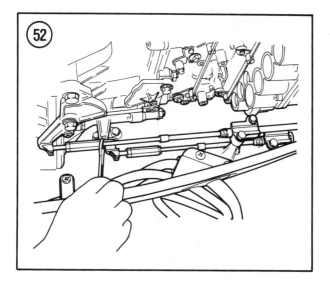

29. Remove the upper oil seal housing.

30. Remove the starter mounting bracket.

31. Note how the lubrication hoses are connected (**Figure 51**), then disconnect and remove them from the power head brackets.

32. Installation is the reverse of removal, plus the following:

   a. Use a new power head gasket.

   b. Install a new upper oil seal housing seal with its lip facing the power head. Lubricate seal lips with Super Grease A (part No. 99000-25030) or equivalent.

   c. Fill the cavity between the lower oil seal and backup oil seal in the lower oil seal housing with water-resistant grease (part No. 99000-25160) or equivalent.

   d. Lightly coat the drive shaft splines with water-resistant grease.

   e. Make sure the locating dowels in the drive shaft support plate are in position, if so equipped.

   f. Rotate the propeller as required to align crankshaft and drive shaft splines.

   g. Coat the power head attaching bolt threads with Silicone Seal (part No. 99000-31120) or equivalent.

   h. Tighten all fasteners to specifications (**Table 1**).

   i. Install the coils in sequence according to the number on the secondary lead. The coil with the lead marked "1" should be installed to the No. 1 cylinder, etc.

   j. Perform engine synchronization and linkage adjustments. See Chapter Five.

**Removal/Installation
(DT 115-DT 140)**

1. Remove the engine top cover.

2. Remove the 4 bolts holding the lower engine holder covers. Lower the covers.

3. Disconnect the negative battery cable.

4. Disconnect the clutch and throttle cables (**Figure 52**).

5. Disconnect the electrical coupler between the remote control cable and power trim unit.

6. Disconnect the spark plug leads. Remove the spark plugs.

7. Remove the battery cables. See **Figure 53**. Disconnect the electrical connector (A, **Figure 53**).

8. Remove the oil injection tank. See Chapter Twelve.

9. Disconnect the water inspection and fuel lines at the lower support housing.

NOTE
At this point, there should be no hoses, wires or linkage connecting the power head to the drive shaft housing. Recheck this to make sure nothing will hamper power head removal.

10. Remove the 8 bolts and 2 nuts holding the power head to the drive shaft housing.

WARNING
If a hoist is not available for use in Step 11, have an assistant help with power head removal to avoid possible serious personal injury.

11. Attach a hoist to the engine hooks and remove the power head fron the drive shaft housing.

12. Check the power head base for alignment dowel pins. If any came off with the power head, remove and reinstall in the drive shaft housing mounting flange.

13. Place the power head on a clean workbench or suitable power head stand.

14. Remove the starter motor. See Chapter Eight.

15. Remove the junction box cover and disconnect all electrical leads.

16. Remove the choke solenoid.

17. Remove the electrical parts holder (**Figure 54**).

18. Remove the flywheel as described in this chapter.

19. Remove the 3 screws holding the stator and timer sensor assembly. Remove the assembly.

20. Remove the 4 nuts holding the link rods and throttle cam assembly. Remove the assembly.

21. Remove the carburetor silencer cover and gasket. Remove the silencer case and gasket.

22. Remove the starter bracket.

23. Remove the fuel filter and the fuel pump/insulator assembly. See Chapter Six.

24. Disconnect the oil injection pump control rod. Remove the oil injection pump and driven gear retainer. See Chapter Twelve.

25. Remove the upper oil seal housing.

26. Installation is the reverse of removal, plus the following:

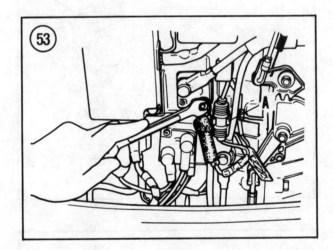

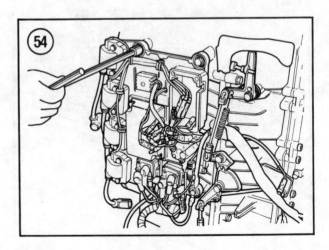

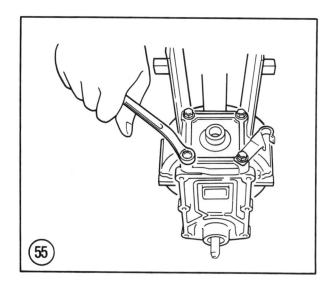

a. Use a new power head gasket.

b. Install a new upper oil seal housing seal with its lip facing the power head. Lubricate seal lips with Super Grease A (part No. 99000-25030) or equivalent.

c. Fill the cavity between the lower oil seal and backup oil seal in the lower oil seal housing with water-resistant grease (part No. 99000-25160) or equivalent.

d. Lightly coat the drive shaft splines with water-resistant grease.

e. Make sure the locating dowels in the drive shaft support plate are in position, if so equipped.

f. Rotate the propeller as required to align crankshaft and drive shaft splines.

g. Coat the power head attaching bolt and nut threads with Thread Lock 1341 (part No. 99000-32050) or equivalent.

h. Tighten all fasteners to specifications (**Table 1**).

i. Install the coils in sequence according to the number on the secondary lead. The coil with the lead marked "1" should be installed to the No. 1 cylinder, etc.

j. Perform engine synchronization and linkage adjustments. See Chapter Five.

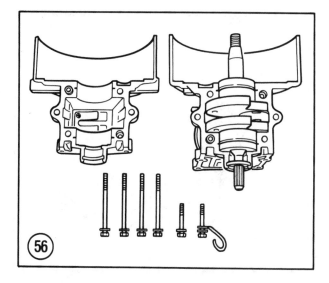

Disassembly
(DT 2)

1. Remove the carburetor and intake manifold assembly.

2. Loosen the 4 cylinder head nuts (**Figure 55**) in several stages to prevent head warpage. Remove the head and gasket. Discard the gasket.

3. Loosen the 6 crankcase bolts in several stages. Carefully pry apart and separate the crankcase halves (**Figure 56**).

4. Remove the O-ring from the crankshaft lower end. Hold the crankshaft in one hand and carefully pull the cylinder block off the piston (**Figure 57**).

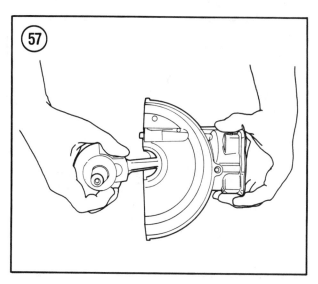

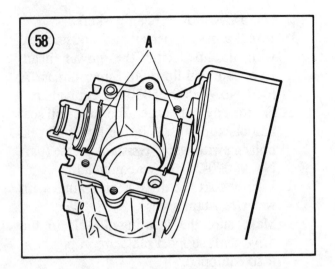

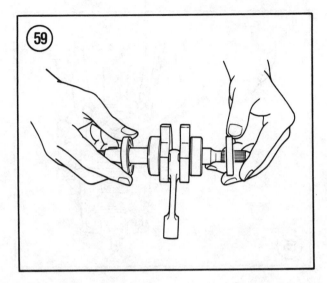

5. Remove the crankshaft thrust rings (A, **Figure 58**).

6. If the piston is to be removed from the connecting rod:

    a. Cup one hand around the piston and carefully pry out the piston pin circlip, catching it as it comes free. Repeat this step to remove the opposite piston pin circlip.

    b. Push the piston pin from the piston/connecting rod with a suitable size drift.

    c. Remove the piston and caged needle bearing from the connecting rod.

7. Remove the upper and lower crankshaft oil seals (**Figure 59**).

8. Carefully spread and remove the piston rings as shown in **Figure 60**.

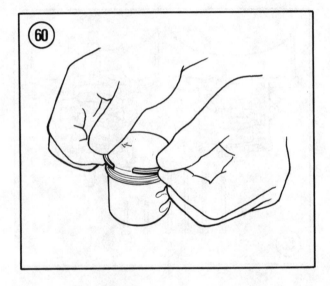

Disassembly (DT 3.5)

1. Remove the carburetor, intake manifold and reed valve assembly.

2. Loosen the 4 cylinder head nuts (**Figure 55**) in several stages to prevent head warpage. Remove the head and gasket. Discard the gasket.

3. Remove the inlet case bolts and inlet case.

4. Loosen the 4 crankcase bolts in several stages. Carefully pry apart and separate the crankcase halves.

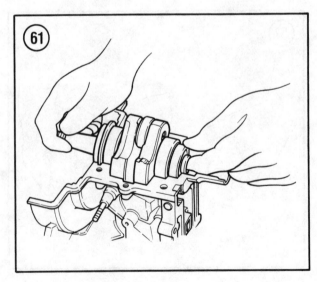

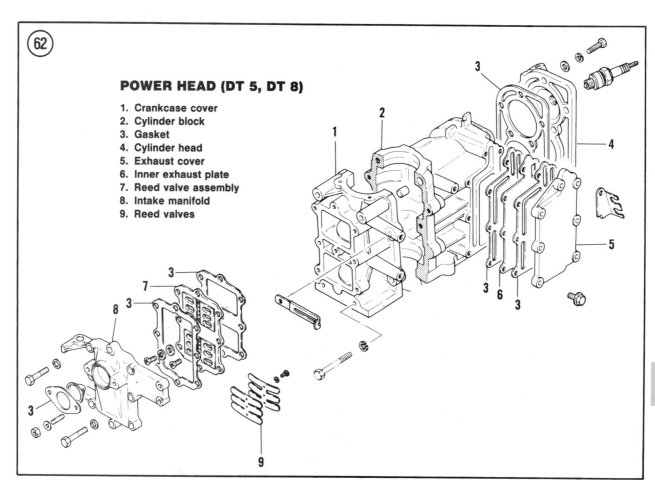

POWER HEAD (DT 5, DT 8)

1. Crankcase cover
2. Cylinder block
3. Gasket
4. Cylinder head
5. Exhaust cover
6. Inner exhaust plate
7. Reed valve assembly
8. Intake manifold
9. Reed valves

5. Carefully lift the crankshaft from the crankcase half (**Figure 61**).

6. If the piston is to be removed from the connecting rod:

   a. Cup one hand around the piston and carefully pry out the piston pin circlip, catching it as it comes free. Repeat this step to remove the opposite piston pin circlip.

   b. Push the piston pin from the piston/connecting rod with a suitable size drift.

   c. Remove the piston and caged needle bearing from the connecting rod.

7. Remove the upper crankshaft bearing. Remove the lower crankshaft oil seal and bearing.

8. Carefully spread and remove the piston rings as shown in **Figure 60**.

Disassembly
(All 2-cylinder Engines)

A large number of bolts and screws of different lengths are used to secure the various covers and components. It is a good idea to use a cupcake tin or similar compartmented container to hold the various fasteners removed from each cover or component. This will make reassembly easier and faster.

Some power heads have pry points in the casting for easier removal of each component. If no pry points are provided, break the gasket seal with a wide-blade putty knife and mallet, then carefully separate the components.

Refer to **Figures 62-64** (typical) for this procedure.

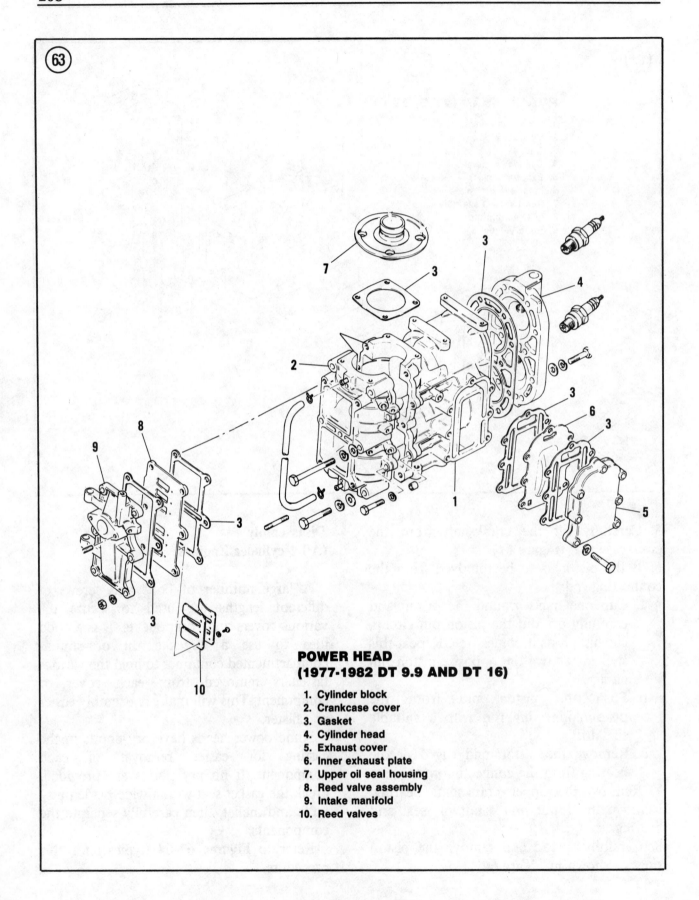

POWER HEAD
(1977-1982 DT 9.9 AND DT 16)

1. Cylinder block
2. Crankcase cover
3. Gasket
4. Cylinder head
5. Exhaust cover
6. Inner exhaust plate
7. Upper oil seal housing
8. Reed valve assembly
9. Intake manifold
10. Reed valves

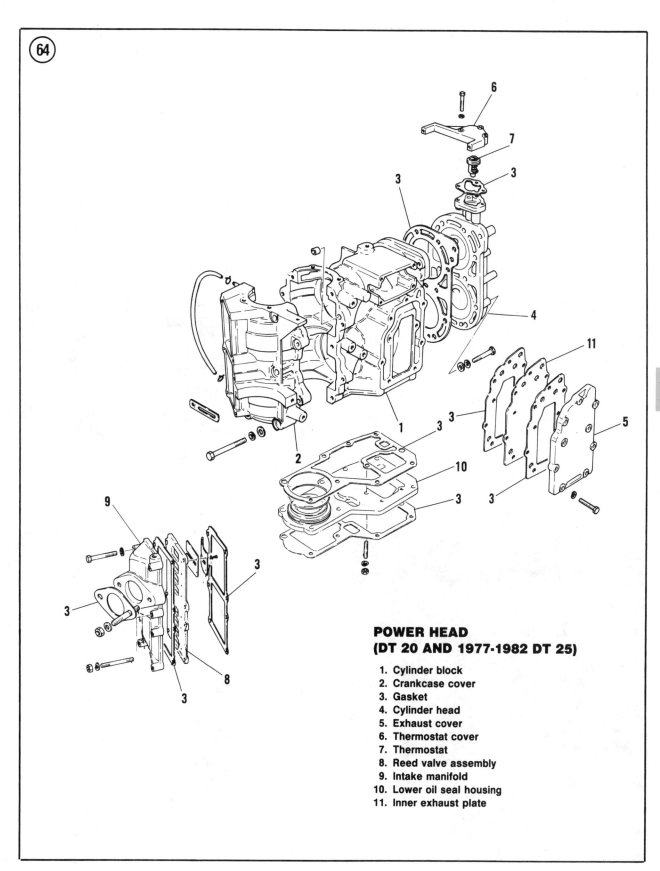

8

**POWER HEAD
(DT 20 AND 1977-1982 DT 25)**

1. Cylinder block
2. Crankcase cover
3. Gasket
4. Cylinder head
5. Exhaust cover
6. Thermostat cover
7. Thermostat
8. Reed valve assembly
9. Intake manifold
10. Lower oil seal housing
11. Inner exhaust plate

1. Disconnect the lubrication hose, if so equipped. Remove the intake manifold bolts. Remove the manifold and gasket. Discard the gaskets.

2. Remove the reed valve assembly. See **Figure 65** (typical).

3. Remove the exhaust cover bolts. Remove the exhaust cover and gasket. See **Figure 66** (typical). Discard the gasket.

4. Remove the inner exhaust plate and gasket, if so equipped. Discard the gasket.

5. 1977-1982 DT 9.9 and DT 16—Remove the water tube holder (**Figure 67**).

6. Remove the lower oil seal housing bolts. Remove the housing. See **Figure 68** (typical).

7. Remove the cylinder head bolts. Remove the cylinder head and gasket. See **Figure 69** (typical). Discard the gasket.

8A. Remove the water valve and spring from the cylinder block, if so equipped. See A and B, **Figure 70**.

8B. Remove the thermostat and spring from the cylinder block, if so equipped. See **Figure 71**.

9. 1983-on DT 25 and DT 30—Remove the 2 bolts holding the cylinder head cover to the cylinder head. With the assembly on a solid surface, carefully pry the cover and head apart using a suitable pry tool at the pry points provided. See **Figure 72**. Separate the cover and head.

10. Remove the crankcase cover bolts. See **Figure 73** (typical).

11. With the crankcase and cylinder block on a solid surface, carefully pry the cover and

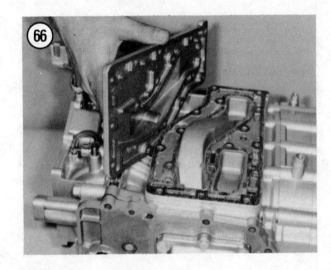

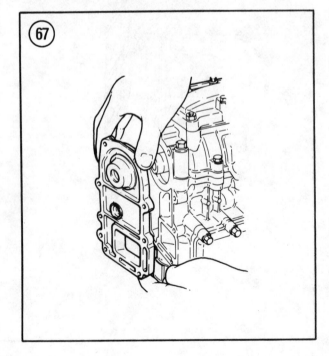

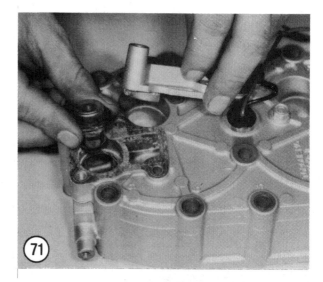

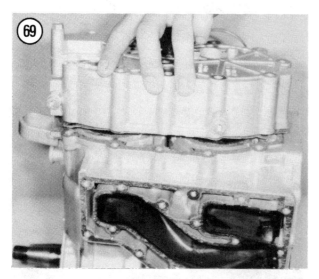

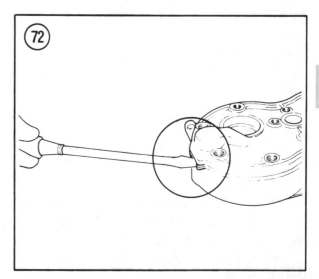

8

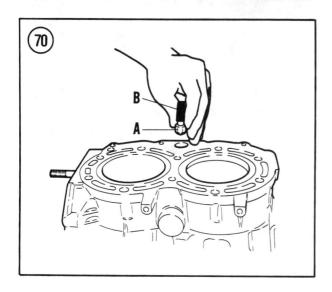

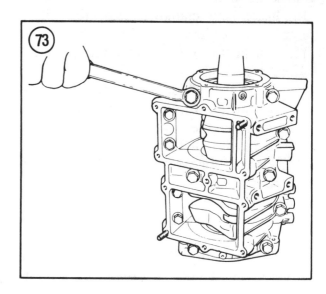

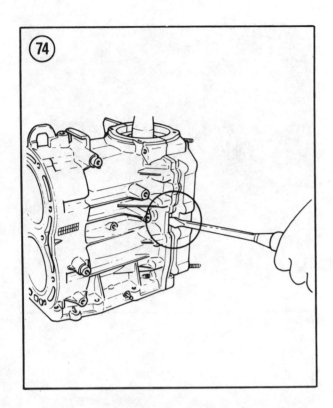

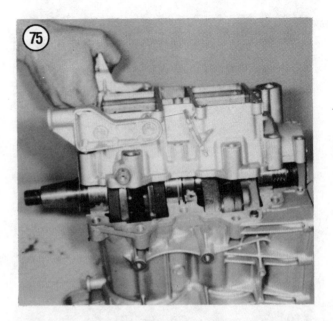

block apart using a suitable pry tool at the pry points provided. See **Figure 74**.

12. Remove the crankcase cover from the block (**Figure 75**).

13. Carefully lift the crankshaft assembly up and out of the cylinder block (**Figure 76**). If necessary, lightly tap on underside of crankshaft taper with a rubber mallet to break the seal.

14. Install the crankshaft assembly on a suitable power head stand, if available.

15. If a piston is to be removed from the connecting rod:

    a. Mark the cylinder number on the top of the piston with a felt-tipped pen.

    b. Remove the piston pin circlip with a hooked tool (**Figure 77**). Repeat this step to remove the opposite piston pin circlip.

    c. Push the piston pin from the piston/connecting rod with a suitable size drift.

    d. Remove the piston and caged needle bearing (**Figure 78**) from the connecting

rod. Keep the piston and bearing together for reinstallation.

16. Carefully spread and remove the piston rings as shown in **Figure 79**.

Disassembly
(All 3-cylinder Engines)

A large number of bolts and screws of different lengths are used to secure the

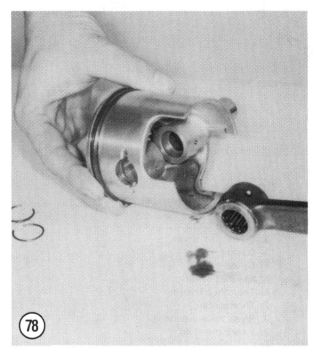

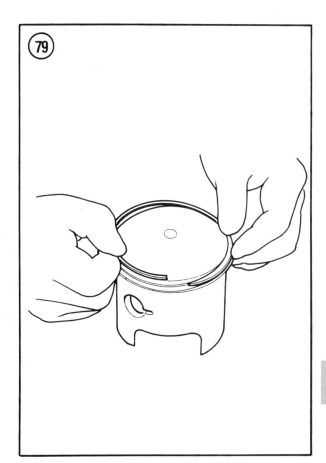

8

various covers and components. It is a good idea to use a cupcake tin or similar compartmented container to hold the various fasteners removed from each cover or component. This will make reassembly easier and faster.

Some power heads have pry points in the casting for easier removal of each component. If no pry points are provided, break the gasket seal with a wide-blade putty knife and mallet, then carefully separate the components.

Refer to **Figure 80** for this procedure.

1. Use pliers to slide each lubrication tube hose clamp away from the fitting enough to disconnect the tube. Pull the tube off the intake manifold. See **Figure 81**.

2. Remove the intake manifold bolts. Remove the manifold and reed valve assembly.

3. Remove the screws holding the thermostat cover to the cylinder head. See **Figure 82**. Remove the cover, gasket and thermostat.

4. Remove the cylinder head bolts (**Figure 83**). Remove the cylinder head and gasket. Discard the gasket.

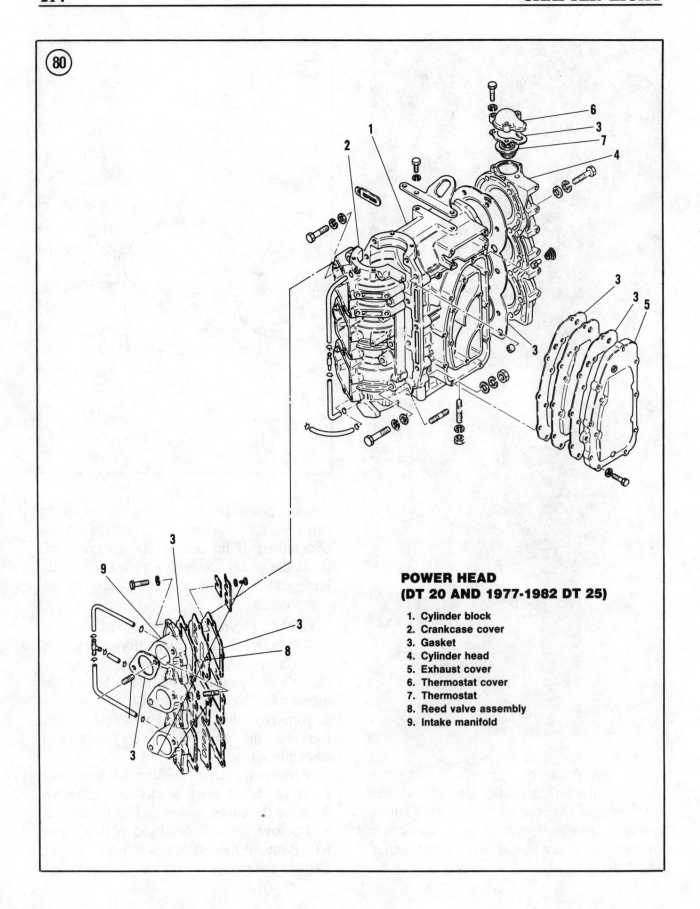

**POWER HEAD
(DT 20 AND 1977-1982 DT 25)**

1. Cylinder block
2. Crankcase cover
3. Gasket
4. Cylinder head
5. Exhaust cover
6. Thermostat cover
7. Thermostat
8. Reed valve assembly
9. Intake manifold

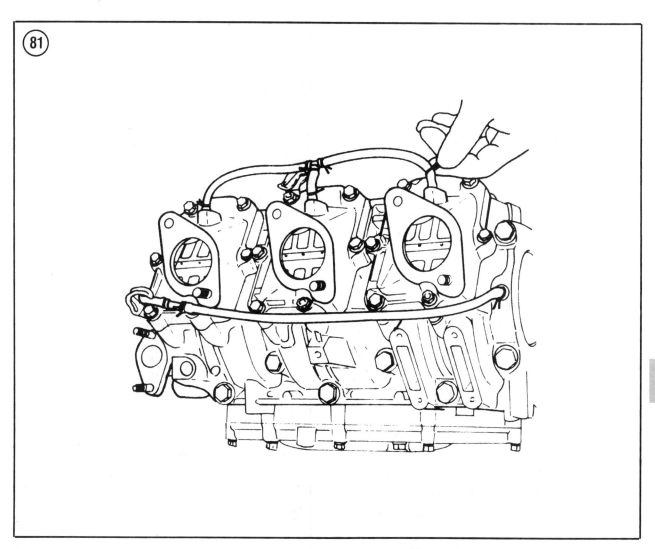

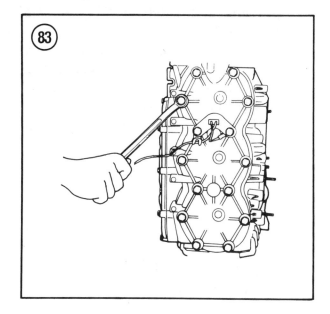

5. Remove the water valve and spring. See A and B, **Figure 84**.

6. Remove the crankcase cover bolts. See **Figure 85** (typical).

7. With the crankcase and cylinder block on a solid surface, carefully pry the cover and block apart using a suitable pry tool at the pry points provided.

8. Remove the crankcase cover from the block.

9. Carefully lift the crankshaft assembly up and out of the cylinder block (**Figure 86**). If necessary, lightly tap on underside of crankshaft taper with a rubber mallet to break the seal.

10. Install the crankshaft assembly on a suitable power head stand, if available.

11. Remove the exhaust cover bolts. Remove the cover and gasket. Discard the gasket.

12. Remove the upper and lower crankshaft oil seals (**Figure 87**).

13. If a piston is to be removed from the connecting rod:

    a. Remove the piston pin circlip with a hooked tool or needlenose pliers. Repeat this step to remove the opposite piston pin circlip.

    b. Push the piston pin from the piston/connecting rod with a suitable size drift.

    c. Remove the piston, caged needle bearing and washer from the connecting rod. Keep the piston and bearing together for reinstallation.

14. Carefully spread and remove the piston rings as shown in **Figure 79**.

Disassembly
(All 4-cylinder Engines)

A large number of bolts and screws of different lengths are used to secure the

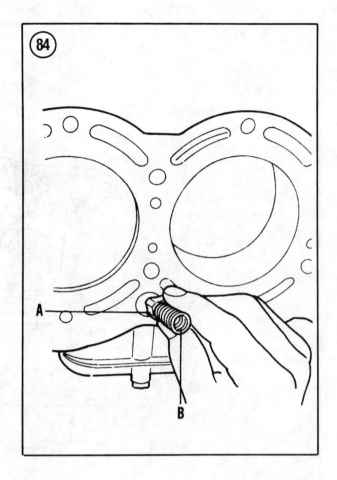

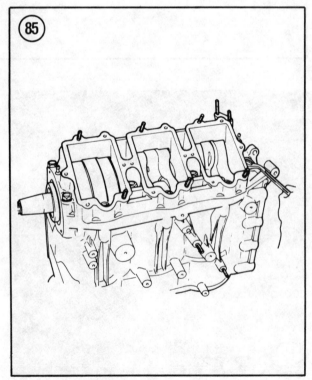

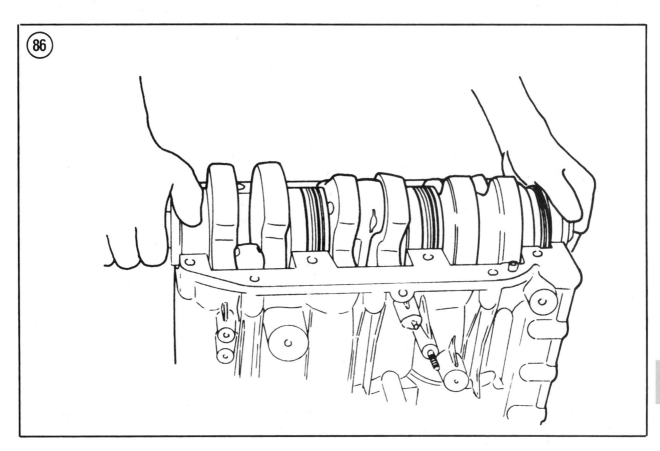

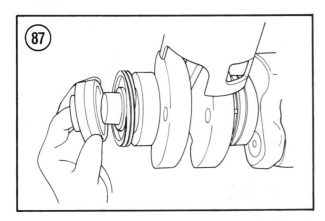

various covers and components. It is a good idea to use a cupcake tin or similar compartmented container to hold the various fasteners removed from each cover or component. This will make reassembly easier and faster.

Some power heads have pry points in the casting for easier removal of each component. If no pry points are provided, break the gasket seal with a wide-blade putty knife and mallet, then carefully separate the components.

Refer to **Figure 88** for this procedure.

1. Remove the intake manifold bolts. Remove the manifold and gasket. Discard the gasket.

2. Remove the reed valve assembly and gasket (**Figure 89**). Discard the gasket.

3. Remove the cylinder head bolts. Remove the cylinder head and gasket. Discard the gasket.

4. Remove the temperature switch (**Figure 90**) from the cylinder head cover.

NOTE
The cylinder head cover is a 2-piece assembly on 4-cylinder power heads.

5. Remove the bolts from each cylinder head cover. Remove the covers and gasket. Discard the gasket.

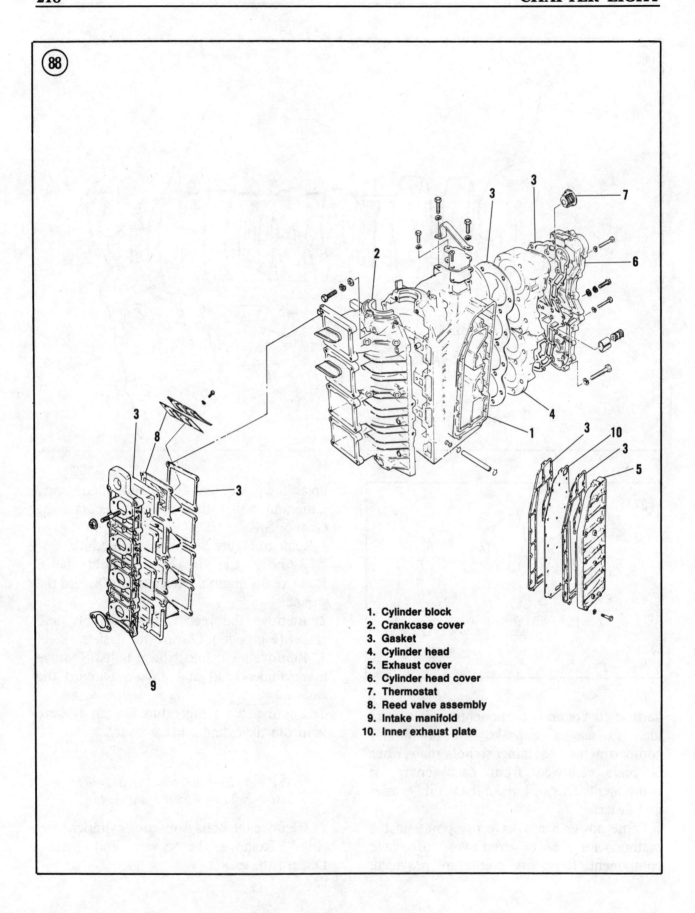

1. Cylinder block
2. Crankcase cover
3. Gasket
4. Cylinder head
5. Exhaust cover
6. Cylinder head cover
7. Thermostat
8. Reed valve assembly
9. Intake manifold
10. Inner exhaust plate

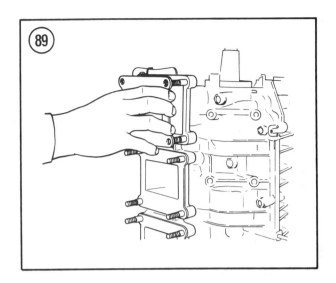

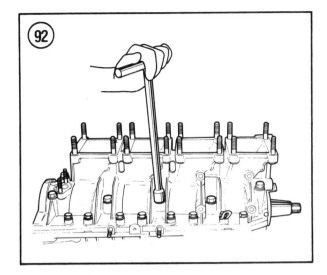

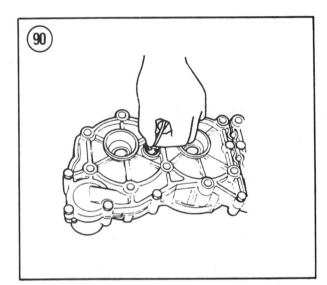

6. Remove the 3 cylinder head connectors (**Figure 91**).

7. Remove the thermostat from the cylinder head (A, **Figure 91**).

8. Remove the crankcase cover bolts. See **Figure 92** (typical).

9. With the crankcase and cylinder block on a solid surface, carefully pry the cover and block apart using a suitable pry tool at the pry points provided.

10. Remove the crankcase cover from the block.

11. Mark the connecting rods and caps. Remove each connecting rod cap, roller bearings and bearing cage. Place bearings and cage from each rod in separate containers.

12. Remove the crankshaft from the cylinder block. If necessary, lightly tap on crankshaft taper with a rubber mallet to break the seal.

13. Remove the remaining connecting rod roller bearings and cages. Place in their respective container.

14. Remove the exhaust cover bolts. Remove the cover and gasket. Discard the gasket.

15. Reinstall each rod cap to its respective connecting rod. Carefully push each piston and connecting rod assembly from its cylinder and remove from the top of the cylinder block.

8

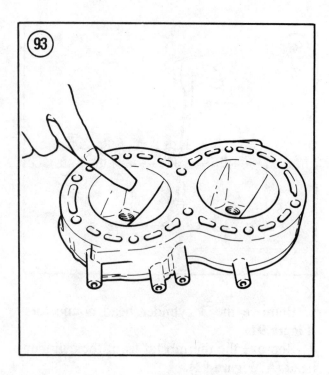

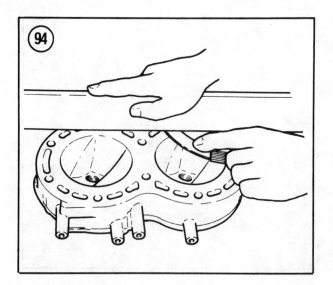

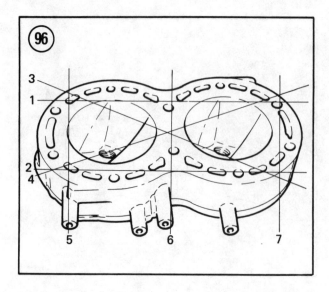

16. Mark the cylinder number on the top of the piston with a felt-tipped pen.

17. If a piston is to be removed from the connecting rod:

    a. Remove the piston pin circlip with a hooked tool or needlenose pliers. Repeat this step to remove the opposite piston pin circlip.

    b. Push the piston pin from the piston/connecting rod with a suitable size drift.

    c. Remove the piston, caged needle bearing and washers. Keep the piston and bearing together for reinstallation.

18. Carefully spread and remove the piston rings as shown in **Figure 79**.

**Cylinder Block and Crankcase
Cleaning and Inspection
(All Engines)**

Suzuki outboard cylinder blocks and crankcase covers are matched and line-bored assemblies. For this reason, you should not attempt to assemble an engine with parts

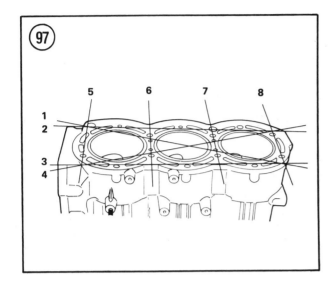

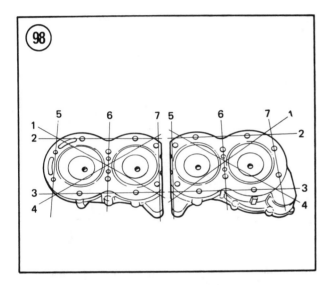

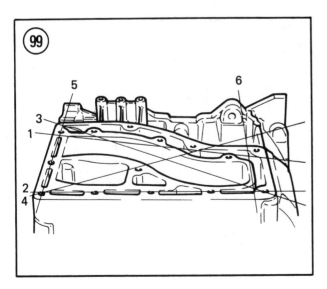

salvaged from other blocks. If inspection indicates that either the block or cover requires replacement, replace both as an assembly.

Carefully remove all gasket and sealant residue from the cylinder block and crankcase cover mating surfaces with lacquer thinner. Clean the aluminum surfaces carefully to avoid nicking them. A dull putty knife can be used, but a piece of Lucite with one edge ground to a 45 degree angle is more efficient and will also reduce the possibility of damage to the surfaces. When reassembling the crankcase cover and cylinder block, both mating surfaces must be free of all sealant residue, dirt and oil or leaks will develop.

1. Remove all carbon deposits from the combustion chambers, exhaust ports and cylinder head. See **Figure 93**. Use a hardwood or Lucite scraper and solvent. Be careful to not scratch or gouge the areas while cleaning.

2. Once all carbon is removed, clean the cylinder block and cylinder head thoroughly with solvent and a brush.

3. Carefully remove all gasket and sealant residue from the mating surfaces.

4. Check the cylinder head gasket mating surface with a straightedge and flat feeler gauge (**Figure 94**). Check for warpage in the directions shown in **Figures 95-98**.

5. If warpage exceeds 0.0012 in. (0.03 mm) in any direction, place a large sheet of No. 400 (or finer) sandpaper on a pane of glass or surface plate. Apply a slight amount of pressure and move the component in a figure-8 pattern. Remove the component and repeat Step 4 to recheck surface flatness.

6. Check the cylinder block-to-head surface for warpage as described in Step 4. Follow the directions shown in **Figures 95-98**. If warpage exceeds 0.0012 in. (0.03 mm) in any direction, correct as described in Step 5.

7. Check the exhaust port surfaces for warpage as described in Step 4. Follow the directions shown in **Figure 99** (2-cylinder),

8

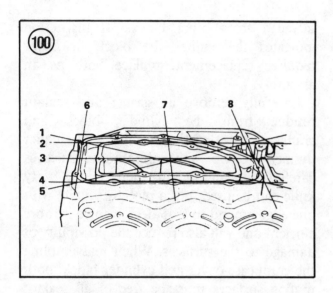

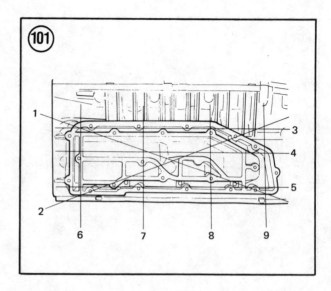

Figure 100 (3-cylinder) or **Figure 101** (4-cylinder). If warpage exceeds 0.0012 in. (0.03 mm) in any direction, correct as described in Step 5.

8. Check the block, cylinder head and cover for cracks, fractures, stripped bolt or spark plug threads or other defects.

9. Check the gasket mating surfaces for nicks, grooves, cracks or excessive distortion. Any of these defects will cause compression leakage. Replace as required.

10. Check all oil and water passages in the block and cover for obstructions. Make sure any plugs installed are properly tightened.

> *NOTE*
> *With older engines, it is a good idea to have the cylinder walls lightly honed with a medium stone even if they are in good condition. This will break up any glaze that might reduce compression.*

11. Check each cylinder bore for signs of aluminum transfer from the pistons to the cylinder walls. If scoring is present but not excessive, have the cylinders honed by a dealer or qualified machine shop.

12. Measure each cylinder bore with an inside micrometer or bore gauge (**Figure 102**) at points A, B and C in **Figure 103**

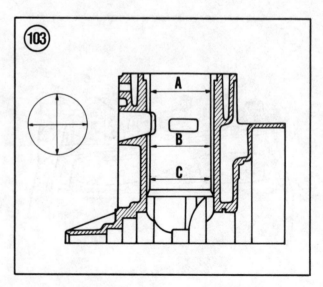

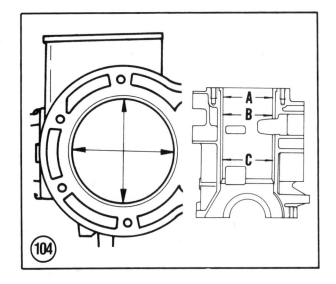

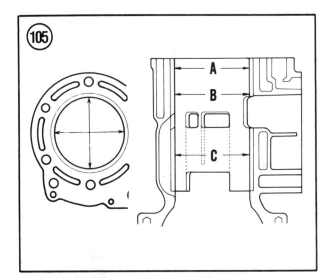

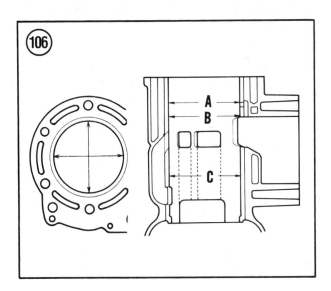

(1-cylinder), **Figure 104** (2-cylinder), **Figure 105** (3-cylinder) or **Figure 106** (4-cylinder). Record the readings.

13. Turn the cylinder 90° and repeat the measurements. Subtract the smallest from the largest reading. If the difference between the 2 measurements exceeds 0.004 in. (0.1 mm), have the cylinders rebored by a dealer or qualified machine shop and install oversize pistons.

NOTE
Obtain the new pistons and measure them before having the cylinders bored. This allows for variations in piston size due to manufacturing tolerances.

Crankshaft and Connecting Rod Bearings Cleaning and Inspection (All Engines)

Bearings can be reused if they are in good condition. To be on the safe side, however, it is a good idea to discard all removable bearings and install new ones whenever the engine is disassembled. New bearings are inexpensive compared to the cost of another overhaul caused by the use of marginal bearings.

1. Remove any sealer from outer edge of ball bearings with a scraper, then clean bearing surface with kerosene.

2. Place ball bearings in a wire basket and submerge in a suitable container of fresh kerosene. The bottom of the basket should not touch the bottom of the container.

3. Agitate basket containing bearings to loosen all grease, sludge and other contamination.

4. Dry ball bearings with dry filtered compressed air. Be careful not to spin the bearings.

5. Lubricate the dry bearings with a light coat of Suzuki Outboard Oil and inspect for

8

rust, wear, scuffed surfaces, heat discoloration or other defects. Replace as required.

6. If caged roller bearings are to be reused, repeat Steps 2-5, cleaning one set at a time to prevent any possible mixup. Check bearings for flat spots. If one roller is defective, replace the entire bearing.

Piston Cleaning and Inspection (All Engines)

1. Check the piston(s) for signs of scoring, cracking, cracked or worn piston pin bosses or metal damage. Replace piston and pin as an assembly if any of these defects are noted.

2. Remove any carbon deposits on the piston crown with a hardwood or plastic scraper.

> *NOTE*
> *To remove stubborn carbon deposits in Step 3, carefully scrape the ring groove with the recessed end of a broken ring. Do not use an automotive ring groove cleaning tool as it can damage the piston groove locating pin.*

3. Check piston ring grooves for distortion, loose ring locating pins or excessive wear. If the flexing action of the rings has not kept the lower surface of the ring grooves free of carbon, clean with a bristle brush and solvent.

4. Immerse pistons in a carbon removal solution to remove any carbon deposits not removed in Step 3. If the solution does not remove all of the carbon, carefully use a fine wire brush and avoid burring or rounding of the machined edges. Clean the piston skirt with crocus cloth.

5. Measure the piston diameter at right angles to the piston pin with a micrometer. See A, **Figure 107**. Refer to **Table 2** for exact measurement point on piston skirt according to engine.

6. Measure the piston bore diameter with bore gauge at the point indicated in **Table 2**.

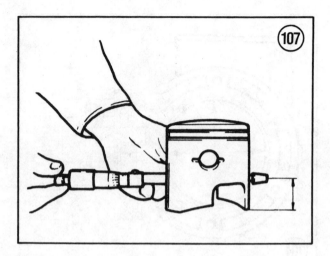

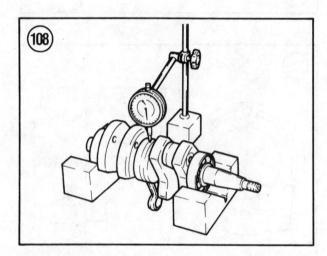

7. Subtract the measurement obtained in Step 5 from the Step 6 measurement to determine the cylinder-to-piston clearance. Compare clearance to specifications (**Table 2**). If clearance exceeds specifications, have the cylinder block rebored by a dealer or machine shop and install oversize pistons.

> *NOTE*
> *Obtain the new pistons and measure them before having the cylinders bored. This allows for variations in piston size to manufacturing tolerances.*

Crankshaft Cleaning and Inspection (All Engines)

Only 4-cylinder engine connecting rods can be disassembled from the crankshaft. If either

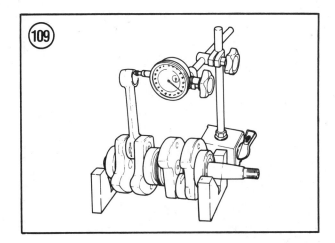

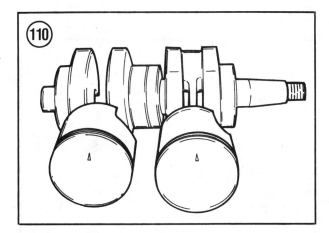

5. Lubricate ball bearing with Suzuki Outboard Motor oil and rotate outer race. Replace bearing if it sounds or feels rough or if it does not rotate smoothly.

6. Support the crankshaft on a pair of V-blocks and check runout with a dial indicator (**Figure 108**). Divide runout reading in half to determine crankshaft deflection. If deflection exceeds 0.0012 in. (0.03 mm) for DT 2-DT 3.5 or 0.002 in. (0.05 mm) for all others, replace the crankshaft assembly.

7. With all pistons removed and the crankshaft on V-blocks, install a dial indicator as shown in **Figure 109** to check wear and condition of the big end of the connecting rod. Hold crankshaft steady and move connecting rod up and down. If dial indicator reading exceeds the following specifications, replace the crankshaft assembly:

    a. DT 2-DT 3.5—0.12 in. (3mm).
    b. 1983-on DT 9.9-DT 15—0.16 in. (4 mm).
    c. All others—0.20 in. (5 mm).

Piston and Connecting Rod Assembly (All Engines)

If the pistons were removed from the connecting rods, they must be correctly oriented when reassembling. The arrow on the piston crown must face downward on DT 2-DT 3.5 engines and toward the exhaust port on all others. To install the piston properly on DT 5-DT 85 engines, place the crankshaft with its flywheel side on the right and position each piston with the arrow on its crown facing upward. See **Figure 110** (typical).

1. Coat piston pin and piston pin/connecting rod small end bores with Suzuki Outboard Motor oil.

2. Check the piston dome number made during disassembly and match piston with its correct connecting rod.

the rod(s) or crankshaft is defective on 1-, 2- or 3-cylinder engines, replace the entire assembly.

1. Clean the crankshaft thoroughly with kerosene and a brush. Blow dry with dry filtered compressed air and lubricate with a light coat of Suzuki Outboard Motor oil.

2. Check the crankshaft journals and crankpins for scratches, heat discoloration or other defects.

3. Check drive shaft splines, flywheel taper threads, keyway and oil injection pump drive gear (if so equipped) for wear or damage. Replace crankshaft as required.

4. If lower crankshaft ball bearing has not been removed, grasp inner race and try to work it back and forth. Replace bearing if excessive axial play is noted.

8

3. Insert caged bearing in connecting rod small end bore. If washers are used, position on each side of bore.

4. With the piston properly oriented, fit the piston over the connecting rod small end, align the piston and small end bores, then work the pin through the piston and connecting rod small end bores.

5. Install piston pin circlips with snap ring pliers. Sharp edge of circlip should face outward and circlip opening should face directly up or down. Make sure circlips seat in piston grooves.

6. Repeat procedure for each remaining piston.

Piston Ring Installation (All Engines)

Some pistons use a keystone design top ring and a flat design bottom ring. Check new rings carefully before installation and install them in their proper grooves.

1. Check end gap of new rings before installing on piston. Place ring in cylinder bore just above the intake and exhaust ports, then square it up by inserting the bottom of an old piston. Measure the gap with a feeler gauge (**Figure 111**) and compare to specifications (**Table 3**).

2. If ring gap is excessive in Step 1, repeat the step with the ring in another cylinder. If gap is also excessive in that cylinder, discard and replace with another new ring.

3. If ring gap is insufficient in Step 1, the ends of the ring can be filed slightly. Clean ring thoroughly and recheck gap as in Step 1.

> *NOTE*
> *Piston rings must be installed in Step 4 and Step 5 with the mark on the end of the ring facing the piston crown. See Figure 112.*

4. Once the ring gaps are correctly established, spread the ring just enough to fit

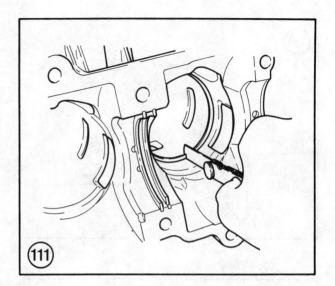

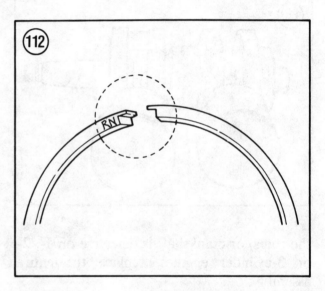

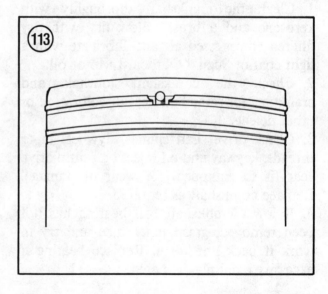

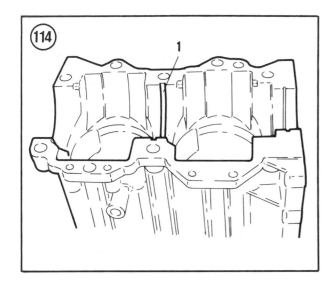

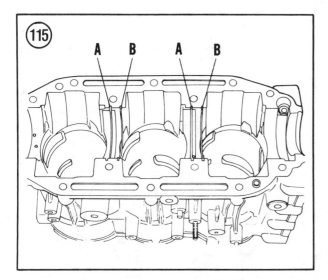

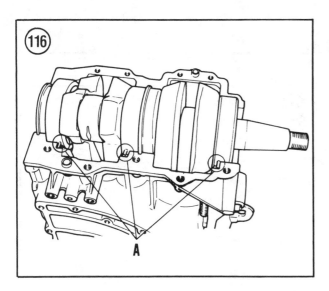

it over the piston head and into position. Repeat this step to install the upper ring.

5. Position each ring so that the piston groove locating pin fits in the ring gap (**Figure 113**). Proper ring positioning is necessary to minimize compression loss and prevent the ring ends from catching on the cylinder ports.

Piston, Connecting Rod and Crankshaft Installation (Except DT 115-DT 140)

1. Coat the piston(s), rings and cylinder bore(s) with Suzuki Outboard Motor oil.

2. Install any labyrinth seals (**Figure 114**) or thrust rings (**Figure 115**) in the crankcase.

3. With the crankcase on a clean flat surface, carefully lower the crankshaft assembly until the pistons start to enter the cylinder bore(s). Compress the rings on one piston with your fingers, making sure that the end gaps fit over the locating pin, and slowly work the piston/ring assembly into the cylinder. Repeat this step to fit each remaining piston into its bore.

4. When all piston/ring assemblies have entered the cylinder bores, apply sufficient downward pressure to seat the pistons in their bores and the crankshaft in the crankcase.

5. Reach through the exhaust ports and lightly depress each ring with a pencil point or small screwdriver blade. The ring should snap back when pressure is released. If it does not, the ring was broken during piston installation and will have to be replaced.

6. DT 2—Wipe a new crankshaft O-ring with water-resistant grease (part No. 99000-25160 or equivalent) and install on lower end of crankshaft. Coat the splined end of the crankshaft with water-resistant grease.

7. Make sure oil seal flanges fit into crankcase cutouts. Rotate each bearing to position its locating pin in the crankcase cutout. See **Figure 116** (typical).

8

Piston and Connecting Rod Installation (DT 115-DT 140)

1. Coat the pistons, rings and cylinder bores with Suzuki Outboard Motor oil.

2. Check the piston dome number made during disassembly and match piston with its correct cylinder bore.

3. Insert the piston into its cylinder bore with the arrow on its crown facing the exhaust side of the cylinder block. Make sure the rings are properly positioned in their grooves and that the locating pins are positioned in the ring gaps.

4. Install a suitable ring compressor over the piston dome and rings. With compressor resting on cylinder head, tighten it until the rings are compressed sufficiently to enter the bore. See **Figure 117**.

5. Hold the connecting rod end with one hand to prevent it from scraping or scratching the cylinder bore and slowly push piston into cylinder.

6. Remove the ring compressor tool and repeat the procedure to install remaining pistons.

7. Reach through the exhaust ports and lightly depress each ring with a pencil point or small screwdriver blade. The ring should snap back when pressure is released. If it does not, the ring was broken during piston installation and will have to be replaced.

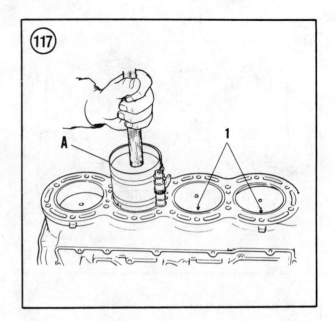

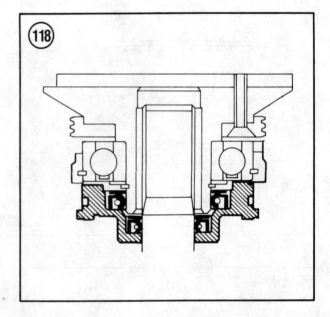

Crankshaft Installation (DT 115-DT 140)

1. Install new seals in the lower oil seal housing as shown in **Figure 118**. Fill the cavity between the seals with water-resistant grease (part No. 99000-25160 or equivalent).

2. Install a new O-ring on the lower oil seal housing. Wipe O-ring with water-resistant grease.

3. Install lower oil seal housing on crankshaft.

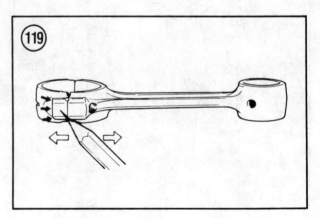

4. Remove the connecting rod caps. Coat connecting rod bearing surfaces and bearing cages with Suzuki Outboard Motor oil. Install a bearing cage in the rod.

5. Lubricate the crankshaft with Suzuki Outboard Motor oil and install in the cylinder block.

6. Position the connecting rod under the crankshaft and pull it up to the crankpin.

7. Lightly coat the exposed part of the crankpin with Suzuki Outboard Motor oil. Install the other bearing cage.

8. Install new connecting rod cap screws and tighten finger-tight.

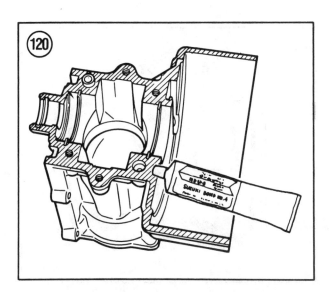

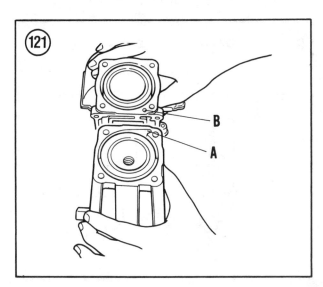

CAUTION
The procedure detailed in Step 9 is very important to proper engine operation as it affects bearing action. If not done properly, major engine damage can result. It can also be a time-consuming and frustrating process. Work slowly and with patience. If alignment cannot be achieved, replace the connecting rod.

9. Run a dental pick or pencil point along the cap match marks to check cap offset. See **Figure 119**. Rod and cap must be aligned so that the dental pick or pencil point will pass smoothly across the fracture line at each of the 3 faces indicated by the arrows in **Figure 119**. If alignment is not correct, gently tap cap with a plastic hammer. When rod and cap are properly aligned, tighten cap screws to specifications (**Table 1**).

10. Rotate the crankshaft to check for binding. If the connecting rod does not float freely over the full length of the crankpin, loosen the rod cap and repeat Step 9.

Assembly (DT 2 and DT 3.5)

1. Apply Suzuki Bond No. 4 (part No. 99000-31030) or equivalent to the mating surfaces on both halves of the crankcase. See **Figure 120**.

2. Install the crankcase cover and tighten the bolts to specifications (**Table 1**) in a diagonal pattern.

3. DT 3.5—Apply a liberal quantity of Suzuki Outboard Motor Oil to the connecting rod big end through the reed valve opening, then install the reed valve and intake manifold/carburetor assembly.

4. Rotate the crankshaft several turns to check for binding. If crankshaft does not turn easily, disassemble and correct the interference.

5. Install the cylinder head with a new gasket. On DT 2 engines, make sure that the water passages in the cylinder head, gasket and crankcase align. See **Figure 121**. Tighten

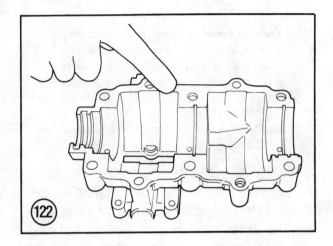

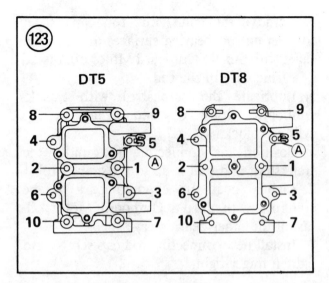

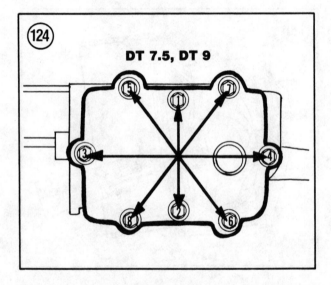

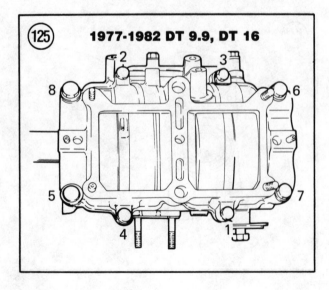

the cylinder head bolts to specifications (**Table 1**) in a diagonal pattern.

6. DT 2—Install the intake manifold and carburetor assembly.

7. Install the power head as described in this chapter.

Assembly
(All 2-cylinder Engines)

Refer to **Figures 62-64** (typical) for this procedure.

1. Apply Suzuki Bond No. 4 (part No. 99000-31030) or equivalent to the mating surfaces on both halves of the crankcase. See **Figure 122**.

2. Install the crankcase cover to the cylinder block and tighten the bolts to specifications (**Table 1**) following the appropriate sequence as shown in **Figures 123-129**.

3. Rotate the crankshaft several turns to check for binding. If crankshaft does not turn easily, disassemble and correct the interference.

4. Apply a liberal quantity of Suzuki Outboard Motor Oil to each connecting rod big end through the reed valve openings.

5. Install new seals in the lower oil seal housing (**Figure 130**). The crankshaft seal lip (A, **Figure 131**) should face away from the crankshaft; the drive shaft seal lip (B, **Figure 131**) should face toward the crankshaft.

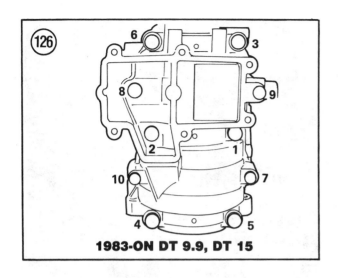

1983-ON DT 9.9, DT 15

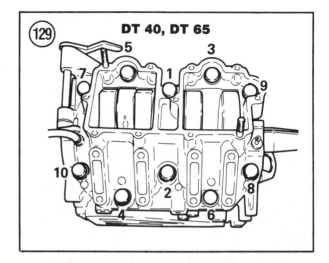

DT 40, DT 65

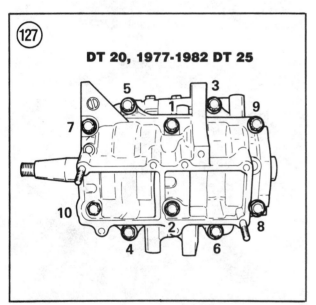

DT 20, 1977-1982 DT 25

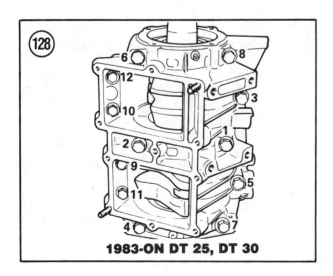

1983-ON DT 25, DT 30

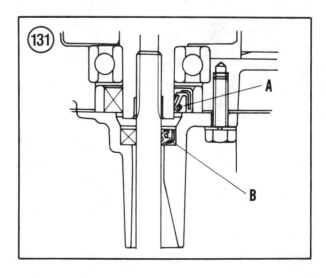

8

6. Fill the cavity between the seals with water-resistant grease (part No. 99000-25160 or equivalent) and install the lower oil seal housing.

7. 1977-1982 DT 9.9 and DT 16—Install a new seal in the water tube holder with the lip facing outward. Coat the seal lip with water-resistant grease (**Figure 132**). Install water tube holder.

8. Install the inner exhaust plate with a new gasket, if so equipped.

9. Install the exhaust cover with a new gasket (**Figure 133**).

10. Install the reed valve assembly with the reed side facing the crankshaft. See **Figure 134** (typical).

11. Install the intake manifold with a new gasket. See **Figure 135** (typical).

12. Connect the lubrication hose, if so equipped. See **Figure 136** (typical).

13. 1983-on DT 25 and DT 30:

  a. Install the thermostat in the cylinder head cover with its air breather hole facing upward.

  b. Install the cylinder head cover to the cylinder head with a new gasket.

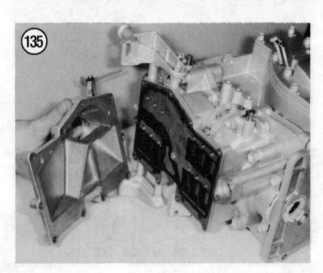

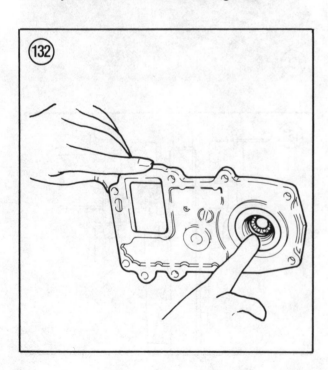

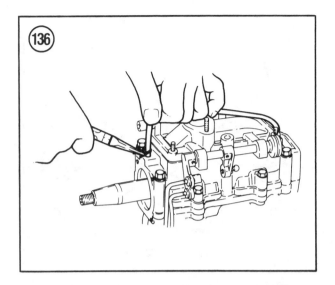

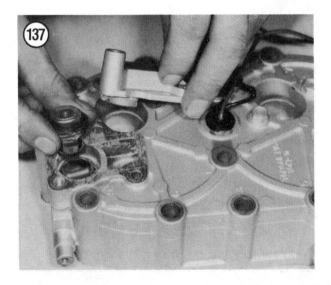

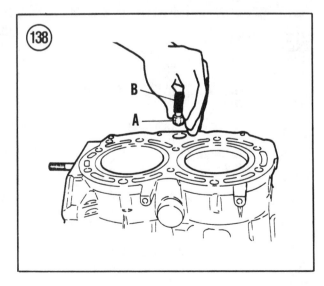

14. All engines so equipped—Install the spring and thermostat in the cylinder block. See **Figure 137**.

15. Install the water valve and spring in the cylinder block, if so equipped. See A and B, **Figure 138**.

16. Install the cylinder head with a new gasket. See **Figure 139** (typical).

17. Install the head bolts and tighten to specifications (**Table 1**) following the appropriate sequence shown in **Figures 140-146**.

18. Install any mounting brackets removed during disassembly.

19. Install the power head as described in this chapter.

**Assembly
(All 3-cylinder Engines)**

Refer to **Figure 80** for this procedure.

1. Apply Suzuki Bond No. 4 (part No. 99000-31030) or equivalent to the mating surfaces on both halves of the crankcase. See **Figure 147**.

2. Install the crankcase cover to the cylinder block and tighten the bolts to specifications (**Table 1**) following the appropriate sequence as shown in **Figure 148**. Be sure to install the J-clamp under the head of bolt No. 6 (A, **Figure 148**).

3. Rotate the crankshaft several turns to check for binding. If crankshaft does not turn easily, disassemble and correct the interference.

4. Apply a liberal quantity of Suzuki Outboard Motor Oil to each connecting rod big end through the reed valve openings.

5. Install new seals in the lower oil seal housing (**Figure 149**). The crankshaft seal lip should face away from the crankshaft (A, **Figure 149**); the drive shaft seal lip should face toward the crankshaft (B, **Figure 149**).

6. Fill the cavity between the seals with water-resistant grease (part No. 99000-25160)

8

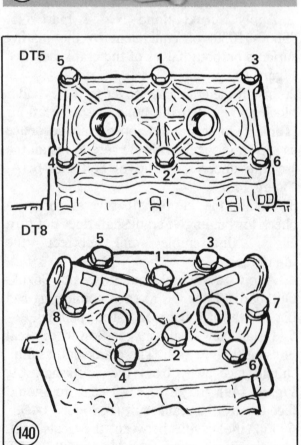

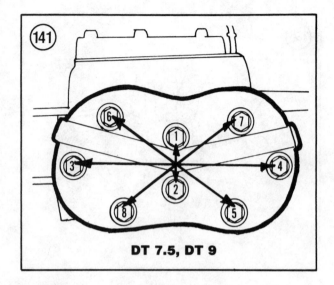

DT 7.5, DT 9

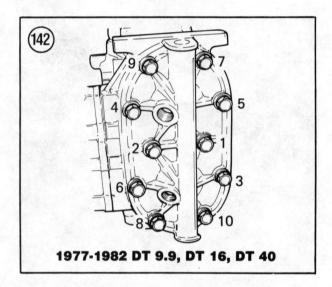

1977-1982 DT 9.9, DT 16, DT 40

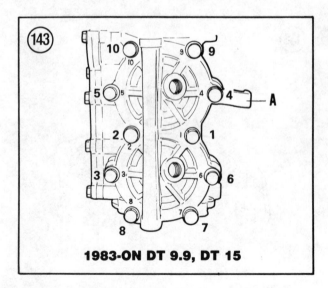

1983-ON DT 9.9, DT 15

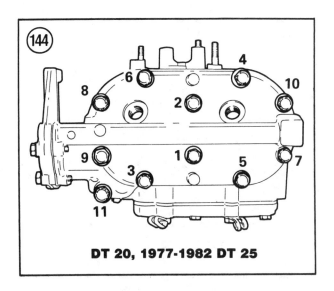

DT 20, 1977-1982 DT 25

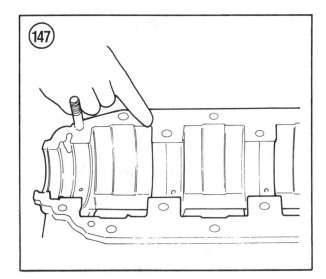

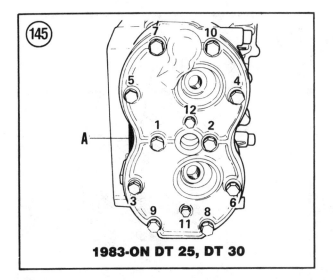

1983-ON DT 25, DT 30

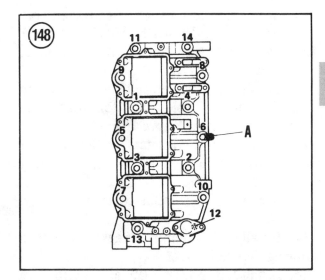

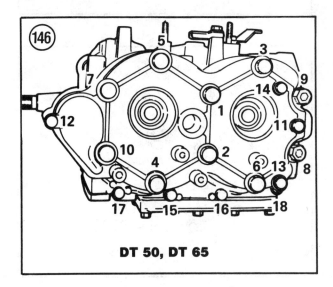

DT 50, DT 65

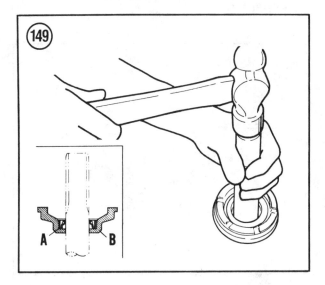

8

or equivalent and install the lower oil seal housing. Make sure that the seal flange (A, **Figure 150**) fits snugly in the crankcase groove (B, **Figure 150**).

7. Install the reed valve assembly and intake manifold. Install the lubrication tube hoses and slide the hose clamps onto the fittings. See **Figure 151**.

8. Install the water valve and spring in the hole provided in the cylinder block.

9. Install the cylinder head with a new gasket. Coat the thermo unit with Thermo Unit Grease (part No. 34855-95550) or equivalent and install in the cylinder head. See **Figure 152**.

10. Install the heat switch over the thermo unit in the cylinder head. Attach the black lead under the head bolt to provide ground. See **Figure 153**.

11. Install and tighten all head bolts to specifications (**Table 1**) following the sequence shown in **Figure 154**.

12. Install the thermostat in the cylinder head with the flange mark facing to the rear (**Figure 155**).

13. Install the thermostat cover with a new gasket.

14. Install any mounting brackets removed during disassembly.

15. Install the power head as described in this chapter.

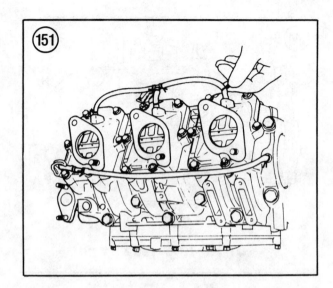

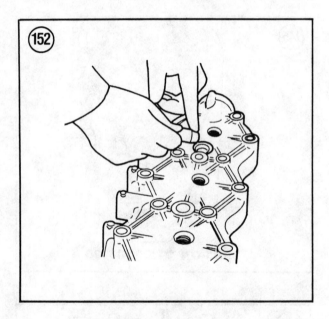

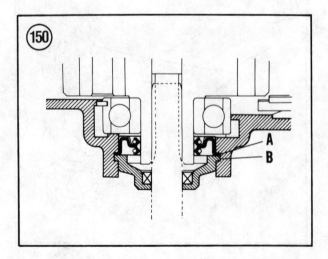

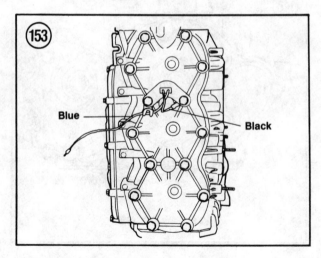

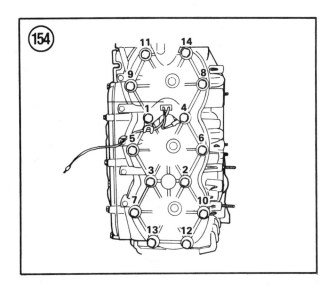

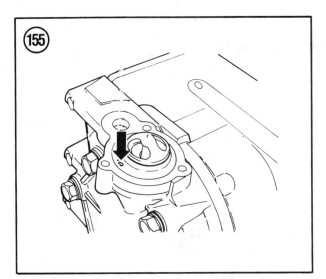

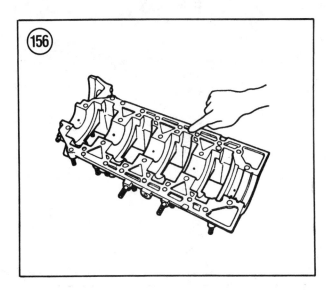

Assembly
(All 4-cylinder Engines)

Refer to **Figure 88** for this procedure.

1. Apply Suzuki Bond No. 4 (part No. 99000-31030) or equivalent to the mating surfaces on both halves of the crankcase. See **Figure 156**.

2. Install the crankcase cover to the cylinder block and tighten the bolts to specifications **(Table 1)** following the appropriate sequence as shown in **Figure 157**.

3. Rotate the crankshaft several turns to check for binding. If crankshaft does not turn easily, disassemble and correct the interference.

4. Apply a liberal quantity of Suzuki Outboard Motor Oil to each connecting rod big end through the reed valve openings.

5. Install the reed valve assemblies with new gaskets. Install the intake manifold with new gaskets. Tighten the bolts securely in an alternating pattern.

6. Install the 3 cylinder head connectors. Install the thermostat in the upper cylinder head with the mark on its flange facing upward.

7. Install the cylinder head covers with a new gasket. Install the temperature switch in the cylinder head cover. Attach the black lead

8

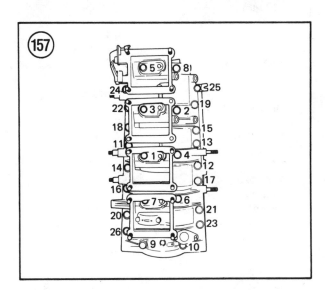

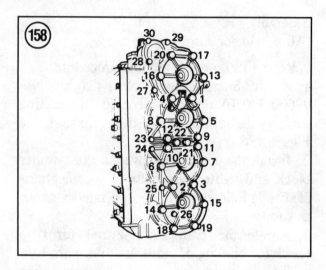

under one of the cover bolts to provide ground.

8. Install the cylinder head assembly to the block with a new gasket. Install and tighten the head bolts to specifications (Table 1) following the sequence shown in Figure 158. Be sure to install the J-clamp under the head of bolt No. 13.

9. Install the exhaust cover with a new gasket.

10. Install any mounting brackets removed during disassembly.

11. Install the power head as described in this chapter.

Table 1 TIGHTENING TORQUES*

Fastener	ft.-lb.	N·m
Connecting rod bolt		
DT 115, DT 140	22-25	30-35
Cylinder head bolt		
DT 2	6-8.5	8-12
DT 3.5	13-20	18-28
DT 5, DT 8. DT 16	11-14.5	15-20
DT 7.5, DT 9	13-16.5	18-23
DT 9.9		
1977-1982	11-14.5	15-20
1983-on	14.5-19	20-26
DT 15	14.5-19	20-26
DT 20, 1977-1982 DT 25	13-20	18-28
1983-on DT 25, DT 30		
10 mm	6-8.5	8-12
12 mm	14.5-19	20-26
DT 40		
6 mm	6-7	8-10
10 mm	14.5-16.5	20-23
DT 50-DT 140		
6 mm	6-8.5	8-12
10 mm	29-43.5	40-60
Crankcase bolt		
DT 2, DT 3.5	6-8.5	8-12
DT 5, DT 8	4.5-8	6-11
DT 7.5, DT 9	5-7.5	7-10
DT 9.9		
1977-1982		
6 mm	4.5-6.5	6-9
8 mm	11-14.5	15-20
1983-on		
10 mm	6-8.5	8-12
12 mm	14.5-19	20-26

(continued)

Table 1 TIGHTENING TORQUES* (continued)

Fastener	ft.-lb.	N·m
DT 15, 1983-on DT 25, DT 30		
10 mm	6-8.5	8-12
12 mm	14.5-19	20-26
DT 20, 1977-1982 DT 25	13-20	18-28
DT 40		
6 mm	6-8.5	8-12
10 mm	29-43.5	40-60
DT 50-DT 85	29-43.5	40-60
DT 115, DT 140		
8 mm	13-20	18-28
10 mm	29-43.5	40-60
Exhaust cover bolt		
DT 5, DT 8, DT 9.9, DT 16	3-5	4-7
DT 20, 1977-1982 DT 25,		
DT 50-DT 140	6-8.5	8-12
DT 40	6-7	8-10
Flywheel nut		
DT 2, DT 3.5	29-36	40-50
DT 5, DT 8	43.5-50.5	60-70
DT 7.5, DT 9	21.5-29	30-40
DT 9.9		
1977-1982	50.5-58	70-80
1983-on	58-65	80-90
DT 15	58-65	80-90
DT 16	50.5-58	70-80
DT 20, 1977-1982 DT 25	72.5-79.5	100-110
1983-on DT 25, DT 30	94-108.5	130-150
DT 40	144.5	200
DT 50-DT 85	144.5-152	200-210
DT 115, DT 140	173.5-188	240-260
Power head mounting bolts		
DT 2	4.5-7	6-10
DT 3.5, DT 9.9 (1983-on),		
DT 15, 1983-on DT 25, DT 30	11-14.5	15-20
DT 50-DT 85		
8 mm	11-14.5	15-20
10 mm	24.5-29.5	34-41
12 mm	40.5-46.5	56-64
DT 115, DT 140	24.5-29.5	34-41
Reed plate bolt	0.5	0.75
Standard torque values		
Bolt head marked "4"		
5 mm	1.5-3	2-4
6 mm	3-5	4-7
8 mm	7-11.5	10-16
10 mm	16-25.5	22-35
Bolt head marked "7"		
5 mm	2-4.5	3-6
6 mm	6-8.5	8-12
8 mm	13-20	18-28
10 mm	29-43.5	40-60

(continued)

8

Table 1 TIGHTENING TORQUES* (continued)

Fastener	ft.-lb.	N·m
Stainless steel bolt		
5 mm	1.5-3	2-4
6 mm	4.5-7	6-10
8 mm	11-14.5	15-20
10 mm	24.5-30	34-41

* Use standard torque values for any fasteners not specifically listed.

Table 2 CYLINDER AND PISTON SPECIFICATIONS

Engine	Piston measurement point*	Cylinder measurement point		Piston-to-cylinder clearance
		Above exhaust port	Below cylinder top	
DT 2	0.59 in. (15 mm)	0.20 in. (5 mm)		0.0021-0.0026 in. (0.053-0.080 mm)
DT 3.5	0.79 in. (20 mm)		0.98 in. (25 mm)	0.0020-0.0026 in. (0.052-0.067 mm)
DT 4.5	Not available			
DT 5- DT 9	0.59 in. (15 mm)	0.20 in. (5 mm)		0.0018-0.0030 in. (0.045-0.075 mm)
DT 9.9 1977-1982	0.83 in. (21 mm)	0.20 in. (5 mm)		0.0017-0.0023 in. (0.042-0.058 mm)
1983-on	0.83 in. (21 mm)		1.10 in. (28 mm)	0.0020-0.0026 in. (0.052-0.067 mm)
DT 15	0.083 in. (21 mm)		1.10 in. (28 mm)	0.0020-0.0026 in. (0.052-0.067 mm)
DT 16	0.79 in. (20 mm)	0.20 in. (5 mm)		0.0017-0.0023 in. (0.042-0.058 mm)
DT 20	0.98 in. (25 mm)		1.18 in. (30 mm)	0.0024-0.0035 in. (0.060-0.090 mm)
DT 25 1977-1982	0.98 in. (25 mm)		1.18 in. (30 mm)	0.0024-0.0035 in. (0.060-0.090 mm)
1983-on	0.94 in. (24 mm)		1.57 in. (40 mm)	0.0026-0.0032 in. (0.067-0.082 mm)
DT 30	0.94 in. (24 mm)		1.57 in. (40 mm)	0.0026-0.0032 in. (0.067-0.082 mm)
DT 40	1.18 in. (30 mm)		1.57 in. (40 mm)	0.0024-0.0032 in. (0.061-0.082 mm)
DT 50- DT 60	1.38 in. (35 mm)		1.57 in. (40 mm)	0.0038-0.112 in. (0.097-0.0044 mm)
DT 65- DT 85	1.38 in. (35 mm)		1.57 in. (40 mm)	0.112-0.127 in. (0.0044-0.0050 mm)
DT 115- DT 140	1.06 in. (27 mm)		1.18 in. (30 mm)	0.0032-0.0035 in. (0.08-0.09 mm)

* Above base of skirt.

Table 3 PISTON RING END GAP

	Standard	Limit
DT 2	0.0039-0.0098 in. (0.1-0.25 mm)	0.024 in. (0.6 mm)
DT 3.5, DT 7.5, DT 9, DT 9.9, DT 15, DT 16, DT 20	0.0059-0.0138 in. (0.15-0.35 mm)	0.028 in. (0.7 mm)
DT 4.5	Not available	
DT 5, DT 6, DT 8	0.0039-0.0118 in. (0.10-0.30 mm)	0.024 in. (0.6 mm)
DT 25-DT 140	0.08-0.016 in. (0.2-0.4 mm)	0.032 in. (0.8 mm)

8

Chapter Nine

Gearcase

Torque is transferred from the engine crankshaft to the gearcase by a drive shaft. A pinion gear on the drive shaft meshes with a drive gear in the gearcase to change the vertical power flow into a horizontal flow through the propeller shaft. The power head drive shaft rotates clockwise continuously when the engine is running, but propeller rotation is controlled by the gear train shifting mechanism.

On Suzuki outboards with a reverse gear, a sliding clutch engages the appropriate gear in the gearcase. This creates a direct coupling that transfers the power flow from the pinion to the propeller shaft. **Figure 1** (typical) shows the operation of the gear train.

Smaller outboards with a neutral but no reverse gear utilize a spring-loaded clutch to shift between neutral and forward gear. Gear train operation is shown in **Figure 2** (disengaged) and **Figure 3** (engaged).

The gearcase can be removed without removing the entire outboard from the boat. This chapter contains removal, overhaul and installation procedures for the propeller, gearcase and water pump. **Table 1** is at the end of the chapter.

The gearcases covered in this chapter differ somewhat in design and construction over the years covered and thus require slightly different service procedures. The chapter is arranged in a normal disassembly/assembly sequence. When only a partial repair is required, follow the procedure(s) for your gearcase to the point where the faulty parts can be replaced, then reassemble the unit.

Since this chapter covers a wide range of models from 1977-on, the gearcases shown in the accompanying illustrations are the most common ones. While it is possible that the components shown in the pictures may not be identical with those being serviced, the

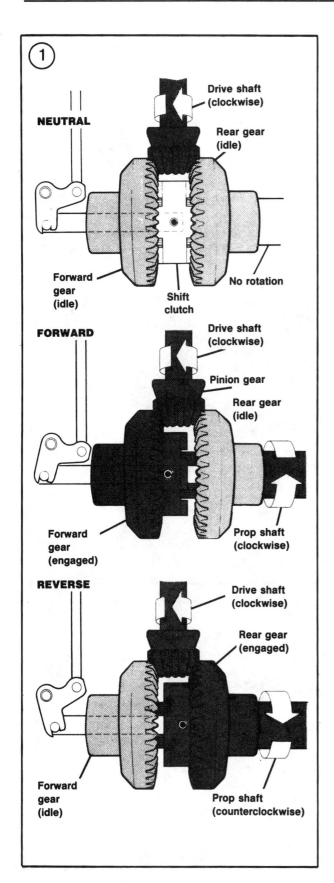

1

NEUTRAL

Drive shaft
(clockwise)

Rear gear
(idle)

Forward
gear
(idle)

Shift
clutch

No rotation

FORWARD

Drive shaft
(clockwise)

Pinion gear

Rear gear
(idle)

Forward
gear
(engaged)

Prop shaft
(clockwise)

REVERSE

Drive shaft
(clockwise)

Rear gear
(engaged)

Forward
gear
(idle)

Prop shaft
(counterclockwise)

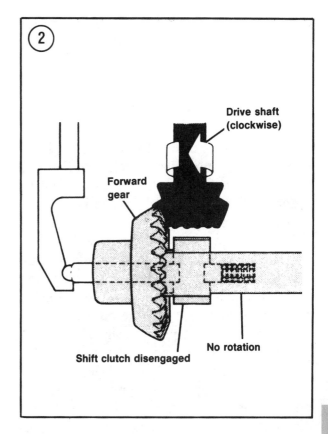

2

Drive shaft
(clockwise)

Forward
gear

Shift clutch disengaged

No rotation

9

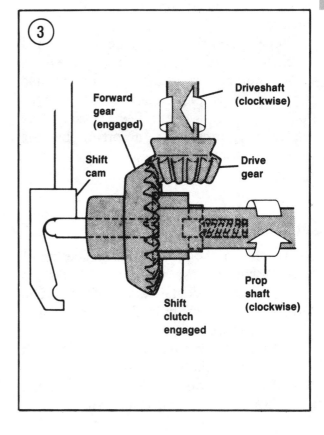

3

Forward
gear
(engaged)

Shift
cam

Driveshaft
(clockwise)

Drive
gear

Shift
clutch
engaged

Prop
shaft
(clockwise)

step-by-step procedures may be used with all models covered in this manual.

PROPELLER

The outboards covered in this manual use variations of 2 propeller attachment designs. Smaller gearcases use a drive pin that engages a slot in the propeller hub, which is retained by a cotter pin.

Some gearcases use a separate hub nut retained by a cotter pin. See **Figure 4**. In this design, a metal pin installed in the propeller shaft engages a recessed slot in the propeller hub. As the shaft rotates, the pin rotates the propeller. The drive pin is designed to break if the propeller hits an obstruction in the water. This design has 2 advantages. The pin absorbs the impact to prevent possible propeller damage. It also alerts the user to the fact that something is wrong, since the engine speed will increase immediately if the pin breaks.

Propellers on the larger gearcases ride on a ratchet-type rubber bushing or a spline drive rubber hub and are retained by a castellated nut and cotter pin or a nut and tab-type lockwasher arrangement. See **Figure 5**. Any underwater impact is absorbed by the propeller bushing/hub.

Removal/Installation

1. To remove the propeller on smaller units:
   a. Disconnect the spark plug lead(s) to prevent accidental starting of the engine.
   b. Remove and discard the cotter pin (**Figure 6**).
   c. Remove drive pin from propeller with an appropriate punch (**Figure 7**).
   d. Remove propeller and O-ring (if used). Discard the O-ring (**Figure 8**).

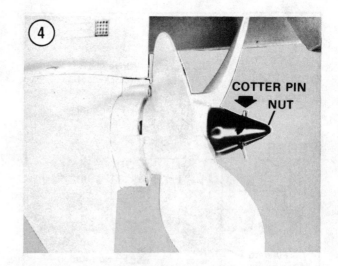

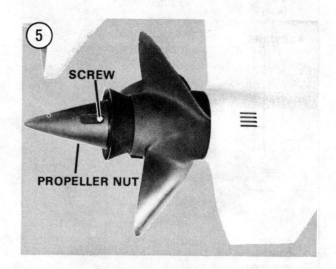

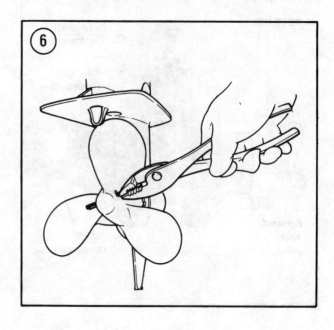

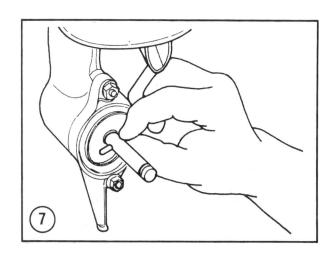

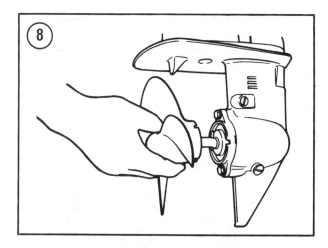

NOTE
The propeller shaft on DT 2 and DT 3.5 models is not splined but should be cleaned in Step e.

e. Clean propeller shaft splines thoroughly. Inspect the pin engagement slot in the propeller hub and shaft for wear or damage.

f. Installation is the reverse of removal. Lubricate the propeller shaft with water-resistant grease (part No. 99000-25160 or equivalent). Use new drive and cotter pins.

2. To remove the propeller on larger units:
   a. Disconnect the spark plug lead(s) to prevent accidental starting of the engine.
   b. Remove the propeller nut cotter pin or straighten the tab lockwasher. If a cotter pin is used, discard it.
   c. Remove the propeller nut from the shaft (**Figure 9**).
   d. Remove the tab lockwasher (if used) and prop nut spacer from the shaft.
   e. Remove the propeller and bushing stopper from the shaft (**Figure 10**).

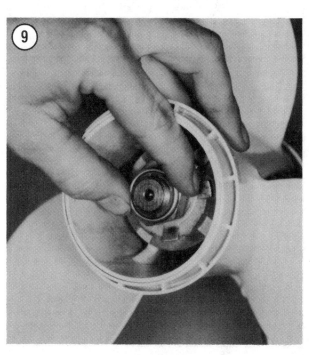

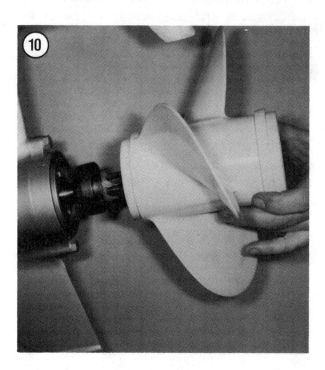

f. Clean the propeller shaft splines thoroughly.

g. Installation is the reverse of removal. Lubricate propeller shaft with water-resistant grease. If a tab lockwasher is used, check washer tab condition and replace as required. If a cotter pin is used, install a new one.

WATER PUMP

The water pump is mounted on top of the gearcase housing on all outboards covered in this manual, except the DT 2. The DT 2 water pump is mounted in a pump case installed on the propeller shaft between the gearcase housing and propeller.

The DT 2 pump impeller is secured to the propeller shaft by a pin that fits into the propeller shaft and a similar cutout in the impeller hub. The impeller on other small gearcases is secured to the drive shaft in the same manner. On larger gearcases, a drive shaft key engages a flat on the drive shaft and a cutout in the impeller hub. As the drive shaft rotates, the impeller rotates with it. Water between the impeller blades and pump housing is pumped up to the power head through the water tube.

The offset center of the pump housing causes the impeller vanes to flex during rotation. At low speeds, the pump acts as a displacement type; at high speeds, water resistance forces the vanes to flex inward and the pump becomes a centrifugal type. See **Figure 11**.

All seals and gaskets should be replaced whenever the water pump is removed. Since proper water pump operation is critical to outboard operation, it is also a good idea to install a new impeller at the same time.

Do not turn a used impeller over and reuse it. The impeller rotates in a clockwise direction with the drive shaft and the vanes

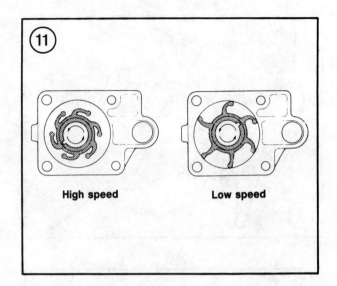

High speed   Low speed

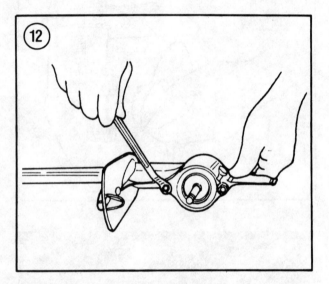

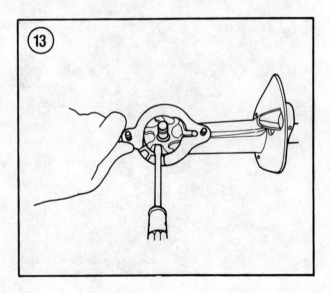

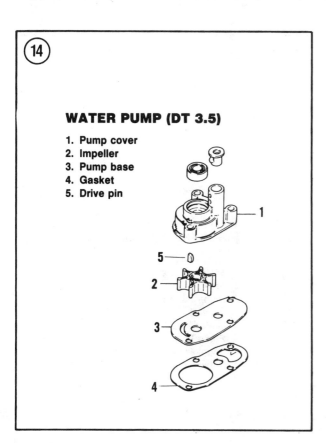

WATER PUMP (DT 3.5)

1. Pump cover
2. Impeller
3. Pump base
4. Gasket
5. Drive pin

(14)

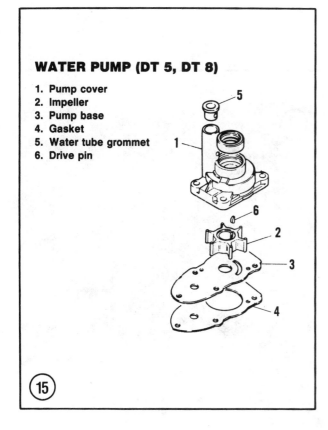

WATER PUMP (DT 5, DT 8)

1. Pump cover
2. Impeller
3. Pump base
4. Gasket
5. Water tube grommet
6. Drive pin

(15)

gradually take a set in one direction. Turning the impeller over will cause the vanes to move in a direction opposite to that which caused the set. This will result in premature impeller failure and can cause extensive power head damage.

Removal and Disassembly (DT 2)

The water pump can be serviced on this model without removing the gearcase from the drive shaft housing.

1. Remove the propeller as described in this chapter.
2. Place a suitable container under the gearcase. Remove the drain screw and drain the lubricant from the unit.
3. Remove the 2 bolts holding the water pump case cover to the gearcase housing (**Figure 12**).
4. Carefully pry the impeller from the water pump case, then remove the impeller drive pin from the propeller shaft (**Figure 13**).

Removal and Disassembly (DT 3.5-DT 65)

The water pumps used on these models vary primarily in shape and size. All use the same basic components and are serviced in essentially the same way. It is not necessary to remove the drive shaft bearing housing to service the water pump. See **Figure 14** (DT 3.5), **Figure 15** (DT 5 and DT 8) and **Figure 16** (1983-on DT 9.9 and DT 15) as typical examples.

1. Remove the gearcase as described in this chapter.
2. Secure the gearcase in a suitable holding fixture or a vise with protective jaws. If protective jaws are not available, position the gearcase upright in the vise with the skeg between wooden blocks.

9

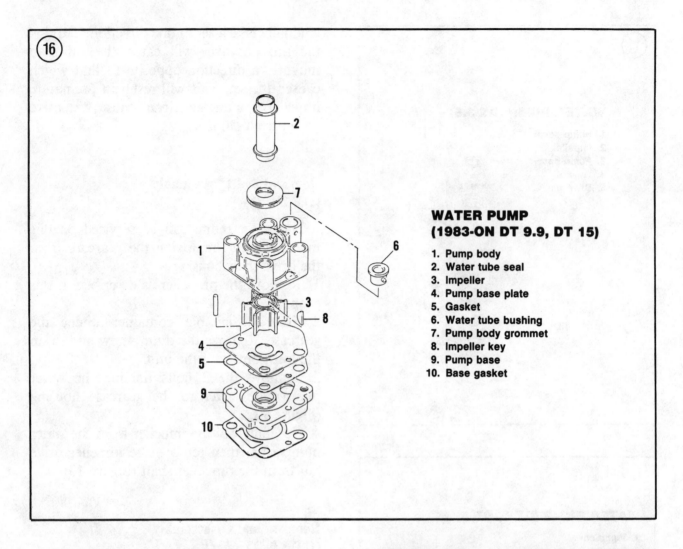

**WATER PUMP
(1983-ON DT 9.9, DT 15)**

1. Pump body
2. Water tube seal
3. Impeller
4. Pump base plate
5. Gasket
6. Water tube bushing
7. Pump body grommet
8. Impeller key
9. Pump base
10. Base gasket

3. Remove the water pump bushing from the pump cover, if so equipped.

4. Remove the fasteners holding the water pump cover in place (**Figure 17**). Remove the pump cover.

5. If the impeller does not come off with the cover, slide it off the drive shaft (**Figure 18**).

6. Remove the impeller drive pin or key from the drive shaft (**Figure 19**).

> *NOTE*
> *The DT 3.5 pump base is held in place by a nut. Remove the nut before performing Step 7.*

7. Carefully pry the pump base plate and gasket assembly (if so equipped) free of the gearcase housing.

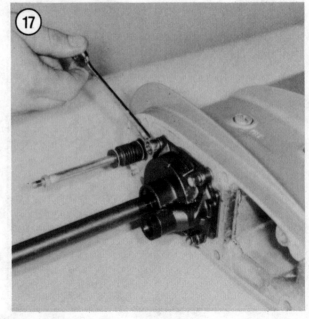

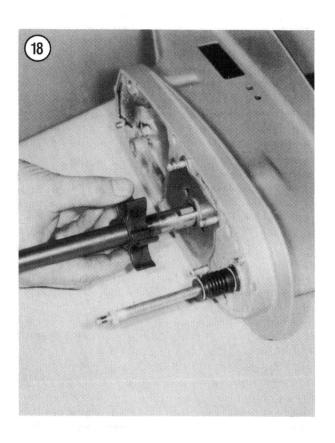

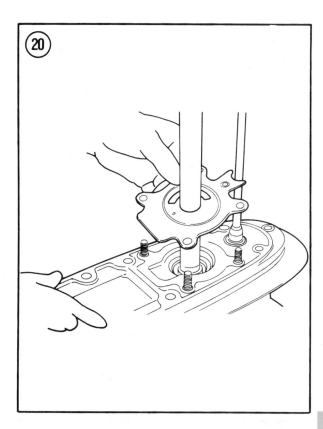

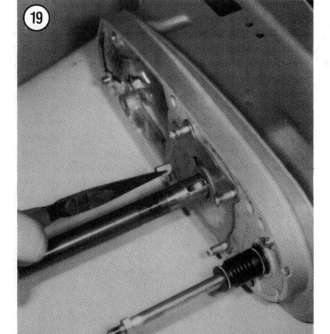

8. Remove the pump base and gasket (**Figure 20**). Discard the gasket.

9. Remove the water inlet housing and gasket, if so equipped. Discard the gasket.

Removal and Disassembly (DT 75-DT 140)

The water pumps used on these models vary primarily in shape and size. All use the same basic components and are serviced in essentially the same way. It is not necessary to remove the drive shaft bearing housing to service the water pump. See **Figure 21** (DT 75-DT 85) or **Figure 22** (DT 115-DT 140) as typical examples.

1. Remove the gearcase as described in this chapter.

2. Secure the gearcase in a suitable holding fixture or a vise with protective jaws. If protective jaws are not available, position the gearcase upright in the vise with the skeg between wooden blocks.

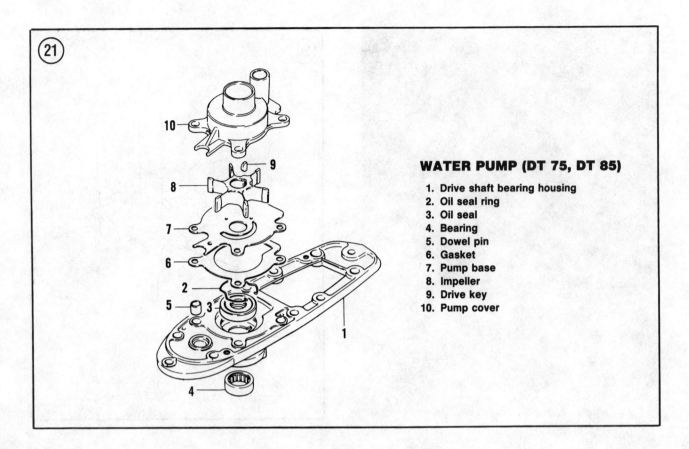

WATER PUMP (DT 75, DT 85)

1. Drive shaft bearing housing
2. Oil seal ring
3. Oil seal
4. Bearing
5. Dowel pin
6. Gasket
7. Pump base
8. Impeller
9. Drive key
10. Pump cover

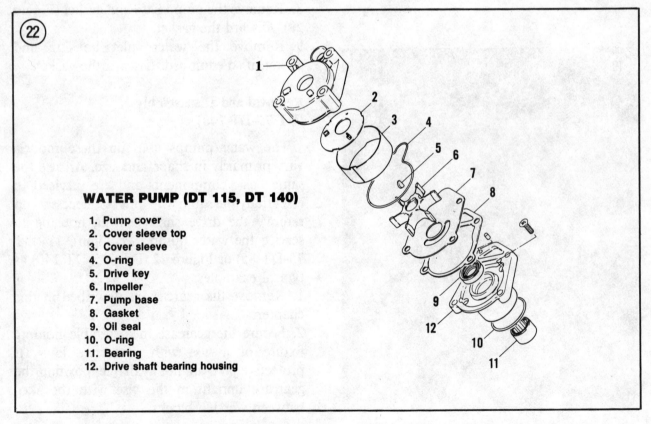

WATER PUMP (DT 115, DT 140)

1. Pump cover
2. Cover sleeve top
3. Cover sleeve
4. O-ring
5. Drive key
6. Impeller
7. Pump base
8. Gasket
9. Oil seal
10. O-ring
11. Bearing
12. Drive shaft bearing housing

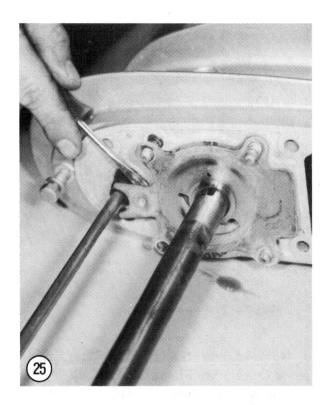

3. Remove the water tube from the pump cover.

4. Remove the bolts holding the pump cover to the gearcase. Slide the pump cover up and off the drive shaft (**Figure 23**).

5. Remove the impeller from the pump cover. If it did not come off with the cover, slide the impeller up and off the drive shaft. See **Figure 24**.

6. Remove the impeller drive key (arrow, **Figure 24**) from the drive shaft flat.

7. Carefully pry the pump base and gasket from the gearcase housing (**Figure 25**). Remove the base and discard the gasket.

Cleaning and Inspection

When removing seals from water pump cover, note and record the direction in which each seal lip faces for proper reinstallation.

1. Remove the shift rod grommet (if so equipped) and water tube seal from the pump cover.

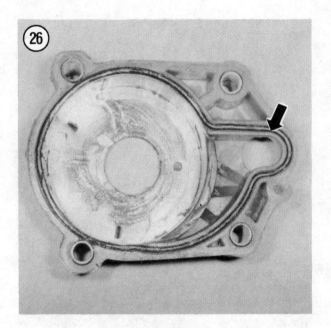

2. Remove and discard the water pump cover O-ring. See **Figure 26** (typical).

3. Check the pump cover for cracks, distortion or melting. Replace as required.

4. Clean the pump cover and base plate in solvent and blow dry with compressed air, if available.

5. Carefully remove all gasket residue from the mating surfaces.

6. If original impeller is to be reused, check bonding to hub (**Figure 27**). Check side seal surfaces and vane ends for cracks, tears, wear or a glazed or melted appearance. If any of these defects are noted, do *not* reuse impeller.

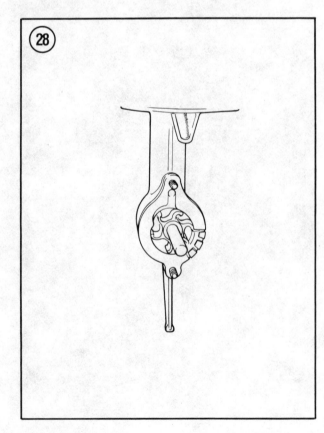

Assembly and Installation (DT 2)

1. Insert impeller drive pin in propeller shaft slot.

2. Install the impeller in the pump body with a rotating counterclockwise motion. When properly installed, the impeller vanes should be positioned as shown in **Figure 28**.

3. Install the pump case cover and tighten the fasteners to specifications (**Table 1**).

9

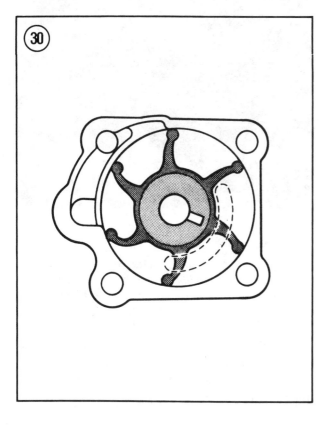

Assembly and Installation
(DT 3.5-DT 65)

1. Install the water inlet housing (if so equipped) with a new gasket.

2. Install the pump base (if so equipped) with a new gasket (**Figure 29**).

3. DT 3.5—Install and tighten the pump base stud nut.

> *CAUTION*
> *If the original impeller is to be reused, install it in the same rotational direction as removed to avoid premature failure. The drive pin groove should be visible and the curl of the blades positioned as shown in **Figure 30**.*

4. Install the impeller in the water pump cover.

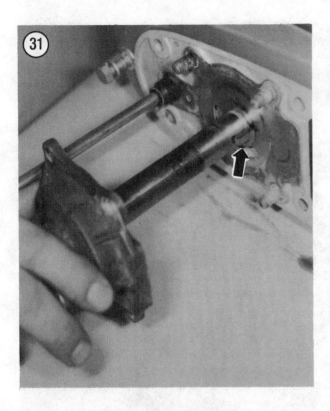

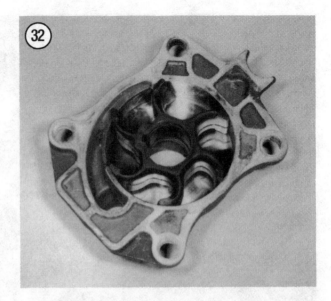

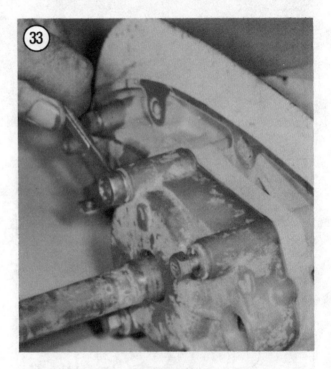

5. Slide the water pump cover down the drive shaft. Align the impeller slot with the drive shaft flat. Install impeller key on drive shaft slot and seat pump cover. See **Figure 31**.

> *CAUTION*
> *Correct housing fastener torque is important in Step 6. Excessive torque can cause the pump to crack during operation; insufficient torque may result in leakage and exhaust induction which will cause overheating.*

6. Coat the water pump cover fastener threads with Thread Lock 1342 (part No. 99000-32050). Install and tighten to specifications (**Table 1**).

**Assembly and Installation
(DT 75-DT 140)**

1. Install the pump base with a new gasket.

> *CAUTION*
> *If the original impeller is to be reused, install it in the same rotational*

direction as removed to avoid premature failure. The drive pin groove should be visible and the curl of the blades positioned as shown in **Figure 30**.

2. Install the impeller in the water pump cover (**Figure 32**).
3. Install a new O-ring in the pump cover base, if so equipped. See **Figure 26**.

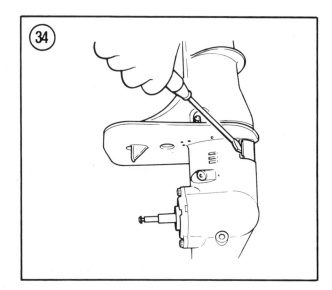

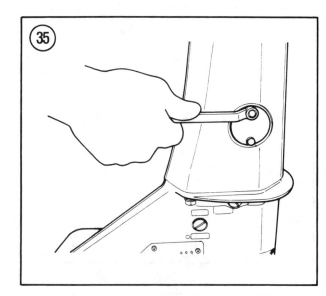

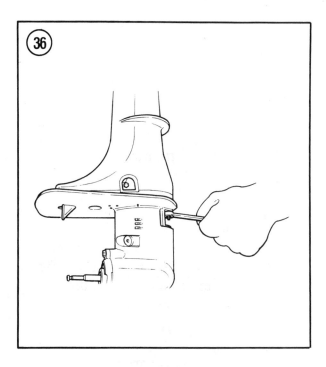

6. Install the water pump cover bolts (**Figure 33**) and tighten to specifications (**Table 1**).

7. Install the water tube in the pump cover.

9

GEARCASE

Removal/Installation
(DT 2-DT 9)

1. Remove the engine cover and disconnect the spark plug lead(s) as a safety precaution to prevent any accidental starting of the engine during lower unit removal.

2. Place the shift lever in FORWARD.

3. Remove the propeller as described in this chapter.

4A. DT 2, DT 3.5, DT 7.5 and DT 9—Pry the clip from the front of the drive shaft housing with a screwdriver. See **Figure 34** (typical).

4B. All others—Pry or unbolt the shift lever hole cover as required from the drive shaft housing, then remove the shift rod connector bolt. See **Figure 35** (typical).

5A. DT 2, DT 3.5 and DT 4.5—Remove the 2 nuts or bolts holding the gearcase to the drive shaft housing (**Figure 36**).

4. Lubricate the O-ring with water-resistant grease (part No. 99000-32160 or equivalent).

5. Slide the water pump cover down the drive shaft. Align the impeller slot with the drive shaft flat. Install impeller key on drive shaft slot and seat pump cover.

> *CAUTION*
> *Correct housing fastener torque is important in Step 6. Excessive torque can cause the pump to crack during operation; insufficient torque may result in leakage and exhaust induction which will cause overheating.*

5B. DT 5, DT 6 and DT 8—Remove the 4 bolts holding the gearcase to the drive shaft housing (**Figure 37**).

5C. DT 7.5 and DT 9—Remove the 4 nuts holding the gearcase to the drive shaft housing (**Figure 38**).

6. Tilt the drive shaft housing up and carefully separate it from the gearcase. Remove the gearcase from the drive shaft housing.

7. Install the gearcase in an appropriate holding fixture.

8. Place a suitable container under the gearcase. Remove the drain screw (**Figure 39**). Drain the lubricant from the unit.

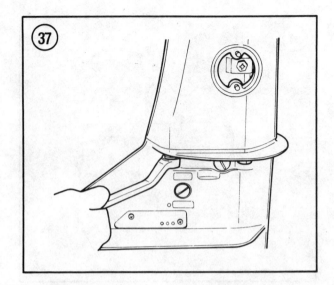

NOTE
If the lubricant is creamy in color or metallic particles are found in Step 9, the gearcase must be completely disassembled to determine and correct the cause of the problem.

9. Wipe a small amount of lubricant on a finger and rub the finger and thumb together. Check for the presence of metallic particles in the lubricant. Note the color of the lubricant. A white or creamy color indicates water in the lubricant. Check the drain container for signs of water separation from the lubricant.

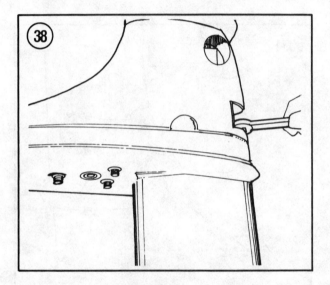

CAUTION
Do not grease the top of the drive shaft in Step 10. This may excessively preload the drive shaft and crankshaft when the mounting fasteners are tightened and cause a premature failure of the power head or gearcase.

10. To reinstall the gearcase, make sure the shift rod is in the FORWARD position (DT 3.5-DT 9) and lightly lubricate the drive shaft splines with water-resistant grease (part No. 99000-25160) or equivalent.

11. Apply a thin but uniform coat of Silicone Seal (part No. 99000-31120) or equivalent to

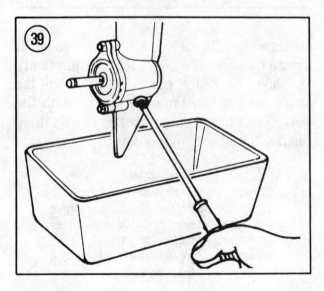

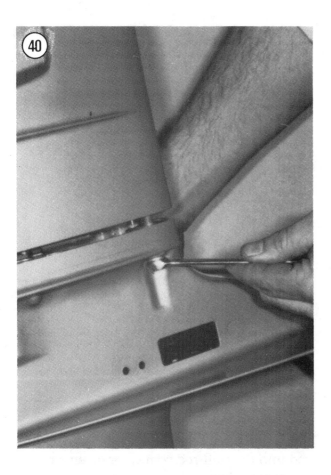

the gearcase and drive shaft housing mating surfaces.

12. DT 2—Wipe the drive shaft housing bolt threads with Thread Lock 1342 (part No. 99000-32050 or equivalent).

13. Position the gearcase under the drive shaft housing. Align the drive shaft splines with the crankshaft, insert the water tube into the water pump case and fit the upper shift rod into the shift rod connector.

CAUTION
Do not rotate the flywheel counterclockwise in Step 14. This can damage the water pump impeller.

14. Seat the gearcase against the drive shaft housing, rotating the flywheel clockwise as required until the drive shaft and crankshaft engage.

15. Install the gearcase fasteners and tighten to specifications (**Table 1**).

16. DT 3.5-DT 9—Make sure the engine shift lever is in FORWARD and install the shift rod connector bolt. Place the shift lever in NEUTRAL and make sure the propeller rotates freely, then shift back into FORWARD and make sure the propeller will only rotate clockwise. If the propeller does not rotate as indicated, loosen the shift rod connector bolt and readjust the position of the connector or rods as required.

17. All except DT 2—Install the shift lever hole cover. If cover is retained by 2 nuts, use a new cover gasket (pry-type covers have no gasket).

18. Install the propeller as described in this chapter.

19. Reconnect the spark plug lead(s) and refill the gearcase with proper type and quantity of lubricant. See Chapter Four.

9

Removal/Installation
DT 9.9-DT 40

1. Remove the engine cover and disconnect the spark plug leads as a safety precaution to prevent any accidental starting of the engine during lower unit removal.

2. Shift the engine into FORWARD.

3. Remove the propeller as described in this chapter.

4. Remove the shift coupler cover from the front of the drive shaft housing, if so equipped.

5. Loosen the lower shift rod connector bolt or locknut. Loosen the upper shift rod turnbuckle (if so equipped) and separate the shift rods. **Figure 40** shows the turnbuckle connection.

6. Remove the fasteners holding the gearcase to the drive shaft housing.

7. Tilt the drive shaft housing up and carefully separate it from the gearcase.

Remove the gearcase from the drive shaft housing.

8. Install the gearcase in an appropriate holding fixture.

9. Place a suitable container under the gearcase. Remove the vent and drain screws. Drain the lubricant from the unit.

> *NOTE*
> *If the lubricant is creamy in color or metallic particles are found in Step 10, the gearcase must be completely disassembled to determine and correct the cause of the problem.*

10. Wipe a small amount of lubricant on a finger and rub the finger and thumb together. Check for the presence of metallic particles in the lubricant. Note the color of the lubricant. A white or creamy color indicates water in the lubricant. Check the drain container for signs of water separation from the lubricant.

> *CAUTION*
> *Do not grease the top of the drive shaft in Step 11. This may excessively preload the drive shaft and crankshaft when the mounting fasteners are tightened and cause a premature failure of the power head or gearcase.*

11. To reinstall the gearcase, pull the lower shift rod upward as far as possible to make sure it is in the FORWARD position and lightly lubricate the drive shaft splines with water-resistant grease (part No. 99000-25160 or equivalent).

12. Apply a thin but uniform coat of Silicone Seal (part No. 99000-31120) or equivalent to the gearcase and drive shaft housing mating surfaces.

13. Position the gearcase under the drive shaft housing. Align the drive shaft splines with the crankshaft, insert the water tube into

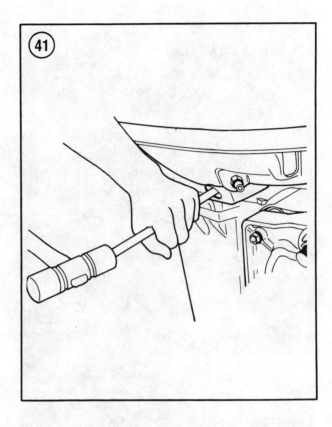

the water pump case and fit the upper shift rod into the shift rod connector or upper shift rod turnbuckle.

> *CAUTION*
> *Do not rotate the flywheel counterclockwise in Step 14. This can damage the water pump impeller.*

14. Seat the gearcase in place, rotating the flywheel clockwise as required until the drive shaft and crankshaft engage.

15. Install the gearcase fasteners and tighten to specifications (**Table 1**).

16. Make sure the engine shift lever is in FORWARD and tighten the shift rod connector or upper shift rod turnbuckle. Place the shift lever in NEUTRAL and make sure the propeller rotates freely, then shift back into FORWARD and make sure the propeller will only rotate clockwise. If the propeller does not rotate as indicated, loosen the shift rod connector or upper shift rod turnbuckle and readjust the position of the

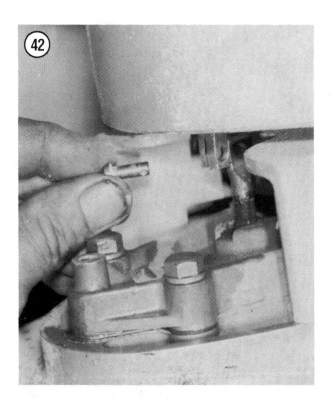

connector/turnbuckle or rods as required. When shift pattern is correct, tighten the shift rod connector or lower shift rod locknut securely.

17. Install the shift coupler cover at the front of the drive shaft housing, if so equipped.

18. Install the propeller as described in this chapter.

19. Reconnect the spark plug leads and refill the gearcase with proper type and quantity of lubricant. See Chapter Four.

Removal/Installation (DT 50-DT 140)

1. Disconnect the spark plug leads as a safety precaution to prevent any accidental starting of the engine during lower unit removal.

2. Place a container under the gearcase. Remove the vent and drain plugs. Drain the lubricant from the unit.

NOTE
If the lubricant is creamy in color or metallic particles are found in Step 3,

the gearcase must be completely disassembled to determine and correct the cause of the problem.

3. Wipe a small amount of lubricant on a finger and rub the finger and thumb together. Check for the presence of metallic particles in the lubricant. Note the color of the lubricant. A white or creamy color indicates water in the lubricant. Check the drain container for signs of water separation from the lubricant.

4. Remove the propeller as described in this chapter.

5. DT 50-65—Place the engine in NEUTRAL and remove the grommet from the starboard side of the lower support. Insert an appropriate socket wrench and remove the clutch shaft nuts, then disconnect the upper and lower shift shafts with a suitable drift and mallet. See **Figure 41**.

6. DT 75-DT 140—Place the engine in NEUTRAL and remove the cover at the front of the drive shaft. Remove and discard the shift rod connector cotter pin (use needlenose pliers). Remove the connector pin (**Figure 42**).

7. Remove the fasteners holding the gearcase to the drive shaft housing.

8. Remove the gearcase from the drive shaft housing and mount it in a suitable holding fixture.

CAUTION
Do not grease the top of the drive shaft in Step 9. This may excessively preload the drive shaft and crankshaft when the mounting bolts are tightened and cause a premature failure of the power head or gearcase.

9. To reinstall the gearcase, lightly lubricate the drive shaft splines with water-resistant grease (part No. 99000-32160) or equivalent.

10. Apply a thin but uniform coat of Silicone Seal (part No. 99000-31120) or equivalent to the gearcase and drive shaft housing mating surfaces.

9

11. Position the gearcase under the drive shaft housing. Align the drive shaft and crankshaft splines, insert the water tube into the water pump case and guide the upper shift rod into the lower shift rod connector.

CAUTION
Do not rotate the flywheel counterclockwise in Step 12. This can damage the water pump impeller.

12. Seat the gearcase in place, rotating the flywheel clockwise as required until the drive shaft and crankshaft engage.

13. Wipe the gearcase bolt threads with Silicone Seal (part No. 99000-31120) or equivalent and tighten to specifications (**Table 1**).

14. DT 50-65—Connect the shift rods and install the 2 nuts. Reinstall the lower support housing grommet.

15. DT 75-DT 140—Connect the shift rods and install the connector pin with a new cotter pin. Install the drive shaft housing cover (**Figure 43**).

16. Place the shift lever in NEUTRAL and make sure the propeller rotates freely, then shift back into FORWARD and make sure the propeller will only rotate clockwise. If the propeller does not rotate as indicated, make sure the gearcase is in NEUTRAL and repeat Step 14 or Step 15 as required until the shift pattern is correct.

17. Install the propeller as described in this chapter.

18. Reconnect the spark plug leads and refill the gearcase with proper type and quantity of lubricant. See Chapter Four.

Disassembly/Assembly (DT 2)

Refer to **Figure 44** for this procedure.

1. Remove the gearcase as described in this chapter.

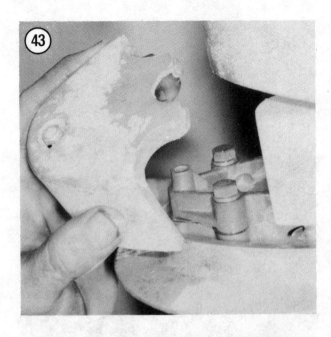

2. Secure the gearcase in a suitable holding fixture or a vise with protective jaws. If protective jaws are not available, position the gearcase upright with the skeg between wooden blocks in the vise.

3. Remove the water pump as described in this chapter.

4. Carefully pry the water pump case free of the gearcase housing (**Figure 45**).

5. Remove the water tube and drive shaft seal pipe (**Figure 46**).

6. Use a pair of screwdrivers as shown in **Figure 47** to pry the E-clip from the pinion gear.

7. Remove the drive shaft, then reach into the gearcase housing and remove the pinion gear and shim(s). See **Figure 48**.

8. Remove the propeller shaft and gear assembly (**Figure 49**). Reach into the gearcase housing and remove the shim(s).

9. Remove the drive shaft seal pipe bushing and oil seal.

10. If inspection of the drive shaft bearings indicates replacement, proceed as follows:

   a. Remove the drive shaft snap ring with pliers (part No. 09900-06108) or equivalent.

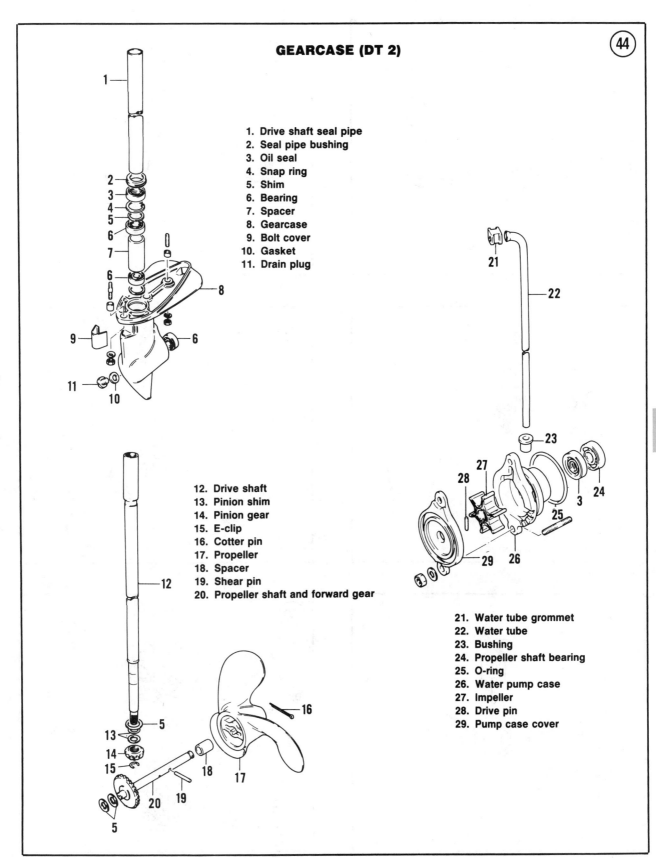

GEARCASE (DT 2) 44

1. Drive shaft seal pipe
2. Seal pipe bushing
3. Oil seal
4. Snap ring
5. Shim
6. Bearing
7. Spacer
8. Gearcase
9. Bolt cover
10. Gasket
11. Drain plug

12. Drive shaft
13. Pinion shim
14. Pinion gear
15. E-clip
16. Cotter pin
17. Propeller
18. Spacer
19. Shear pin
20. Propeller shaft and forward gear

21. Water tube grommet
22. Water tube
23. Bushing
24. Propeller shaft bearing
25. O-ring
26. Water pump case
27. Impeller
28. Drive pin
29. Pump case cover

9

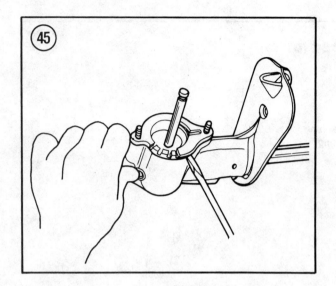

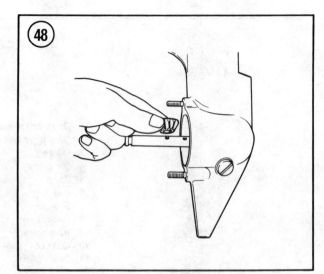

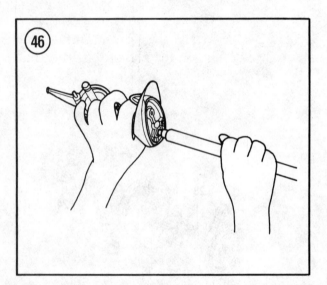

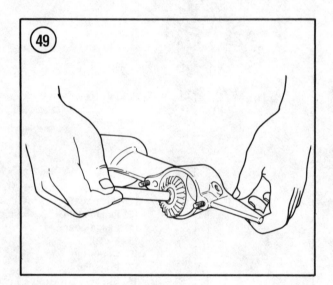

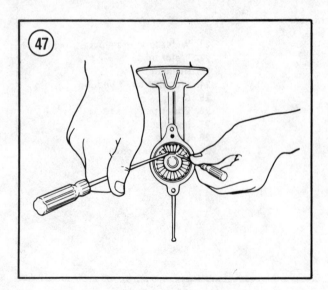

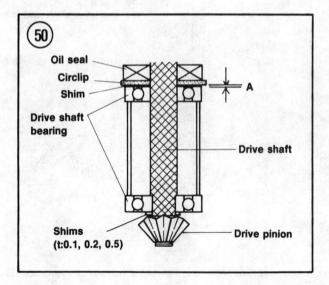

Oil seal

Circlip

Shim

Drive shaft bearing

A

Drive shaft

Shims
(t:0.1, 0.2, 0.5)

Drive pinion

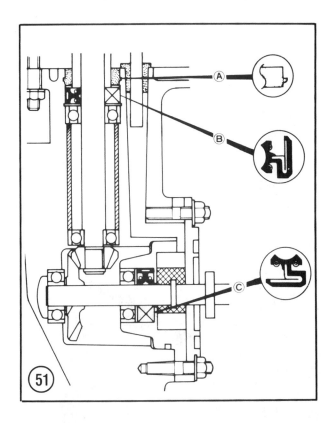

b. Remove the shim(s) from the top drive shaft bearing.

c. Insert a bearing remover handle in the seal pipe bore.

d. Insert the bearing remover in the gearcase bore and attach to the remover handle.

e. Pull the 2 drive shaft bearings and spacer from the gearcase.

11. Clean and inspect all parts as described in this chapter.

12. If the drive shaft bearings were replaced:

a. Install new bearings with the spacer between them using an appropriate bearing installer.

b. Install the shim(s) on the top drive shaft bearing.

c. Install the drive shaft snap ring with pliers (part No. 09900-06180) or equivalent.

d. Temporarily install the drive shaft with the pinion gear and shimming. Pull upward on drive shaft. It should not move more than 0.004 in. (0.1 mm). If movement exceeds this specification, remove the snap ring and exchange the shim(s) as required to bring the clearance within specifications. See **Figure 50**.

13. Once drive shaft bearing shimming is correct, install a new oil seal and drive shaft bushing with their lips positioned as shown in A and B, **Figure 51**. Coat lips with water-resistant grease (part No. 99000-32160 or equivalent).

14. Install the propeller shaft shims and propeller shaft in the gearcase housing.

15. Position the pinion gear and shim(s) in the housing under the drive shaft bore, insert the drive shaft and engage the pinion gear. Install the E-clip on the end of the drive shaft to retain the pinion gear.

16. Install the drive shaft seal pipe and water tube.

17. Remove the water pump case bearing and oil seal.

18. Install a new bearing with an installer (part No. 09914-79510).

19. Install a new oil seal and coat its lips with water-resistant grease.

20. Remove and discard the water pump case O-ring. Lubricate a new O-ring with water-resistant grease and install on case.

21. Install the water pump as described in this chapter.

22. Install the gearcase as described in this chapter. Fill with recommended type and quantity of lubricant. See Chapter Four.

23. Check gearcase lubricant level after engine has been run. Change the lubricant after 10 hours of operation (break-in period). See Chapter Four.

Disassembly/Assembly
(DT 3.5, 1983-on DT 9.9 and DT 15)

Refer to **Figure 52** (DT 3.5) or **Figure 53** (DT 9.9 and DT 15) for this procedure.

9

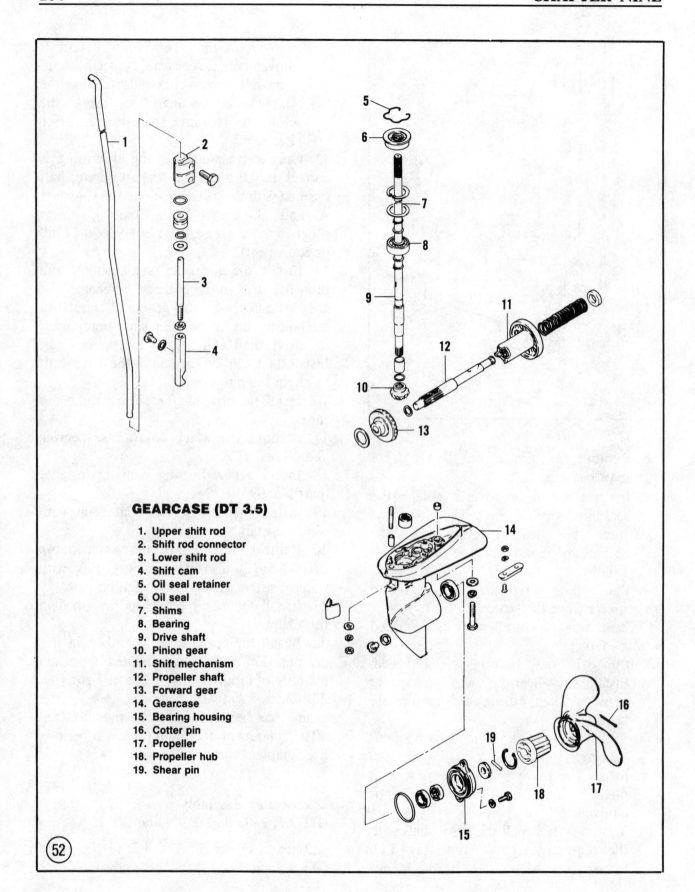

GEARCASE (DT 3.5)

1. Upper shift rod
2. Shift rod connector
3. Lower shift rod
4. Shift cam
5. Oil seal retainer
6. Oil seal
7. Shims
8. Bearing
9. Drive shaft
10. Pinion gear
11. Shift mechanism
12. Propeller shaft
13. Forward gear
14. Gearcase
15. Bearing housing
16. Cotter pin
17. Propeller
18. Propeller hub
19. Shear pin

52

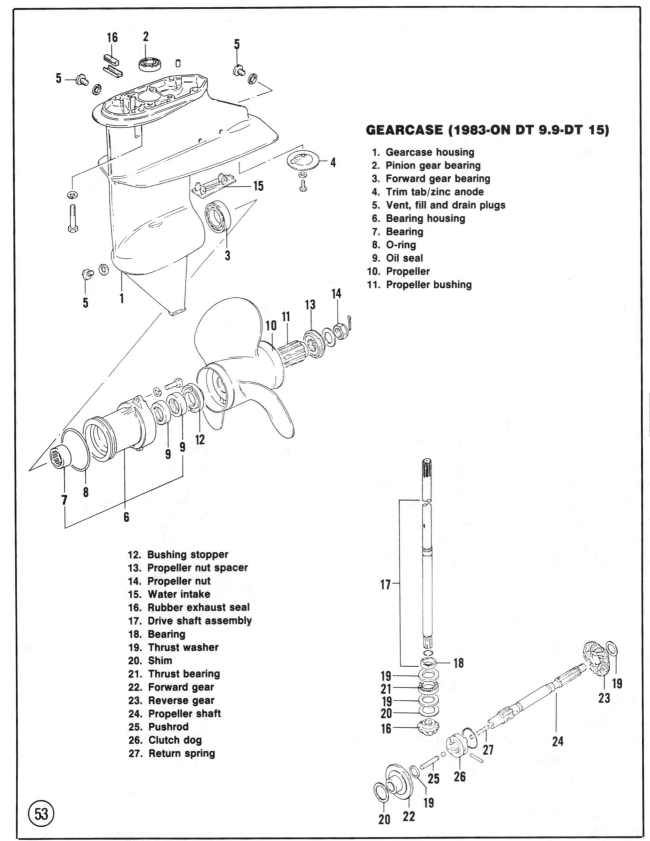

GEARCASE (1983-ON DT 9.9-DT 15)

1. Gearcase housing
2. Pinion gear bearing
3. Forward gear bearing
4. Trim tab/zinc anode
5. Vent, fill and drain plugs
6. Bearing housing
7. Bearing
8. O-ring
9. Oil seal
10. Propeller
11. Propeller bushing

12. Bushing stopper
13. Propeller nut spacer
14. Propeller nut
15. Water intake
16. Rubber exhaust seal
17. Drive shaft assembly
18. Bearing
19. Thrust washer
20. Shim
21. Thrust bearing
22. Forward gear
23. Reverse gear
24. Propeller shaft
25. Pushrod
26. Clutch dog
27. Return spring

9

53

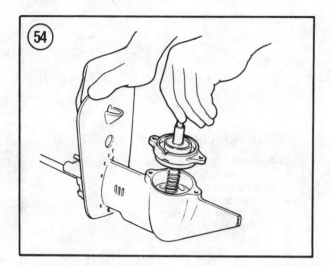

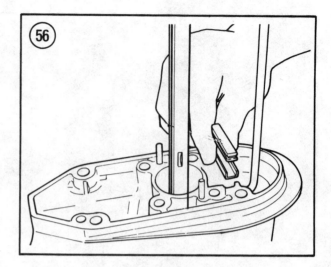

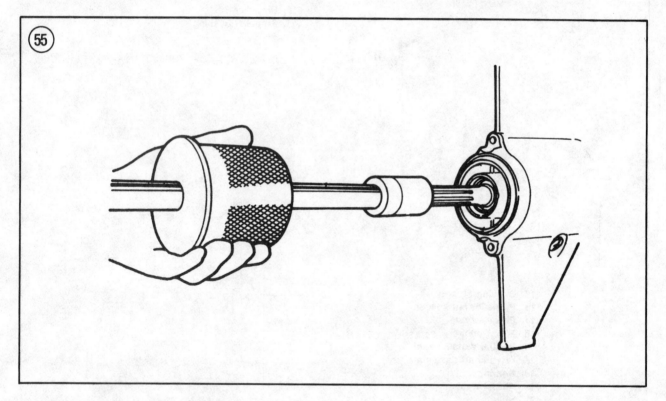

1. Remove the gearcase as described in this chapter.

2. Secure the gearcase in a suitable holding fixture or a vise with protective jaws. If protective jaws are not available, position the gearcase upright with the skeg between wooden blocks in a vise.

3. Remove the water pump as described in this chapter.

NOTE
If bearing housing is corroded in prop shaft bore and cannot be removed easily by hand in Step 4A, tap side of housing cap with a rubber mallet to rotate cap ears and pry off.

4A. DT 3.5—Remove the 2 bearing housing bolts. Remove the bearing housing and propeller shaft assembly (**Figure 54**).

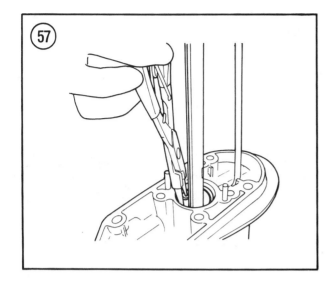

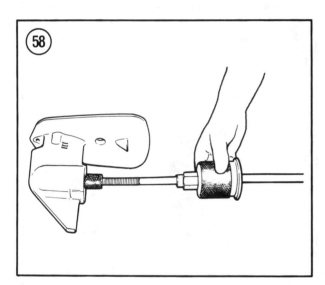

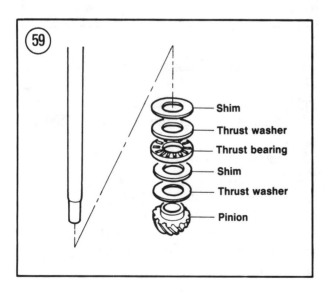

- Shim
- Thrust washer
- Thrust bearing
- Shim
- Thrust washer
- Pinion

4B. DT 9.9-DT 15—Remove the 2 bearing housing bolts. Attach remover tool (part No. 09950-59320 or equivalent) to propeller shaft and connect a slide hammer. Remove the bearing housing and propeller shaft assembly. See **Figure 55**.

5. Slide the bearing housing off the propeller shaft.

6. DT 9.9-DT 15—Remove the rubber exhaust seal (**Figure 56**).

7. DT 3.5—Remove the drive shaft oil seal retaining ring. Pry the seal out and off the shaft.

8. Remove the drive shaft bearing snap ring with pliers part No. 09900-06108 or equivalent (**Figure 57**). Discard the snap ring.

9. Remove the drive shaft from the gearcase housing. The shim pack, thrust bearing and thrust washer(s) should come with it.

10. Reach into the propeller shaft bore and remove the pinion gear, then the forward gear and shim(s).

11. Attach bearing remover (part No. 09913-69911) to a slide hammer and remove the forward gear bearing. See **Figure 58**.

12. DT 9.9-DT 15—Remove the shift rod collar nut. Remove the shift rod.

13. Disassemble the propeller shaft and clutch assembly as described in this chapter.

14. Clean and inspect all parts as described in this chapter.

15. Install a new forward gear bearing with installer part No. 09914-79610 or equivalent.

16. Fit the forward gear shim(s) over the shaft at the rear of the gear and install gear/shim assembly in the prop shaft bore.

17. DT 9.9-DT 15—Insert shift rod assembly in gearcase bore and install collar nut.

18. Insert the pinion gear in the prop shaft bore. Fit the gear into the drive shaft bore and mesh it with the forward gear.

19. Reassemble the bearing, shim pack and thrust washer to the drive shaft in the same order as removed. See **Figure 59**.

9

20. Insert the drive shaft into the gearcase housing with a rotating motion and engage the pinion gear.

21. Install a new drive shaft bearing snap ring. Make sure the snap ring fits properly into its groove.

22. DT 3.5—Install a new drive shaft oil seal. Lubricate the seal lip with water-resistant grease (part No. 99000-32160) or equivalent. Install the retaining ring (**Figure 60**).

23. DT 9.9-DT 15—Install the rubber exhaust seal.

24. Check pinion gear depth and forward gear backlash as described in this chapter.

25. Remove and discard the bearing housing bearing and oil seal.

26. Install a new housing bearing with installer part No. 09914-79610 or equivalent.

27. Install a new oil seal. Coat seal lips with water-resistant grease (part No. 99000-32160 or equivalent).

28. Install a new bearing housing O-ring. Lubricate housing O-ring with water-resistant grease.

29. Insert propeller shaft into housing bore and engage the forward gear.

30. Coat bearing housing outer edges (front and rear) with water-resistant grease.

31. Carefully install bearing housing on propeller shaft.

32A. DT 3.5—Temporarily reinstall bearing housing and check the propeller shaft end play by pushing and pulling the shaft as shown in **Figure 61**. Correct end play should be 0.008-0.016 in. (0.2-0.4 mm). If not within specifications, disassemble the gearcase and change the shim pack thickness. Add shims to decrease or remove shims to increase end play.

32B. DT 9.9-DT15—Check propeller shaft thrust clearance as described in this chapter.

33. When proper propeller shaft end play/thrust clearance has been established, coat the bearing housing bolt threads with Silicone Seal (part No. 99000-31120) or

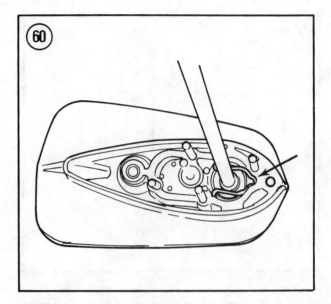

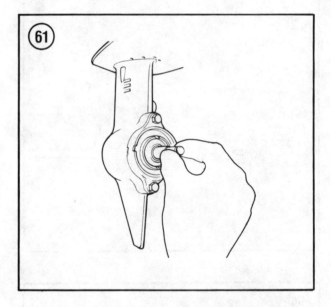

equivalent. Install housing (use installer part No. 09922-59510 with DT 9.9-DT 15) and tighten bolts to specifications (**Table 1**).

34. Install the water pump as described in this chapter.

35. Install the gearcase as described in this chapter. Fill with recommended type and quantity of lubricant. See Chapter Four.

36. Check gearcase lubricant level after engine has been run. Change the lubricant after 10 hours of operation (break-in period). See Chapter Four.

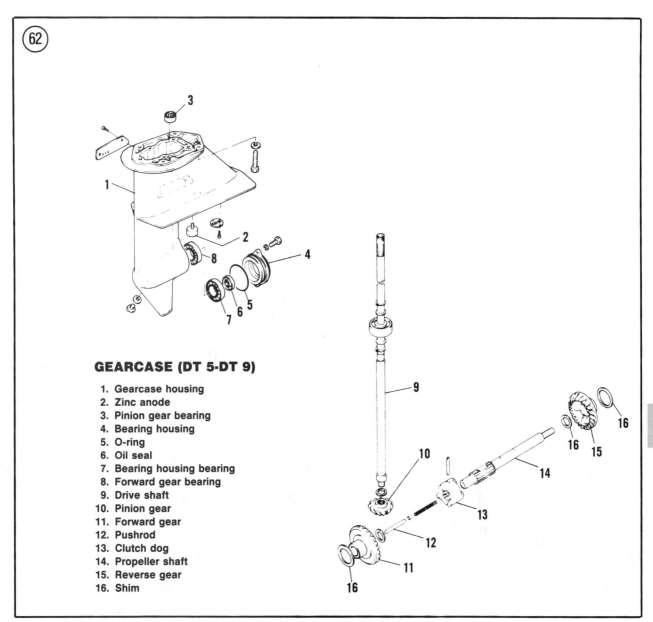

GEARCASE (DT 5-DT 9)

1. Gearcase housing
2. Zinc anode
3. Pinion gear bearing
4. Bearing housing
5. O-ring
6. Oil seal
7. Bearing housing bearing
8. Forward gear bearing
9. Drive shaft
10. Pinion gear
11. Forward gear
12. Pushrod
13. Clutch dog
14. Propeller shaft
15. Reverse gear
16. Shim

9

**Disassembly/Assembly
(DT 5, DT 6, DT 7.5, DT 8, DT 9,
1977-1982 DT 9.9 and DT 16)**

Refer to **Figure 62** (DT 5-DT 9) or **Figure 63** (1977-1982 DT 9.9 and DT 16) for this procedure.

1. Remove the gearcase as described in this chapter.

2. Secure the gearcase in a suitable holding fixture or a vise with protective jaws. If protective jaws are not available, position the gearcase upright with the skeg between wooden blocks in a vise.

3. Remove the water pump as described in this chapter.

NOTE
If bearing housing is corroded in prop shaft bore and cannot be removed easily by hand in Step 4A, tap side of housing cap with a rubber mallet to rotate cap ears and pry off.

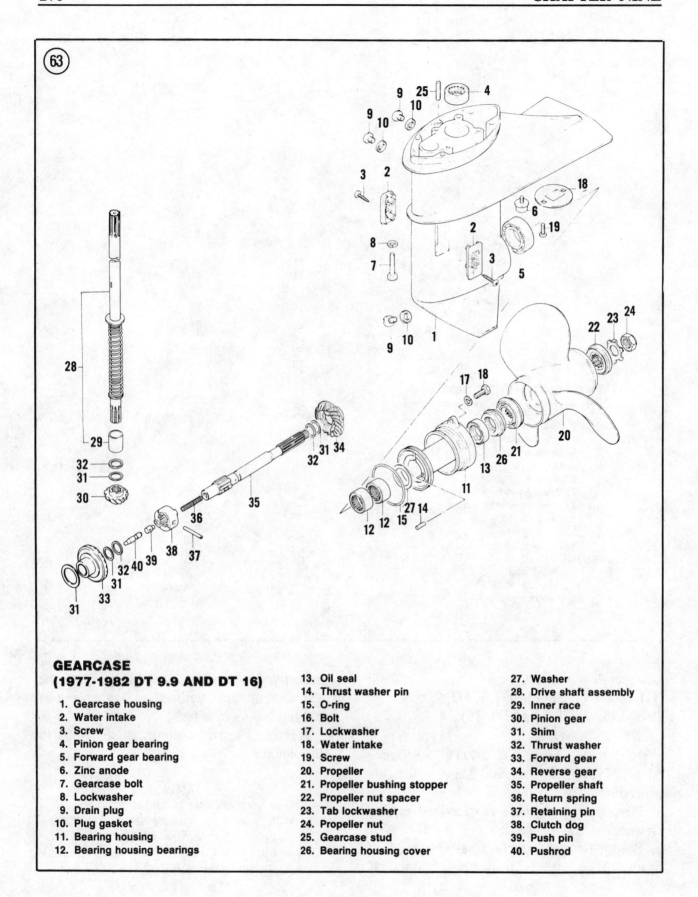

GEARCASE
(1977-1982 DT 9.9 AND DT 16)

1. Gearcase housing
2. Water intake
3. Screw
4. Pinion gear bearing
5. Forward gear bearing
6. Zinc anode
7. Gearcase bolt
8. Lockwasher
9. Drain plug
10. Plug gasket
11. Bearing housing
12. Bearing housing bearings
13. Oil seal
14. Thrust washer pin
15. O-ring
16. Bolt
17. Lockwasher
18. Water intake
19. Screw
20. Propeller
21. Propeller bushing stopper
22. Propeller nut spacer
23. Tab lockwasher
24. Propeller nut
25. Gearcase stud
26. Bearing housing cover
27. Washer
28. Drive shaft assembly
29. Inner race
30. Pinion gear
31. Shim
32. Thrust washer
33. Forward gear
34. Reverse gear
35. Propeller shaft
36. Return spring
37. Retaining pin
38. Clutch dog
39. Push pin
40. Pushrod

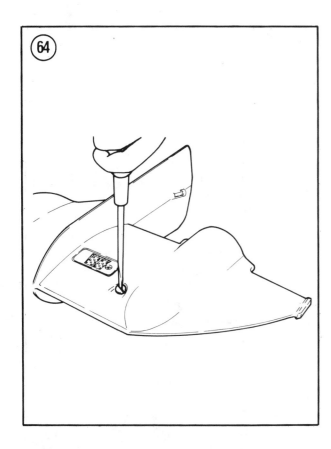

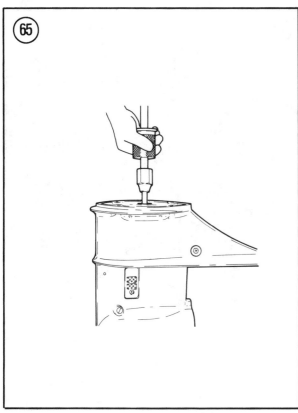

4A. DT 5-DT 9—Remove the 2 bearing housing bolts. Remove the bearing housing and propeller shaft assembly.

4B. DT 9.9-DT 16—Remove the 2 bearing housing bolts. Attach remover tool (part No. 09950-59320 or equivalent) to propeller shaft and connect a slide hammer. Remove the bearing housing and propeller shaft assembly. See **Figure 55**.

5. Unbolt the drive shaft bearing housing. Remove the bearing housing with the drive shaft. On DT 5-DT 9 models, the shift rod assembly will come free with the bearing housing and drive shaft.

6. Remove the drive shaft bearing housing snap ring (if used) and separate the housing from the drive shaft.

7. DT 9.9-DT 16—Loosen the shift cam stop screw (**Figure 64**) and remove the shift rod.

8. Reach into the propeller shaft bore and remove the pinion gear, then the forward gear and shim(s).

9. Attach bearing remover (part No. 09913-69911) to a slide hammer and remove the forward gear bearing.

10. Use the same remover/slide hammer combination to remove the gearcase drive shaft bearing. See **Figure 65**.

11. Clean and inspect all parts as described in this chapter.

12. Install new forward gear and drive shaft bearings with installer part No. 09914-79610 or equivalent.

13. Fit the forward gear shim(s) over the shaft at the rear of the gear and install in the prop shaft bore.

14. Insert the pinion gear with shim(s) in the prop shaft bore. Fit the gear into the drive shaft bore and mesh it with the forward gear.

15. Insert the drive shaft into the gearcase housing with a rotating motion and engage the pinion gear.

16. DT 9.9-DT 16—Lubricate the shift rod O-ring with water-resistant grease (part No. 99000-32160 or equivalent) and insert shift

9

rod assembly in gearcase (**Figure 66**). Install shift cam stop screw (**Figure 64**).

17. Lubricate the drive shaft bearing housing oil seal lip with water-resistant grease. Install the housing on the drive shaft and seat in the gearcase housing. Install housing snap ring (if used) and make sure it fits properly into its groove.

18. DT 5-DT 9—Lubricate the shift rod O-ring with water-resistant grease (part No. 99000-32160 or equivalent) and install with the water pump base as shown in **Figure 67**.

19. Install the drive shaft bearing housing retaining nut.

20. Install the water pump as described in this chapter.

21. Check pinion gear depth and forward gear backlash as described in this chapter.

22. Remove and discard the bearing housing bearing and oil seal.

23. Install a new housing bearing with installer part No. 09914-79610 or equivalent.

24. Install a new oil seal. See **Figure 68** (DT 5-DT 9) or **Figure 69** (DT 9.9-DT 16). Coat seal lips with water-resistant grease.

25. Install a new bearing housing O-ring. Lubricate housing O-ring and end of propeller shaft pushrod with water-resistant grease.

26. Insert propeller shaft into housing bore and engage the forward gear.

27A. DT 5-DT 9—Coat edge of bearing housing with Silicone Seal (part No. 99000-31050) or equivalent.

27B. DT 9.9-DT 16—Coat bearing housing outer edges (front and rear) with water-resistant grease (**Figure 70**).

28. Carefully install bearing housing on propeller shaft.

29. Check propeller shaft thrust clearance as described in this chapter.

30. When proper propeller shaft thrust clearance has been established, coat the bearing housing bolt threads with Silicone Seal (part No. 99000-31120) or equivalent.

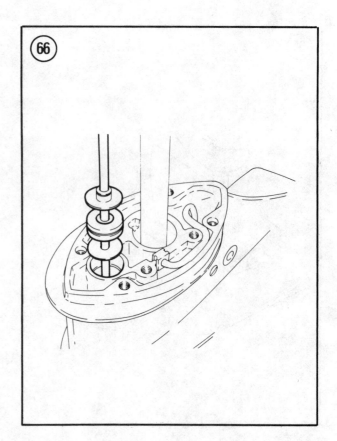

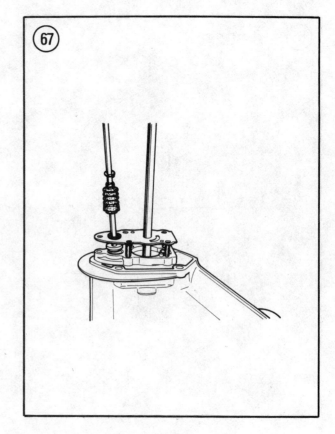

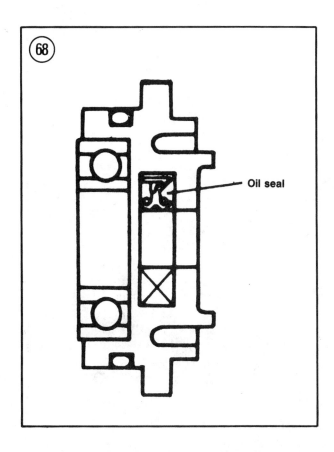

Oil seal

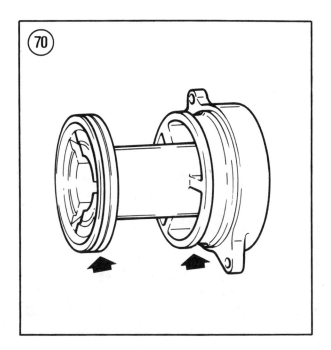

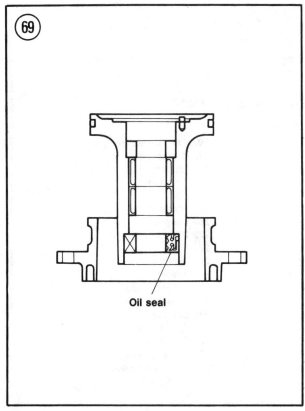

Oil seal

Install housing (use installer part No. 09922-59510 with DT 9.9-DT 16) and tighten bolts to specifications (**Table 1**).

31. Install the gearcase as described in this chapter. Fill with recommended type and quantity of lubricant. See Chapter Four.

32. Check gearcase lubricant level after engine has been run. Change the lubricant after 10 hours of operation (break-in period). See Chapter Four.

Disassembly/Assembly (DT 20, 1977-1982 DT 25)

Refer to **Figure 71** (DT 20P and DT25P) or **Figure 72** (DT 25) for this procedure.

1. Remove the gearcase as described in this chapter.

2. Secure the gearcase in a suitable holding fixture or a vise with protective jaws. If protective jaws are not available, position the gearcase upright with the skeg between wooden blocks in a vise.

3. Remove the water pump as described in this chapter.

4. Invert the gearcase in the holding fixture. Remove the lower gearcase housing bolts.

9

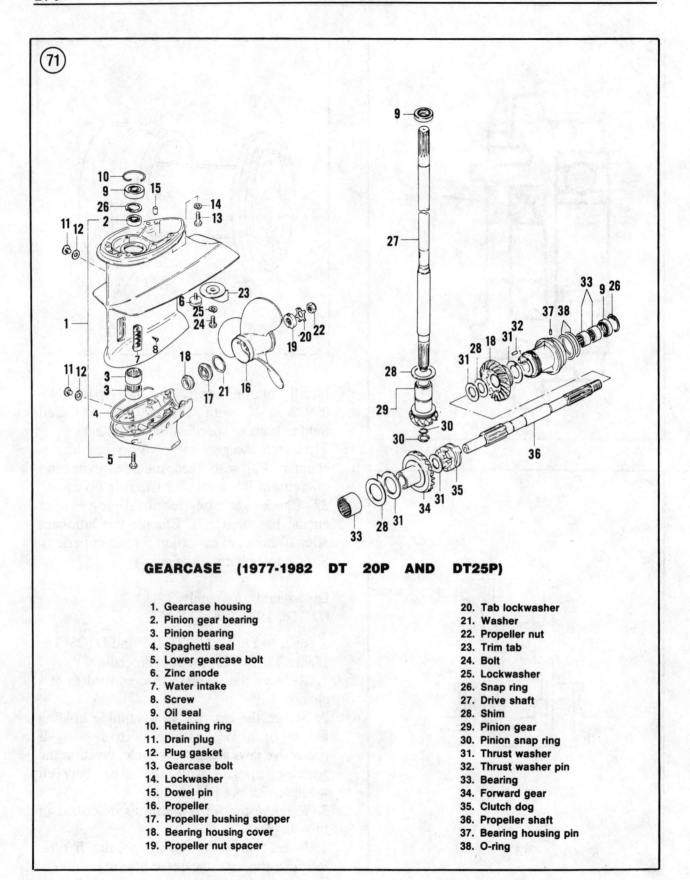

GEARCASE (1977-1982 DT 20P AND DT25P)

1. Gearcase housing
2. Pinion gear bearing
3. Pinion bearing
4. Spaghetti seal
5. Lower gearcase bolt
6. Zinc anode
7. Water intake
8. Screw
9. Oil seal
10. Retaining ring
11. Drain plug
12. Plug gasket
13. Gearcase bolt
14. Lockwasher
15. Dowel pin
16. Propeller
17. Propeller bushing stopper
18. Bearing housing cover
19. Propeller nut spacer
20. Tab lockwasher
21. Washer
22. Propeller nut
23. Trim tab
24. Bolt
25. Lockwasher
26. Snap ring
27. Drive shaft
28. Shim
29. Pinion gear
30. Pinion snap ring
31. Thrust washer
32. Thrust washer pin
33. Bearing
34. Forward gear
35. Clutch dog
36. Propeller shaft
37. Bearing housing pin
38. O-ring

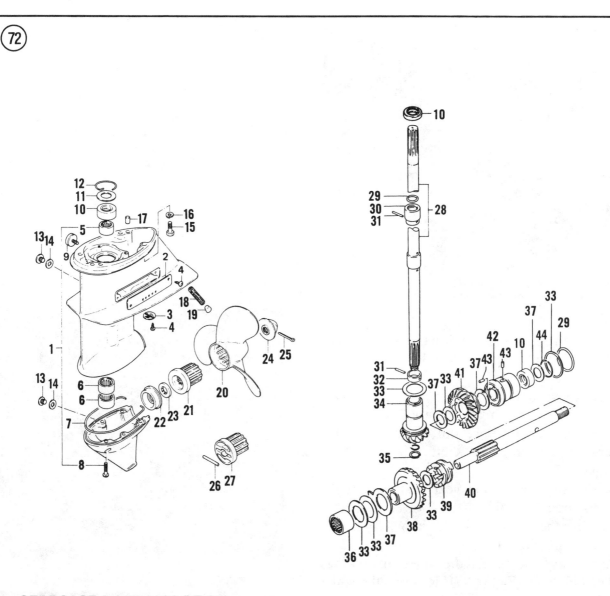

GEARCASE (1977-1982 DT 25)

1. Gearcase housing
2. Side cover
3. Lower cover
4. Screw
5. Pinion gear bearing
6. Pinion bearing
7. Spaghetti seal
8. Lower gearcase bolt
9. Zinc anode
10. Oil seal
11. Washer
12. Retaining ring
13. Drain plug
14. Plug gasket
15. Bolt
16. Lockwasher
17. Dowel pin
18. Water intake filter
19. Plug
20. Propeller
21. Propeller bushing
22. Bearing housing cover
23. Propeller bushing stopper
24. Propeller nut
25. Cotter pin
26. Shear pin
27. Propeller bushing
28. Drive shaft
29. O-ring
30. Upper spacer
31. Pin
32. Lower spacer
33. Shim
34. Pinion gear
35. Pinion snap ring
36. Bearing
37. Thrust washer
38. Forward gear
39. Clutch dog
40. Propeller shaft
41. Reverse gear
42. Bearing housing
43. Dowel pin
44. Snap ring

9

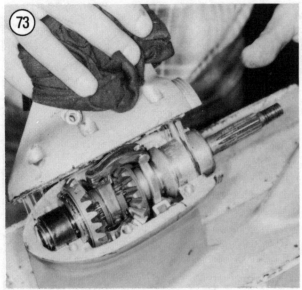

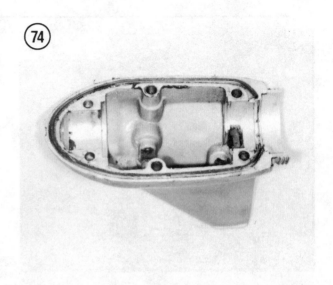

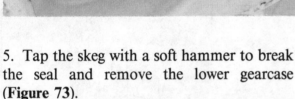

5. Tap the skeg with a soft hammer to break the seal and remove the lower gearcase (**Figure 73**).

6. Remove and discard the spaghetti seal from the lower gearcase (**Figure 74**).

7. Pivot the shift yoke out of the way and remove the propeller shaft assembly. See **Figure 75**.

8. Remove the pinion gear snap ring with pliers (part No. 09900-06107 or equivalent). Remove the pinion gear and shim(s) from the drive shaft (**Figure 76**).

9. Remove and discard the cotter pin holding the shift yoke (**Figure 77**). Remove the shift yoke.

10. Remove the shift rod and drive shaft.

11. Slide all components except the clutch dog from the propeller shaft.

12. Disassemble the propeller shaft clutch assembly as described in this chapter.

13. Clean and inspect all parts as described in this chapter.

14. Install the drive shaft and shift rod.

15. Install the water pump as described in this chapter.

16. Install the pinion gear and shim(s) on the drive shaft. Install the pinion gear snap ring with pliers part No. 09900-06107 (**Figure 78**).

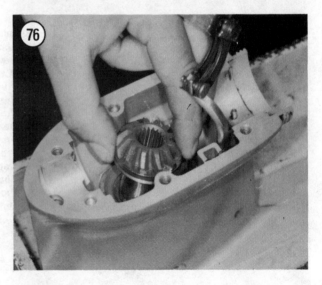

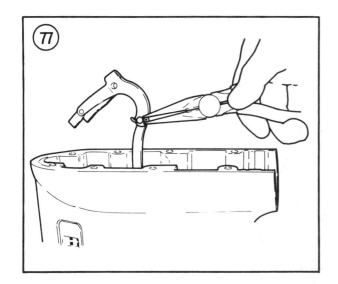

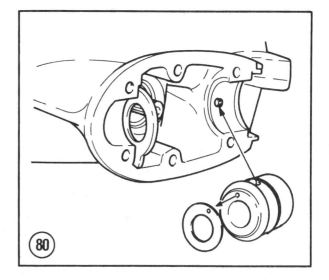

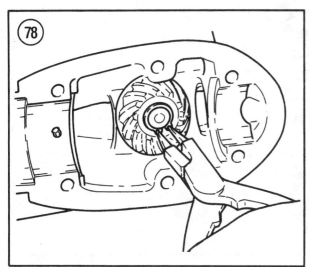

17. Remove and discard the bearing housing oil seal and bearing.

18. Install a new housing bearing with installer (part No. 09914-79610 or equivalent).

19. Install a new housing oil seal. Coat seal lips with water-resistant grease.

20. Assemble the propeller shaft components according to **Figure 71** or **Figure 72**:

  a. Copper side of thrust washers must face gears and locating pin on washer must fit into gearcase groove when assembly is installed. See **Figure 79**.

  b. Bearing housing locating pins must be positioned as shown in **Figure 80** when installed in the gearcase.

21. Install assembled propeller shaft in upper gearcase. Check backlash between the forward and pinion gears with a flat feeler gauge. If not within 0.002-0.012 in. (0.05-0.3 mm), remove the propeller shaft assembly and add shim(s) to decrease or remove shim(s) to increase backlash.

22. Repeat Step 21 to check reverse gear backlash.

23. When forward and reverse gear backlash has been properly established:

  a. Apply a light coat of gear marking compound to 5-6 teeth on each gear.

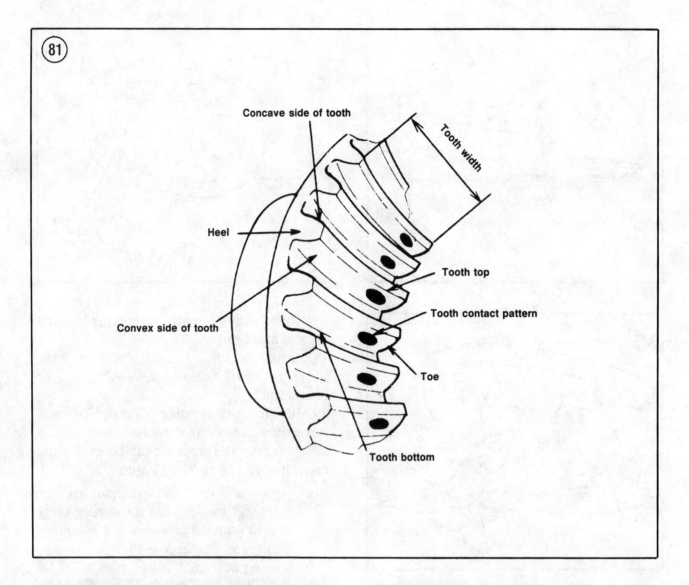

(81)

Concave side of tooth

Tooth width

Heel

Tooth top

Tooth contact pattern

Convex side of tooth

Toe

Tooth bottom

b. Temporarily install the lower gearcase and tighten the bolts snugly.

c. Hold the propeller shaft from moving and rotate the drive shaft about 10 turns.

d. Remove the lower gearcase and check the tooth contact pattern.

e. If contact pattern does not look like that shown in **Figure 81**, repeat Step 21 and/or Step 22 as required.

f. Temporarily reinstall the lower gearcase and check the propeller shaft end play by pushing/pulling the shaft. If it is not within 0.002-0.012 in. (0.05-0.3 mm), replace the washer or shim as shown in **Figure 82** to bring end play within specifications.

24. Once backlash and end play have been correctly established, remove the lower gearcase cover. Apply a thin coat of Silicone Seal (part No. 99000-32050) or equivalent to the upper and lower gearcase mating surfaces.

25. Install a new spaghetti seal in the lower gearcase. See **Figure 83**.

26. Install the lower gearcase to the upper gearcase. Install and tighten the bolts to specifications (**Table 1**).

27. Install the gearcase as described in this chapter. Fill with recommended type and quantity of lubricant. See Chapter Four.

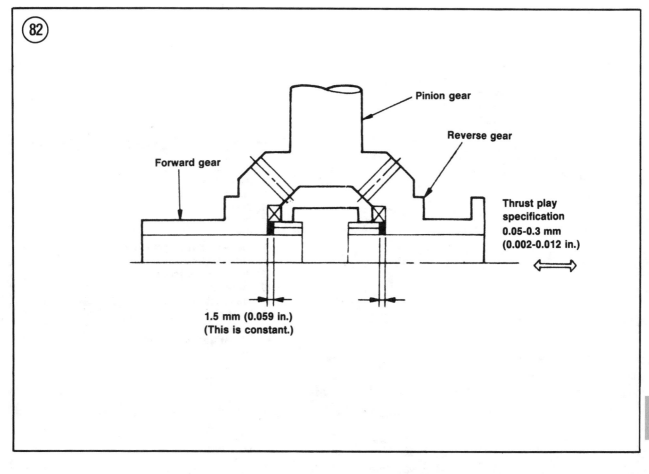

Forward gear

Pinion gear

Reverse gear

Thrust play specification 0.05-0.3 mm (0.002-0.012 in.)

1.5 mm (0.059 in.) (This is constant.)

9

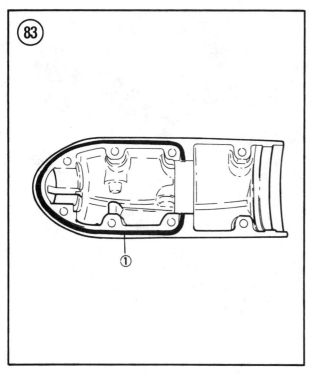

28. Check gearcase lubricant level after engine has been run. Change the lubricant after 10 hours of operation (break-in period). See Chapter Four.

Disassembly/Assembly (1983-on DT 25, DT 30, DT 40-DT 65)

Refer to **Figure 84** (1983-on DT 25 and DT 30), **Figure 85** (DT 40) or **Figure 86** (DT 50-DT 65) for this procedure.

1. Remove the gearcase as described in this chapter.

2. Secure the gearcase in a suitable holding fixture or a vise with protective jaws. If protective jaws are not available, position the gearcase upright with the skeg between wooden blocks in a vise.

3. Remove the water pump as described in this chapter.

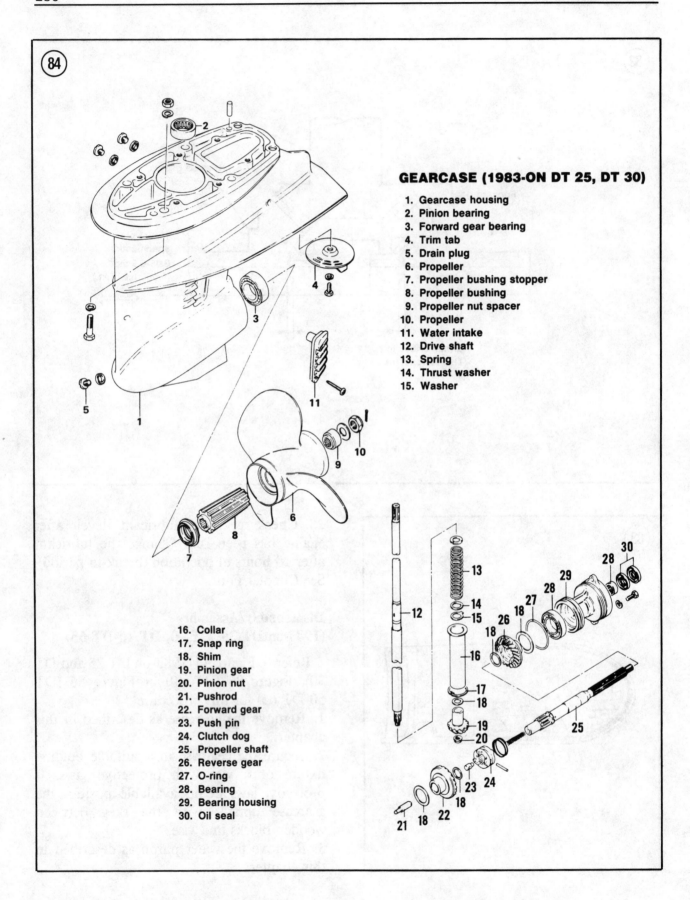

84

GEARCASE (1983-ON DT 25, DT 30)

1. Gearcase housing
2. Pinion bearing
3. Forward gear bearing
4. Trim tab
5. Drain plug
6. Propeller
7. Propeller bushing stopper
8. Propeller bushing
9. Propeller nut spacer
10. Propeller
11. Water intake
12. Drive shaft
13. Spring
14. Thrust washer
15. Washer

16. Collar
17. Snap ring
18. Shim
19. Pinion gear
20. Pinion nut
21. Pushrod
22. Forward gear
23. Push pin
24. Clutch dog
25. Propeller shaft
26. Reverse gear
27. O-ring
28. Bearing
29. Bearing housing
30. Oil seal

GEARCASE (DT 40)

1. Pinion bearing
2. Water intake
3. Trim tab
4. Zinc anode
5. Bearing
6. Water filter
7. Gearcase housing
8. Propeller nut spacer
9. Propeller
10. Propeller bushing stopper
11. Drive shaft
12. Thrust bearing
13. Washer
14. Shim or thrust washer
15. Pin
16. Spring

17. Thrust washer
18. Collar
19. Pinion gear
20. Pinion nut
21. Forward gear
22. Pushrod
23. Push pin
24. Clutch dog
25. Retaining pin
26. Retaining spring
27. Return spring
28. Propeller shaft
29. Reverse gear
30. O-ring
31. Bearing
32. Oil seal
33. Bearing housing
34. Bushing

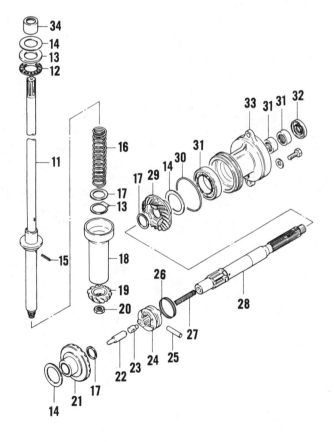

9

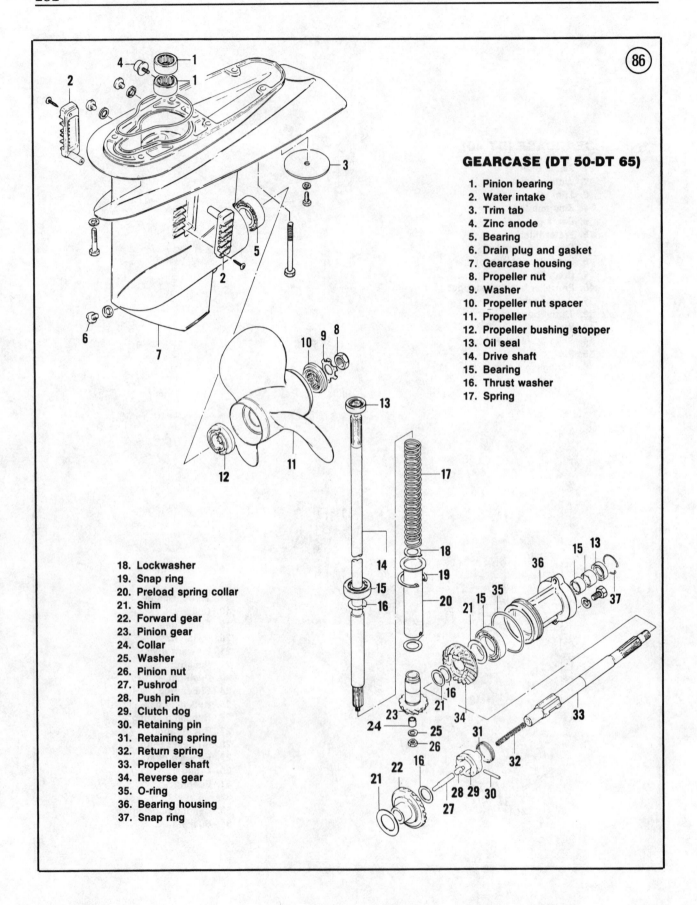

86

GEARCASE (DT 50-DT 65)

1. Pinion bearing
2. Water intake
3. Trim tab
4. Zinc anode
5. Bearing
6. Drain plug and gasket
7. Gearcase housing
8. Propeller nut
9. Washer
10. Propeller nut spacer
11. Propeller
12. Propeller bushing stopper
13. Oil seal
14. Drive shaft
15. Bearing
16. Thrust washer
17. Spring

18. Lockwasher
19. Snap ring
20. Preload spring collar
21. Shim
22. Forward gear
23. Pinion gear
24. Collar
25. Washer
26. Pinion nut
27. Pushrod
28. Push pin
29. Clutch dog
30. Retaining pin
31. Retaining spring
32. Return spring
33. Propeller shaft
34. Reverse gear
35. O-ring
36. Bearing housing
37. Snap ring

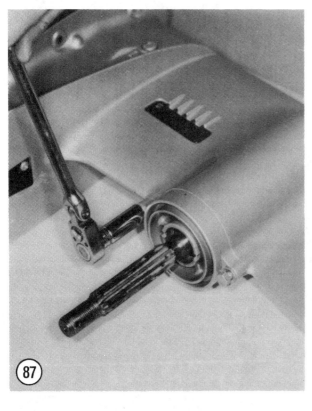

4. Remove the 2 bolts holding the bearing housing (**Figure 87**). Install a propeller shaft remover and remove the propeller shaft/bearing housing assembly with a slide hammer. Use remover part No. 09950-59310 (DT 25 and DT 30) or part No. 09930-30161 (all others).

5. Install a drive shaft holder on the splined drive shaft end. Use part No. 09921-29610 (DT 25 and DT 30) or part No. 09921-29510 (all others).

6. Fit an appropriate size box end wrench over the pinion nut and pad the sides of the prop shaft bore to prevent distortion or damage from contact with the wrench.

7. Holding pinion nut with the wrench installed in Step 6, turn the drive shaft counterclockwise to loosen the pinion nut. See **Figure 88**.

8. Remove the tools. Remove the pinion nut and pinion gear (**Figure 89**).

9

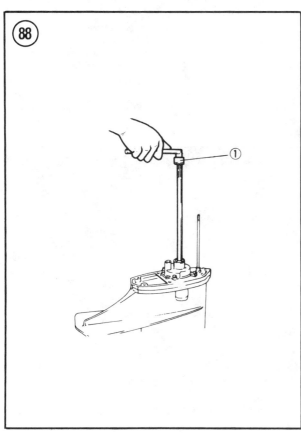

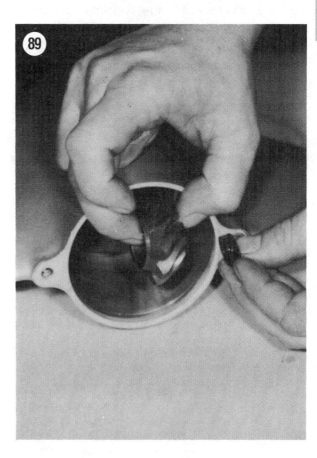

9. Remove the forward gear and any shim(s). See **Figure 90**.

10. DT 25-DT 40—Unbolt the drive shaft bearing housing (**Figure 91**). Pry the bearing housing free and remove the drive shaft and bearing housing from the gearcase as an assembly.

11. DT 25 and DT 30—Remove the pinion gear shim(s) from the drive shaft bore.

12. DT 40—Remove the preload spring, collar and retaining pin.

13. DT 50-DT 65—Remove the drive shaft bearing housing snap ring holding the preload spring collar. Remove the preload spring collar or preload spring. Withdraw the drive shaft and bearing housing assembly from the gearcase.

14. Remove the drive shaft housing screw (above the starboard water intake). Withdraw the shift rod assembly from the gearcase (**Figure 92**).

15. DT 25 and DT 30—Remove the drive shaft bearing housing snap ring holding the preload spring collar. Remove the drive shaft, preload spring, spring collar and washers.

16. Slide all components except the clutch dog from the propeller shaft.

17. Disassemble the propeller shaft clutch assembly as described in this chapter.

18. Clean and inspect all parts as described in this chapter.

19. Remove and discard the propeller shaft bearing housing oil seals and bearing. See **Figure 93** (typical).

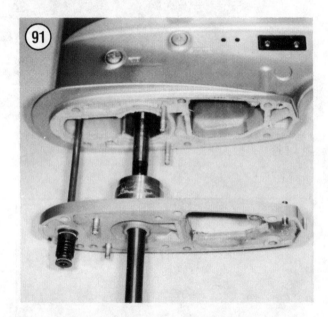

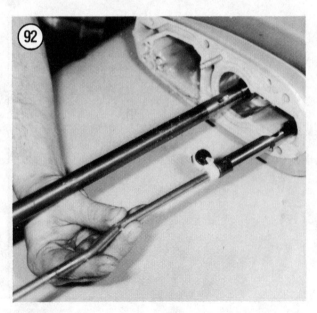

20. Install a new propeller shaft housing bearing with an appropriate installer.

21. Install new propeller shaft housing oil seals and a new housing O-ring. Coat seal lips and O-ring with water-resistant grease (part No. 99000-32160 or equivalent).

22. Remove and discard the drive shaft bearing housing oil seal. See **Figure 94** (typical). Install a new seal with an appropriate installer. Coat seal lips with water-resistant grease.

23. Assemble the propeller shaft components according to **Figures 84-86**.

24. Lubricate all parts with Suzuki Outboard Motor Gear Oil.

25. Lightly lubricate the shift rod guide and boot with water-resistant grease. Install the shift rod assembly in the gearcase. Install the drive shaft housing screw which retains the shift rod guide.

26. Assemble the drive shaft bearing housing to the drive shaft:

   a. DT 40—Install preload spring and retaining pin. See **Figure 95**.

   b. All others—Make sure the end of the preload spring fits into the washer notch provided. See **Figure 96**.

   c. Install the drive shaft bearing housing snap ring to the preload collar, if used.

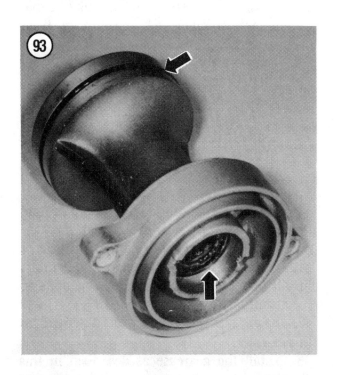

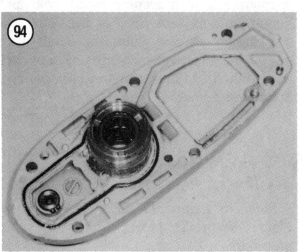

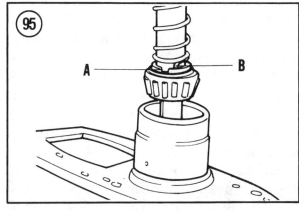

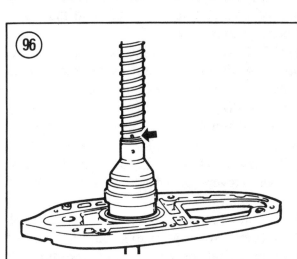

d. Lightly lubricate the bearing housing O-ring with water-resistant grease.

27. DT 40—Install the preload spring collar in the gearcase drive shaft bore.

28. DT 25 and DT 30—Install the pinion gear shim pack in the gearcase drive shaft bore.

29. Install the forward gear and shim pack in the propeller shaft bore.

30. Install the pinion gear in the propeller shaft bore and mesh with the forward gear.

31. Lightly coat mating surfaces of drive shaft bearing housing and gearcase with Silicone Seal (part No. 99000-31120) or equivalent.

32. Holding pinion gear in place, install the drive shaft assembly in the gearcase. Rotate shaft to align its splines with those of the pinion gear and seat gear on shaft.

33. Install and tighten the drive shaft bearing housing fasteners.

34. Coat the pinion nut threads with Thread Lock 1342. Position nut over drive shaft threads in prop shaft bore. Start nut by hand.

35. Hold pinion gear nut with an appropriate size box end wrench and pad side of prop shaft bore to prevent damage from contact with the wrench.

36. Install drive shaft holder on crankshaft end of drive shaft. Use part No. 09921-29610 (DT 25 and DT 30) or part No. 09921-29510 (all others). Rotate drive shaft and tighten to specifications (**Table 1**).

37. Lubricate the propeller shaft bearing housing O-ring and the shift mechanism pushrod with water-resistant grease.

38. Install the propeller shaft/bearing housing assembly in the propeller shaft bore. Use installer part No. 09922-59510.

39. Check pinion gear depth and forward/reverse gear backlash as described in this chapter.

40. When forward and reverse gear backlash has been properly established, remove the propeller shaft/bearing housing assembly:

a. Apply a light coat of gear marking compound to 5-6 teeth on each gear.

b. Temporarily reinstall the propeller shaft/bearing housing assembly. Tighten the bolts snugly.

c. Hold the propeller shaft from moving and rotate the drive shaft about 10 turns.

d. Remove the bearing housing and propeller shaft assembly. Check the tooth contact pattern.

e. If contact pattern does not look like that shown in **Figure 81**, repeat Step 39 as required.

f. Temporarily reinstall the propeller shaft/bearing housing assembly. Install a dial indicator and check the propeller shaft end play by pushing/pulling the shaft. If it is not within 0.002-0.012 in. (0.05-0.3 mm), replace the washer or shim as shown in **Figure 82** to bring end play within specifications.

41. When gear tooth contact pattern and propeller shaft end play are correct, coat the gearcase and bearing housing mating surfaces with Silicone Seal and reinstall assembly. Install and tighten bearing housing bolts to specifications (**Table 1**).

42. Install the water pump as described in this chapter.

43. Install the gearcase as described in this chapter. Fill with recommended type and quantity of lubricant. See Chapter Four.

44. Check gearcase lubricant level after engine has been run. Change the lubricant after 10 hours of operation (break-in period). See Chapter Four.

Disassembly/Assembly (DT 75-DT 140)

Refer to **Figure 97** (DT 75-DT 85) or **Figure 98** (DT 115-DT 140) for this procedure.

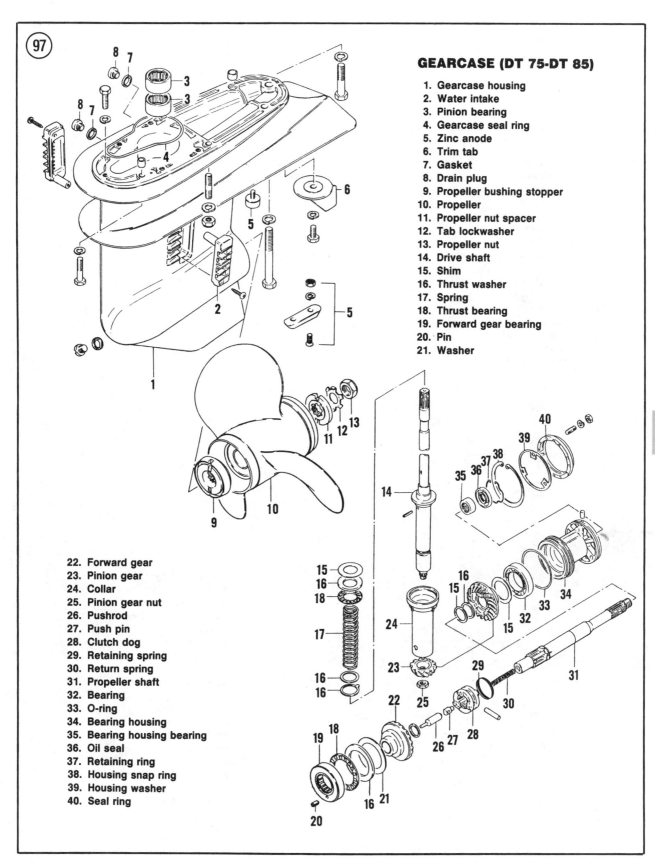

⑨⑦

GEARCASE (DT 75-DT 85)

1. Gearcase housing
2. Water intake
3. Pinion bearing
4. Gearcase seal ring
5. Zinc anode
6. Trim tab
7. Gasket
8. Drain plug
9. Propeller bushing stopper
10. Propeller
11. Propeller nut spacer
12. Tab lockwasher
13. Propeller nut
14. Drive shaft
15. Shim
16. Thrust washer
17. Spring
18. Thrust bearing
19. Forward gear bearing
20. Pin
21. Washer

22. Forward gear
23. Pinion gear
24. Collar
25. Pinion gear nut
26. Pushrod
27. Push pin
28. Clutch dog
29. Retaining spring
30. Return spring
31. Propeller shaft
32. Bearing
33. O-ring
34. Bearing housing
35. Bearing housing bearing
36. Oil seal
37. Retaining ring
38. Housing snap ring
39. Housing washer
40. Seal ring

9

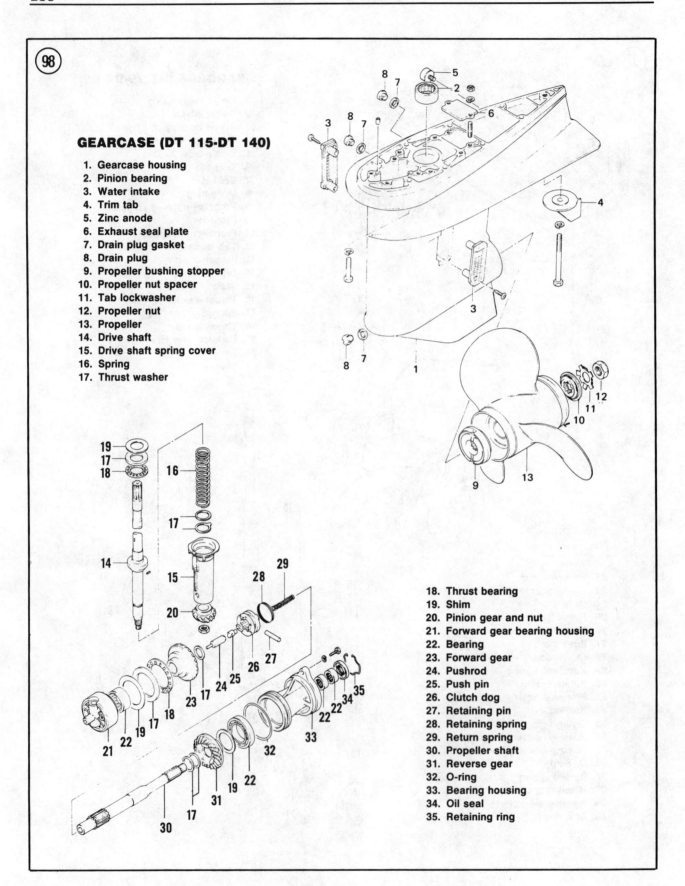

98

GEARCASE (DT 115-DT 140)

1. Gearcase housing
2. Pinion bearing
3. Water intake
4. Trim tab
5. Zinc anode
6. Exhaust seal plate
7. Drain plug gasket
8. Drain plug
9. Propeller bushing stopper
10. Propeller nut spacer
11. Tab lockwasher
12. Propeller nut
13. Propeller
14. Drive shaft
15. Drive shaft spring cover
16. Spring
17. Thrust washer

18. Thrust bearing
19. Shim
20. Pinion gear and nut
21. Forward gear bearing housing
22. Bearing
23. Forward gear
24. Pushrod
25. Push pin
26. Clutch dog
27. Retaining pin
28. Retaining spring
29. Return spring
30. Propeller shaft
31. Reverse gear
32. O-ring
33. Bearing housing
34. Oil seal
35. Retaining ring

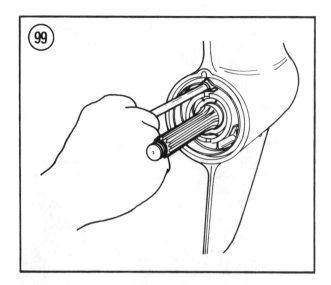

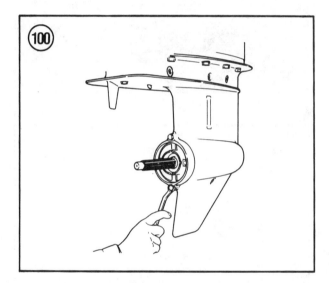

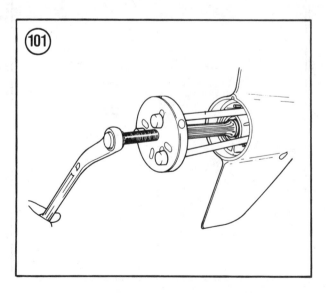

1. Remove the gearcase as described in this chapter.

2. Secure the gearcase in a suitable holding fixture or a vise with protective jaws. If protective jaws are not available, position the gearcase upright with the skeg between wooden blocks in a vise.

3. Remove the water pump as described in this chapter.

4A. DT 75-DT 85—Remove the seal ring and housing washer (**Figure 99**).

4B. DT 115-DT 140—Remove the 2 bolts holding the bearing housing (**Figure 100**).

5. DT 75 and DT 85—Remove the snap ring with pliers part No. 09900-06108 or equivalent.

NOTE
Use the 2 short bolts from tool part No. 09930-39430 to install the remover tool in Step 6 on DT 115 and DT 140 gearcases.

9

6. Install bearing housing remover (part No. 09930-39410) and remove the propeller shaft/bearing housing assembly. See **Figure 101**.

7. DT 115 and DT 140—Remove the drive shaft bearing housing fasteners. Pry the housing free and carefully remove from the drive shaft with the drive shaft thrust bearing and shim.

8. Install a drive shaft holder on the splined drive shaft end. Use part No. 09950-79510 (DT 75 and DT 85) or part No. 09921-29410 (DT 115 and DT 140).

9. Fit an appropriate size box end wrench over the pinion nut and pad the sides of the prop shaft bore to prevent distortion or damage from contact with the wrench.

10. Holding pinion nut with the wrench installed in Step 9, turn the drive shaft counterclockwise to loosen the pinion nut. See **Figure 88**.

11. Remove the tools. Remove the pinion nut and pinion gear (**Figure 102**).

12. Remove the forward gear and thrust washer. See **Figure 103**.

13. DT 75 and DT 85—Remove the drive shaft bearing housing fasteners. Pry the housing free and carefully remove from the drive shaft with the shift rod.

14. Remove the drive shaft, preload spring and thrust bearing as an assembly. See **Figure 104**.

15. Remove the drive shaft spring collar from the gearcase bore. See **Figure 105**.

16. Remove the 2 drive shaft thrust washers from the gearcase bore.

17. DT 115 and DT 140—Remove the clutch rod and shift rod guide from the gearcase. See **Figure 106**.

18. Slide all components except the clutch dog from the propeller shaft.

19. Disassemble the propeller shaft clutch assembly as described in this chapter.

20. Clean and inspect all parts as described in this chapter.

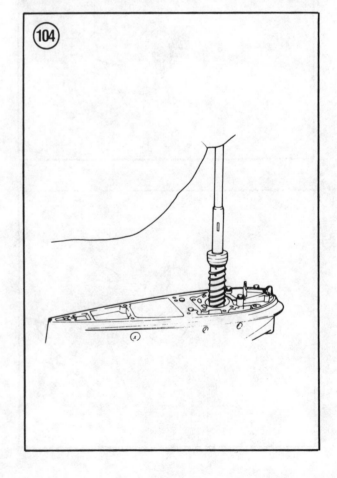

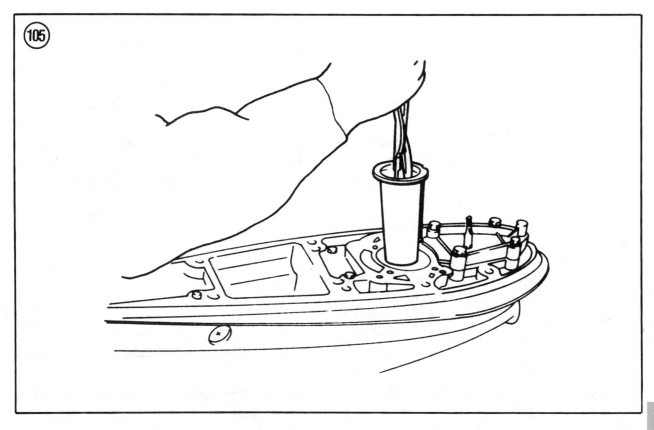

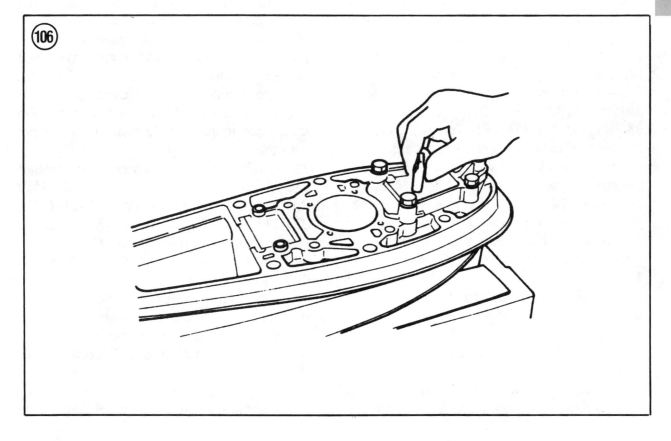

9

21. DT 115 and DT 140—If inspection of the forward gear bearing indicates replacement is necessary:

   a. Install bearing housing remover (part No. 09930-39410) using the 2 long bolts from tool part No. 09930-39430.
   b. Remove forward gear bearing housing with a slide hammer. See **Figure 107**.
   c. Install a new bearing housing with an appropriate installer.

22. Remove and discard the propeller shaft bearing housing oil seals and bearing. See **Figure 93** (typical).

23. Install a new propeller shaft housing bearing with an appropriate installer.

24. Install new propeller shaft housing oil seals and a new housing O-ring. Coat seal lips and O-ring with water-resistant grease (part No. 99000-32160 or equivalent).

25. Remove and discard the drive shaft bearing housing oil seal. See **Figure 94** (typical). Install a new seal with an appropriate installer. Coat seal lips with water-resistant grease.

26. Assemble the propeller shaft components according to **Figure 97** or **Figure 98**.

27. Lubricate all parts with Suzuki Outboard Motor Gear Oil.

28. DT 115 and DT 140—Install the clutch rod and shift rod guide in the gearcase.

29. Install the 2 drive shaft thrust washers in the gearcase bore.

30. Install the drive shaft spring collar in the gearcase bore. See **Figure 105**.

31. Install the drive shaft, preload spring and thrust bearing as an assembly. See **Figure 104**.

32. Install the shift rod assembly.

33. Install the shim, thrust washer and thrust bearing on the forward gear in that order. Install the forward gear assembly in the gearcase.

34. Install the pinion gear in the propeller shaft bore and mesh with the forward gear.

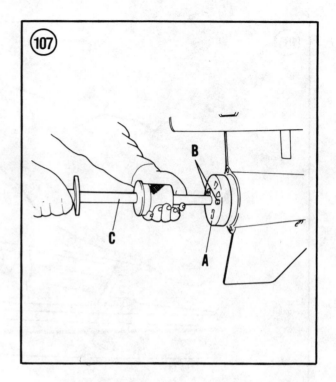

35. Holding pinion gear in place, install the drive shaft assembly in the gearcase. Rotate shaft to align its splines with those of the pinion gear and seat gear on shaft.

36. Coat the pinion nut threads with Thread Lock 1342. Position nut over drive shaft threads in prop shaft bore. Start nut by hand.

37. Hold pinion gear nut with an appropriate size box end wrench and pad side of prop shaft bore to prevent damage from contact with the wrench.

38. Install drive shaft holder on crankshaft end of drive shaft. Use part No. 09950-79510 (DT 75 and DT 85) or part No. 09921-29410 (DT 115 and DT 140). Rotate drive shaft and tighten to specifications (**Table 1**).

39. Check forward gear backlash as described in this chapter.

40. Temporarily install the propeller shaft/bearing housing assembly. Check pinion gear depth, reverse gear backlash and gear tooth contact pattern as described in this chapter.

41. Coat gearcase and drive shaft bearing housing mating surfaces with Silicone Seal

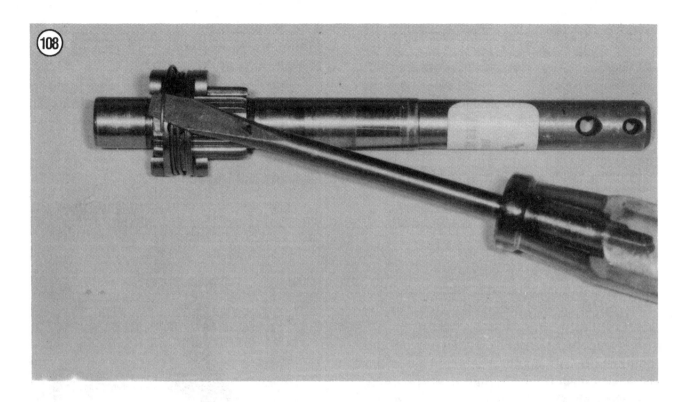

(part No. 99000-31120) or equivalent and install the housing. Tighten fasteners to specifications (**Table 1**).

42. Remove the propeller shaft/bearing housing assembly. Check clutch pushrod dimension as described in this chapter.

43. Lubricate the propeller shaft bearing housing O-ring and the shift mechanism pushrod with water-resistant grease.

44. Install the propeller shaft/bearing housing assembly in the propeller shaft bore. Use installer tool part No. 09922-59410.

45. DT 115 and DT 140—Coat bearing housing bolts with Thread Lock 1342. Install and tighten to specifications (**Table 1**).

46. Install the water pump as described in this chapter.

47. Install the gearcase as described in this chapter. Fill with recommended type and quantity of lubricant. See Chapter Four.

48. Check gearcase lubricant level after engine has been run. Change the lubricant after 10 hours of operation (break-in period). See Chapter Four.

PROPELLER SHAFT CLUTCH

Disassembly/Assembly

Smaller displacement outboards use a staked pin to hold the clutch dog in position on the propeller shaft. Larger displacement outboards use a clutch dog with a retaining spring.

1. Remove the clutch plunger from the front of the propeller shaft.

2A. Staked clutch pin—Insert an appropriate size punch and drive the staked pin from the clutch dog.

2B. Retaining spring design—Carefully lift one end of the clutch dog retaining spring and insert a screwdriver blade under it as shown in **Figure 108**. Holding the screwdriver in one position, rotate the propeller shaft to unwind the retaining spring. Work carefully to avoid stretching the spring.

3. Insert a pencil in the end of the propeller shaft and compress the return spring, then

9

remove the clutch dog pin with a punch or awl. See **Figure 109**.

4. Slide the clutch dog off the propeller shaft and remove the push pin and return spring. **Figure 110** shows the typical components of a disassembled propeller shaft.

5. Clean and inspect all parts as described in this chapter.

6. Lubricate all parts with Suzuki Outboard Motor Gear Oil.

7. Insert return spring and push pin in propeller shaft bore.

8. Align the push pin hole with the propeller shaft slot (**Figure 111**).

9. Install clutch dog on shaft with the stamped letter "F" facing the front of the shaft.

10. Temporarily install clutch pushrod and compress return spring. Align clutch dog pin hole with push pin hole, then insert retaining pin through the clutch dog and push pin holes.

11A. Retaining spring design—Release pressure on the clutch pushrod and install retaining spring over clutch dog. Do not stretch ring excessively during installation.

11B. Staked clutch pin—Center retaining pin in clutch dog and stake each side of clutch dog pin hole to retain pin.

12. Remove clutch pushrod and apply a liberal coat of water-resistant grease to its flat end. Reinstall flat end of pushrod in propeller shaft bore.

Cleaning and Inspection

1. Clean all parts in fresh solvent. Blow dry with compressed air, if available.

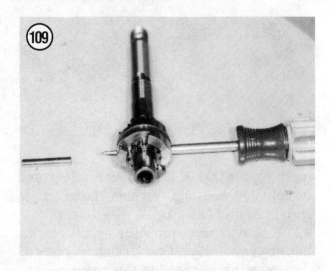

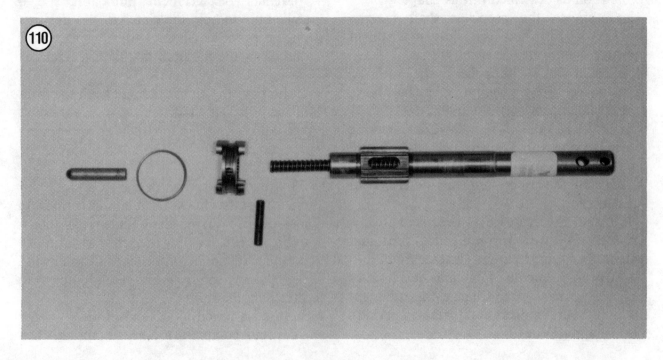

2. Clean all nut and screw threads thoroughly if Silicone Seal has been used. Soak nuts and screws in solvent and use a fine wire brush to remove residue.

3. Remove and discard all O-rings, gaskets and seals. Clean all Silicone Seal residue from mating surfaces.

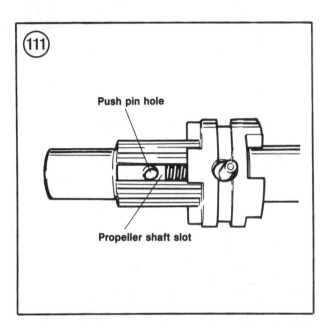

4. Check drive shaft splines for wear or damage. If gearcase has struck a submerged object, the drive shaft and propeller shaft may suffer severe damage. Replace drive shaft as required and check crankshaft splines for similar wear or damage.

5. Check propeller shaft splines and threads for wear, rust or corrosion damage. Replace shaft as necessary.

6. Install V-blocks under the drive shaft bearing surfaces at each end of the shaft. Slowly rotate the shaft while watching the crankshaft end. Replace the shaft if any signs of wobble are noted.

7. Repeat Step 6 with the propeller shaft. Also check the shaft surfaces where oil seal lips make contact. Replace the shaft as required.

8. Check the propeller shaft bearing housing bearing for wear or damage. Replace bearing as required. If bearing wear is excessive, replace bearing housing.

9. Check bearing housing contact points on the propeller shaft. If shaft shows signs of pitting, grooving, scoring, heat discoloration or embedded metallic particles, replace shaft and bearings.

10. Check water pump as described in this chapter.

11. Check all shift components for wear or damage:

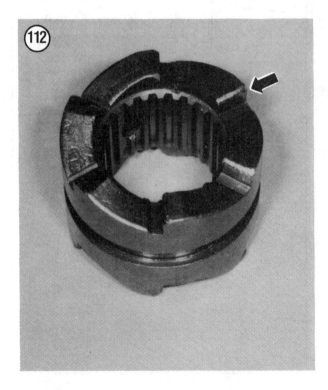

a. Look for excessive wear on the clutch dog and forward/reverse gear engagement surfaces. If clutch dogs are pitted, chipped, broken or excessively worn, replace the gear(s) and clutch dog. See **Figure 112**.

b. Roll the clutch return spring on a flat surface to check straightness. Replace the spring if it does not roll freely.

c. Check clutch dog for cracks at shear point and rounded areas that contact forward gear clutch dogs. Replace as required.

d. Check shift pin and cam for wear. See **Figure 113** (typical) for wear points. Excessive wear on shift cam crests can let the engine drop out of gear. Replace as required.

12. Clean all roller bearings with solvent and lubricate with Suzuki Outboard Motor Gear Oil to prevent rusting. Check all bearings for rust, corrosion, flat spots or excessive wear. Replace as required.

13. Check the forward, reverse and pinion gears for wear or damage. If any teeth are pitted, chipped, broken or excessively worn, replace all gears as a set. Check pinion gear splines for excessive wear or damage. Replace as required.

14. Check the propeller for nicks, cracks or damaged blades. Minor nicks can be removed with a file, taking care to retain the shape of the propeller. Replace any propeller with bent, cracked or badly chipped blades.

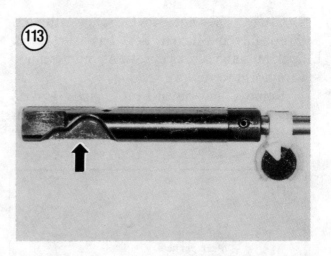

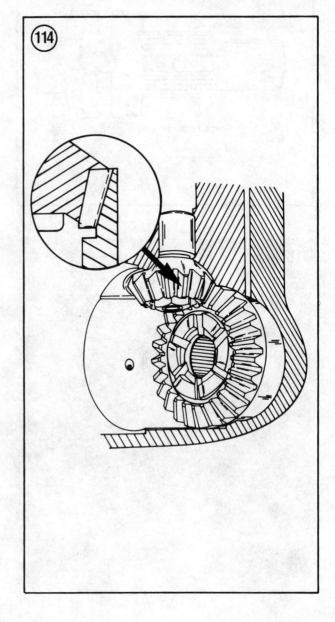

PINION GEAR DEPTH AND FORWARD/REVERSE GEAR BACKLASH

Proper pinion gear engagement and forward and reverse gear backlash are important for smooth operation and long service life. Three shimming procedures may be used to properly set up the gearcase:

a. The pinion gear must be shimmed to a correct depth.

b. The forward gear must be shimmed to the pinion gear for proper backlash.

c. The reverse gear must be shimmed to the pinion gear for proper backlash.

Not all models will require all 3 shimming procedures.

The gearcase on larger displacement outboards requires the use of measuring

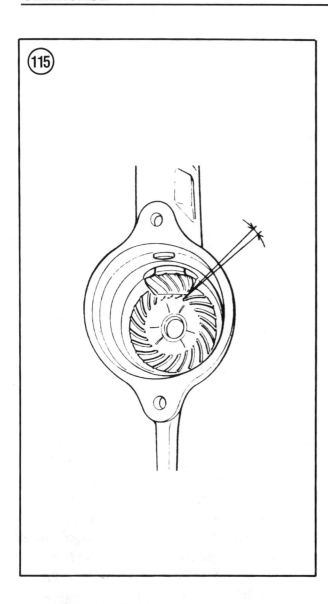

equipment. Smaller displacement models are checked by touch or sight and require some degree of experience to determine if the amount of backlash is within specifications. Suzuki does not provide shimming instructions for the DT 4.5.

Pinion Gear Depth and Forward/Reverse Gear Backlash (DT 3.5, DT 5, DT 6, DT 7.5, DT 8, DT 9, 1977-1982 DT 9.9 and DT 16)

1. Depress and hold the drive shaft.
2. Reach into the prop shaft bore and lightly push the pinion gear upward.

3. Check pinion and forward gear tooth engagement by feel. The entire length of the gear teeth should be in contact as shown in **Figure 114**. There should be a minimum of up and down play in the drive shaft.
4. If the pinion gear is too high or too low, remove the drive shaft and increase or decrease the shim thickness to correct the gear height.
5. When the proper pinion gear depth has been established, depress and hold the drive shaft.
6. Move the forward gear back and forth with a finger. The free play felt is forward gear backlash (**Figure 115**) and should be as follows:

   a. DT 7.5, DT 9, 1977-1982 DT 9.9, DT 16—0.002-0.006 in. (0.05-0.15 mm)
   b. All others—0.004-0.008 in. (0.1-0.2 mm).

7. If forward gear backlash is incorrect, remove the forward gear and increase or decrease the shim thickness to correct the backlash.
8. If forward gear backlash requires adjustment, recheck pinion gear depth after changing the forward gear shim.
9. To check reverse gear backlash:

   a. Check drive shaft thrust play by lifting up and depressing drive shaft.
   b. Temporarily install the propeller shaft/bearing housing assembly.
   c. Repeat Step a. The amount of thrust play should be the same in this step as in Step a. If it is less, remove the propeller shaft/bearing housing assembly. Decrease the shim thickness at the reverse gear and repeat this procedure until thrust play is identical before and after installing the propeller shaft/bearing housing assembly.

10. Check the propeller shaft thrust clearance as described in this chapter.

9

**Pinion Gear Depth and
Forward Gear Backlash
(1983-on DT 9.9, DT 15, DT 40)**

1. Install gear adjusting set (part No. 09951-09510) as shown in **Figure 116**.
2. Depress and hold the drive shaft while setting the dial indicator gauge to zero.
3. Slowly pull the drive shaft up as far as possible and read the indicator gauge. If the backlash exceeds 0.012 in. (0.3 mm), increase the thickness of the pinion and forward gear shims. If the backlash is less than 0.002 in. (0.05 mm), decrease the thickness of the pinion and forward gear shims.
4. Lightly coat the forward gear teeth with gear marking compound.
5. Temporarily install the propeller shaft/bearing housing assembly and engage the forward gear. Hold the propeller shaft from moving and slowly rotate the drive shaft about 5 full turns.
6. Remove the propeller shaft, drive shaft and pinion gear and forward gear.
7. Check the tooth pattern on the forward gear. It should resemble that shown in **Figure 81**:

   a. If it resembles that shown in **Figure 117**, decrease the forward gear shim thickness and increase the pinion gear shim thickness.

   b. If it resembles that shown in **Figure 118**, increase the forward gear shim thickness and decrease the pinion gear shim thickness.

   c. Clean the marking compound from the gear teeth and repeat Steps 4-6 to recheck pattern. Repeat this procedure as required until the tooth contact pattern is correct.

   d. When pattern is correct, remove and clean all marking compound from gear teeth for final reassembly.

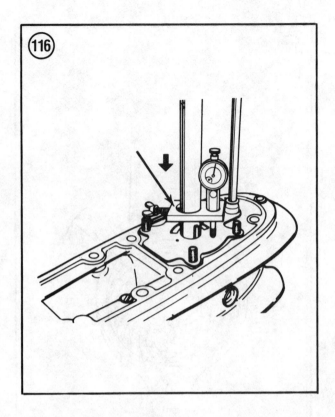

8. To check reverse gear backlash:

   a. Check drive shaft thrust play by lifting up and depressing drive shaft.

   b. Temporarily install the propeller shaft/bearing housing assembly.

   c. Repeat Step a. The amount of thrust play should be the same in this step as in Step a. If it is less, remove the propeller shaft/bearing housing assembly. Decrease the shim thickness at the reverse gear and repeat this procedure until thrust play is identical before and after installing the propeller shaft/bearing housing assembly.

9. Check the propeller shaft thrust clearance as described in this chapter.

**Pinion Gear Depth and
Forward Gear Backlash
(1983-on DT 25, DT 30, DT 75-DT 140)**

1. Depress and hold the drive shaft.
2. Move the forward gear back and forth with a finger. The free play felt is forward gear

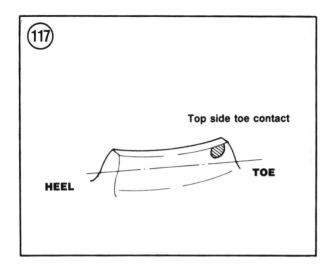

Top side toe contact

HEEL   TOE

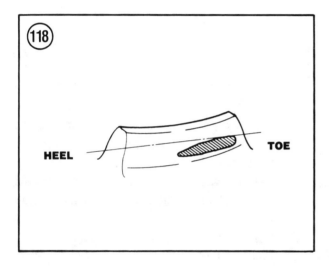

HEEL   TOE

5. Remove the propeller shaft/bearing housing assembly, drive shaft, pinion gear and forward gear.

6. Check the tooth pattern on the forward gear. It should resemble that shown in **Figure 81**:

   a. It if resembles that shown in **Figure 117**, decrease the forward gear shim thickness and increase the pinion gear shim thickness.

   b. If it resembles that shown in **Figure 118**, increase the forward gear shim thickness and decrease the pinion gear shim thickness.

   c. Clean the marking compound from the gear teeth and repeat Steps 4-6 to recheck pattern. Repeat this procedure as required until the tooth contact pattern is correct.

   d. When pattern is correct, remove and clean all marking compound from gear teeth for final reassembly.

7. To check reverse gear backlash:

   a. Check drive shaft thrust play by lifting up and depressing drive shaft.

   b. Temporarily install the propeller shaft/bearing housing assembly.

   c. Repeat Step a. The amount of thrust play should be the same in this step as in Step a. If it is less, remove the propeller shaft/bearing housing assembly. Decrease the thickness of the reverse gear-to-bearing shim and repeat this procedure until thrust play is identical before and after installing the propeller shaft/bearing housing assembly. With DT 115-DT 140 models, the thrust play should be maintained between 0.010-0.016 in. (0.25-0.40 mm).

8A. DT 75-DT 140—If the forward and reverse gear shimming is changed, change the thickness of the shim at the front of the reverse gear according to the increase or decrease in the gear shims to maintain proper

9

backlash and should be 0.002-0.012 in. (0.05-0.3 mm) for DT 75-DT 140 and 0.004-0.008 in. (0.1-0.2 mm) (all others). See **Figure 115**:

   a. If backlash is greater than specified, install thicker forward and pinion gear shims.

   b. If backlash is less than specified, install thinner forward and pinion gear shims.

3. Lightly coat the forward gear teeth with gear marking compound.

4. Temporarily install the propeller shaft/bearing housing and engage the forward gear. Hold the propeller shaft from moving and slowly rotate the drive shaft about 5 full turns.

propeller shaft thrust clearance. For example, if the forward gear shim is increased by 0.004 in. (0.1 mm) and the reverse gear rear shim is decreased by 0.012 in. (0.3 mm), reduce the reverse gear front shim by 0.016 in. (0.04 mm).

8B. All others—Check the propeller shaft thrust clearance as described in this chapter.

Pinion Gear Depth and Forward Gear Backlash (DT 50-DT 65)

1. Depress and hold the drive shaft.
2. Move the forward gear back and forth with a finger. The free play felt is forward gear backlash and should be 0.004-0.012 in. (0.1-0.3 mm). See **Figure 115**:
   a. If backlash is greater than specified, install thicker forward gear shims.
   b. If backlash is less than specified, install thinner forward gear shims.
3. Lightly coat the forward gear teeth with gear marking compound.
4. Make sure the shift cam is properly positioned to accept the propeller shaft clutch pushrod.
5. Temporarily install the propeller shaft/bearing housing assembly and engage the forward gear. Hold the propeller shaft from moving and slowly rotate the drive shaft about 5 full turns.
6. Remove the propeller shaft/bearing housing assembly, drive shaft, pinion gear and forward gear.
7. Check the tooth pattern on the forward gear. It should resemble that shown in **Figure 81**:
   a. It if resembles that shown in **Figure 117**, increase the pinion gear shim thickness.
   b. If it resembles that shown in **Figure 118**, decrease the pinion gear shim thickness.
   c. Clean the marking compound from the gear teeth and repeat Steps 4-6 to

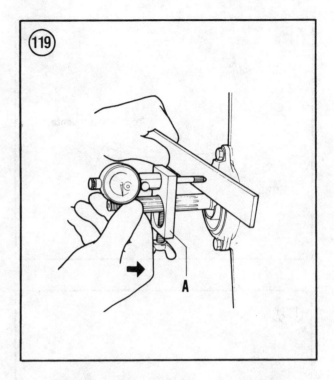

recheck pattern. Repeat this procedure as required until the tooth contact pattern is correct.
   d. When pattern is correct, remove and clean all marking compound from gear teeth.
8. To check reverse gear backlash:
   a. Reinstall the forward gear, pinion gear and drive shaft assembly.
   b. Temporarily install the propeller shaft/bearing housing assembly.
   c. Install a dial indicator as shown in **Figure 119**. Grasp the propeller shaft and pull it out as far as possible. Set the indicator gauge to zero.
   d. Grasp the propeller shaft and push it inward as far as possible. Read the indicator gauge. The thrust clearance should be 0.002-0.012 in. (0.05-0.3 mm).
   e. If the thrust clearance is not within specifications in Step d, remove the reverse gear and increase or decrease the reverse gear shim thickness to bring the clearance into specifications.

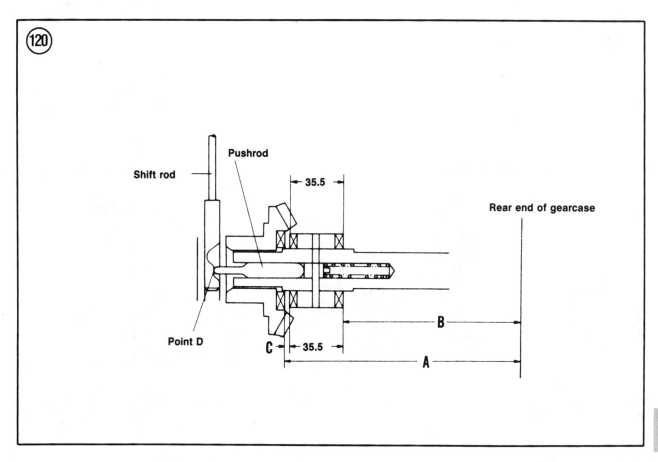

PROPELLER SHAFT THRUST CLEARANCE

This measurement should be taken on DT 3.5-DT 40 models after completing *Pinion Gear and Forward/Reverse Gear Backlash* as described in this chapter. Suzuki does not provide specifications for the DT 4.5.

1. Temporarily install the propeller shaft and bearing housing assembly.

2. Install a dial indicator as shown in **Figure 119**. Grasp the propeller shaft and pull it out as far as possible. Set the indicator gauge to zero.

3. Grasp the propeller shaft and push it inward as far as possible. Read the indicator gauge. The thrust clearance should be as follows:

    a. DT 3.5, 1983-on DT 9.9, DT 15, 1983-on DT 25 and DT 30—0.008-0.016 in. (0.2-0.4 mm).

    b. DT 5, DT 8, 1977-1982 DT 9.9, DT 16—0.002-0.020 in. (0.05-0.50 mm).

    c. DT 7.5, DT 9—0.002-0.006 in. (0.05-0.15 mm).

    d. DT 40—0.002-0.012 in. (0.05-0.3 mm).

4. If thrust clearance is less than specified, install thinner thrust washers on each side of the clutch dog to bring the clearance within specifications.

5. If thrust clearance is greater than specified, install thicker thrust washers on each side of the clutch dog to bring the clearance within specifications.

CLUTCH PUSHROD DIMENSION

This check is made on DT 75-DT 140 models after completing the tooth contact pattern check. Refer to **Figure 120** (DT 75-DT 85) or **Figure 121** (DT 115-DT 140) for this procedure.

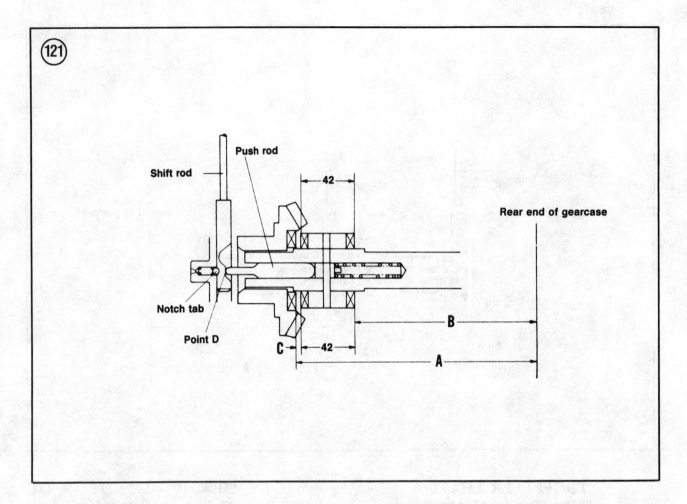

Push rod

Shift rod

42

Rear end of gearcase

Notch tab

Point D

C

42

B

A

1. Place the shift mechanism in the neutral position.

2. With the propeller shaft/bearing housing assembly out of the gearcase, use vernier calipers to measure and record the distance between the clutch engagement surface of the forward gear to the rear edge of the gearcase. See **Figure 122**. This is dimension A.

3. Temporarily install the propeller shaft (without bearing housing) in the gearcase until the front of the pushrod just touches the shift cam detent. See point D, **Figure 120** or **Figure 121**.

4. Use vernier calipers to measure and record the distance between the rear of the clutch dog and the rear edge of the gearcase. See **Figure 123**. This is dimension B.

5. Subtract dimension B from dimension A and record the result.

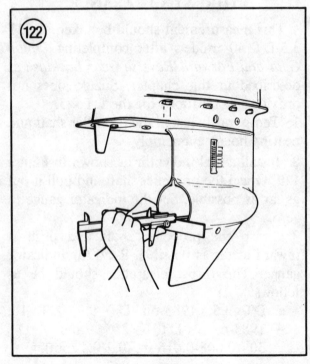

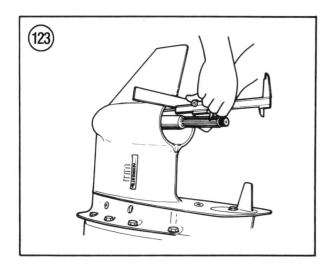

6. Subtract the thickness of the clutch dog from the figure obtained in Step 5 and record the result. This is dimension C. The DT 75-DT 85 clutch dog is 35.5 mm thick; the DT 115-DT 140 clutch dog is 42 mm thick.

7. If the figure obtained in Step 6 (dimension C) is 0.9-1.4 mm (DT 75-DT 85) or 1.3-1.7 mm (DT 115-DT 140), the clutch pushrod length is satisfactory.

8. If dimension C is not within the specifications in Step 7, replace the clutch pushrod with a longer or shorter one as required. See your dealer for available pushrod lengths.

ZINC ANODE

Some gearcases are fitted with a circular screw-in sacrificial zinc alloy anode to reduce galvanic corrosion. See **Figure 124**.

The anode should not be painted, as this destroys its protective value. Check the anode periodically for erosion. If badly eroded, it should be replaced and the source of the erosion located and corrected if possible. Erosion may be caused by faulty wiring in the boat or in a boat moored nearby, as well as by the water.

Table is on the following page.

Table 1 TIGHTENING TORQUES*

Fastener	ft.-lb.	N•m
Bearing housing bolt		
DT 2-DT 30	4.5-7	6-10
DT 40-DT 140		
1977-1982	36-43.5	50-60
1983-on	11-14.5	15-20
Drain plug	11-12.5	15-17
Gearcase attaching nut/bolt		
DT 2	4.5-7	6-10
1977-1982 DT 3.5-DT 65	11-14.5	15-20
1977-1982 DT 85		
8 mm	11-14.5	15-20
10 mm	25-30	34-41
1977-1982 DT 115-DT 140	25-30	34-41
1983-on DT 3.5-DT 40	11-14.5	15-20
1983-on DT 50M		
8 mm	11-14.5	15-20
10 mm	25-30	34-41
1983-on DT 115-DT 140	25-30	34-41
Pinion nut		
1977-1982 DT 40-DT 65	22-29	30-40
1977-1982 DT 85	44-51	60-70
1977-1982 DT 115-DT 140	58-65	80-90
1983-on DT 25-DT 30	13-16	18-22
1983-on DT 40-DT 50	22-29	30-40
1983-on DT 60-DT 85	51-58	70-80
1983-on DT 115-DT 140	72-80	100-110
Propeller nut		
1983-on DT 25, DT 30	20-22	27-30
All others	36-43.5	50-60
Standard torque values		
Bolt head marked "4"		
5 mm	1.5-3	2-4
6 mm	3-5	4-7
8 mm	7-11.5	10-16
10 mm	16-25.5	22-35
Bolt head marked "7"		
5 mm	2-4.5	3-6
6 mm	6-8.5	8-12
8 mm	13-20	18-28
10 mm	29-43.5	40-60
Stainless steel bolt		
5 mm	1.5-3	2-4
6 mm	4.5-7	6-10
8 mm	11-14.5	15-20
10 mm	24.5-30	34-41

* Use standard torque values for any fastener not specifically listed.

Chapter Ten

Automatic Rewind Starters

All manual start (and some electric start) models are equipped with a rope-operated rewind starter. Electric start models not equipped with a rewind starter have a flywheel drive cup and starter rope for emergency starts.

Two types of starters are used: a Bendix or spool starter bracket-mounted to the side of the power head (**Figure 1**) and an overhead starter mounted in a housing above the flywheel (**Figure 2**).

Pulling the rope handle causes the starter spindle or spool shaft to rotate against spring tension, moving the drive pawl or pinion gear to engage the flywheel and turn the engine over. When the rope handle is released, the spring inside the assembly reverses direction of the spindle or spool shaft and winds the rope around the pulley or spool.

A neutral starter interlock (NSI) prevents starter operation unless the shift lever is in NEUTRAL. A circuit in the ignition system provides the interlock feature on most models. On models without the ignition system NSI circuitry, interlock is accomplished by a mechanical interlock device. Only the mechanical interlock device affects the servicing of the starters discussed in this chapter.

Automatic rewind starters are relatively trouble-free; a broken or frayed rope is the most common malfunction.

NOTE
Suzuki does not provide and service instructions for the DT 4.5.

BENDIX STARTER

This starter type is used on some DT 5, DT 6, DT 8, DT 9.9 DT 16, DT 20 and DT 25 models.

Removal/Installation

1. Remove the engine cover.
2. Disconnect the spark plug wires to prevent the engine from accidentally starting.
3. Pry the rope handle retainer free and remove the rope from the retainer.

4. Grasp the rope from inside the lower cover and let the spring unwind slowly. When the rope passes through the lower cover grommet, tie a slip knot in the end.

5. Remove the bolts holding the starter housing to the power head (**Figure 3**). Remove the starter housing.

6. Installation is the reverse of removal. Pull the starter rope to make sure that the pinion gear and flywheel teeth mesh properly.

Disassembly/Assembly

Refer to **Figure 4** (DT 5-DT 8) or **Figure 5** (DT 9.9-DT 25) for this procedure.

> *WARNING*
> *Disassembling this starter mechanism without holding the spring in place can result in the spring unwinding violently and can cause serious personal injury. Wear safety glasses and gloves during this procedure.*

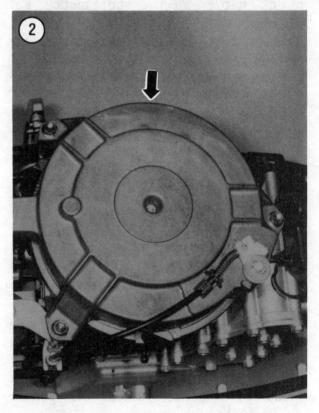

③

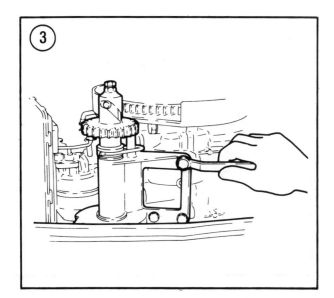

④

BENDIX STARTER (DT 5-DT 8)

1. Pinion gear
2. Friction spring
3. Snap ring
4. Bushing
5. Housing
6. Spring
7. Roll pin
8. Starter spool
9. Handle

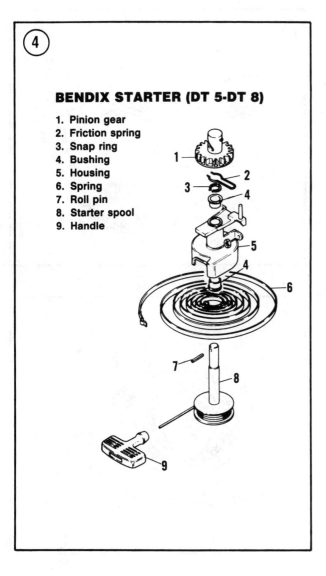

⑤

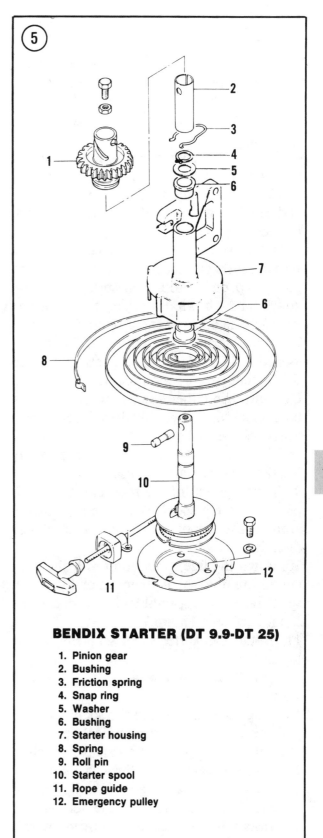

BENDIX STARTER (DT 9.9-DT 25)

1. Pinion gear
2. Bushing
3. Friction spring
4. Snap ring
5. Washer
6. Bushing
7. Starter housing
8. Spring
9. Roll pin
10. Starter spool
11. Rope guide
12. Emergency pulley

10

1. DT 9.9-DT 25—Remove the bolt located at the top of the pinion gear (**Figure 6**).

2. Place the starter housing on a flat surface, support the pinion gear and drive out the roll pin with a pin punch. See **Figure 7**.

3. Remove the pinion gear, bushing and spring assembly.

4. Remove the snap ring inside the housing bore with snap ring pliers.

5. Cover the starter housing with shop cloths and carefully withdraw the starter spool from the housing.

6. If the spring requires replacement, place starter housing on the floor (right side up) and gently tap on its top. The spring will drop down and unwind inside the housing. Remove the housing and discard the spring.

7. If the spring was removed, insert the looped end (A, **Figure 8**) of a new spring into the cutout in the housing (B, **Figure 8**). Carefully wind the spring into the housing bore clockwise, then lightly lubricate with water-resistant grease.

8. Make sure the bushings are properly installed on the starter housing.

9. Insert the end of the rope into the notch provided in the spool. Wind the rope tightly around the spool pulley in a clockwise direction.

10. Align the free spring loop with the pawl cutout on the spool, then carefully install spool into housing until spring loop engages spool pawl. See **Figure 9**.

11. Install the starter spool snap ring in the housing bore.

12. Install the pinion gear, bushing and spring on the spool.

13. Align the pin holes in the spool, bushing and gear. Support the pinion gear and reinstall the roll pin with a suitable punch.

14. Pull the starter rope through the cutout in the spool (**Figure 10**) and tie a slip knot in the end. Wind the rope into the housing.

15. Install the starter as described in this chapter.

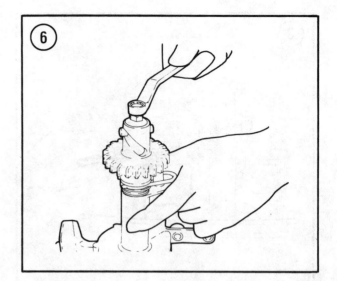

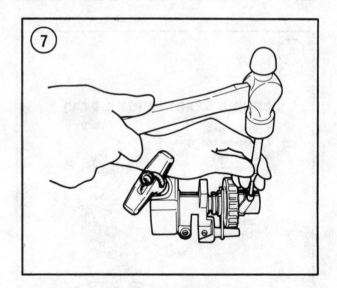

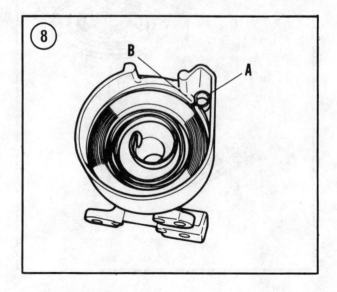

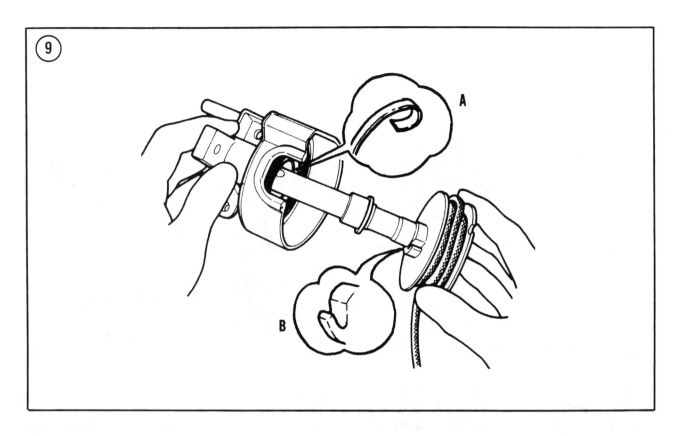

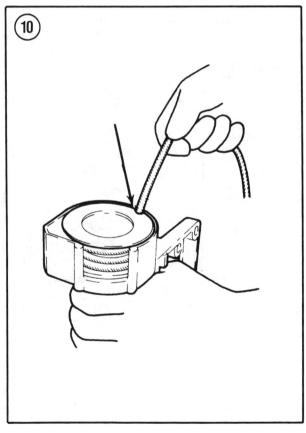

16. DT 9.9-DT25—Install the bolt at the top of the pinion gear. See **Figure 6**.

OVERHEAD STARTER

This type of starter is mounted in a housing on top of the power head. The starter rope is wound around a spring-loaded pulley. A pawl plate attached to the pulley engages the flywheel drive cup when the rope is pulled. A mechanical neutral safety interlock device is used on some models to prevent the engine from being started in gear.

Several variations of the basic design have been used on Suzuki outboards. Disassembly and assembly of each variation is covered separately.

Removal/Installation
(All Models)

1. Remove the engine cover.
2. Disconnect the spark plug wire(s) to prevent accidental starting of the engine.

10

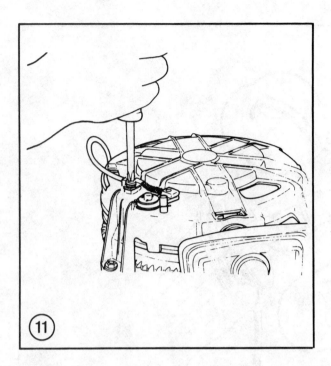

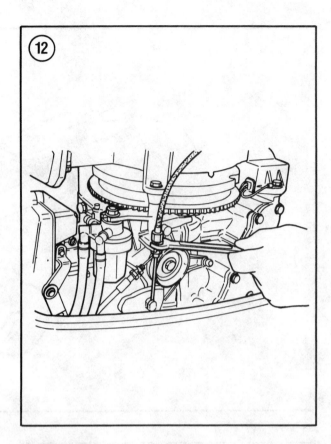

3. DT 25-DT 30 (1983-on)—Remove the starter interlock cable holder and disconnect the cable from the interlock arm (**Figure 11**).

4. DT 9.9-DT 15 (1983-on)—Loosen the starter interlock cable locknut and disconnect the cable from the throttle (**Figure 12**).

5. Remove the 3 bolts holding the starter housing to the power head (**Figure 13**). Remove the starter housing.

6. Installation is the reverse of removal. Pull starter rope to engage the pawl assembly with the drive cup before tightening the screws. Adjust the starter interlock (if so equipped) as described in this chapter.

Disassembly/Assembly
(DT 2, DT 3.5, DT 5, DT 6 and DT 8)

> *WARNING*
> *Disassembling this starter mechanism without holding the spring in place can result in the spring unwinding violently and can cause serious personal injury. Wear safety glasses and gloves during this procedure.*

Refer to **Figure 14** (DT 2) or **Figure 15** (all others) for this procedure.

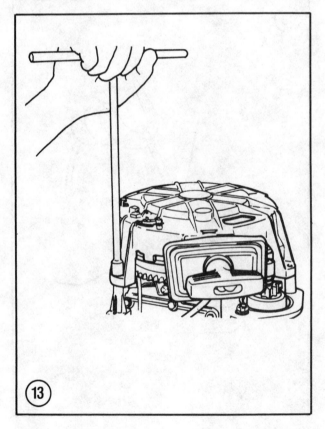

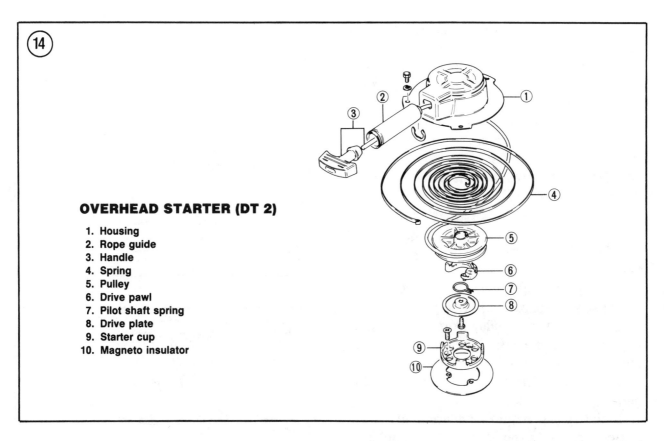

OVERHEAD STARTER (DT 2)

1. Housing
2. Rope guide
3. Handle
4. Spring
5. Pulley
6. Drive pawl
7. Pilot shaft spring
8. Drive plate
9. Starter cup
10. Magneto insulator

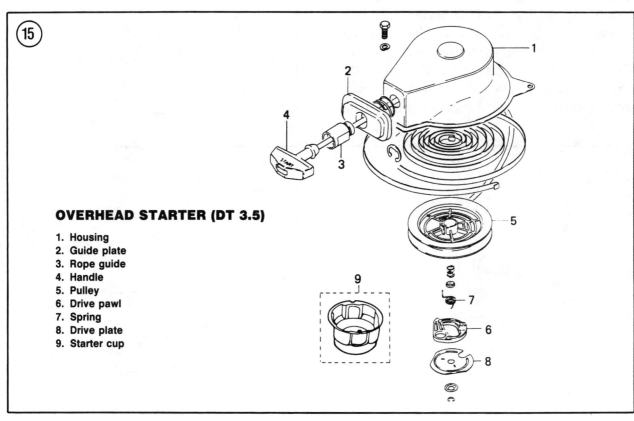

OVERHEAD STARTER (DT 3.5)

1. Housing
2. Guide plate
3. Rope guide
4. Handle
5. Pulley
6. Drive pawl
7. Spring
8. Drive plate
9. Starter cup

10

1. Invert the starter housing and pull the rope out as far as possible. Hold in this position and apply downward pressure on the starter pulley to prevent it from pulling the rope back in.

2. Hook the rope on the pulley notch. Let the pulley slowly rotate clockwise to release the spring tension. See **Figure 16**.

3A. DT 2—Remove the bolt in the center of the pulley (**Figure 17**).

3B. All others—Pry the circlip from the drive shaft in the center of the pulley (**Figure 18**).

4A. DT 2—Remove the drive plate and pawl.

4B. All others—Remove the drive plate, return spring, spacer and drive pawl.

5. Carefully lift the pulley from the housing. If pulley does not come out easily, insert a screwdriver in the pulley hole as shown in **Figure 19** and push the spring loop out of the pulley groove.

6. If the spring requires replacement, place starter housing on the floor (right side up) and gently tap on its top. The spring will drop down and unwind inside the housing. Remove the housing and discard the spring.

7. If the spring was removed, insert the looped end of a new spring into the housing bore and carefully wind the remainder of the

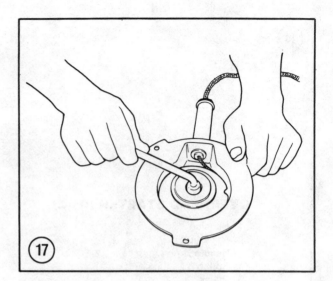

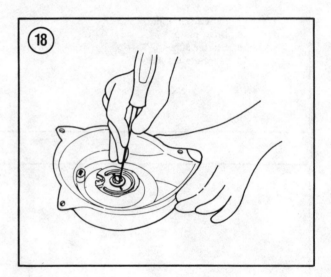

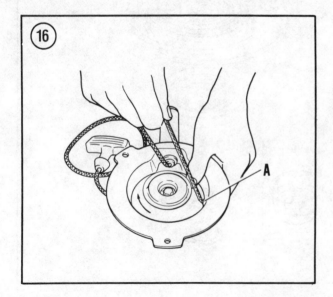

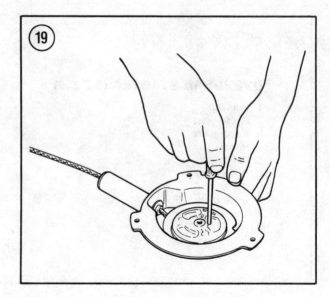

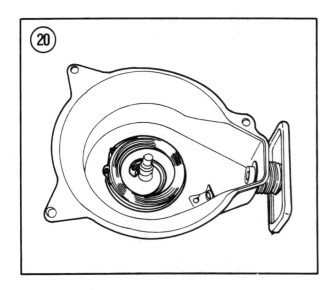

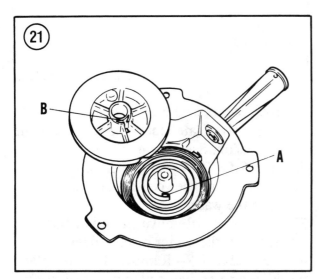

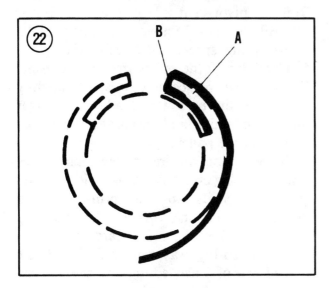

spring into the housing bore clockwise. When properly installed, it will rest in the bore as shown in **Figure 20**.

8. If the rope requires replacement, attach the new rope to the starter pulley.

9. Install the pulley in the housing so the bent end of the spring will engage the groove in the pulley. See **Figure 21**. Rotate the drum slightly counterclockwise. If the spring end and pulley groove have engaged properly, tension will be felt.

10. If no tension is felt in Step 9, insert a screwdriver in the pulley hole and rotate the pulley slightly, using the screwdriver to guide the spring over the pulley groove as shown in **Figure 22**.

11. Lubricate all parts with water-resistant grease.

12A. DT 2—Install the washer (A, **Figure 23**). Position the drive pawl (B, **Figure 23**) in housing and engage pilot shaft plate spring over the drive pawl pivot pin (C, **Figure 23**). Seat pilot shaft plate on drive pawl. Install and tighten the pulley bolt.

10

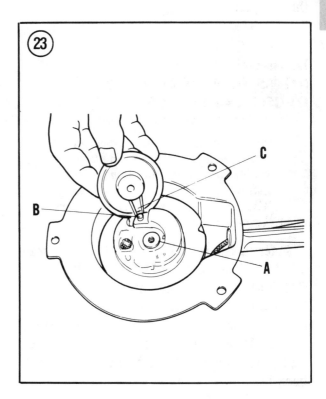

12B. All others—Install the drive pawl and spacer. Engage one end of the return spring in the drive plate hole (A, **Figure 24**). Engage the other end of the spring in the drive pawl hole (B, **Figure 24**). Install the washer and circlip.

13. Feed the rope through the housing and attach the handle.

14. Hook the rope on the pulley notch and rotate the pulley counterclockwise 6 turns.

15. Apply finger pressure to the pulley, then unhook the rope from the pulley notch and slowly allow the pulley to wind the rope under spring tension.

16. Connect a spring balance to the pulley handle and pull the rope out. It should require 3-5 pounds of pull. If the pull required is not within this specification, repeat Step 1, Step 2 and Steps 14-16, rotating the pulley more or fewer turns than specified in Step 14 to bring the pull within specifications. More turns create more tension; fewer turns create less tension.

17. Install the starter housing as described in this chapter.

Disassembly/Assembly (DT 7.5, DT 9, DT 20, 1977-1982 DT 25, DT 40 and DT 50)

> *WARNING*
> *Disassembling this starter mechanism without holding the spring in place can result in the spring unwinding violently and can cause serious personal injury. Wear safety glasses and gloves during this procedure.*

Refer to **Figure 25** (DT 7.5-DT 9), **Figure 26** (1977-1982 DT 20-DT 25) or **Figure 27** (DT 40-DT 50) for this procedure.

1. Invert the starter housing and pull the rope out as far as possible. Hold in this position and apply downward pressure on the starter pulley to prevent it from pulling the rope back in.

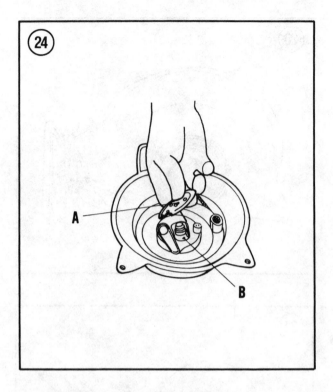

2. Hook the rope on the pulley notch. Let the pulley slowly rotate clockwise to release the spring tension. See **Figure 28**.

3A. DT 7.5-DT 9—Pry the circlip from the drive shaft in the center of the pulley. Remove the washer.

3B. All others—Remove the pivot bolt and washer from the center of the pulley.

4A. DT 7.5-DT 9—Remove the drive plate, pawls, return spring, coil spring and washer from the pivot shaft.

4B. All others—Remove the drive plate, return spring, spacer and drive pawls.

5. Carefully lift the pulley from the housing. If pulley does not come out easily, carefully insert the tip of a thin-blade screwdriver under the pulley and disengage the spring loop from the pulley.

6. If the spring requires replacement, place starter housing on the floor (right side up) and gently tap on its top. The spring will drop down and unwind inside the housing. Remove the housing and discard the spring.

7. If the spring was removed, insert the looped end of a new spring into the housing

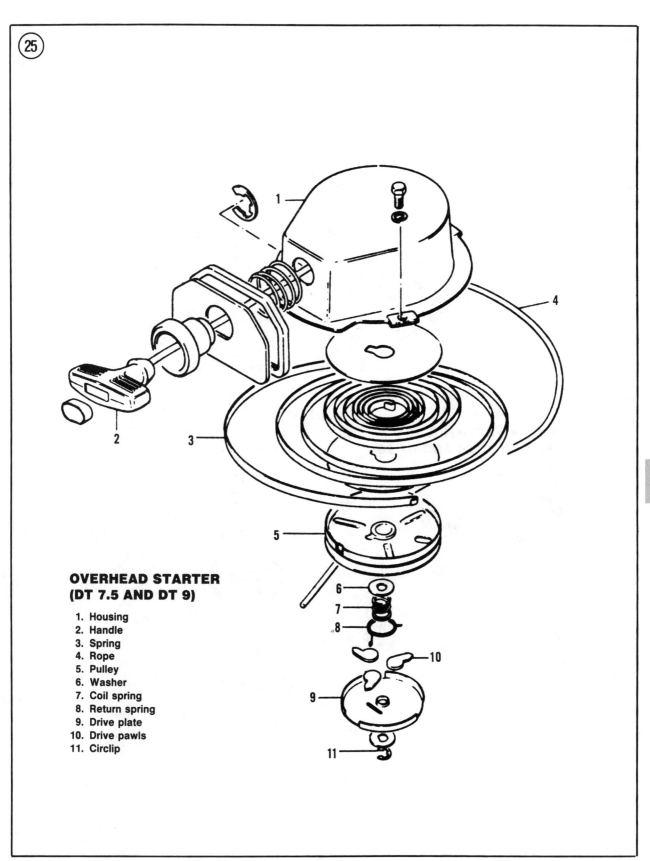

㉕

OVERHEAD STARTER
(DT 7.5 AND DT 9)

1. Housing
2. Handle
3. Spring
4. Rope
5. Pulley
6. Washer
7. Coil spring
8. Return spring
9. Drive plate
10. Drive pawls
11. Circlip

10

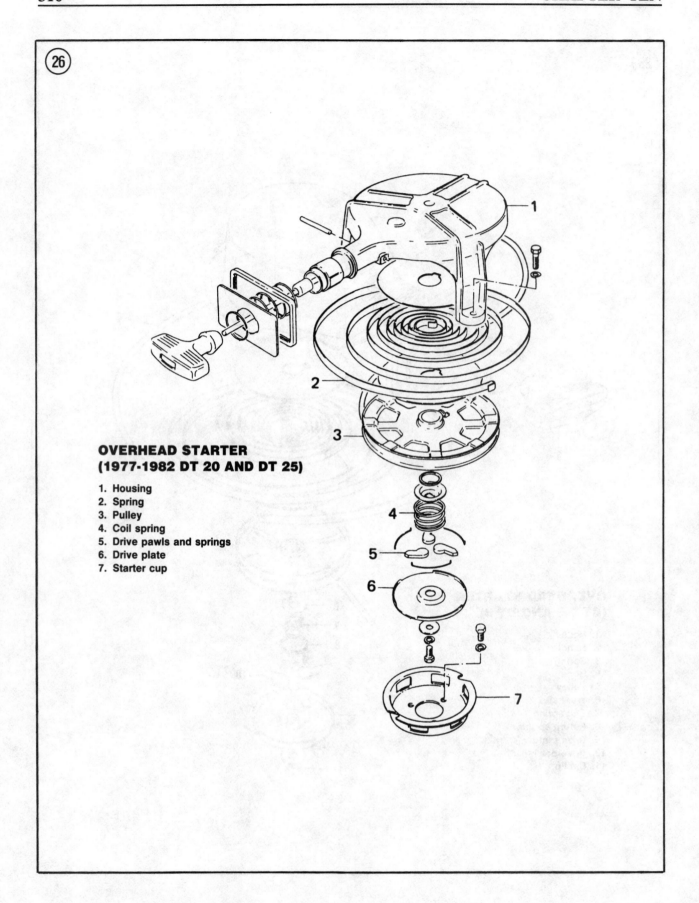

26

OVERHEAD STARTER
(1977-1982 DT 20 AND DT 25)

1. Housing
2. Spring
3. Pulley
4. Coil spring
5. Drive pawls and springs
6. Drive plate
7. Starter cup

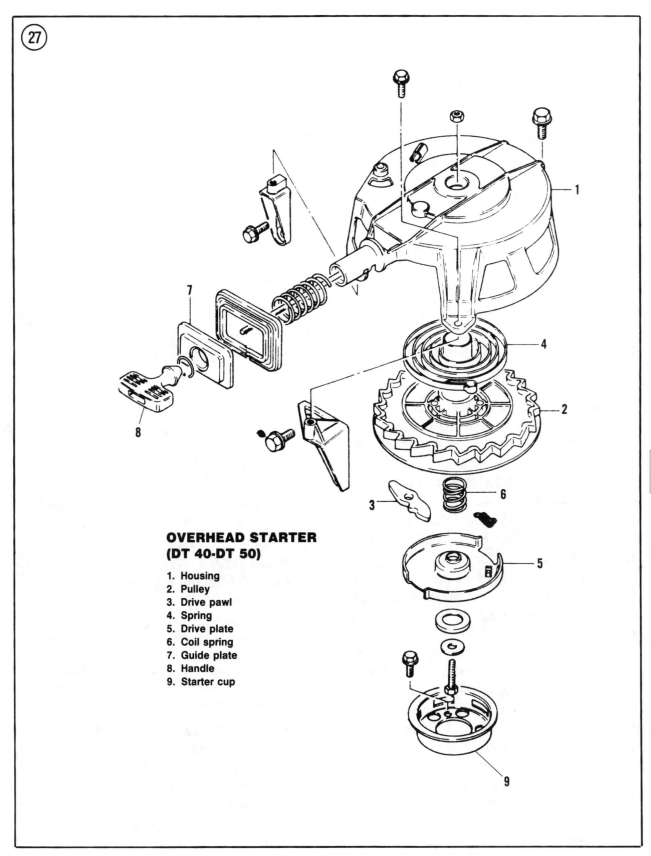

**OVERHEAD STARTER
(DT 40-DT 50)**

1. Housing
2. Pulley
3. Drive pawl
4. Spring
5. Drive plate
6. Coil spring
7. Guide plate
8. Handle
9. Starter cup

10

bore and carefully wind the remainder of the spring into the housing bore. See **Figure 29**.

8. If the rope requires replacement, attach the new rope to the starter pulley.

9. Lubricate all parts with water-resistant grease.

10. Install the pulley in the housing so the bent end of the spring will engage the groove in the pulley. Rotate the drum slightly counterclockwise. If the spring end and pulley groove have engaged properly, tension will be felt.

11. If no tension is felt in Step 10, carefully remove the pulley, realign the spring loop and pulley groove and repeat Step 10.

12A. DT 7.5-DT 9—Install the washer. Install the drive pawls in the pulley cutouts. Install the coil and return springs. Fit the drive plate in position and install the washer and circlip.

12B. All others—Install the return spring, drive pawl springs and pawls. Fit the drive plate in position. Install and tighten the pulley bolt.

13. Feed the rope through the housing and attach the handle.

14. Hook the rope on the pulley notch and rotate the pulley counterclockwise 5-6 turns (DT 7.5-DT 9) or 3-4 turns (all others).

15. Apply finger pressure to the pulley, then unhook the rope from the pulley notch and slowly allow the pulley to wind the rope under spring tension.

16. Connect a spring balance to the pulley handle and pull the rope out. It should require 3.5-5.5 pounds of pull. If the pull required is not within this specification, repeat Step 1, Step 2 and Steps 14-16, rotating the pulley more or fewer turns than specified in Step 14 to bring the pull within specifications. More turns create more tension; fewer turns create less tension.

17. Install the starter housing as described in this chapter.

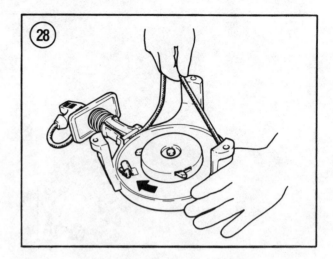

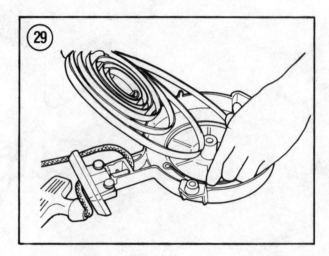

**Disassembly/Assembly
(1983-on DT 9.9, DT 15,
1983-on DT 25 and DT 30)**

> *WARNING*
> *Disassembling this starter mechanism without holding the spring in place can result in the spring unwinding violently and can cause serious personal injury. Wear safety glasses and gloves during this procedure.*

Refer to **Figure 30** (DT 9.9-DT 15) or **Figure 31** (DT 25-DT 30) for this procedure.

1. Invert the starter housing and pull the rope out as far as possible. Hold in this position and apply downward pressure on the starter pulley to prevent it from pulling the rope back in.

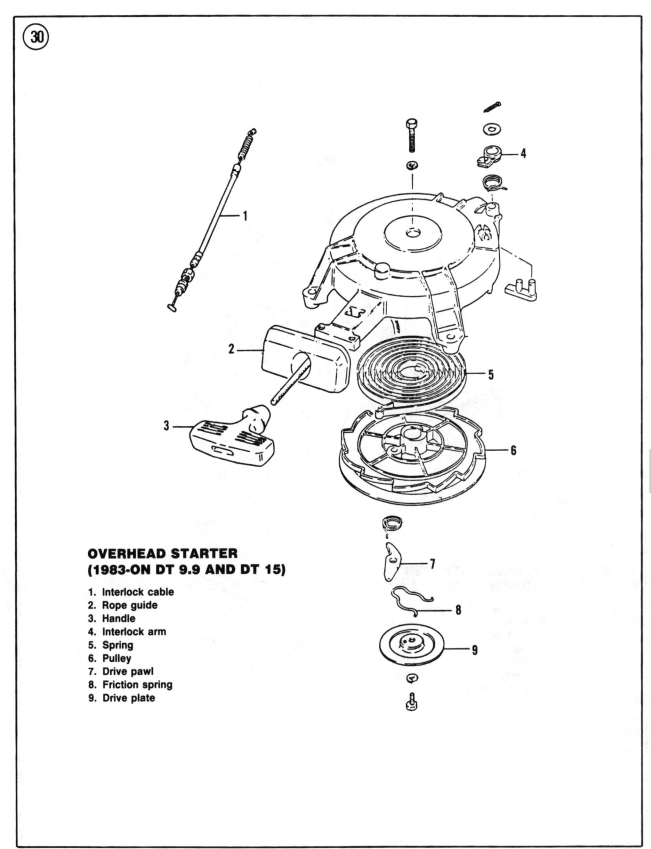

30

OVERHEAD STARTER
(1983-ON DT 9.9 AND DT 15)

1. Interlock cable
2. Rope guide
3. Handle
4. Interlock arm
5. Spring
6. Pulley
7. Drive pawl
8. Friction spring
9. Drive plate

10

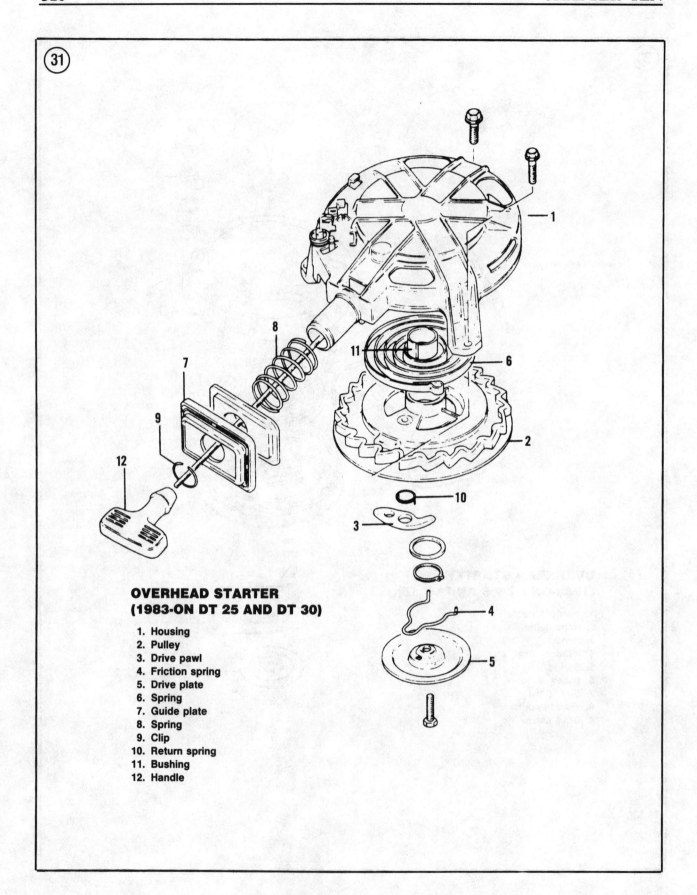

(31)

OVERHEAD STARTER
(1983-ON DT 25 AND DT 30)

1. Housing
2. Pulley
3. Drive pawl
4. Friction spring
5. Drive plate
6. Spring
7. Guide plate
8. Spring
9. Clip
10. Return spring
11. Bushing
12. Handle

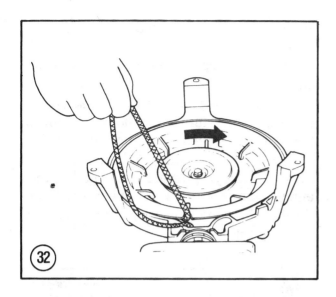

(32)

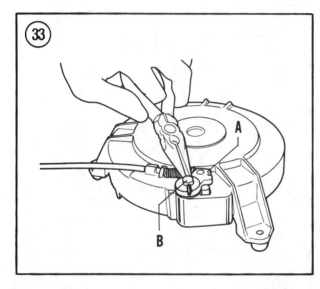

(33)

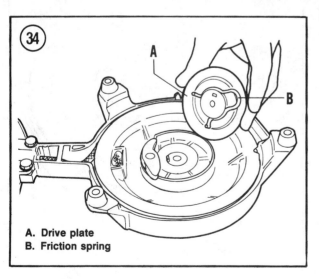

(34)

A. Drive plate
B. Friction spring

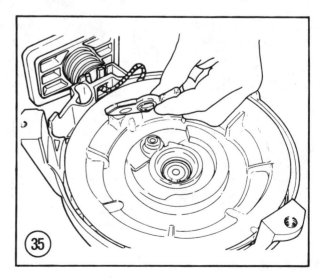

(35)

2. Hook the rope on the pulley notch. Let the pulley slowly rotate clockwise to release the spring tension. See **Figure 32**.

3. Remove the cotter pin and washer from the interlock device. Remove the interlock arm (A, **Figure 33**) from the pivot (B, **Figure 33**). Remove the interlock spring and pivot.

4A. DT 9.9-DT 15—Remove the drive plate bolt. Remove the drive plate with friction spring. See **Figure 34**.

4B. DT 25-DT 30—Remove the drive plate bolt. Remove the drive plate with friction spring and the spacer.

5. Remove the drive pawl and spring from the pulley. See **Figure 35**.

6. DT 25-DT 30—Remove the circlip from pulley bore with snap ring pliers.

7. Carefully lift the pulley from the housing. If pulley does not come out easily, carefully insert the tip of a thin-blade screwdriver under the pulley and disengage the spring loop from the pulley.

8. Remove the interlock device.

9. If the spring requires replacement, place starter housing on the floor (right side up) and gently tap on its top. The spring will drop down and unwind inside the housing. Remove the housing and discard the spring.

10. Lubricate all parts with water-resistant grease.

10

11. If the spring was removed, insert the looped end of a new spring into the housing bore and carefully wind the remainder of the spring into the housing bore. See **Figure 36**.

12. If the rope requires replacement, attach the new rope to the starter pulley.

13. Install the interlock device (A, **Figure 37**).

14. Install the pulley in the housing so the bent end of the spring (B, **Figure 37**) will engage the groove in the pulley (C, **Figure 37**). Rotate the pulley slightly counterclockwise. If the spring end and pulley groove have engaged properly, tension will be felt.

15. If no tension is felt in Step 14, carefully remove the pulley, realign the spring loop and pulley groove and repeat Step 14.

16. DT 9.9-DT 15—Install the circlip in the pulley bore.

17. Insert the short bent end of the drive pawl spring in the pulley hole, then connect the long bent end to the drive pawl groove (A, **Figure 38**). Install drive pawl.

18. Install drive plate with friction spring. Align drive plate hole with housing boss, and spring end with pulley groove. See **Figure 39**. Seat drive plate in position.

19. Install pulley bolt and washer. Tighten securely.

20. Feed the rope through the housing and attach the handle.

21. Wind the rope counterclockwise around the pulley 2 1/2 turns, then hook the rope on the pulley notch. Rotate the pulley counterclockwise another 4 full turns.

22. Apply finger pressure to the pulley, then unhook the rope from the pulley notch and slowly allow the pulley to wind the rope under spring tension.

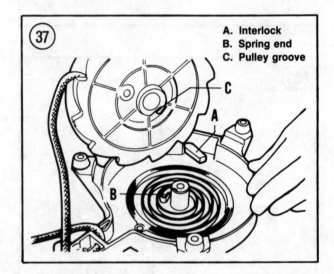

A. Interlock
B. Spring end
C. Pulley groove

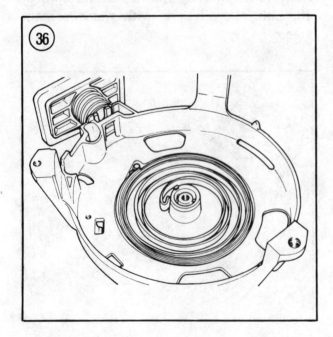

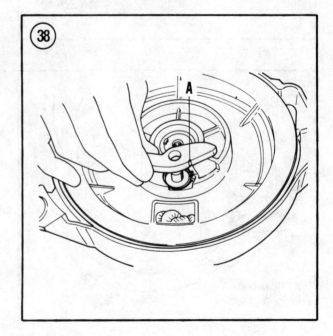

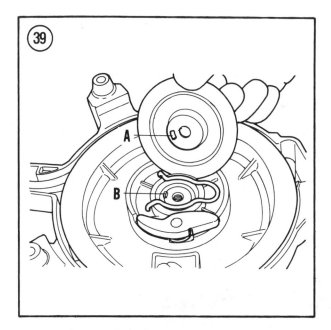

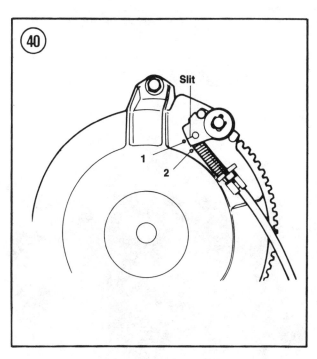

23. Install the starter interlock pivot and spring. Connect the interlock arm to the pivot. Install the washer and a new cotter pin. See **Figure 33**.

24. Install the starter housing as described in this chapter.

Starter Interlock Adjustment (1983-on DT 9.9-DT 15)

1. Make sure the shift lever is in NEUTRAL.
2. Loosen the interlock cable locknut (**Figure 12**) and turn the adjusting nut until the slit on the starter housing interlock arm aligns with the forward mark on the housing (1, **Figure 40**).
3. Move the shift lever first to FORWARD, then to REVERSE. If the interlock arm slit does not align with the rear mark on the housing (2, **Figure 40**) in each position, repeat Step 2.

Starter Interlock Adjustment (1983-on DT 25-DT 30)

1. Make sure the shift lever is in NEUTRAL.
2. Connect the end of the interlock cable to the interlock arm on the starter housing.
3. Apply sufficient tension on the cable to align the slit on the interlock arm with the forward mark on the housing (1, **Figure 40**), then tighten the cable clamp (**Figure 11**).
4. Move the shift lever first to FORWARD, then to REVERSE. If the interlock arm slit does not align with the rear mark on the housing (2, **Figure 40**) in each position, repeat Step 3.

10

Chapter Eleven

Power Trim and Tilt System

OPERATION, MAINTENANCE AND TROUBLESHOOTING

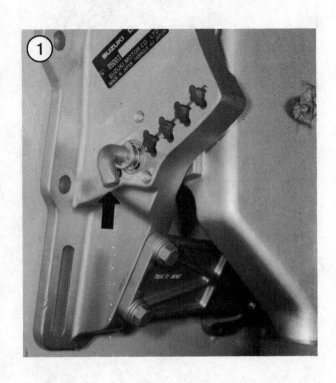

The usual method of raising and lowering the outboard gearcase is a mechanical one, consisting of a series of holes in the transom mounting bracket. To trim the engine, an adjustment stud (**Figure 1**) is removed from the bracket, the outboard is repositioned and the stud reinserted in the proper set of holes to retain the unit in place.

A power trim and tilt system is optional on DT 50-DT 65 and standard on DT 75-DT 140 models. Power trim provides low-effort control when the boat is underway or at rest.

Two- and three-cylinder engines are fitted with twin trim/tilt cylinders mounted inside the clamp brackets (**Figure 2**). The 4-cylinder engines use a dual trim and single tilt cylinder assembly mounted inside the clamp brackets (**Figure 3**).

Early models are fitted with a Prestolite pump. A Shinko pump is used on 1983-on models.

This chapter includes maintenance, troubleshooting procedures and hydraulic pump and trim/tilt cylinder replacement for both power trim/tilt designs.

Components (DT 50-DT 85)

This system consists of a hydraulic pump (containing an electric motor, oil reservoir,

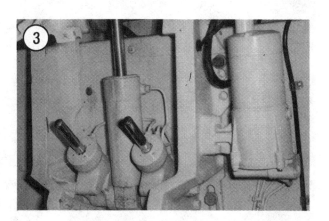

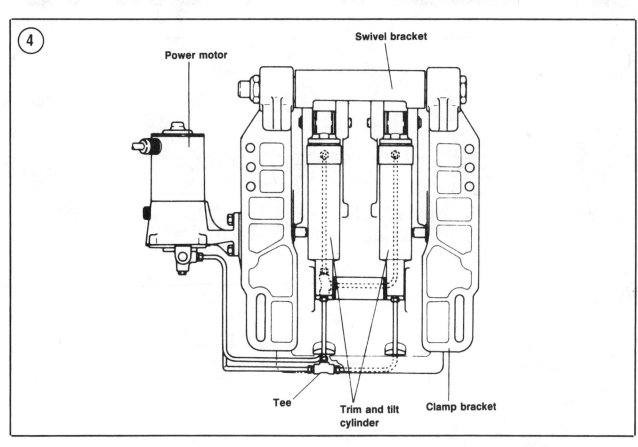

11

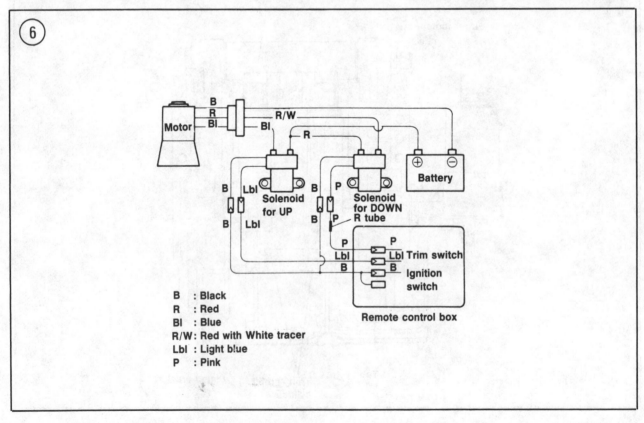

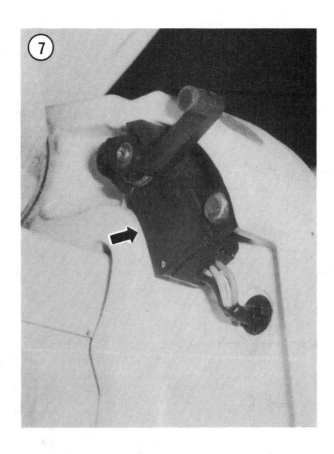

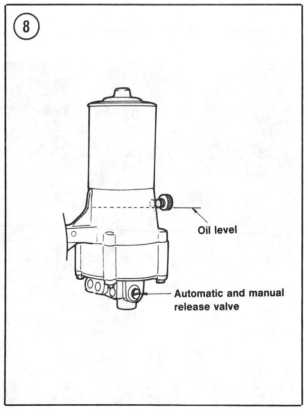

Oil level

Automatic and manual
release valve

oil pump and valve body) and 2 hydraulic trim/tilt cylinders. See **Figure 4**. Up/down solenoids are mounted on the power head (**Figure 5**). An indicator sender and gauge, trim/tilt switch and the necessary hydraulic and electrical lines complete the system. **Figure 6** shows the electrical schematic for this system.

Operation (DT 50-DT 85)

Moving the trim switch to the UP position closes the pump motor circuit. The motor drives the oil pump, forcing oil into the up side of the trim/tilt cylinders. The engine will move upward until it reaches its maximum position.

Moving the trim switch to the DOWN position also closes the pump motor circuit. The reversible motor runs in the opposite direction, driving the oil pump to force oil into the down side of the trim/tilt cylinders and bringing the engine back to the desired position.

The power trim/tilt system will temporarily maintain the engine at any angle within its range to allow shallow water operation at slow speed, launching, beaching or trailering.

To prevent damage from striking an underwater object, a relief valve in the hydraulic pump opens to allow the outboard to pivot upward quickly and return slowly, absorbing the shock.

An optional trim gauge sending unit is located on the inside of the starboard clamp bracket. See **Figure 7** (typical). Access to the sending unit requires the engine to be fully tilted.

Shinko pumps are equipped with a manual release valve (**Figure 8**). Opening this valve by turning its hex head up to 2 full turns permits manual raising and lowering of the engine if the electrical system fails.

11

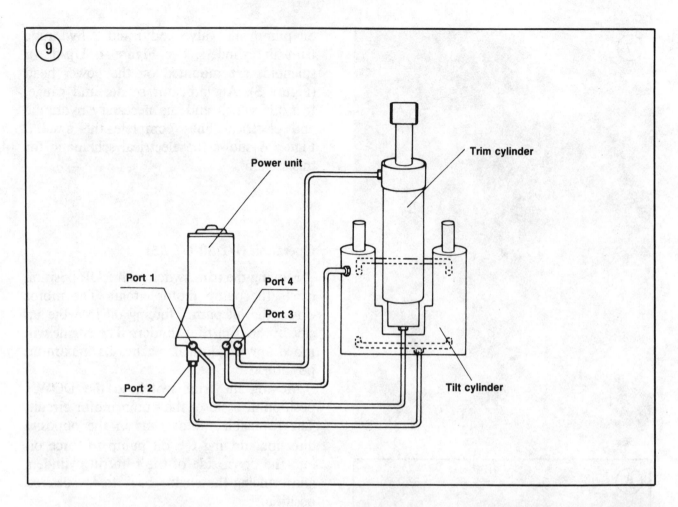

⑨

Power unit

Trim cylinder

Port 1

Port 4

Port 3

Port 2

Tilt cylinder

Components (DT 115-DT 140)

This system consists of a manifold containing a combination hydraulic tilt cylinder and 2 hydraulic trim cylinders which also act as shock absorbers. A hydraulic pump (containing an electric motor, oil pump, reservoir and all valving) is attached to the manifold. See **Figure 9**. The up/down solenoids are mounted on the power head (**Figure 10**). A trim/tilt switch, indicator gauge, sending unit and the necessary hydraulic and electrical lines complete the system. **Figure 6** shows the electrical schematic for this system.

Operation (DT 115-DT 140)

Moving the trim switch to the UP position closes the pump motor circuit. The motor

⑩

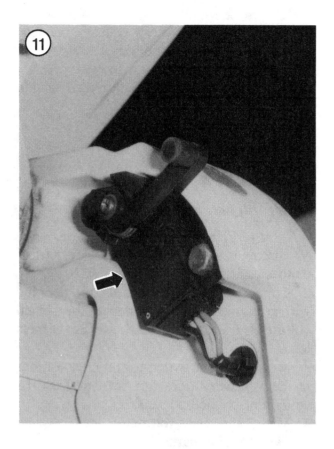

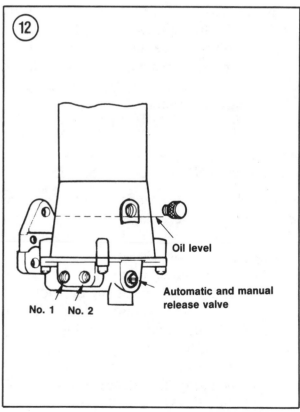

Oil level

Automatic and manual
release valve

No. 1   No. 2

drives the oil pump, forcing oil into the up side of the trim cylinders. The trim cylinder pistons push on the swivel bracket thrust pads to trim the engine upward. Once the trim cylinders are fully extended, the hydraulic fluid is diverted into the tilt cylinder, which now moves the engine throughout the remaining range of travel.

Moving the trim switch to the DOWN position also closes the pump motor circuit. The reversible motor runs in the opposite direction, forcing oil into the tilt cylinder and bringing the engine back to a position where the swivel brackets rest on the trim cylinder pistons. The pistons then lower the engine the remainder of the way.

The power trim/tilt system will temporarily maintain the engine at any angle within its range to allow shallow water operation at slow speed, launching, beaching or trailering.

To prevent damage from striking an underwater object, a relief valve in the hydraulic pump opens to allow the outboard to pivot upward quickly and return slowly, absorbing the shock.

A trim gauge sending unit is located on the inside of the starboard clamp bracket (**Figure 11**). Access to the sending unit requires the engine to be fully tilted.

Shinko pumps are equipped with a manual release valve (**Figure 8**). Opening this valve by turning its hex head up to 2 full turns permits manual raising and lowering of the engine if the electrical system fails.

11

Hydraulic Pump Fluid Check

> *CAUTION*
> *Do not fill pump reservoir with the outboard in the UP position or the valve body assembly may be damaged.*

1. Tilt the outboard to its full DOWN position.

2. Clean area around pump fill plug. Remove the plug (**Figure 12**) and visually check the

fluid level in the pump reservoir. It should be at the bottom of the fill hole threads.

3. Top up if necessary with DEXRON automatic transmission fluid.

Hydraulic Pump Fluid Refill

Follow this procedure when a large amount of fluid has been lost due to an overhaul of the system or a leakage that has been corrected. See **Figure 12**.

1. Remove the fill plug and top off the reservoir with DEXRON automatic transmission fluid.

2. Operate the trim switch to raise the engine to its full tilt up position, adding more DEXRON as required to keep the fluid level at the bottom of the fill plug hole.

3. Bring the engine back to its full tilt down position.

4. Install the fill plug and operate the engine up and down several times.

5. Remove the fill plug and add DEXRON to the reservoir as required to keep the fluid level at the bottom of the fill plug hole.

6. Repeat Step 4 and Step 5 until the fluid level stabilizes at the bottom of the fill plug hole. Install and tighten the fill plug securely.

7. Recharge the battery. See Chapter Seven.

Troubleshooting

Whenever a problem develops in the power trim/tilt system, the initial step is to determine whether the problem is in the electrical or hydraulic system. Electrical and hydraulic tests are given in this chapter. If the problem appears to be in the hydraulic system, refer it to a dealer or qualified specialist for necessary service.

1. Make sure the plug-in connectors are properly engaged and that all terminals and wires are free of corrosion. Tighten and clean as required.

2. Make sure the battery is fully charged. Charge or replace as required.

3. Check the system fuse, if so equipped.

4. Check the fluid level as described in this chapter. Top off if necessary.

5. Make sure the manual release valve is fully closed (Shinko pump).

Motor will not run

Refer to **Figure 6** for this procedure.

1. Disconnect the pump motor electrical connector from the wiring harness.

2. Connect the red voltmeter lead to the blue wiring harness lead. Connect the black voltmeter lead to the black wiring harness lead.

3. Move the trim switch to the UP position. If the voltmeter does not read at least 12 volts, replace the up solenoid.

4. Move the red voltmeter lead to the red/white wiring harness lead.

5. Move the trim switch to the DOWN position. If the voltmeter does not read at least 12 volts, replace the down solenoid.

6. If the voltmeter readings are as specified in Step 3 and Step 5 and the motor still does not run, replace the motor.

Motor runs, will not raise outboard

1. Check the hydraulic fluid level as described in this chapter.

2. On Shinko pumps, make sure the manual release valve is fully closed.

3. Check the hydraulic lines and fittings for signs of leakage while operating the motor up and down. If leakage is found, tighten fittings to 60-65 in.-lb. and repeat this step to determine if fittings still leak.

4. Disconnect the line and fitting at the No. 1 port on the pump. See **Figure 12** (DT 50-DT 85) or **Figure 9** (DT 115-DT 140).

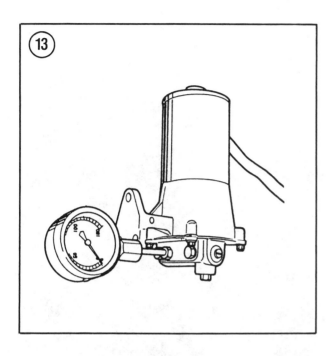

⑬

5. Install a suitable plug in the No. 1 port on the pump. Move the trim switch to the UP position.

6. If the motor runs freely in Step 5, the pump is defective. If the motor and pump go into a hydraulic stall, the trim/tilt cylinders are defective.

7. Remove the plug and install a 2,000 psi pressure gauge (part No. 09915-79410) in the No. 1 port. See **Figure 13** (DT 50-DT 85) or **Figure 9** (DT 115-DT 140).

8. Move the trim switch to the UP position and note the pressure gauge reading:

    a. If it does not indicate a minimum of 1,000 psi (DT 50-DT 85) or 1,500 psi (DT 115-DT 140), the pump is defective.

    b. If it indicates and holds a minimum of 1,000 psi (DT 50-DT 85) or 1,500 psi (DT 115-DT 140), the trim/tilt cylinders are defective.

Motor tilts up but leaks down

1. Disconnect the line and fitting at the No. 1 port on the pump. See **Figure 12** (DT 50-DT 85) or **Figure 9** (DT 115-DT 140).

2. Install a 2,000 psi pressure gauge (part No. 09915-79410) in the No. 1 port. See **Figure 13** (DT 50-DT 85) or **Figure 9** (DT 115-DT 140).

3. Move the trim switch to the UP position and hold until the motor and pump go into a hydraulic stall.

4. Move the switch back to the OFF position and wait several seconds, then run the motor back up and note the pressure gauge reading:

    a. If the pump holds its pressure reading but leaks down more than 200 psi in 5 minutes, the trim/tilt cylinders are defective.

    b. If the pump does not hold its pressure reading, the pump and motor assembly is defective.

Motor tilts up but not down

The servo-spool in the pump valve body is defective. Remove the motor and have the valve body replaced by a dealer or qualified specialist.

Motor tilts up when operated in reverse

1. Disconnect the line and fitting at the No. 2 port (DT 50-DT 85) or No. 3 port (DT 115-DT 140) on the pump. See **Figure 12** (DT 50-DT 85) or **Figure 9** (DT 115-DT 140).

2. Install a 2,000 psi pressure gauge (part No. 09915-79410) in the No. 2 port (DT 50-DT 85) or No. 3 port (DT 115-DT 140).

3. Move the trim switch to the DOWN position and note the pressure gauge reading:

    a. If it does not indicate a minimum of 240 psi (DT 50-DT 85) or 400 psi (DT 115-DT 140) or if it cannot hold whatever pressure is developed and leaks down to 0 psi, the pump is defective.

11

b. If it indicates and holds a minimum of 240 psi (DT 50-DT 85) or 400 psi (DT 115-DT 140), the trim/tilt cylinders are defective.

Trim/Tilt Cylinder Testing

If the troubleshooting procedures indicate that the trim/tilt cylinders are defective, perform this procedure to determine which one is at fault.

DT 50-DT 85

1. Place a suitable container underneath the tee in the lift line and disconnect one of the cylinders from the lift line. See **Figure 4** or **Figure 14** for tee location.
2. Install a suitable plug in nipple of the disconnected tee line.
3. Move the trim switch to the UP position. If the cylinder that is still connected to the tee will lift and hold the motor, the disconnected cylinder is defective.
4. If the cylinder connected to the tee will not lift and hold the motor, disconnect that cylinder at the tee and reconnect the cylinder disconnected in Step 1.
5. Move the trim switch to the UP position. If the cylinder that is connected to the tee will lift and hold the motor, the disconnected cylinder is defective. If neither cylinder lifts and holds the motor, both are defective.

DT 115-DT 140

1. Place a suitable container under the port trim cylinder and disconnect the top hydraulic line at the cylinder. See **Figure 9**.
2. Cap the line to prevent leakage and install a suitable plug in the cylinder fitting.
3. Move the trim switch to the UP position:
   a. If the starboard cylinder lifts the motor and does not leak down, the port trim cylinder is defective.

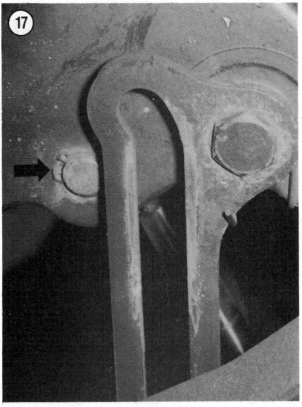

b. If the motor does not lift, the starboard trim cylinder is defective.

c. If the motor raises to the full tilt position and then leaks down, the tilt cylinder is defective.

COMPONENT REPLACEMENT

Service to the trim/tilt cylinders is much easier and quicker if the outboard motor has been removed from the boat. On some boat installations, outboard motor removal may be necessary to provide sufficient access to the hydraulic fittings to prevent damage to the lines.

Hydraulic Pump/Motor
Removal/Installation

1. Disconnect the pump/motor electrical connector from the wiring harness.
2. Place a container under the pump and disconnect all hydraulic lines. Cap the lines to prevent leakage.
3. Remove the bolts holding the pump to the clamp bracket (**Figure 15**). Remove the pump.

Trim/Tilt Cylinder
Removal/Installation
(DT 50-DT 85)

1. Support the motor in the full up position.
2. Disconnect the hydraulic line at the cylinder. Cap the line to prevent leakage.

NOTE
Some installations use a single piston rod pin to hold both cylinder pistons in place; others use individual pins for each cylinder.

3. Remove the cotter pin on the inner side of each cylinder piston rod pin. See **Figure 16**.
4. Remove the circlip on the outer side of each rod pin. See **Figure 17**.

11

5. Remove the piston rod pin(s).

6. Remove the 2 bolts and 2 nuts holding the cylinder support bracket to the clamp bracket assembly. See **Figure 18**.

7. Remove the cylinder support bracket with the cylinders attached.

8. Remove the lower cylinder shaft fasteners. Slide the shaft from the support bracket and cylinders. Remove the cylinders.

9. Installation is the reverse of removal. Coat the piston rod pin(s) and lower cylinder shaft with water-resistant grease. Refill the hydraulic pump as described in this chapter.

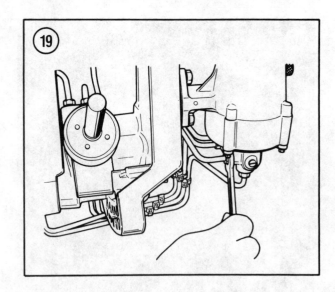

Trim/Tilt Cylinder
Removal/Installation
(DT 115-DT 140)

1. Support the motor in the full up position.

2. Disconnect the hydraulic lines at the pump (**Figure 19**). Cap the lines to prevent leakage.

3. Remove the pump as described in this chapter.

4. Remove the snap ring at each end of the tilt cylinder upper shaft (**Figure 20**). Carefully drive the upper shaft out.

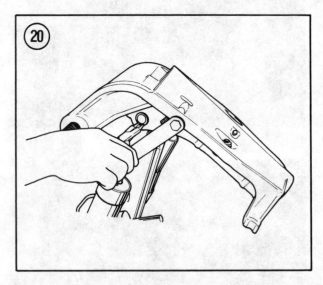

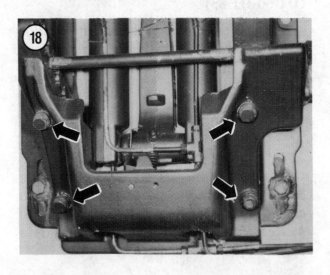

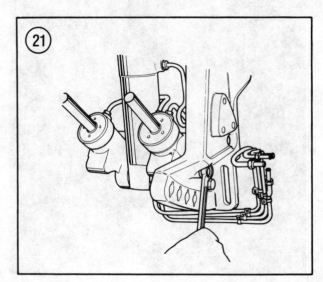

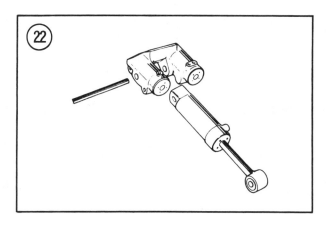

5. Remove the tilt lock pin.

6. Remove the 3 bolts on each clamp bracket holding the manifold in place (**Figure 21**). Remove the manifold.

7. Drive the tilt cylinder lower shaft from the manifold. Remove the tilt cylinder. See **Figure 22**.

8. Installation is the reverse of removal. Coat the upper and lower shafts with water-resistant grease. Refill the hydraulic pump as described in this chapter.

11

Chapter Twelve

Oil Injection System

The fuel-oil ratio required by outboard motors depends upon engine demand. Without oil injection, oil must be hand-mixed with gasoline at a 50:1 ratio to assure that sufficient lubrication is provided at all operating speeds and engine load conditions. This ratio is adequate for high-speed operation, but contains more oil than required to lubricate the engine properly during idle and low-speed operation.

With oil injection, the ratio of oil provided with the fuel sent to the engine cylinders can be varied instantly and accurately to provide the optimum ratio for proper lubrication at any operating speed or engine load condition. Late-model Suzuki DT 40-DT 140 outboards are equipped with a mechanical oil injection system using a crankshaft-driven injection pump and integral oil tank. The pump draws oil from the oil tank and

supplies it under pressure to intake manifold nozzles where it is sprayed into the air-fuel mixture. See **Figure 1**. A control cable (DT 40-DT 60) or rod (DT 75-DT 140) connects the pump to the throttle and varies the pump stroke according to throttle opening. The fuel-oil ratio ranges between 120:1 (DT 40-DT 85) or 125:1 (DT 115-DT 140) at idle to 50:1 at wide-open throttle.

This chapter covers the operation and service required by the oil injection system.

SYSTEM COMPONENTS

The Suzuki oil injection system is a factory-installed standard feature on 1980-on DT 85-DT 140, 1983-on DT 60-DT 75 and 1984 DT 40-DT 50 outboards. Models equipped with oil injection use a

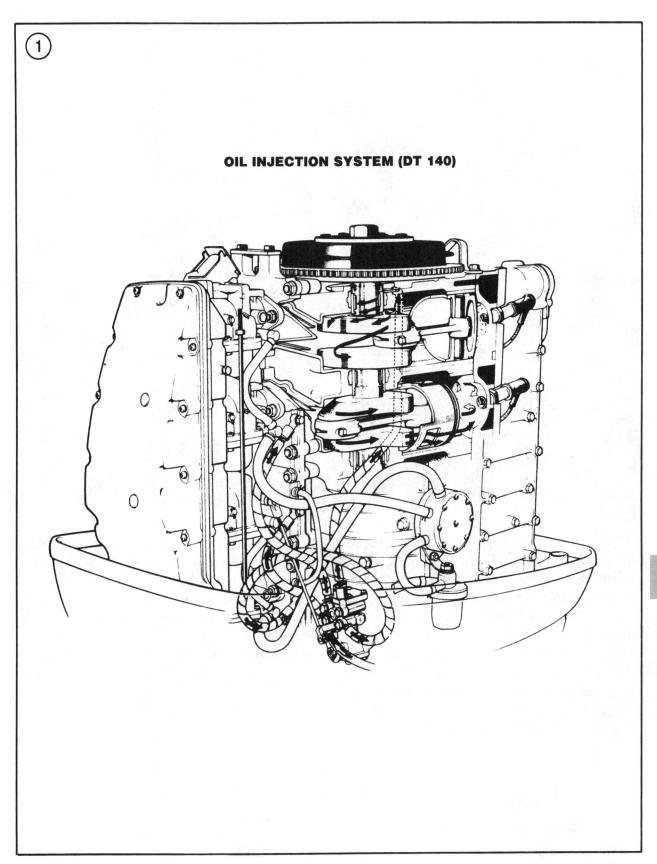

OIL INJECTION SYSTEM (DT 140)

12

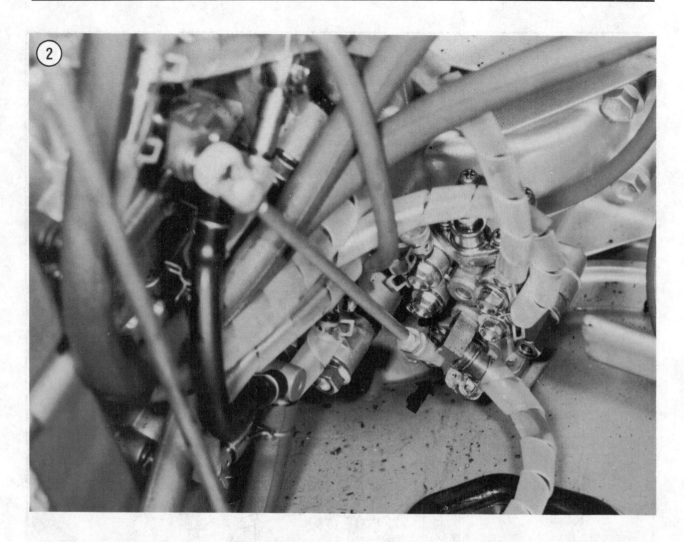

self-contained oil pump on the powerhead (**Figure 2**) in addition to the fuel pump. The pump is connected to the throttle by a control cable or rod. An oil tank or reservoir is mounted on the power head. See **Figure 3** (typical). When full, the tank contains sufficient oil for approximately 2 hours (DT 40-DT 85) or 5 hours (DT 115-DT 140) of continuous wide-open throttle operation. A warning buzzer located in the remote control box monitors oil level in the tank.

on the crankshaft engages a driven gear in the oil pump. This driven gear transmits crankshaft rotation through a series of reduction gears inside the pump, controlling the stroke of the pump plunger according to crankshaft speed. Since the pump is mechanically linked to the throttle, it supplies the proper amount of oil according to engine speed.

OPERATION

Suzuki's injection system supplies oil to the engine separately from the fuel. A drive gear

NOTE
The oil injection pump is sealed at the factory and is serviced by replacement if defective. Any attempt to disassemble the pump will void the factory warranty.

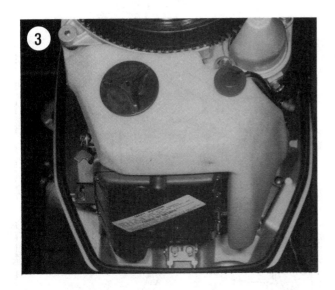

Oil travels to and from the oil pump through transparent lines (except 1980 models). This permits visual confirmation that the system is functioning properly.

The overheat warning buzzer in the remote control box is connected to a sensor in the oil tank. This buzzer gives off a warning sound when the engine is started (with the choke actuated) to indicate that the system is working. A steady sound of the buzzer during cruising indicates that the engine is either overheating or that the oil tank level has dropped below a safe level. An intermittent sounding of the buzzer during cruising indicates that the oil tank level is decreasing.

Break-in Procedure

The first 30 gallons (5 full tanks) of fuel used in a new or rebuilt oil-injected engine should be a 50:1 fuel-oil mixture (see Chapter Four) *in addition* to the lubricant supplied by the injection pump. Mark the oil level on the translucent oil tank mounted to the power head, then periodically check to make sure that the system is working (oil level diminishing) before switching over to plain

gasoline at the end of the 30 gallon fuel-oil mixture used during the break-in period. This applies both to engines that have been overhauled and new engines out of the box.

WARNING BUZZER

A warning buzzer is installed in the remote control box. The buzzer serves a dual function on oil-injected models. The sending unit in the power head oil tank is connected to the warning buzzer through the key switch and grounded to the engine. If the oil level in the tank drops below 17 ounces (DT 40-DT 85) or 34 ounces (DT 115-DT 140), the warning buzzer will sound continuously to alert the user to a low oil level.

If the buzzer indicates a low oil level and there is no reserve supply of oil aboard the boat, Suzuki recommends that engine speed be reduced to approximately 1,500 rpm. This will provide about one hour of cruising after the buzzer has sounded before the oil is used up.

A temperature sending unit is installed in the cylinder head on all models and connected to the warning buzzer through the key switch to warn of an overheat condition. If the power head temperature exceeds 212-220° F, the buzzer sounds continuously. Backing off on the throttle will shut the buzzer off as soon as power head temperature reaches approximately 190° F, unless a restricted engine water intake is causing the overheat condition. If the water pump indicator does not deliver a steady stream or if the buzzer continues sounding after 2 minutes, the engine should be shut off immediately to prevent power head damage.

CAUTION
If the engine overheats and the warning buzzer sounds, retorque the cylinder head fasteners after the engine cools to minimize the possibility of power head damage from a blown head gasket.

12

Testing

The warning buzzer should be tested periodically to make sure that it is functioning properly. A buzzer test unit is mounted on DT 115-DT 140 power heads. Use the following procedure to check the buzzer on DT 40-DT 85 models.

1. Locate the electrical wire between the warning buzzer and temperature switch. Move the insulating sleeve back to provide access to the disconnect point in the wire.

2. Turn the key switch ON and ground the disconnect point to the engine.

3. If the buzzer does not sound, check the wiring and buzzer.

4. Reposition the insulating sleeve over the disconnect point in the wire.

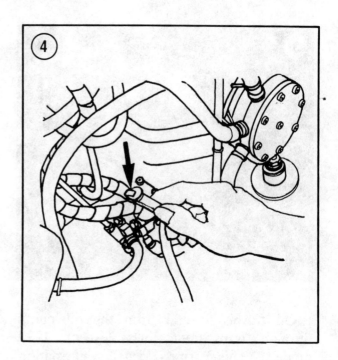

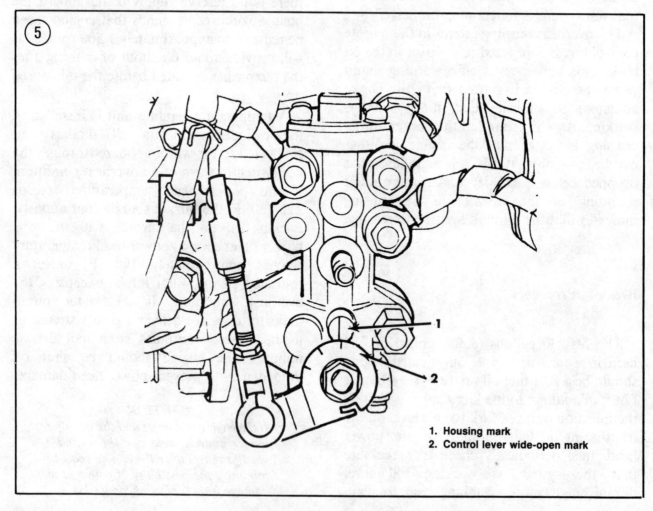

1. Housing mark
2. Control lever wide-open mark

OIL PUMP SERVICE

Oil Pump Bleeding

The oil pump must be gravity-bled to remove any air whenever the system is serviced or when the outboard has not been used for a lengthy period of time.

1. Remove the engine cover.

2. Make sure that the engine is in an upright position. If tilted in a trailering position, tilt the engine upright.

3. If the oil pump has been removed, fill the oil lines with oil before reconnecting them to the pump fittings.

4. Open the bleed bolt on the injection pump 3-4 turns counterclockwise. See **Figure 4**.

5. Wait several seconds and turn the bleed bolt clockwise to close it. Tighten bolt snugly.

Oil Pump Discharge Adjustment

This adjustment should only be required if the oil pump is removed for service.

1. Remove the engine cover.

2. Move the throttle to the wide-open position.

3. Check the full-open mark on the oil pump control lever. It should align with the match mark on the pump housing. See **Figure 5** (typical).

4. Close the throttle. The full-closed mark on the control lever should align with the pump housing match mark. See **Figure 6** (typical).

5. If the marks do not align in Step 3 or Step 4, open or close the throttle as required and proceed as follows:

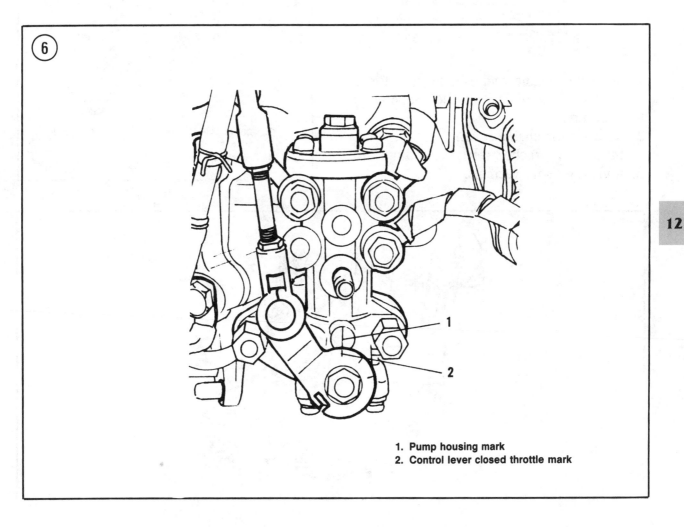

6

1. Pump housing mark
2. Control lever closed throttle mark

12

a. DT 40-DT 60—Loosen the control cable locknut and turn the cable adjusting nut until the marks align, then retighten the locknut. See **Figure 7**.

b. DT 75-DT 140—Disconnect the control lever rod from the control lever. Loosen the rod connector locknut and rotate connector as required to align match marks when reinstalled. See **Figure 5** or **Figure 6** (typical), as required.

Oil Pump Delivery Rate Test

CAUTION
The engine should be operated with a 50:1 fuel-oil mixture in the fuel tank during this procedure.

1. Start the engine and run at idle for 5 minutes or until it reaches operating temperature.
2. Remove the engine cover.
3. Install a tachometer according to manufacturer's instructions.

4. Install measuring cylinder (part No. 09900-21602) as shown in **Figure 8**.
5. Disconnect the control rod or cable at the oil pump control lever. See **Figure 9** (control rod shown).
6. Manually move the control lever to the full-open position (match marks aligned). See **Figure 5** (typical).
7. The pump should discharge 4.6-5.6 ml (DT 40-DT 60), 6.5-7.9 ml (DT 75-DT 85) or 10-12 ml (DT 115-DT 140) of oil in 2 minutes.

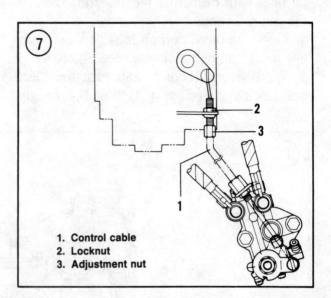

1. Control cable
2. Locknut
3. Adjustment nut

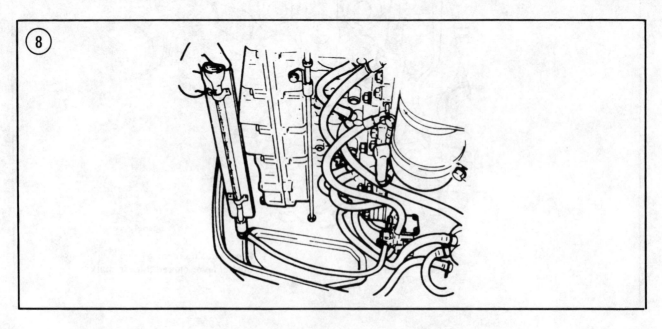

8. Manually move the control lever to the full-closed position (match marks aligned). See **Figure 6** (typical).

9. The pump should discharge 1.6-2.1 ml (DT 40-DT 60), 2.4-3.0 ml (DT 75-DT 85) or 3.6-4.4 ml (DT 115-DT 140) of oil in 3 minutes.

10. If the pump does not perform as described in Step 7 or Step 9, check the injection lines for possible leakage or restrictions. If none are found, replace the pump.

COMPONENT REPLACEMENT

Oil Tank Removal/Installation

1. Remove the engine cover.

2A. DT 115-DT 140—Remove the oil tank band and support rod nut, if so equipped. See **Figure 10**.

12

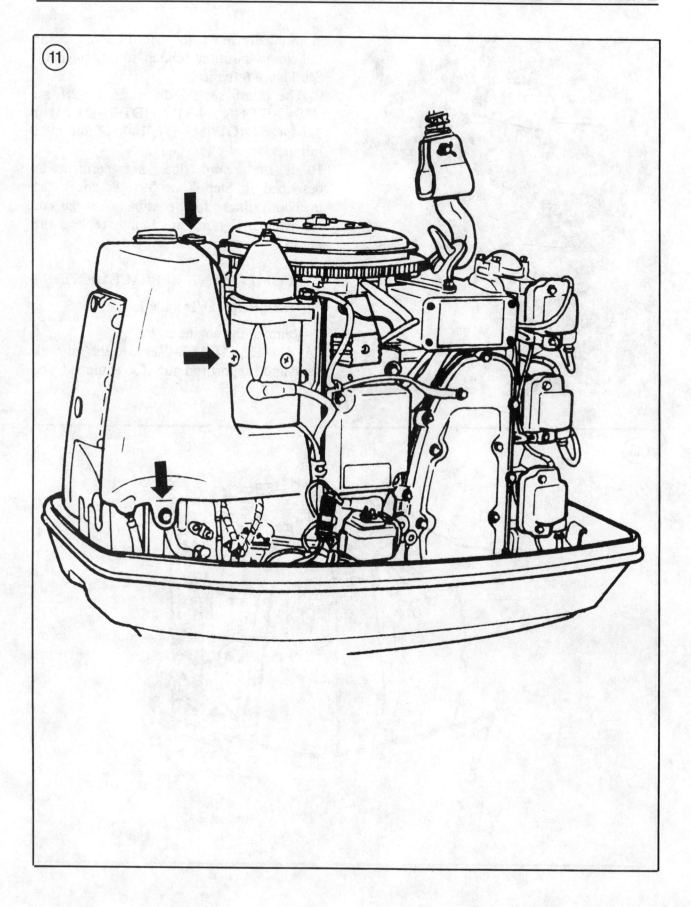

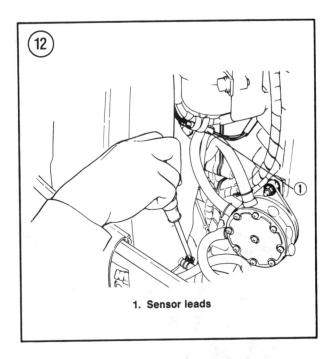

1. Sensor leads

2B. DT 50-DT 85—Remove the oil tank fasteners. See **Figure 11** (typical).

3. Move the tank away from the power head and disconnect the sensor leads. See 1, **Figure 12**.

4. Loosen the clamp holding the oil line to the tank (**Figure 12**). Pull the line from the tank fitting. Cap the tank fitting and plug the oil line to prevent leakage.

5. Installation is the reverse of removal.

Oil Pump Removal/Installation

> *CAUTION*
> *Proper oil hose routing and connections are important. The hose unions which connect to the power head and oil pump look the same but contain check valves of differing calibrations. Oil hoses must be installed between the pump and power head correctly and connected to the proper cylinder fitting on the intake manifold.*

1. Disconnect the negative battery cable.

2. Remove the engine cover.

3. Remove the oil tank as described in this chapter.

4. Disconnect the oil pump control cable or rod at the throttle. **Figure 9** shows the control rod; the control cable attachment is similar.

5. Label the power head location of each oil line banjo fitting with masking tape and a felt-tipped pen for correct reinstallation reference, then disconnect each fitting. See **Figure 13**.

6. Remove the 2 oil pump attaching nuts (**Figure 14**). Remove the oil pump from the power head.

7. Carefully break the driven gear retainer gasket seal with a putty knife or screwdriver

12

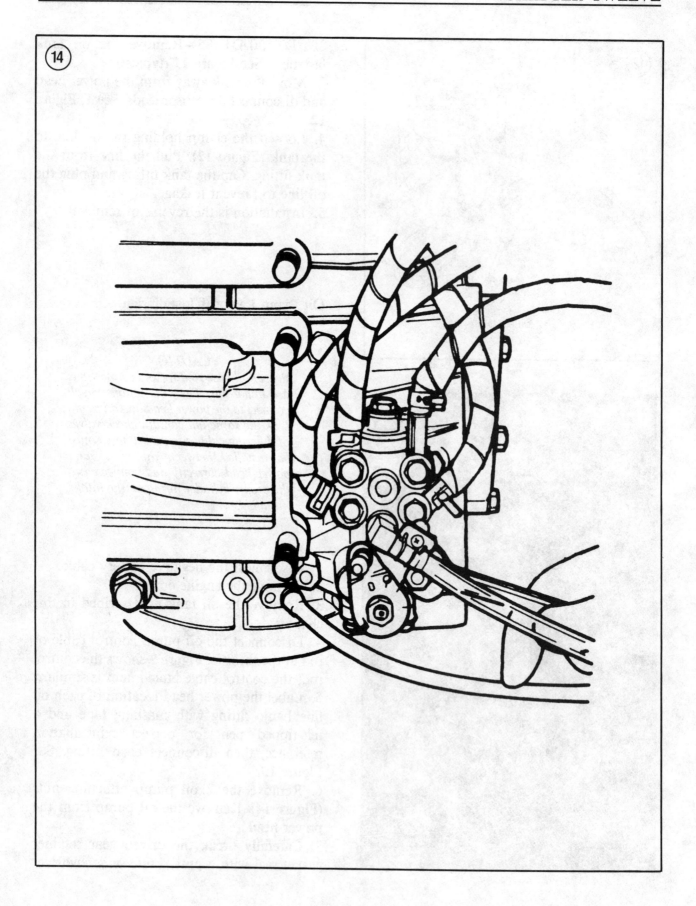

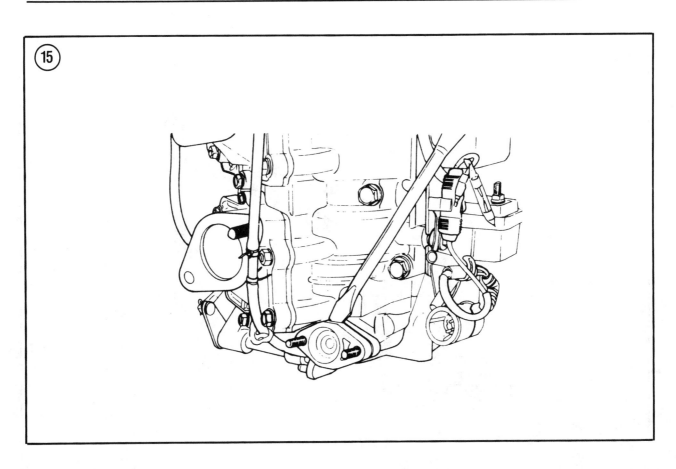

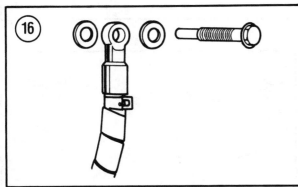

blade (**Figure 15**), then remove the retainer and driven gear assembly from the power head.

8. Clean the power head and retainer mating surfaces of all gasket residue.

9. If the pump is to be replaced but the oil lines and banjo fittings reused:

   a. Unbolt one line at a time from the pump and discard the banjo fitting gaskets.

b. Use new gaskets on either side of the banjo fitting (**Figure 16**) and install it to the same position on the new pump.

c. Be sure to install the banjo fitting with its brass side facing the pump.

12

CAUTION
If the oil lines are disconnected from the banjo fitting to replace the check valve or oil line, they must be reinstalled with the same type of clamps as removed. The use of worm clamps will damage the vinyl hose while tie straps will not provide sufficient clamping pressure.

10. If the oil pump and banjo fittings are to be reused but the oil lines require replacement:

   a. Compress the oil line clamp with pliers, slide it away from the banjo fitting and

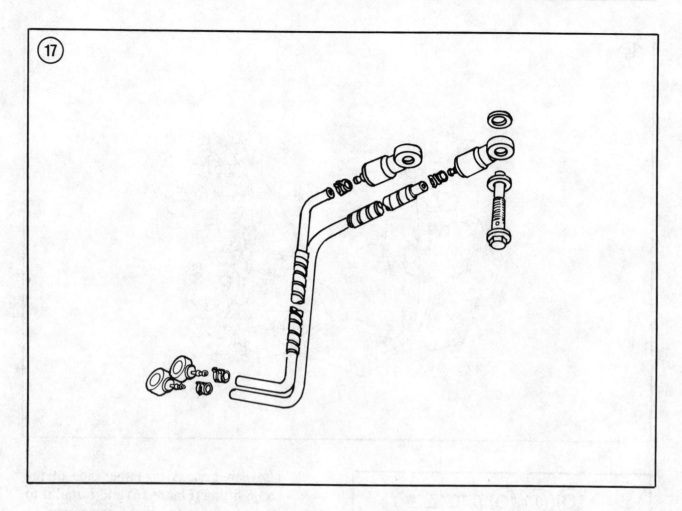

pull the old line off the fitting. See **Figure 17**.

b. Compress a new oil line clamp with pliers and fit it over the new oil line.

c. Compress the clamp and slide it in position over the banjo fitting nipple.

d. Repeat the procedure to install the line to the other banjo fitting.

11. If the banjo fitting check valve is to be replaced, disconnect the oil line as described in Step 10 and install the line to the new banjo fitting.

12. Align the oil pump shaft with the driven gear retainer groove and fit the pump to the retainer (**Figure 18**). Install the assembly to the power head with a new gasket and tighten the attaching nuts securely.

13. If oil lines were removed or replaced, loosen the banjo fitting bolts slightly and

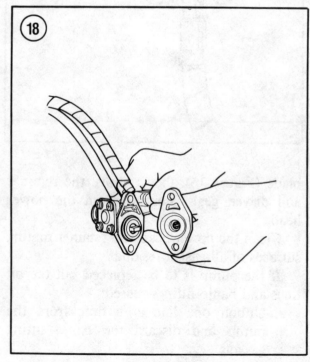

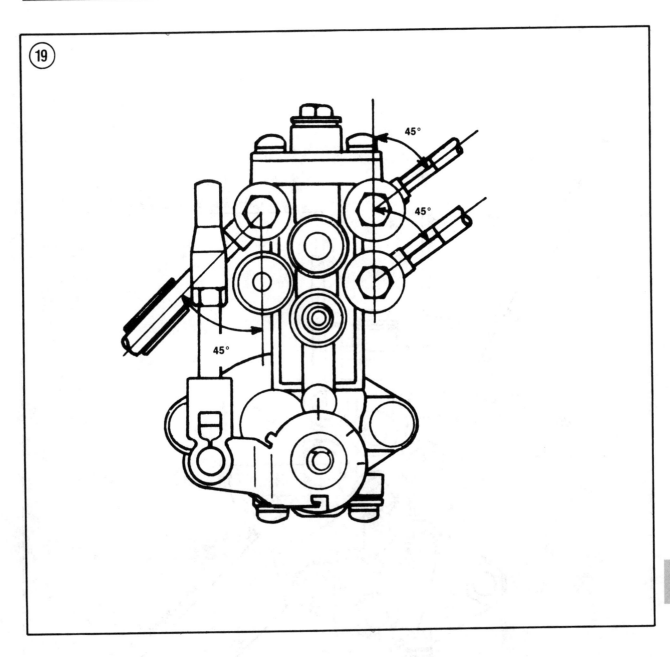

position the lines as shown in **Figure 19** or **Figure 20**, then retighten the bolts securely.

14. Install the oil lines to the intake manifold with new banjo fitting gaskets as shown in **Figure 21** (DT 115-DT 140) or **Figure 22** (all others).

15. Connect the control cable or rod and perform the *Injection Pump Discharge Adjustment* described in this chapter.

16. Compress the banjo fitting clamps and disconnect the outlet hoses. Fill the hoses with Suzuki CCC 50:1 Outboard Oil, then reconnect the hoses to the fittings.

17. Bleed the injection pump as described in this chapter.

18. Carefully check all hoses and connections for signs of oil leakage before starting the engine in Step 19.

19. Check the injection pump delivery rate as described in this chapter.

12

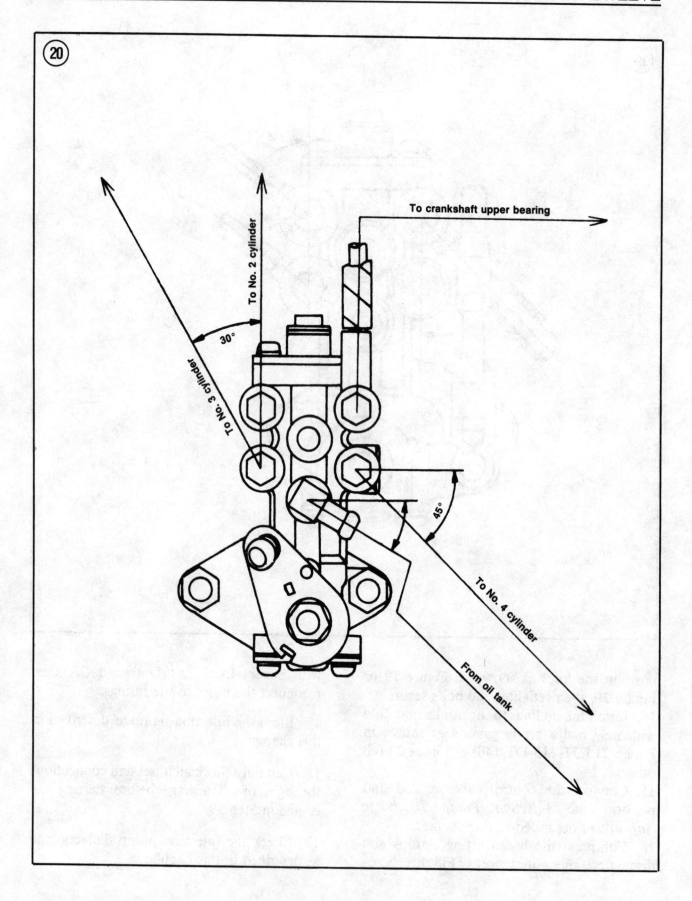

⑳

To crankshaft upper bearing

To No. 2 cylinder

30°

To No. 3 cylinder

45°

To No. 4 cylinder

From oil tank

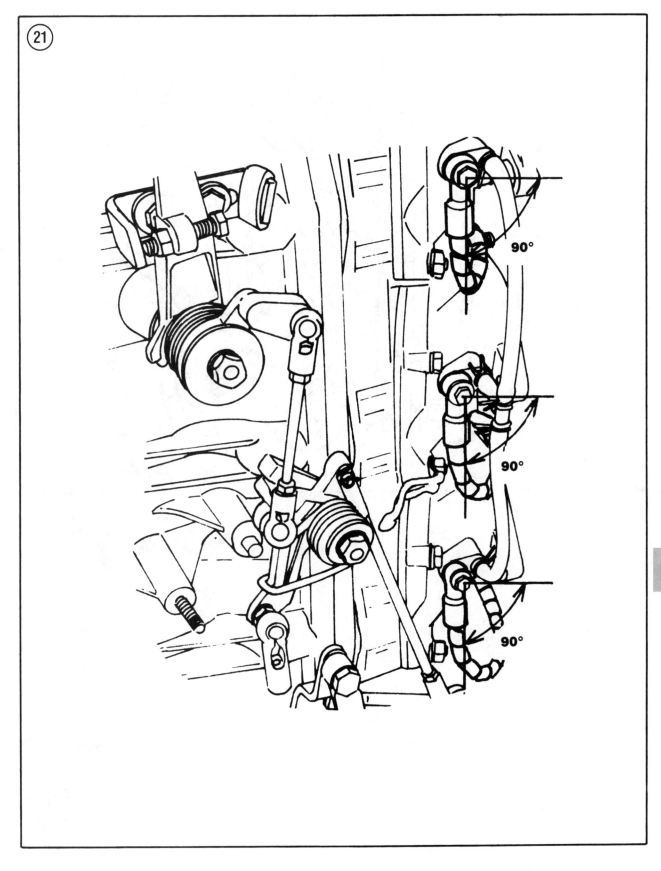

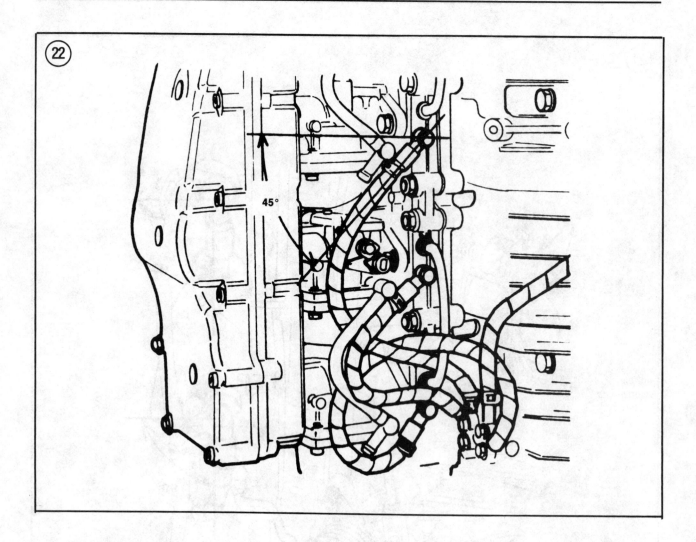

INDEX

13

13

Wiring Diagrams

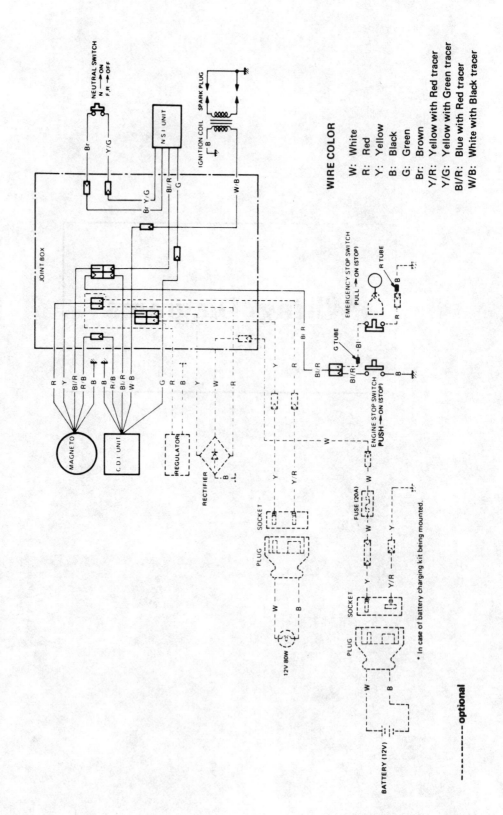

1981-1982 DT 20P/DT 25/DT 25P/DT 28

WIRE COLOR

W: White
R: Red
Y: Yellow
B: Black
G: Green
Br: Brown
Y/R: Yellow with Red tracer
Y/G: Yellow with Green tracer
Bl/R: Blue with Red tracer
W/B: White with Black tracer

* In case of battery charging kit being mounted.

------- optional

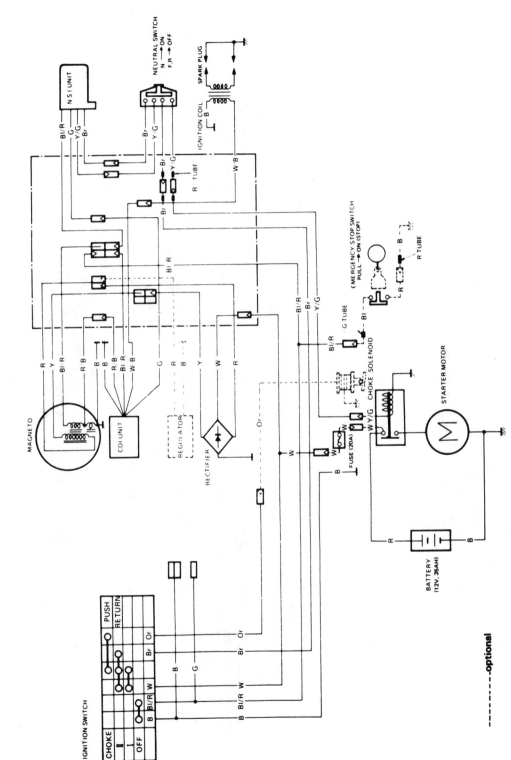

1981-1982 DT 25PE/DT 28E

14

1983 DT 50M

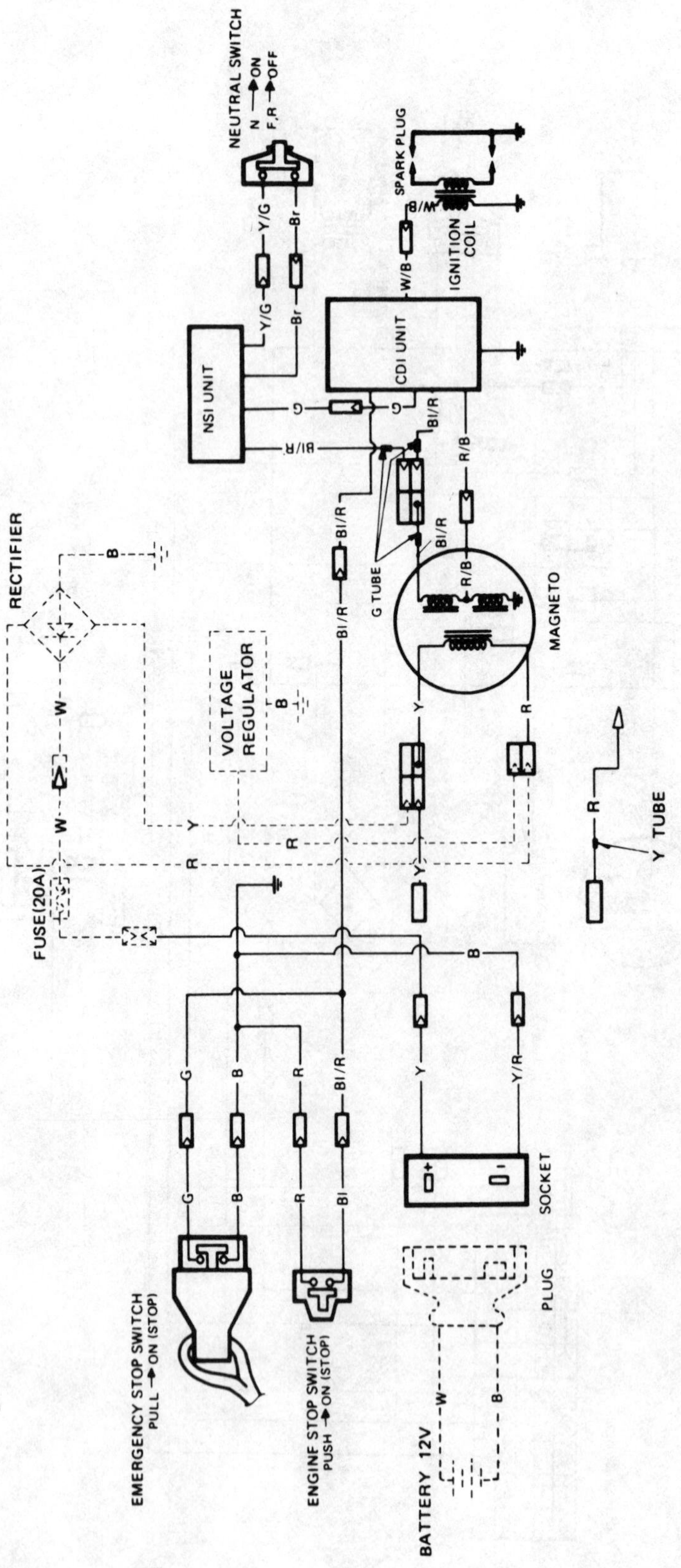

.... : Option

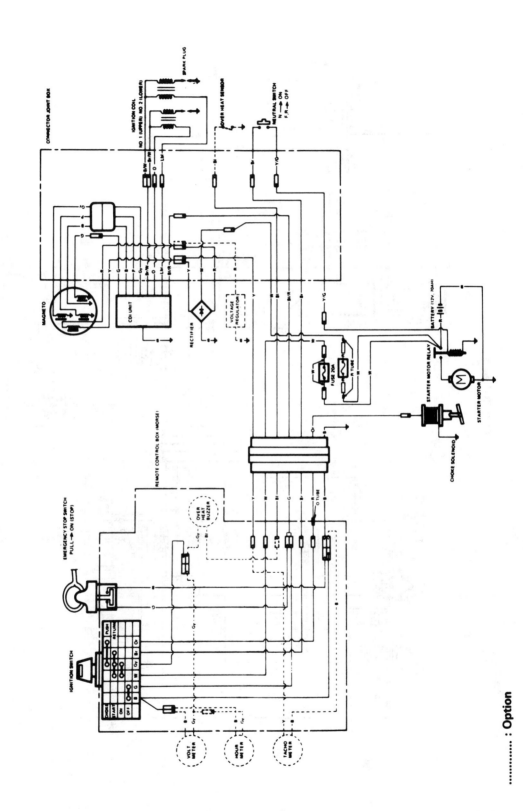

1983 DT 50/DT 50W

⋯⋯⋯ : **Option**

14

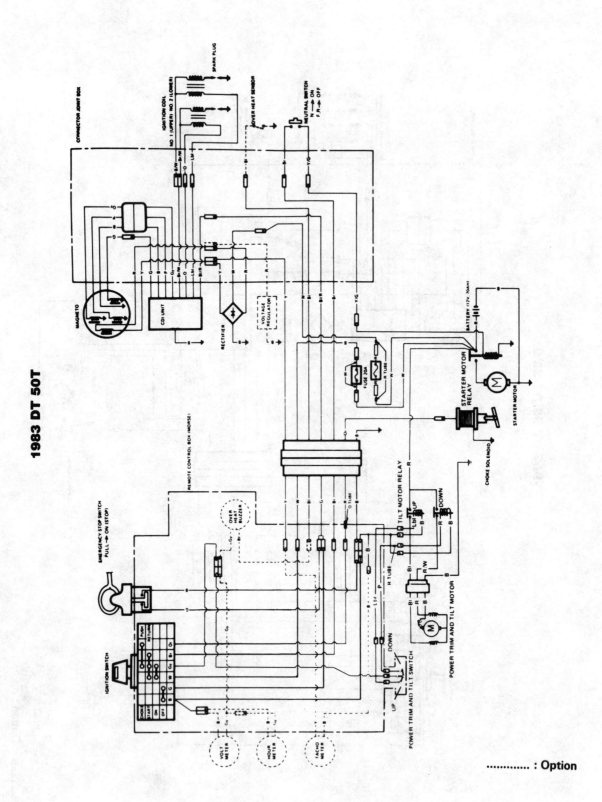

1983 DT 50T

.... : Option

1983 DT 60

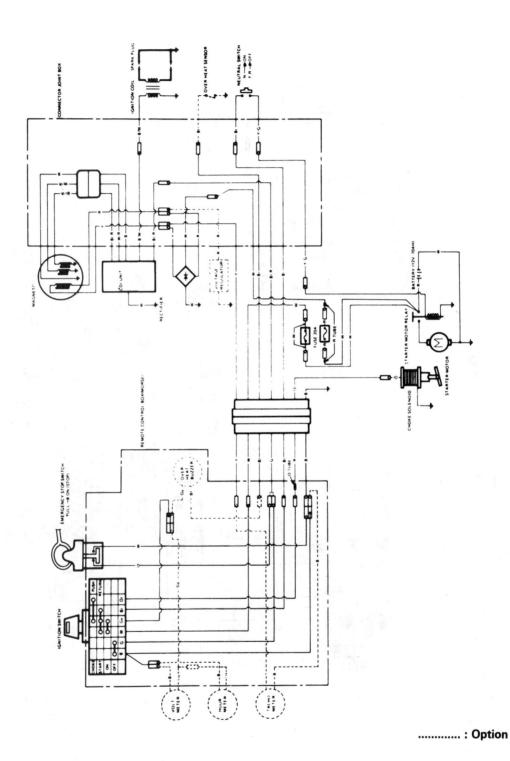

.... : **Option**

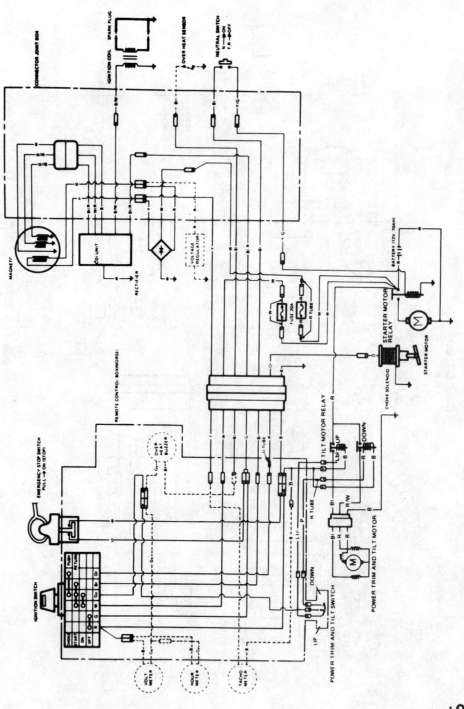

1984 DT 60

.... : Option

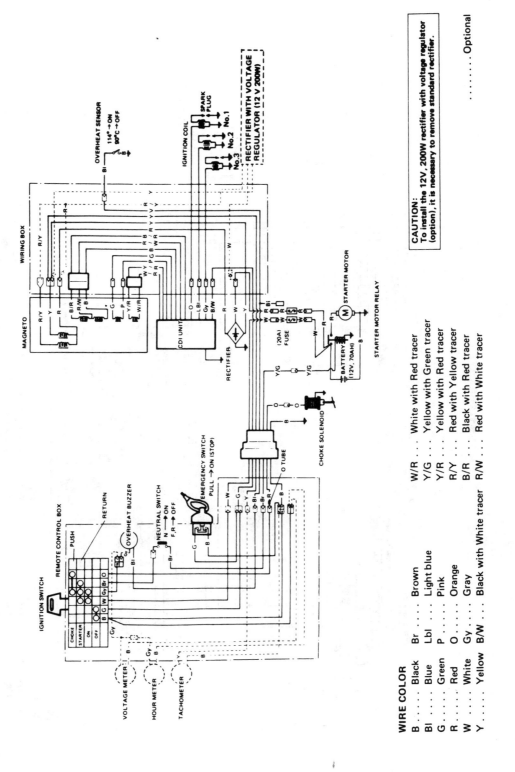

DT 65 AND DT 85

WIRE COLOR

B	Black	Br	Brown	W/R	White with Red tracer
Bl	Blue	Lbl	Light blue	Y/G	Yellow with Green tracer
G	Green	P	Pink	Y/R	Yellow with Red tracer
R	Red	O	Orange	R/Y	Red with Yellow tracer
W	White	Gy	Gray	B/R	Black with Red tracer
Y	Yellow	B/W	Black with White tracer	R/W	Red with White tracer

CAUTION:
To install the 12V, 200W rectifier with voltage regulator (option), it is necessary to remove standard rectifier.

. . . . Optional

14

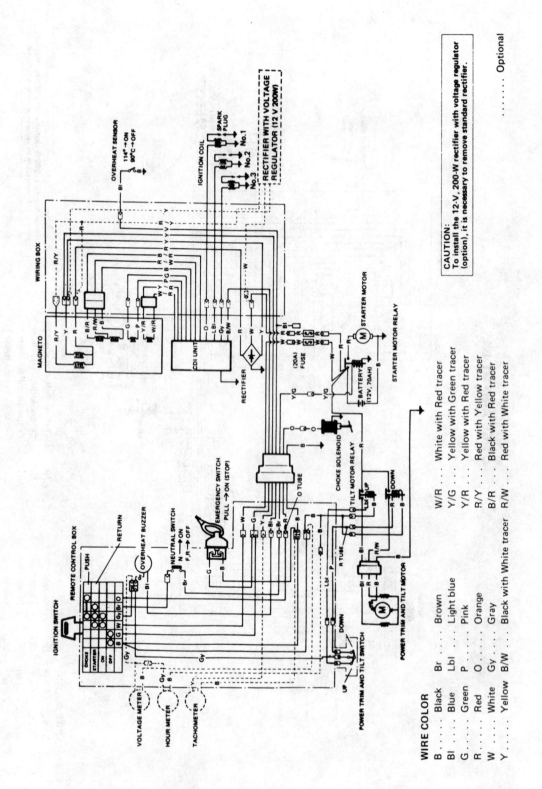

1981-1983 DT 85T

WIRE COLOR

B	Black	Br	Brown	W/R	White with Red tracer
Bl	Blue	Lbl	Light blue	Y/G	Yellow with Green tracer
G	Green	P	Pink	Y/R	Yellow with Red tracer
R	Red	O	Orange	R/Y	Red with Yellow tracer
W	White	Gy	Gray	B/R	Black with Red tracer
Y	Yellow	B/W	Black with White tracer	R/W	Red with White tracer

CAUTION:
To install the 12-V, 200-W rectifier with voltage regulator (option), it is necessary to remove standard rectifier.

.... Optional

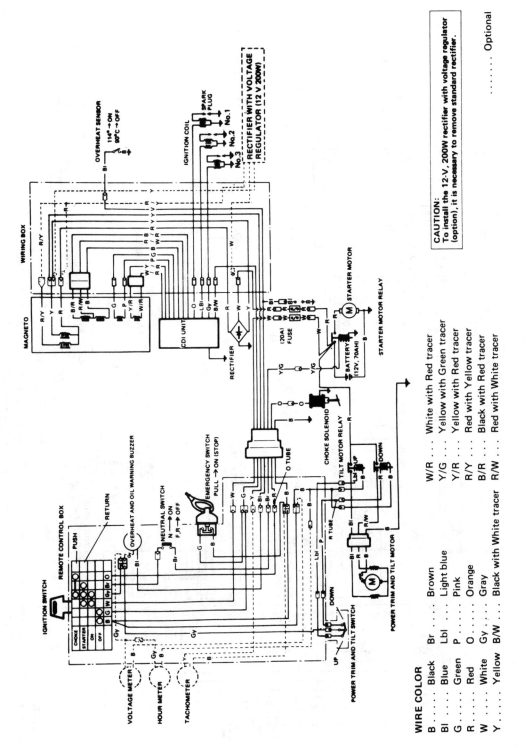

1981-1983 DT 85TC

WIRE COLOR

B	. . . . .	Black	Br	. . . . .	Brown
Bl	. . . . .	Blue	Lbl	. . . . .	Light blue
G	. . . . .	Green	P	. . . . .	Pink
R	. . . . .	Red	O	. . . . .	Orange
W	. . . . .	White	Gy	. . . . .	Gray
Y	. . . . .	Yellow	B/W	. . . . .	Black with White tracer

W/R	. . .	White with Red tracer
Y/G	. . .	Yellow with Green tracer
Y/R	. . .	Yellow with Red tracer
R/Y	. . .	Red with Yellow tracer
B/R	. . .	Black with Red tracer
R/W	. . .	Red with White tracer

CAUTION:
To install the 12-V, 200W rectifier with voltage regulator (option), it is necessary to remove standard rectifier.

. . . . Optional

14

1982 DT 115/DT 140

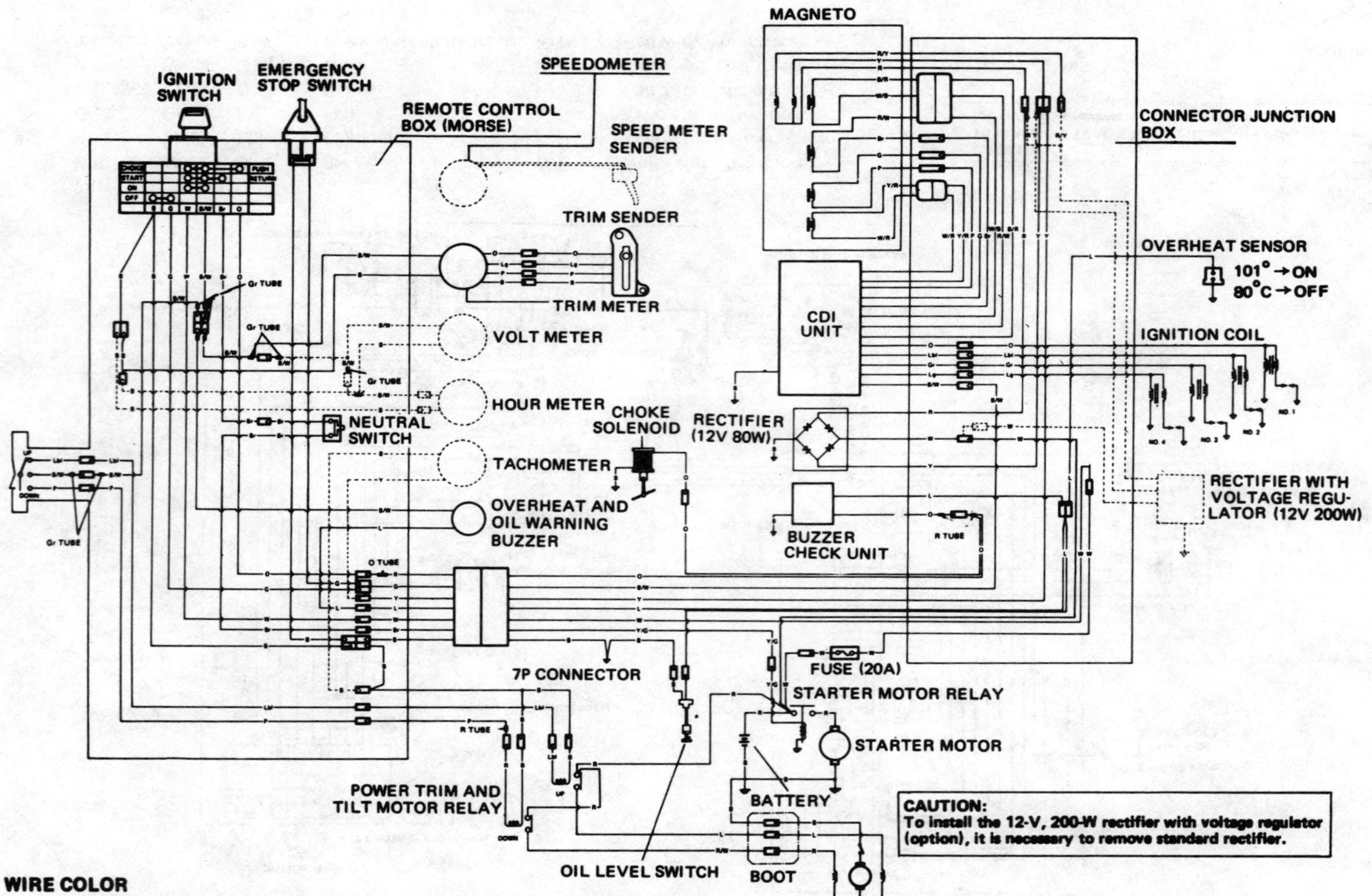

CONNECTOR JUNCTION BOX

OVERHEAT SENSOR 101° → ON 80°C → OFF

IGNITION COIL

RECTIFIER WITH VOLTAGE REGULATOR (12V 200W)

MAGNETO

CDI UNIT

RECTIFIER (12V 80W)

BUZZER CHECK UNIT

FUSE (20A)

STARTER MOTOR RELAY

STARTER MOTOR

BATTERY

BOOT

POWER TRIM AND TILT MOTOR

CAUTION:
To install the 12-V, 200-W rectifier with voltage regulator (option), it is necessary to remove standard rectifier.

SPEEDOMETER

SPEED METER SENDER

TRIM SENDER

TRIM METER

VOLT METER

HOUR METER

CHOKE SOLENOID

TACHOMETER

OVERHEAT AND OIL WARNING BUZZER

7P CONNECTOR

OIL LEVEL SWITCH

POWER TRIM AND TILT MOTOR RELAY

REMOTE CONTROL BOX (MORSE)

EMERGENCY STOP SWITCH

IGNITION SWITCH

NEUTRAL SWITCH

Bl/R	Blue with Red tracer
R/B	Red with Black tracer
W/B	White with Black tracer
W/R	White with Red tracer
Y/G	Yellow with Green tracer
Y/R	Yellow with Red tracer

WIRE COLOR

B	Black	Br	Brown
Bl	Blue	Lbl	Light blue
G	Green	P	Pink
R	Red	O	Orange
W	White	Gr	Gray
Y	Yellow	B/W	Black with White tracer